FACE
THE
FUTURE

by the same author

THE POLITICS OF DEFENCE

IN SICKNESS AND IN HEALTH
The Politics of Medicine

HUMAN RIGHTS

DAVID OWEN

FACE
THE
FUTURE

JONATHAN CAPE
THIRTY BEDFORD SQUARE LONDON

First published 1981

© 1981 by David Owen

Jonathan Cape Ltd, 30 Bedford Square, London WC1

British Library Cataloguing in Publication Data
Owen, David
Face the future
1. Socialism in Great Britain
I. Title
335'.00941   HX246

ISBN 0-224-01956-2

Photoset in Baskerville by Robcroft Ltd, London
Printed in Great Britain by
Billings & Sons Ltd,
Guildford, London and Worcester

Contents

To Tristan, Gareth and Lucy,
whose future it is.

Acknowledgments

My first debt is to my wife and three children for all their support, particularly in cheerfully accepting that our time together has been constantly eroded while the book was being written. Many friends and experts have been extremely generous with their time and advice and I wish to thank them all. No one has taken a greater burden of the work than Margaret Smart and I am deeply grateful to her and to my research assistant, Alan Robinson. All at Jonathan Cape have willingly accepted a heavy workload and none more so that Jill Sutcliffe and Xandra Hardie.

D.O.

Part One
Social Democracy

1

The Values of Socialism

Let us face facts: The British nation has been ill served by its political parties over the last quarter of a century.

Social, political and racial tensions grow and a country which was once envied by the world appears unable to shake itself free, to revive its self-confidence, to unleash its energies and restore its fortunes. Adversary politics continue to fan the embers of class divisions. Our standard of living as a nation and as individuals is falling behind that of our neighbours in Europe. The present economic decline is deep-seated and shows every sign of continuing against a mood of despair and disillusionment. Except for a few short periods of reasonably successful economic management between 1957-9, 1968-70 and 1976-8, the record overall is one of failure.

Government is not the sole or even the major factor in ensuring economic prosperity and social stability but the nation has suffered deeply from not having had a sustained period of good government. Britain, a country once so strong, so resilient, so resourceful and bold, cannot allow this drift to continue. The future must be faced with resolution.

Socialism in its philosophy and practice covers a far wider span of principles, values, ideals and policies than have been or are ever likely to be encompassed by any one political party. The Labour Party has been the main vehicle of socialism in Britain for many years but it does not have exclusive rights to be the sole party representing socialist ideals. It was challenged early in this century by the Independent Labour Party.

The events of 1980 and resolutions passed at the Labour

3

Party Conference have dramatically changed the policies, image and direction of the Labour Party. Given the strength of the social democratic approach to politics in Europe, it will be disastrous if socialism in Britain does not start to reflect that experience and success. At present the Labour Party is further removed from being a social democratic party than at any time in its history.

It has to be faced that many of the principles central to the success of the 1945-51 Labour government are now under profound challenge. The Labour Party of 1981 is very different from the party which in 1951 lost power but won the support of the largest number of voters ever to support any political party in this country. That there are differences is not necessarily wrong, for the problems of the 1980s are vastly changed in character and in kind from those facing the post-war Labour government. Yet it must be recognised that the 1981 Labour Party is even more centralist in its attitudes to the role of the state than the 1945-51 Labour government was. It is the bureaucratic centralisers, the corporatists, who now dominate British socialism and their influence, far from being checked, is growing; the mood of authoritarianism is not being held back by a counterbalancing libertarian streak; the state is seen as the main instrument of reform and its greater power is being advocated along with narrow nationalism.

The two fundamental cleavages in socialist thought are between revolutionaries and reformists, and between centralisers and decentralisers. One of the earliest Fabian tracts, published in 1886, said that 'English socialism is not yet anarchist or collectivist, not yet defined enough in point of policy to be classified. There is a mass of socialistic feeling not yet conscious of itself as socialism. But when the unconscious socialists of England discover their position, they also will probably fall into two parties – a collective party supporting a strong central administration and a counterbalancing anarchist party defending individual initiative against that administration.'[1] Nearly a century later it is this argument which is seriously dividing socialists.

The centralist–decentralist socialist split and the complex issues it raises have little relevance to the rather facile press

4

labelling of Left and Right which has always dominated public comment about arguments within the British Labour movement. Yet it is the question of decentralisation which now forms the real divide in the politics of the Left. The last decade has seen a growing public debate on the merits of small-scale institutions, a reaction to the centralisation of government, and criticism of the growth in the size of industrial companies, hospitals and schools. The Labour Party has virtually ignored these criticisms, and has been part of the drift towards centralisation. It is not surprising that electoral support for the Labour Party has ebbed away and that the main intellectual critique of Labour Party policy has come from outside the Party. The challenge is to develop a philosophy that will be welcomed by those voters who identify with socialist values yet who are reluctant to see further nationalisation or a growth in bureaucracy. There is a yearning for a fresh and valid socialist alternative, a widespread realisation that the continuation or extension of past trends and policies is no way forward for the future. The policies of Tribunite socialists and Fabian socialists in the Labour movement often occupy the same intellectual ground. The so-called move to the Left at the 1980 Annual Conference was not a radical movement but rather a reiteration of the old policies of more state involvement, more centralised direction, a strangely negative combination of unilateral action, protection, prohibition and withdrawal.

What is needed is a socialist philosophy outside the restrictive confines of much of the present polarised political debate, which asserts the radical democratic libertarian tradition of decentralised socialism, which revives the concept of fellowship and community within a participatory democratic society, and which sees change not as a threat but as a challenge. Change carries with it the assumption of choice and choice implies values, judgment and balance. 'Liberty–Equality–Fraternity' the old radical cry still emphasises an eternal truth: that none of the three can properly be fulfilled without being combined in some measure with the other two. For more than a century political thought has been dominated by the interaction and balance between liberty and equality, but surprisingly little attention has been given to the other element of this historic triad, fraternity, representing the sense of fellowship, co-operation, neighbourliness, community and citizenship. This neglect of fraternity, particularly by socialist thinkers, has meant that the espousal of equality has lacked a unifying force to bridge the gaps and contradictions between equality and liberty. Even more importantly, the foundations for the values and attitudes which must underpin a democratic socialist society are lacking a strong and secure base. Even the most fervent proponents of liberty feel it necessary to qualify the description of a state of liberty or freedom as being 'that condition of man in which coercion of some by others is reduced as much as is possible in society'.[2] Without fraternity neither liberty nor equality will flourish.

Socialist thinking has concentrated too much on the mechanics of equality and has paid insufficient attention to the attitudes which underpin the pursuit of equality, particularly how to foster altruism, which is the human drive behind the aspiration to eradicate inequalities and to strive for a more egalitarian society. 'No money values can be attached to the presence or absence of a spirit of altruism in a society. Altruism is giving to a stranger . . . it may touch every aspect of life and affect the whole fabric of value. Its role in satisfying the biological need to help – particularly in modern societies – is another unmeasurable element.'[3]

For all socialists, whether they use the label social democrat, democratic socialist, or whatever position they may occupy in the political spectrum of socialism, there is common ground in one particular set of beliefs, the need to redress poverty and to reduce inequality. At the heart of socialism lies the combination of an abhorrence of the misery which poverty brings and positive belief in the virtues of a just and equal society in which equality of means, treatment and respect lay the fraternal foundation for any community.

Equality is a noble ideal. We know it will not be achieved, but that of itself does not invalidate an aspiration – any more than the fact that wages and salaries will reflect different responsibilities and opportunities means that it is wrong to strive for a system which endeavours to make financial rewards fairer. Right wing propaganda which portrays the

6

socialist desire for a greater measure of equality as nothing more than pure envy of the rich, a blind vindictiveness and hatred of the successful[4] is simply the weakest defence of vested interest and privilege. A more powerful argument from the Right is that the real choice is between more equality with low living standards for all and on the other hand greater, or at least some, inequality but with higher standards for all. This is at least a practical argument and though it exaggerates the effect of inequality as a motivating force for economic growth it at least does not criticise the attempt to reduce poverty, to alleviate the problems of families haunted by a lack of basic necessities and the desire to free people from the shackles of low income and of low status.

It is the insensitivity to those in society, a high percentage of people, who are unable to compete and achieve, which is the unattractive face of the Right and the counterpart of those on the Left who allow envy to predominate. When the Prime Minister, Mrs Thatcher, asks, 'What is it that impels the powerful and vocal lobby in Britain to press for greater equality – for total equality even, when there is little evidence to show that ordinary people want it? Undoubtedly one important pressure is the *simpliste* desire to help the under-privileged. But more often the reasons boil down to an undistinguished combination of envy and what might be termed "bourgeois guilt",[5] she reveals the fundamental insensitivity which to date at least has narrowed her capacity to lead the whole nation. The desire to help is not just *simpliste*, it is deep, genuine and basic. Envy of course exists and can demean the movement for greater equality, but it is a minority motive. 'Bourgeois guilt' exists too, and when coupled with a wish to deny one's own upbringing or to ape the social background of others, is deeply unattractive, but guilt is not a motive to be so lightly disparaged if it can engender concern and a wish that others shall enjoy the same benefits.

Arguments against socialist redistribution are made by the Right's social theorists, who are convinced that equality is undesirable on the grounds that it is unobtainable, and that therefore the search for it is futile. Reference is sometimes made by the more extreme participants in the debate to genetics, environment and intelligence, and undigested and erroneous deductions are drawn from the works of Professors Jensen, Bernstein and Eysenck. The arguments continue despite the evidence that social class is not determined by IQ, that educational success depends less on IQ than on family background and that biological inequality does not necessarily dictate that society should be hierarchical and rigidly stratified.[6] The Right have also argued that any society will always have so-called functional stratification, in which important decision-makers will either have more status or more material rewards than the mass of the people, and that this kind of inequality will inevitably remain in any complex industrialised society, whether free-market or state-controlled. This theory assumes that individuals will always be motivated predominantly by a desire to maximise their own or their families' financial rewards or status and that it is impossible to create a climate where rewards based on job satisfaction or an ethos of public service tend to predominate.

There is a Right-wing theory that though social and financial inequalities clearly are very great and difficult to justify, it is doubtful whether they can be removed except at unacceptable cost. This argument is stronger, for a democratic system allows the privileged to organise in defence of their position and tends to accept as the price for democracy a measure of individual freedom which does run counter to what may statistically or theoretically be in the best interests of the whole of society. Democratic socialists are rightly unwilling to put at risk or to dismantle Western liberties and democracy in order to remove inequality. Gradual persuasion in a democracy is the only sure way of bringing about greater equality without socialism degenerating into the kind of undemocratic and restrictive society that is spawned by authoritarian state control. This will necessitate a more value-orientated discussion of politics, and while some socialists, particularly those who profess no religious belief, may be wary of such an approach, that reluctance must be challenged. For it is this very reluctance which has prevented discussion of issues like fraternity and altruism, and encourages socialists to espouse equality while confining their theories to the mechanics of distribution.

8

That socialism is about much more than just equality was a theme William Morris well understood when he wrote that socialism was 'a condition of society in which there should be neither rich nor poor, neither master nor master's man, neither idle nor overworked, neither brain sick workers nor heart sick workers; in a word, in which all men would be living in equality of condition, and would manage their afairs unwastefully and with full consciousness, that harm to one would mean harm to all.'[7] The use of the terms 'brain sick' and 'heart sick hand workers' is an evocative reminder that there is much more to the process of living than the redistribution of material wealth, and a clear pointer to the relevance of industrial democracy in attaining job satisfaction and encouraging job enrichment. The emphasis on managing our affairs unwastefully involves the use of words which evoke part of the current ecological debate, which is rightly a dominant concern for many and an issue in which socialists should be particularly engaged. The quality of our social environment is as important as the quantity of social provision. The concept of harm to one meaning harm to all goes deeper and wider than more familiar phrases.

If socialism depicts equality only in terms of distribution, then, when inequalities persist or when socialists and socialist governments not only perpetuate but defend certain inequalities of income in terms of differential payment for different tasks, a deep sense of failure is engendered, leading to disillusionment, and this will be used as a justification for abandoning liberty in order to be sure of achieving equality. The record of state controlled societies in overcoming inequality is not such as to make any thinking democrat change his or her predisposition for liberty.

Unfair distribution of talents does not preclude equality of respect, for this can be applied equally to men or women, to the habitual drunkard, to a judge or a doctor, to the mentally handicapped, or to a sporting personality, regardless of social status or professional earning capacity. Equality of respect covers equality under the democratically passed laws essential for the maintenance of liberty. Again and again one is driven back to the democratic imperative as the means for resolving the conflicts and contradictions of life. 'If we wish to remain human, there is only one way, the way into the open society. We must go into the unknown, the uncertain and insecure, using what reason we may have to plan for both security and freedom.'[8]

Yet such an outlook runs counter to what is, together with democracy, one of the constant themes of Western political thinking in recent centuries, the quest for certainty. This quest is not unique to political thought, but runs strongly through much religious, scientific and economic thinking. Some of the frustration and even despair of modern thought and writing stems from the inability of those who search to find simple answers or solutions to ever more complex problems. Many socialists in particular search endlessly for an all-embracing unity of political purpose and thought. Sensing the value of collective action they turn in varying degrees to totalitarian bureaucratic or democratic collectivism. The attraction of the totalitarian analysis stems from the security and faith its all-embracing structure engenders among its adherents.

Certainty is easier to achieve if one can totally abandon or lower the priority given to democracy. It is impossible to give the highest priority to democracy and still find a great measure of certainty. Democracy carries with it an acceptance of the infinite spectrum of views, aspirations and demands of human beings that cannot be perfectly structured or systemised. Democratic politics carries with it the necessity to put the sum of human happiness before philosophy, dogma or doctrine. Even to categorise human behaviour is fraught with danger. No one falls perfectly within any category. Yet that risk has already been faced by two writers who have had a powerful effect on contemporary thought, Isaiah Berlin and G.D.H. Cole. Isaiah Berlin's 'The Hedgehog and the Fox'[9] defines two personalities using the saying of the Greek poet, Archilochus, 'The fox knows many things, but the hedgehog knows one big thing'. The personality of hedgehog relates 'everything to a single central vision, one system less or more coherent or articulate, in terms of which they understand, think and feel –a single, universal organising principle.' The foxes 'pursue many ends, often unrelated and even contradictory, connected, if at all, only in some *de facto* way, for some psychological or physiological cause.' The foxes are the decentralisers who 'lead lives, perform acts, and entertain ideas that are centrifugal rather than centripetal'. Behind this admittedly over-simplified classification lies one of the great divides of thought and writing. Isaiah Berlin used the classification to identify intellectual and artistic personalities, but it can also be applied to political personalities. The greatest dangers to democracy come from those politicians whose certainty means that they espouse dogma and doctrine when facing the complex decision-making of our modern society.

G.D.H. Cole was deeply conscious of the need to develop a form of socialism that would be appropriate to British values and institutions. But he also sought to combine the insights of Marx and Proudhon in a manner that would stress fellowship and community rather as William Morris had done, avoiding collectivism or anarchic libertarianism. Cole recognised that the Marxist ideas of the class war and the dictatorship of the proletariat were both unattractive to the electorate, and likely, if ever carried out, to sweep away many of the liberties that Britain had gradually built up. He rejected those forms of socialism that neglected liberty and fraternity in the overriding quest for equality and he saw democratic participation as the key to maintaining communities and achieving social change that was attuned to the needs of working people.

A political classification to which G.D.H. Cole often referred was originally used by Beatrice Webb: the 'A's' and the 'B's' – the 'anarchists' and the 'bureaucrats'. The 'B's' have long been in the ascendancy in the Labour movement in Britain and the welfare state and the post-war nationalisation programme were the crowning achievements of 'B' thought.[10] Few in the Labour movement have championed the anarchists' dislike of the state and centralisation. The label 'anarchist' is clearly inappropriate for Cole since his thought was more deeply influenced by a socialist theory of power rather than by Proudhon's mutualism, and he was firm in his advocacy of social justice and in his support for welfare policies. The Labour Party has always lacked a theory to explain how the distribution of power was to be altered in order to achieve socialism and how power was to be distributed in a socialist society. These questions have been neglected since it was too easily assumed that the achievement of a much greater degree of state ownership would of itself spread to all citizens the power previously held by private business. In practice, however, the redistribution of power in favour of Whitehall, the executive, the civil service and a huge administrative apparatus has not automatically achieved the socialist objective of common ownership. It has in practice impeded the creation of a participatory democracy by removing the power to take initiatives from the community and encouraging 'corporatism' and rule by committee.

That nationalisation was an insufficient basis for changing society was always accepted by G.D.H. Cole. He identified the task ahead as stimulating democratic activism and wrote, 'this is precisely what the 'B's' are temporarily unfitted to do by themselves: only the 'A's', held in check by the 'B's' can do it in any effective way'.[11] Throughout his life and in numerous writings Cole advocated 'A' socialism though firmly within a democratic society. Extending democracy and championing the expression of a vigorous plurality of viewpoint undoubtedly make decision taking more time consuming but the decisions become more sustainable once they have been taken. Pluralism offers the prospect of a more interesting, relevant and stimulating democracy, where difficult problems will evoke different solutions and where decisions more fully reflect the wishes of particular communities.

The pluralism which Isaiah Berlin advocates is not a soft consensus but has been characterised by Aileen Kelly as being 'much more tough-minded and intellectually bold; it rejects the view that all conflicts of values can be finally resolved by synthesis and that all desirable goals may be reconciled. It recognises that human nature is such that it generates values which, though equally sacred, equally ultimate, exclude one another, without there being any possibility of establishing an objective hierarchical relation between them. Moral conduct therefore may involve making agonising choices, without the help of universal criteria, between incompatible but equally desirable values. This permanent possibility of moral uncertainty is . . . the price that must be paid for recognition of the true nature of one's freedom: the individual's right to self-direction, as opposed to direction by state or church or party, is plainly of supreme importance if one holds that the diversity of human goals and aspirations cannot be evaluated by any universal criteria, or subordinated to some transcendent purpose.'[12]

Such a philosophical atittude, if linked to a political approach which is unequivocally democratic and socialist, radical and bold, could appeal to those who identify with the past values of the British Labour Party but who now see its political counterpart in the social democracy successfully practised by many other socialist governments in Western Europe. It is an approach within the socialist debate which is not uniquely or even predominantly British. French socialism, which was born out of revolution and has never been as resolutely reformist as British socialism, is currently involved in a similar debate. At the 1977 Congress of the Socialist Party at Nantes Michel Rocard challenged the centralist orthodoxy and spoke of the two political cultures within the French Left; the one which had dominated for a long time was 'jacobin, centralising, étatist, nationalist and protectionist'. The second culture was 'decentralising, regionalist, refuses arbitrary domi-nations, the domination of employers as well as that of the state. This culture fears regulations and administrations. It prefers instead basic collectivities and experiment.'[13]

This approach is neither syndicalist nor anarchistic but is concerned with freedom, is sceptical about more power to the state, and believes that workers should have rights in the workplace. British socialism has in the past rejected many of these themes as being idealistic or wildly impracticable but they are more relevant after the obvious failure of state ownership, continued alienation, and the failure to achieve industrial democracy. That a strong and centralised state has contributed greatly to the welfare of the British population in the last fifty years is not in doubt; it was perhaps naive of nineteenth century anarchists to believe that a strong state was not needed to start the erosion of the dominance of private ownership and the move towards common ownership. The state has, however, now not so much outlived its usefulness but has become itself an impediment to further change towards the development of a participatory democracy, wider ownership, co-operation and community. The state has a continuing role; modern society cannot do away with the state, and those who regard any attempt to reform and redefine its role as being completely insufficient to safeguard freedom, are detached from reality.

Democracy in Britain cannot just be limited to the political life of the country and be confined to the cyclical elections for the Westminster parliament, the European parliament and the local authority. A true democracy will mean a progressive shift of power from Westminster out to the regions, to the county and town halls, to communities, neighbourhood, patients, tenants and parents. Such a diffusion of power will be resisted by the machine politicians, some trade union leaders, industrial managers, and the bureaucrats, all of whose current power base, status and authority will be challenged. To introduce radical reforms it will be necessary to harness the frustration and to retain the support of a public, which, while affected by a myriad of decisions, as yet feel little enthusiasm for participation even in those areas which do interest them, since they do not believe that their participation will have any influence on decision-making. There is now abundant evidence that the relevance and importance of industrial ownership in transforming attitudes within industry has been exaggerated: the two polarised viewpoints that economic prosperity and social progress come from either private ownership or state ownership alone are facile. The emphasis needs to be placed instead on co-operative ownership and industrial democracy, and on distinguishing the different problems facing public and private ownership and developing where appropriate different policies for pricing, profits, wage-bargaining and investment in those sectors. The major argument is that parliamentary democracy by itself is not enough and needs to be buttressed and enriched by an extension of democracy from the community upwards. The trade unions will need to adapt to more varied patterns of ownership in which their members share in the management, and unions will need to make a greater distinction in how they organise to represent the interest of workers within the public and private sectors. The unions must also be prepared to accept a greater measure of democracy and balloting and to encourage their members to develop different forms of industrial democracy within various patterns of ownership.

In advocating devolution we should reject the inward restrictive emotions of nationalism: whether English, Welsh, Scottish, Irish or British, we should enjoy the simple pleasure of genuine patriotism and at the same time the cultural delight and diversity of retaining the distinctive characteristics of the nation state. In espousing internationalism there needs to be a deep-seated commitment to negotiations for a new world economic order and a new world security order. The challenge for British socialism is to rediscover traditional values, to re-order many current priorities, to redefine future goals. This calls for a radical reorientation towards a more decentralised society where the immense task ahead is 'that of passing beyond the welfare state, in which people get given things, to the kind of society in which they find satisfaction in doing things for themselves and for one another'.[14]

There is a very genuine and probably growing opinion that Britain should adopt a low growth strategy, create a low energy society, resist tne employment and social implications of the new technology, sustain old industries, refuse robots, keep the conventional office, return to the land and dismantle the industrial society. It is easy to scoff at these ideas, but they have appeal because of the despair felt at the consequences of present policies. For people to be persuaded to reject such a strategy, as not just backward looking but as a counsel of despair that will itself bring more misery than happiness, they must be able to relate to a future where there is the prospect of a society which they control and where they do not feel the slaves of that society, a future which holds the prospect of individuals coming together freely to master the system under which they all will live. The key to such a new direction lies in persuasion, not in imposition, and the challenge is to design a political system which allows for persuasion. No one single measure can begin to solve the complex issues which face us all but a shift of attitudes in favour of a more involved democracy where persuasion and consent predominate, and away from authoritarianism, bureaucracy and corporatism, is desirable world-wide. Even higher economic growth against the likely world industrial trends looks harder to achieve and its competitive drive has itself substituted values which have contributed to the destruction of community feeling and to widespread alienation and dissatisfaction.

As Britain is forced to grapple with the world's problems so it will be necessary to adapt society, as well as our own material aspirations, to lower growth. The assumption, prevalent in the 1950s and 1960s, that high growth would automatically transform the problems of poverty, squalor, inequality and injustice has clearly been proven wrong. There is now a greater wish to explore the underlying values within our society: to question, though not to reject, materialism; to ponder, though not to embrace, the morality of sharing fairly the fruits of the earth. Yet all experience indicates that it will be more difficult to correct fundamental inequalities in a situation of low economic growth. A low energy strategy which takes as its central assumption the desirability of low growth can logically argue for a moratorium on the development of nuclear power. Yet aiming for higher economic growth means that, while one can reduce energy consumption more rigorously than in the past, and while much of the new technology is itself less energy-demanding, there will still be a need to provide more energy as a precondition of economic growth.

The dilemma is well illustrated by the Western democracies' most vigorous current public debate which is about the future role of nuclear power. The leaders of communist and developing countries have been able to espouse nuclear power without any debate. Yet, so far, all Western democratic leaders have found it necessary to argue for the continuation of a nuclear power generation programme, in the face of legitimate public anxieties about nuclear waste disposal and a less justified, though nevertheless widely felt, public fear associated with the more remote risks of a serious incident involving a nuclear power station.

Britain is better supplied than most countries with coal, gas and oil, and energy self sufficiency looks feasible, at least for twenty years, which allows us to proceed with more caution over nuclear power. Diversifying our energy sources and progressively developing alternative decentralised sources of energy is a prudent policy on economic, social and environmental grounds. Yet there will continue to be a need for national energy policies and an energy grid for electricity and natural gas; and few who want higher economic growth feel able to square likely forward energy demand with a moratorium on further nuclear power electricity generation.

It is similarly impossible to aim for higher economic growth and to shut out the new technology, to turn one's back on the micro-chip, abandon the office revolution or hold off the robot factory with one one manned shift out of three. Such developments have profound social implications for our traditional way of life, but we are responding to the challenge with little imagination and in the belief that the old political structures and attitudes can cope with the new challenges. In Britain more than in most countries we have suffered for some time from a lack of national self-confidence. The British resistance to change is very pervasive and is well documented as existing long before the Great Depression – itself part of the legacy of our being the first country into the industrial revolution. The pessimism that came with the Great Depression was fostered by the savage unemployment and its memory lived on. It became institutionalised within the trade union movement, within management and within Whitehall. Helped by the Second World War, the memory fed the development of corporatism. The growth of centralism and its manifestation in corporatism are described later in some detail, but here it is only necessary to assert that it is this institutional trend, the committee consensus, which has contributed to the peculiar reluctance in Britain to welcome and adapt to change. Our European neighbours and most comparable industrial competitors have shown – in France in the last two decades, through most of this century in Germany – a greater readiness to make the industrial changes which have contributed to their far more impressive economic performance.

Yet even over the last decade, with all its disappointments, there has been in Britain a steady rise in the standard of living.

Although European comparisons show it to be relatively lower than in other countries, it has nevertheless contributed to a clear improvement in the overall standard of life. In 1970 virtually no manual workers had four weeks' paid holiday. In 1980 over 35 per cent did. Real personal disposable income in fixed prices rose from £1,000 in 1970 to £1,400 in 1980. These are but two statistics indicative of the general improvement.

The industrialised developed world, or the North as it is referred to in the context of the North-South dialogue, has little real understanding of the depth of poverty existing in the Third World, the underdeveloped South. The television screen brings home to many people's sitting rooms the ravages of famine, floods and earthquakes, but the poverty, illiteracy, malnutrition and illness which haunt vast tracts of the world are difficult to comprehend. The Report of the Independent Commission on International Development Issues under the Chairmanship of Willy Brandt is the most readable and authoritative account of the problems that is easily available.[15] The World Bank estimates that 800 million people can be classified as destitute. Some 40 per cent of the people in the South are not able to secure the basic necessities of life. Four large countries – India, Pakistan, Bangladesh and Indonesia – account for around two-thirds of the world's poor. The bare statistics can easily have a deadening effect. Between 20 to 25 million children below the age of five die every year in developing countries and a third of these deaths are from diarrhoea due to drinking polluted water.

To provide safe drinking water is an achievable goal and the UN in 1977 aimed to do this by 1990. Yet three years later it was clear that the target would not be reached without a doubling of rates of investment in the urban areas and a fourfold increase in rural areas. The 1980s have been declared a 'Decade for Drinking Water and Sanitation'. The cost of simple standpipes or wells is estimated at $10 per person for water in rural areas; for sanitation the cost is $5 per person in rural areas. Some sceptics decry international action and believe that fixing ambitious world targets is the wrong approach; yet the World Health Organisation's successful smallpox eradication programme in the 1970s vindicates such

18

an approach and demonstrates what can be done by a united and determined world.

The Brandt Report necessarily aims at rich governments, whether in the industrialised West or OPEC. It therefore takes as a major theme the divide between North and South and aims to convince powerful Western interest groups that substantial cash transfers to the South, reflationof the world economy by increasing demand, and the rejection of protectionism, are mutual or common interests. It is arguing, however, for economic expansion at a time when the dominant view in Britain and in much of the West is against monetary inflation. Instead the world is experiencing monetary restraint which it is hoped will cut down inflation and not harm medium to longer term production. It is very hard to see how, until there is a greater consensus of view amongst governments about the basic tenets of economic policy and how they run their own national economies, there can be a concerted international response to the world's economic problems. It is, therefore, important that in stressing – rightly – enlightened self-interest politicians do not play down or neglect the arguments of common humanity.

This particularly applies to the eradication of hunger where the arguments of self-interest are not easily discernible and yet where the moral case for action is widely accepted. The need for this duality of purpose, self-interest and common humanity, is important not just to convince the Western industrialised world, but also the OPEC countries. In a world where *Realpolitik* dominates, and is likely to continue to dominate, the most rapid movement in tackling the problems of the South will come if OPEC, which is in a pivotal position, decides to force the Western countries to respond. Because of their oil and gas reserves, they are uniquely placed to use their power and leverage. Hitherto their key decision makers have had little self-interest in changing the world economic order; but as OPEC changes its political leaders, as the tension between the older and younger leaders grows, their links with Third World countries strengthen. As a grouping of predominantly Muslim nations, they draw on their moral traditions. The balance of power is very slowly but inexorably changing.

The West has believed for far too long that it has a monopoly of civilised and moral values. The quickest, most dramatic and probably the most radical way of tackling the economic imbalance in the world would be for the OPEC countries to negotiate with the North not only on their own behalf but also on behalf of the South. If they agreed to keep up oil production levels and to recycle their forward surpluses only on condition that the North also expanded their economies and opened up their trading patterns, this would be a powerful force for change, since it could be backed by the realistic threat of cutting back on oil production. As OPEC becomes progressively more radical, so it will be less influenced by the monetarist theories which tend to be favoured by many of their highly traditional banking sources of financial advice. They are listening more to the grievances of the Third World even if they retain their traditional royal family leaderships. If they ignore the South and OPEC puts its interests exclusively in with those of the North, the prospects for any real negotiations taking place over a new economic order in the next decade are very slight.

At the start of the 1980s all the key trends point in the wrong direction. It is amazing how few leading political figures seem aware of the perilous state of many Third World countries' finances. The chance of a major country defaulting on debt repayment is now very high unless there are more generous write-offs, better debt recycling and greater commodity price stability. Deflation in the West has limited the ability of many of the Western countries to purchase goods from the Third World yet we continue to lend to them at previous levels; the risk of a default is also compounded by the continuing rise in oil prices, adding to the Third World countries' costs. A major default would precipitate a financial crisis, since some large financial institutions in the United States in particular are by now severely over-exposed. The repercussions would be very serious and it can be in no one's interest for this chain of events to be triggered. Nor should private banks be allowed to continue to lend at high risk and therefore at high interest to countries which then use all their much needed aid to finance these debts. Aid itself is dropping all the time, as politicians seize on the fashionable questioning of the purposes of aid to reduce their aid budgets. OECD countries in 1961 gave 0·54 per cent of GNP in aid, their highest ever level. This had dropped to 0·31 per cent by 1977, and with the subsequent fall in the rate of growth in the US and the UK, the OECD percentage must be dropping still further. The 1979 Conservative government totally reversed the previous Labour government's forward expenditure priorities which allowed for a 6 per cent per year real terms' increase in the aid budget. Britain has been singled out for criticism by the President of the World Bank for planning to cut aid to 0·38 per cent of GNP by 1985 from the 0·49 per cent average for 1977-9. A more short-sighted policy would be hard to contrive.

The Brandt Report stresses the case for untied aid, automatic disbursement and programme lending and suggests financing it by taxes on foreign trade, energy consumption and arms sales. These are all praiseworthy recommendations, but they stand little chance of being adopted other than under pressure from OPEC by a West which already feels itself economically beleaguered, and only too eager to excuse itself by pointing to the abysmal record on aid of the Soviet Union and other COMECON countries. The reluctance of some Western leaders to discuss the Brandt programme for survival should be a signal to the Third World to give a higher priority to trying to persuade OPEC to negotiate on their behalf with the West in the various world negotiating forums. If the West see this as a possible development, they might move to open discussions with OPEC as a pre-emptive action. There is no justification for inaction, for a resigned acceptance of continued world economic recession; a mixture of inactivity and pessimism will result in continued decline.

Here in Britain politicians need to heed André Malraux's aphorism as we enter the 1980s that a mixture of pessimism and activism breeds fascism. The new Conservative government elected in 1979 showed an untypical activism in the sense that it started as a radical government with initially considerable optimism. Then pessimism took over as the government acted to reduce employment, reduce services and cut the money supply. If the public mood matches this resigned fatalism, pessimism could easily become a way of life, fed by headlines that highlight only what goes wrong. Britain could become so fearful of unemployment, nuclear war and nuclear melt-down, so alarmed about the finite nature of resources, whether of energy or food, so concerned about the breakdown of values and of traditional family life, and so fatalistic about progressive de-industrialisation, that it is unable to see a different perspective.

The start of the 1980s with very high unemployment may not appear the best time to advocate a new perspective, but there are well-founded grounds for believing that over the next two decades we will grope towards a new economic and security order, a world that does ease poverty and hunger, does control the arms race, develops new safe sources of energy, new sources of protein, adopts new patterns of child care with a new family structure, works less and has more flexible hours and patterns of work involving far more leisure. The highly centralised society of the Western industrialised democracies will either give way to a more decentralised, disaggregated way of life or it will become more authoritarian and centralised. The question is whether politicians in the Western democracies chart the course of a more decentralised democratic society or resist. Do we develop our democracy so that we become the masters of our destiny, or do we become more state controlled, more subservient to the system? There is already plentiful evidence that individuals within society are straining to be given more choice and to take more responsibility for their lives. The most important part of a new approach is to allow that feeling to surface and to extend democracy. At present only twenty to thirty of the member states of the United Nations can be classified as genuine democracies; governments everywhere centralise and bureaucratise and, in doing so, stifle the roots of democracy. The new politics must challenge the increasing centralisation of society which is fast becoming the hallmark of government in East and West, North and South, and insist on a greater measure of decentralisation as the natural partner of genuine democracy.

2

The Decentralist Tradition

In reviving the decentralist strand of socialist thinking and in advocating specific policies for the 1980s it is worth first re-examining the historical debate. The socialist societies of the 1880s and 1890s, with their mixed membership of socialists and anarchists, focused most of their attention on the issue of *decentralised worker-control* versus *nationalisation*. William Morris, although not an anarchist, criticised both the Fabian definition of socialism and the means by which the Fabians expected socialism to be realised. Morris wrote that the Fabians' 'municipal socialism' might seem to work but, 'it may do nothing of the kind: the highly centralised municipal administration of the Roman Empire did not in the least alter the economic basis of chattel slavery.' The mistake of the Webbs, Morris argued, was 'to over-estimate the importance of the mechanism of a society apart from the end to which it may be used.'[1] The decade which included the First World War saw the Fabian view prevail. The belief in centralisation and nationalisation was given a further boost by the Russian Revolution and the world economic situation. Margaret Cole wrote that 'it was the Russian Revolution itself which soon spelt the end of Guild Socialism as an organised movement. Immediately the Russian factory workers did in fact take over control of factories, and the resultant chaos was so disastrous that the Bolsheviks quickly put a stop to it and introduced centralised discipline.'[2]

The outcome of that debate profoundly influenced the political thought of the Labour movement and in particular the policies of the Labour Party. The flavour of debate is best captured through the contrasting words of two of the key participants, not so much for their particular policies or suggested structures but for what they reveal about their underlying attitudes to people. Looking back on that debate in 1934, G.D.H. Cole wrote that, 'the familiar brands of collectivist socialism were somehow things one wanted for other people rather than oneself, in order to eradicate the deprivations of injustices of capitalism, whereas the Guild doctrine offered me a kind of socialism that I could want as well as think right' . . . 'as having personalities to be expressed as well as stomachs to be filled.'[3]

It is salutary to contrast this with the paternalistic attitude of Sidney Webb, in a lecture entitled 'A Stratified Democracy'. 'The great mass of the people,' he said, 'will always be found apathetic, dense, unreceptive to any unfamiliar ideas, and your eager active spirit with the unfamiliar idea . . . frets and fumes at being held in check by this apathetic mass. But after all, the apathetic mass are individually God's creatures, and entitled to have a vote, and it is no use kicking against their apathy and denseness. You have got to work your governmental machine in some way that will enable you to get on notwithstanding their denseness.'[4]

At the February 1918 Labour Party Conference the Fabian collectivist tradition emerged as the dominant influence in formulating the wording of the Labour Party constitution. Clause 3 of the constitution stated ' . . . to secure for the producers by hand and by brain the full fruits of their industry and the most equitable distribution thereof that may be possible, upon the basis of the common ownership of the means of production, and the best obtainable system of popular administration and control of each industry or service.' The latter part was a bow to the Guild Socialists but the direction was henceforth towards nationalisation. In 1929 Clause 4, para 4 of the constitution, which was to become so contentious after the electoral defeat of 1959, emerged. 'Means of production' was altered to 'means of production, distribution, and exchange', and 'producers' was amended to 'workers'. It is interesting that the early debate between the centralists and decentralists was so dominated by the discussion over workers' control and did not widen out to cover other areas in the centralist – decentralist debate. The reason was probably that the Labour Party in Parliament and in the boroughs was still building up its support. It had not yet held power and there was a tendency therefore to concentrate on the main industrial issue on which decisions had to be taken and which from day to day divided both the Party and the Trade Union movement.

It was significant that the Webbs, while being strong advocates of the consumer co-operative movement, were suspicious of industrial co-operatives. The Webbs did not object to the profits of retail co-ops being distributed to the population at large but they were very sceptical of the ability of workers to manage factories and preferred that industry should be nationalised and professional managers be employed. For Morris, influenced by his romantic notion of a return to the dignity and craftsmanship of the medieval guilds, this was an inadequate vision. In criticising Graham Wallas, one of the Fabian essayists, he wrote that, 'Socialism is emphatically not merely "a system of property-holding" but a complete theory of human life, founded indeed on a distinct system of religion, ethics and conduct, which . . . will not indeed enable us to get rid of the tragedy of life . . . but will enable us to meet it without fear and without shame.'[5] There was no dissent about the need for democracy: the argument was about the form democracy should take. Common ownership was seen to be of fundamental importance; the issue was whether ownership should be by the state on behalf of everyone, or by workers within the organisation. The Webbs and their fellow Fabians stressed the virtues of collective action in every sphere, not only in the ownership of industry but also in social activities. As Anthony Crosland put it in *The Future of Socialism*, they thought that 'any extension of collective [action] at the expense of individual activity constitutes an advance towards socialism, including the registration by the state of playing-card makers, hawkers, dogs, cabs, places of worship and dancing rooms.'[6] Yet while mocking these collectivist Fabian attitudes Crosland also questioned the reality of the all-

25

embracing participatory society, when he wrote, 'if what is meant by participation is an active and continuous process of participating in decision-making, then all experience shows that only a small minority of the population will wish to participate . . . the fact is that the majority will continue to prefer to lead a full family life and cultivate their gardens. And a very good thing too. For a continuous political activism by the great bulk of the population would not only run counter to most people's desires for privacy and a leisured family life, but it would also (as G.D.H. Cole used often to say) pose a real threat to the stability of our democracy. Indeed it would mark the breakdown of normal social cohesion.'[7] That criticism evokes Oscar Wilde's supposed comment that socialism would take too many evenings. Yet participation and political activity cannot be so lightly dismissed. John Stuart Mill was right when he argued that liberty is morally better than slavery, that even if slaves like being slaves it is still right to free them, because only free men are fully human.

It is of course true that the movement towards greater participation will always operate within the bounds of human nature; for some growing vegetables on the allotment will always be of more concern than air pollution. But plan to cut a motorway through an allotment area and suddenly activism will be unleashed. The momentum towards participation has its roots in the very educational advances for which socialists and others have striven. In no area is this drive for participation more difficult for established authority to comprehend than in the industrial place of work. Yet no other activity occupies so much time in an individual's life and should more naturally be at least subject to that person's influence.

The movement in favour of workers' control grew out of syndicalism, the revolutionary trade union movement which arose after 1880 in France and in the United States. Its leading advocates were the American Marxist, Daniel DeLeon and the Frenchman, Georges Sorel. In Britain syndicalist doctrines were spread most effectively by the trade union leader, Tom Mann. In South Wales the syndicalists formed the Unofficial Reform Committee of the South Wales Miners Federation, and in 1912 the Committee published a pamphlet entitled *The*

Miners' Next Step in which they rejected nationalisation and instead favoured a process by which each industry would be run by the workers with the various industries of the country being controlled by a Central Production Board. This they asserted 'would mean real democracy in real life, making for real manhood and womanhood. Any other form of democracy is a delusion and a snare.'[8] The National Union of Mineworkers (NUM) to this day is resistant to any form of worker representation on the National Coal Board, preferring the Tripartite mechanism for representation, with the Unions, National Coal Board and Government discussing the wider issues affecting the industry, and with all retaining independence for negotiations on wages and conditions. The NUM, itself a deeply federalist union with considerable autonomy given to the union leaders in different parts of the country, has maintained its legendary unity largely by the widespread use of the pit-head ballot.

The influence of the syndicalists was minimal in Britain because their revolutionary doctrine and advocacy of direct action through the general strike had little appeal. Most union leaders who were interested preferred the theory of Guild Socialism elaborated initially by two journalists, A.R. Orage and S.G. Hobson on the Left-wing weekly *New Age*. The Guild Socialists differed from the syndicalists in that they did not believe that the state should be abolished or that revolutionary means should be adopted. They argued that the best basis for representation was by function rather than by territory since modern legislators could not reflect all the diverse interests and opinions of their constituents. They felt that a democratic system based on the workplace or industry would more fully reflect the interests of the workers and would help to prevent the dilution of democracy which occurs when representatives are overstretched or remote. The Guild Socialists believed that the means of production should be collectivised but be controlled by guilds rather than by the state. Guildsmen would elect their own legislatures and executives and these would select representatives to serve on a council of all the important guilds. This council would co-ordinate the plans of the guilds and settle disputes between them but would not act as a replacement for parliament.

27

The disparity of thinking can be seen by analysing the two viewpoints presented to the Sankey Commission on the coal industry in 1919. Sidney Webb supported the formation of joint committees of workers and managers to offer advice and criticism to the owners, whereas G.D.H. Cole called for the establishment at once of the greatest amount of industrial democracy – meaning direct control by the workers and their unions – that was practicable, and for the most rapid subsequent extension of that control that was practicable. Beatrice Webb saw the self-governing workshop as 'that "charmer" within the order of thought, but "gay deceiver" within the order of things.'[9] This slightly deprecating and condescending judgment still represents the tenor of much establishment thinking within the Labour movement even today. Workers' control is seen as a romantic idea, harmless provided it does not get too strong, a potential but remote threat to the authority of the trade union movement: but basically irrelevant to the real issues of managing the economy. Industrial co-operatives are something to which lip service may be paid, or which can be disparaged with a knowing smile and an evocative reference to the well-publicised failures of KME in Kirby, or the *Scottish Daily News*, and a question about the Meriden Motor-Cycle Co-operative. These attitudes fail to absorb the impact of the quantum shift in the educational level of the industrial labour force. The wish to have more say and greater involvement in the decisions which dictate a person's daily pattern of work is not just a feature of education but also of greater leisure and security. Even seventy years ago, however, some powerful trade unions like the National Union of Railwaymen were sympathetic to workers' control. The issue split the Independent Labour Party but with the Miners Federation, the Post Office Workers and others there was an influential minority within the Labour movement sympathetic to the concept of workers' control.

Guild Socialism was essentially a movement of middle class intellectuals and as such it was limited in its appeal. Trade union leaders were reluctant to adopt the very radical solution that the Guild Socialists favoured and without union support the Guild Socialists could not hope to confront the hostility of private owners. The advocacy of workers' control was also coming at a time when many workers and all women still did not have the vote and the proposed downgrading of parliament and the civil service was far too radical for many people sympathetic to the broad idea. There was also considerable doubt by those who favoured central control that the degree of economic planning which they favoured could be achieved by the national guilds. As a result, after the collapse of the building guilds, Guild Socialism has left only a theoretical legacy. But these early debates did ensure that the Webbs moved off their initial position of total opposition to worker participation in industrial control and their 'Constitution for the Socialist Commonwealth' did allow for participation within a system of organised groups. It was a shift of emphasis, an acceptance of worker directors – like those in 1977 on the Post Office Board and in 1967 for the regional Boards of British Steel – and it was illustrated by their seeing as a 'real social gain that the General Secretary of the Swiss Railwaymen's Trade Union should sit as one of the five members of the supreme governing body of the Swiss railway administration'.[10]

The concept of the public corporations evolved from the writings and speeches of Herbert Morrison. It is too easy, however, to see Morrison himself as the archetypal centralist. He was in fact the most committed supporter of local government who has ever held senior Cabinet office in the Labour Party. In the 1945-51 Labour government it was frequently Herbert Morrison who challenged the accretion of powers to the state particularly if they were taken from local government, as they were over the NHS. Morrison, ever the practical politician, wanted to establish in the 1930s a detailed management structure for nationalised industry which would allow for a clear-cut decision making procedure, and this was far more important to him than a theory of democratic control. The concept of nominated members of public corporations was, however, strongly challenged by the advocates of greater worker representation and the Labour programme of 1934 said, 'the employees in a socialised industry have a right which should be acknowledged by law, to an effective share in the control and direction of the industry'.[11] But the 1945 Labour government was not committed to the concept. Stafford Cripps could say in 1946, 'there is not yet a very large number of workers in Britain capable of taking over large enterprises . . . until there has been more experience by the workers of the managerial side of industry. I think it would be almost impossible to have worker controlled industry in Britain, even if it were on the whole "desirable".'[12] This comment reflected a confusion which remains to this day between the concept of workers acting as managers, and the more realistic objective of managers acting for workers or with them, rather than for capital.

The government of which Stafford Cripps was such a prominent member was deeply rooted in the Fabian collectivist centralist tradition – like all its successors. The dominance of this tradition contributed to the fact that by the 1979 election the Tory philosophical Right was the radical challenger to the status quo in relation to the debate about public sector industry and public services generally. The Right had picked up the public's concern about government bureaucracy and cleverly created a political climate in Britain which identified the target for these concerns as being the Labour Party. The Labour government and the Party appeared intellectually exhausted: standing pat on the status quo. It was the Right which stood against nationalisation, bureaucracy, state inter-ventionism, for a materialistic personal freedom and the privatisation of industry which, against an intellectual vacuum and lack-lustre espousal of trade union dominated industrial democracy from the Left, meant that the Right had a more than passing appeal – around 40 per cent of trade unionists voted Conservative, among them many workers in state industries. At no time since the end of the 1920s had the Labour movement seriously engaged in the intellectual debate about the role of the individual in relation to the state, the company and the community. With few new ideas to invigorate its supporters and with which to chart a course for the 1980s, the Labour government was bound to appear defensive, and even though there was a Manifesto commitment to industrial democracy, it never came alive as an issue, in part because the key democratic issues had not been resolved.

In contrast nationalisation in the 1945 Manifesto was not a vote loser and it had considerable public support. It was natural then to retain much of the machinery evolved in wartime, to continue to plan the economy, so as to ease the transition to a peacetime system of production and to ensure that full employment was maintained. There was a strong practical case, which had been argued over the past few decades, for the 1945 government to take the large public utilities into state ownership. Yet many socialists even then saw nationalisation as much more than a practical industrial policy. It represented a means of achieving greater socialism in the long run by easing the conditions of manual workers through better paid and more secure jobs and by allowing the economy to be planned. Tawney wrote that nationalisation 'will benefit the mine-worker by removing the downward pressure of capitalism on his standard of life, by making room for considerations of social well-being which are at present subordinated to the pursuit of dividends, and by securing him an effective voice in the policy and organisation of the industry.'[13] Some of these advantages have been achieved, but mainly through the pressure of collective bargaining and the role of the state as a good employer, not through the involvement of those who work in the industry. In the 1960s, when the coal industry was deliberately run down by both Conservative and Labour governments, not many miners were convinced that nationalisation had brought great benefits to their industry. In comparison to the attitudes of the coal owners in the 1930s there had been great changes, but these had also taken place over the same period in most of British industry, both private and public. In 1972 it took the first miners' strike since 1926 for miners' wages to start to improve their relative position. The fourfold increase in oil prices saw the coal industry, in 1974, at last experiencing the steady investment and government support that it had lacked for the first twenty-five years of nationalisation. The record of nationalised industries is not as bad as its critics pretend but neither has it lived up to the hopes of its early advocates. Not one State Industry can point to a really pioneering role in relation to workers' control.

31

Sadly no Labour government can point to any significant measure of decentralisation. Only Richard Crossman showed in government a genuine radical wish to change the structure of government. In 1966, when he was Minister of Housing and Local Government, he established a Royal Commission with terms of reference designed to produce positive reform. As Lord President of the Council he also attempted to reform both the House of Commons and the House of Lords. The Labour Party in Opposition in the 1950s never challenged the centripetal tendency of post-war Britain. In government in the 1960s Labour advocated large-scale industry and large government departments, and argued for economies of scale and the extension of the public sector.

The establishment of the Royal Commission on the Constitution under Lord Kilbrandon in 1969 could and should have been a constitutional landmark, a turning point in our history. Instead it was a cynical reaction to the electoral success of the Scottish Nationalist Party, taken not as a convinced devolutionist response to a genuine issue but as a way to defuse a new and threatening political force. The subsequent ten-year debate which ended in the referendum and parliamentary debacle of 1979 was no more than an accurate reflection of a deep division of opinion, both in the Labour Party and in the country, that had been glossed over under the threat of a continuous SNP challenge to the Labour Party in Scotland. The Royal Commission on Local Government's Report[14] came too late in the lifetime of the 1964-70 government to be implemented, as did the proposals to end the tripartite structure of the National Health Service. It was left to another centralist government, the Tory one of 1970-4, to bureaucratise and nearly destroy the structure of local government and the National Health Service. Social historians will probably judge these as the two most disastrous administrative reforms this century. The 1979 Conservative government is demonstrating an even stronger centralist sentiment in its control of local government.

Even the establishment of the Committee on Local Government Finance in 1974[15] reflected a short-term political reaction to protests over rate increases. It never had as its prime motivation a wish to examine seriously the case for greater financial autonomy for local authorities. The virtual rejection of its recommendations in the Layfield Report, while the ink was still wet, was a triumph for centralism amongst both politicians and civil servants. The decision to appoint the Enquiry into Industrial Democracy was also flawed by the acceptance of demands for terms of reference which circumscribed the enquiry so as to emphasise the centralist, legislative, trade union dominated, option for industrial democracy. As a result the Bullock Report[16] gave some consideration to the other more radical options, but reflected in its membership and in its approach, the centralist approach.

In the aftermath of the 1979 electoral defeat British socialism can either continue with old attitudes locked within a centralist consensus, or it can break the mould and try to develop and build a fresh decentralised philosophy, and put forward a detailed programme of legislative and administrative reforms to diffuse power in Britain. To carry electoral support such a programme will need to have an inner coherence, and honestly face the genuinely conflicting arguments and attitudes that are posed within the centralist–decentralist dilemma. How great is the risk of widening inequalities by decentralising, and how effective is centralisation in achieving equality, are vital questions for socialists; how efficient is a question for everyone. Most postwar British governments have at times said that they are in favour of administrative and political decentralisation but they have failed to pursue these beliefs when it has been realised that the result would be a reduction in their existing powers. What is needed is nothing less than a radical reappraisal of British society. It will not be resolved by referring those political issues to a civil service bureaucracy or establishing another round of Royal Commissions or Committees of Enquiry. It needs a fresh political philosophy and commitment. It needs to be a society where quality is weighed with quantity, where diversity is the friend of order not its enemy.

This is not a prescription for consensus, middle of the road politics. There are hard choices to be made, large bureaucracies to be dismantled, vested interests to be challenged, whether represented by the First Division of the Civil Service Association or the National Union of Public Employees, whether that of the Institute of Directors or the Transport and General Workers Union, the British Medical Association or the National Union of Teachers. What is required is a break with the past not a revolution; not replacing an extremism of the Right by an extremism of the Left but an evolution of attitudes, which is the only democratically acceptable method of making change and ensuring that the changes last beyond the lifetime of one government. A society founded on decentralised socialist values faces a more radical challenge than a society dominated by the centralist belief in state control and nationalisation. A decentralised society widens the goals which socialists seek to realise and it takes on more of the existing centres of power than does a strategy that has the relatively narrow goal of transferring power from the private to the public sector.

Enhancing democracy is a long-term policy. John Stuart Mill argued that men would learn by being free, that freedom produces morally better people because it forces them to develop their potentialities. Only change of attitude will produce lasting social change. By deliberately increasing the opportunities for the individual to become involved, a decentralised society can focus the attention of a wider section of the population on its economic weaknesses, social failings and persistent inequalities. The task is to explain more about the nature of society or to enable voters to find out for themselves rather than merely to trade in single slogans such as 'nationalisation' or 'private enterprise'. Political values ought to underpin the appeal of any political party to the electorate. Socialists need to elaborate theirs more if they are to change the political climate. The values of the Right have made headway recently and these were shown in 1979 to be as important in terms of voter appeal as detailed policies or manifestos.

The most stimulating writer on socialism in the 1950s was Anthony Crosland, though his analysis was surprisingly centralist in concept. This was masked to some extent by Crosland's own personality and his ability lightly to deride every facet of any organisation and to extol individualism in a way which made his form of socialism beguilingly sensitive, warm and attractive. Who could fail to respond to a plea for liberty and gaiety in private life? 'We need not only higher exports and old-age pensions, but more open-air cafés, brighter and gayer streets at night, later closing hours for public houses, more local repertory theatres, better and more hospitable hoteliers and restaurateurs, brighter and cleaner eating-houses, more riverside cafés, more pleasure-gardens on the Battersea model, more murals and pictures in public places, better designs for furniture and pottery and women's clothes, statues in the centre of new housing-estates, better-designed street-lamps and telephone kiosks, and so on *ad infinitum.* The enemy in all this will often be in unexpected guise; it is not only dark Satanic things and people that now bar the road to the new Jerusalem, but also, if not mainly, hygienic, respectable, virtuous things and people, lacking only in grace and gaiety.'[17]

Crosland asserted in 1950 that 'Britain has in all essentials, ceased to be a capitalist country'[18] and later in 1974 that 'I see no reason to alter the revisionist thesis that government can generally impose its will (provided it has one) on the private corporation'.[19] The revisionist case was that fundamental changes were needed in the structure of society but that these changes could be imposed. They tended to under-estimate the importance of changing attitudes seeing change in terms of legislative or administrative reform. Being dominated by the need to obtain economic growth, the Crosland analysis spent little time on capitalism or aspects of alienation.

Crosland was firmly in the tradition of those, such as Tawney, who emphasised the ability of the government to bring socialism about by economic reforms. Despite his appeal for 'grace and gaiety' he tended to believe that a combination of politicians and administrators would be able to cure social problems with only minimal involvement by the bulk of the population. Little attention was given to how to achieve a fundamental change in attitudes in the values of community by eroding the values of capitalism, and by the involvement of individuals in decision-making at their place of work. Marxists who argue that economic changes precede changes in values and that the economic basis of capitalism must be removed before any change in values can be expected also ignore the importance of attitudinal change. Both under-estimate the ability of old value systems to adapt to institutional changes in such a way that despite radical-sounding legislation little real change results. That changes in values and structures need to proceed together in order to achieve significant changes in the actual working of institutions is one of the major lessons that should be derived from the revisionist experience through the 1960s and 1970s. The revisionists formed a coalition with the corporatists without realising the extent to which that very corporatism had embraced capitalist values and had become a stultifying brake on introducing any radical change. Crosland was not unaware of this when writing in 1962 that: 'A dogged resistance to change now blankets every segment of our national life. A middle-aged conserva-tism, parochial and complacent, has settled over the country; and it is hard to find a single sphere in which Britain is pre-eminently in the forefront . . . Our Parliament and Civil Service, brilliantly adapted to the needs of a bygone age, and which we still seek to export unmodified to ex-colonial territories, are in fact in need of drastic modernisation.'[20] Successive Labour governments saw change as primarily arising out of structural organisational and administrative reform. So 1964-80 saw the establishment of endless Commit-tees of Enquiry, Royal Commissions and Inter-departmental Working Parties. Their findings were implemented by poli-ticians only if they did not pose a challenge to the role of the centralised state. Few socialists saw that corporatism was as much the enemy of socialism as capitalism, perhaps more so because it proved a less obvious challenge – more adaptive and just as corrosive. Yet it is with corporatism that British socialism has unwittingly become ever more closely identified. The decentralist socialist case which at the start of the century was diffuse and utopian, was in retrospect bound to be defeated by the organisational and practical arguments for centralised socialism, particularly when that form of socialism had never even been tried. Half a century later, after the experience of centralised government through the two post-war periods, it is possible to identify its off-spring, corporatism. For the decentralist analysis to carry conviction the nature of corporatism must be exposed and its further extension rejected.

3

The Growth of Corporatism

There is clearly a legitimate and responsible role for the state and in certain areas such as defence, international relations and world trade, its tasks are obvious. The state has also developed a role in domestic policy which has been sufficiently successful to make it difficult to argue in principle against the welfare state; the question is whether the trend towards increasing the role of the state can be checked or reversed so as to shift towards a more decentralised society.

The argument that Britain has begun to move inexorably towards a corporate state is not new, and in recent years that critique has been vigorously mounted from the New Left as well as from the Hayek Right. The year 1979 saw the return of a Conservative government which, for the first time, meant a government that was openly critical of the corporate state. The challenge to British socialism is not to allow this political critique to be mounted only from the viewpoint of the Right, but to ensure that the Left is also heard to be reassessing the strength of the corporate state with conviction and coherence. Hitherto the dominant tradition within the Labour Party has been centralist, and large sections of the Party are so deeply embedded in the structure of the state that they see an attack on the corporate state as an attack on them. The signs are that the Labour Party will become so defensive that it will automatically oppose all of the Conservative Party attitudes to the corporate state, to the extent of becoming the defender of the bureaucracy and resisting any cutback in the tasks and functions of the state.

Driven to accept the inevitability of the continued private ownership of much of industry yet disliking the concept of market forces, many socialists seek to control private industry through the apparatus of the state. Such socialists do not accept the Marxist[1] analysis that corporatism is a capitalist strategy for subordinating labour when for a variety of reasons the normal capitalist device of market forces is not operating. They see corporatism as a way of enhancing the position of labour through agreement, forming a tripartite negotiating forum between trade union organisations, the state and employer organisations. Hitherto many Conservatives have found that the mix between private and public ownership is inevitable and have tried to instil artificial disciplines of market forces into the public sector through the apparatus of the state. Between the Conservative and Labour position corporatism develops as a system where the traditional distinction between capitalism and socialism is eroded. Instead of the majority view prevailing as is the essence of democracy, committee decision-making produces a consensus which erodes decisive democratically elected and responsible decision making. This form of Conservative status quo corporatism is in marked contrast to the attempt at a redistributive corporatism in Scandinavia or the bland mixture of the kind that has evolved in Britain under Labour governments.

The growth of the interventionist state began in Britain with the social welfare reforms of the 1906-14 Liberal governments. This was a radical change, the first example of the state actively promoting social goals for a large sector of the population. By 1914 expenditure on the social services had doubled and the First World War saw an acceleration of this trend and a qualitative change in the role of the state under the challenge of total war. Trade union and business co-operation was essential for victory and so the state adapted its structure and role to ensure their co-operation.

The historian, A.J.P.Taylor, has described the impact of the war in the following terms: 'until August 1914 a sensible, law-abiding Englishman could pass through life and hardly notice the existence of the state, beyond the post office and the policeman . . . All this was changed by the impact of the Great

War. The mass of people became, for the first time, active citizens. Their lives were shaped by orders from above; they were required to serve the state instead of pursuing exclusively their own affairs.'[2]

In the First World War the British government encouraged the growth of labour and employers' organisations to secure public consent for mobilisation, while the organisations welcomed the increase in power. The British government was forced to bargain for the support of the public as it was vital to produce the munitions and obtain the manpower to achieve victory. The state apparatus was partly dismantled after the First World War but several newly created Ministries survived, such as the Ministry of Labour and the Ministry of Transport and 'by 1922 it had become clear that a number of unions and employers' leaders had accepted the need for formal political collaboration with the state. TUC and employers' organisations, crossed a threshold which had not even existed before the war, and behaved thereafter in some degree as estates of the realm, to the detriment of more ancient, obsolete estates, the municipalities, the churches, the "colleges" of professional men, and the panoply of voluntary bodies, so important in the political system of the nineteenth century.'[3] The significance of the 1926 General Strike was that it killed workers' control and the syndicalist tradition and though it did not break trade union power it did turn trade union power in a corporatist direction to work henceforth with employers and government. It publicly demonstrated that TUC and NCEO interests had to be recognised for the country to be governable. The General Strike also brought to prominence trade union leaders such as Ernest Bevin who, despite their records as strike leaders, recognised that there was a place for conciliation rather than conflict in winning better returns for their membership. In 1929 the TUC, the National Conference of Employers' Organisations and the CBI had their first joint meeting without government present and with a wide remit covering the national economy, unemployment and industrial legislation. It was the start of a long road towards institutional co-operation.

In the United States and in Europe during the depression

more interventionist governments adopted many of what we now identify as corporatist remedies. As with Mussolini's Italy, Hitler's Germany could not strictly be termed corporatist since a false consensus was imposed by very effective propaganda, backed by the threat and use of force rather than by consultation and representation. The Italians attempted to reduce the independence of non-state institutions and to create a rigidly hierarchical society, and the same pattern was discernible, too, in Nazi Germany. In the United States, President Roosevelt and 'the New Deal' created a series of institutions to pay out government finance and to influence and plan sectors of the economy. The US trade unions also became more corporatist but given their weak structure there was little danger of these measures developing into full-blown corporatism. Even so Roosevelt was endlessly attacked by big business for whom state intervention lacked any legitimacy. This resistance was fortified by the deeply federal structure of US government with the individual states jealous of any federal government encroachment on their powers.

An intellectual justification for government intervention was provided, in all developed countries, by the economic analysis heralded in Keynes's *General Theory*. Keynes showed that capitalist economies were not self-regulating and in particular that they did not automatically create full employment. Demand-management by the state was legitimised and, with the development of new economic tools by the Keynesians, governments were now able at least to pose as being able to control macro-economic variables such as the level of investment, the rate of inflation and the amount of unemployment. Henceforth, governments could no longer claim that a poor economic performance was due to factors wholly outside their control and in the first flush of enthusiasm governments began to intervene in the economy, claiming that they were creating the economic conditions which would justify their re-election.

Ernest Bevin as Minister of Labour in 1940 acquired powers under the Emergency Powers (Defence) Act that had never been held by central government before. The wages of agricultural workers and railwaymen were raised, and so was excess profit tax. With craftsmen enlisting in the armed services attempts were made to negotiate dilution agreements to use semi-skilled workers. Wages Tribunals were established under the Conditions of Employment and National Arbitration Order No. 1305. Prices were held, real wages increased slightly and the net effect was redistribution of wealth. The foundation was laid for repeated experiments in forms of incomes policy allied, to a lesser or greater extent, to prices and dividend restraint.

The Second World War again accelerated the growth of corporatism. In five years the institutional framework of a semi-planned economy was built up to such an extent that A.J.P. Taylor could write: 'this produced a revolution in British economic life, until in the end direction and control turned Great Britain into a country more fully socialist than anything achieved by the conscious planners of Soviet Russia.'[4] The government intervened in all aspects of industry in order to increase the production of armaments. The financial powers of the banks were curtailed, welfare policies were brought forward to secure the acquiescence of workers and foreign trade was regulated. 'The common struggle against an external enemy provoked in both Labour and Conservative Parties acceptance of the ideas of a mixed economy, a modified imperial role, a welfare state and the perpetuation of institutional consensus.'[5] Many war-time controls were later removed but the process of representation and consultation was now formalised.

The 1945 Labour government, in its centralising measures, was broadly governing within a trend established even before the outbreak of the Second World War. Since then governments have demanded centralised restraint, often with public support, at times of economic crisis, to cope with a collapse in the balance of payments or inflation. Then, as support has been eroded, interest groups have flourished and the restraint has been replaced by a compensatory spiral. The economic crises have followed one another with depressing regularity. Hard choices have been frequently ducked and no fundamental solution has been found, and the pattern of institutional compromise, built up during wartime, has been legitimised and retained in peacetime.

Britain after the Second World War was not compelled to create new institutions to rebuild the economy as were Japan and Germany. Instead old institutions were adapted, particularly parliament, the civil service and local government. The country as a whole shrank from truly radical reform and important permanent institutions such as the universities and schools continued much as before. Even the 1944 Education Act, important though it was, did little to challenge the class structure within Britain.[6] Comprehensive education, bitterly fought over for two decades, has only now gained wider acceptance and is producing good results, and our technical and engineering education is still given far too low a priority.

Britain, the first country to enter the Industrial Revolution, was also the first to confront many of the problems of an industrial society: the alienation of the worker at the place of work, the demoralisation of the assembly line worker, the loss of satisfaction that came with the decline of craftsmanship and the growth of the semi-skilled. With strong and numerous trade unions it has become apparent that many groups of workers, particularly in the public sector, have the potential to cause industrial and social disruption; and the aims of one group often depend on the support of other like-minded groups for success. Division of labour is now so complex that as workers, consumers and citizens we have all come to depend on the actions of other people. The pensioner depends on the single large civil service computer for his or her weekly pension, the housewife on the water engineers, the surgeon on the electricians. A society which recognises that a degree of co-ordination is necessary in order to make life tolerable soon develops the framework for co-ordinating institutions, committees, representation procedures and, to support it all, proliferating administration. The state not surprisingly soon develops a role as integrator, regulator and arbiter, and this happens even in countries where belief in the free market economy has produced a far less interventionist state than in Britain. Yet just as the complexity of life makes it easy for the state to adopt this central role the centralisation makes society strangely vulnerable.

The peculiar nature of British corporatism owes much to

the strange way in which the mixed economy has come to mean a mix not just between public and private ownership but a mixing of objectives and management attitudes within each sector. A public corporation under Labour governments adopts the accounting techniques of private enterprise, its profits are expressed and its productivity measured in line with the practice of private enterprise despite the fact that this may then pose a challenge to the very purpose of having the corporation publicly controlled in the first place. The fact that the railways are a public service becomes secondary or that the National Coal Board has a strategic energy function is ignored in pursuit of profit in its annual accounts. The quantification of service in terms of consumer satisfaction or strategic return is forgotten. A similar criticism can be made of the private sector which, while publicly criticising state intervention, has quietly exploited state intervention and the corporate attitudes of Ministers and civil servants for its own advantage. 'State intervention in economic life in fact largely means intervention for the purpose of helping capitalist enterprise. In no field has the notion of the "welfare state" had a more precise and apposite meaning than here: there are no more persistent and successful applicants for public assistance than the proud giants of the private enterprise system.'[7] It is a perfectly fair criticism that successive British governments have been prepared to pay out public money to firms that not only refuse to follow government guidelines but frequently do not respect regional policy or even minimal criteria of trade union recognition and good employer practice.

Advocates of the mixed economy must be prepared to question the extent to which it is desirable to mix the objectives of the public and private sectors – the extent to which inducing a sense of social responsibility in the private sector is compatible with the economic dynamic that should come from the private entrepreneur. While it is true that Anthony Crosland argued that 'a mixed economy is essential to social democracy', his revisionism has been criticised for, 'in the increasingly controlled bureaucratised and centrally directed economy now prevailing and always favoured by Crosland . . . a firm will hang on to its profits, export more

44

than is economically justified, butter up its trade unions, never dismiss redundant workers, charge only "fair" prices, site new plants where the government wants it to, operate expensive welfare programmes, make gifts to education, patronise the arts, and participate in local community affairs: "Its goals are a 'fair' rather than a maximum profit, reasonably rapid growth, and the warm glow which comes from a sense of public duty" – and a title doubtless for the chairman to boot . . . Crosland thus sees managers as floating rudderless in a sort of vacuum, blown hither and thither by alternate gusts of public duty and non-economic self-interest, responsible to nobody in particular and to everyone in general.'[8] It is a serious criticism that socialists who advocate a mixed economy must face up to; that they risk emasculating the private sector, by constraining its driving force, so limiting its scope for initiative that its strengths and economic contribution are fatally sapped. The charge has substance. It would be better to give the private sector more freedom from central governmental detailed control and legislate instead for local democratic rights for its own employees, freeing it to operate commercially as a force within the economy with the differences between the private and public sector being openly recognised, not incorporated or amalgamated.

A very wide range of institutions is possible and viable within the framework of western industrialised countries. 'The dozen developed capitalist economies are more alike in the goals they pursue than the specific policy techniques and institutions used to achieve them. Each country has its own style in managing the economy, determined largely by its political institutions and social history. The French have contrived a technique of economic planning which requires intimate collaboration between civil servants and private business firms of a sort which English and American tradition abhors. Italy has had success with mixed enterprises owned jointly by government and private stockholders. Swedish co-operatives play stronger economic roles than those in other countries . . . '[9]

In the 1980s Labour Party policy shows every sign of still giving an unquestioned central and dominant role to the state

but, while state intervention has been advocated in every area
of political activity, there has never been agreement about the
role of the state in relation to the trade unions. Trade unionists
and the trade union leaders may call for more state intervention
in industry, but the majority of trade union leaders have never
accepted that the state should interfere with free collective
bargaining and most are opposed to any statutory interference
in industrial relations. It is an odd position to be advocating
state intervention into other people's activities but resenting
any state intervention in one's own trade union activities. A
breakdown in the relationship between Labour governments
and the trade unions has been at the root of the last two
election defeats. There was genuine anger at the attempted
legislation by the Labour government in 1968 into the
conduct of trade unionism. In 1978 and 1979 there was
bitterness over the attempt to impose a fourth year of incomes
policy. A root cause of these two breakdowns in relations has
been that while Labour governments have continued to foster
centralised socialism the trade union movement itself has
been progressively moving towards a more decentralised
structure. The Royal Commission on the Trade Unions
chaired by Lord Justice Donovan, in its major report published
in 1968[10] recognised that there had been a shift in the
bargaining strength of unions from the official structures to
the shopfloor. Since the nineteenth century some unions have
had representatives at the workplace to collect subscriptions
and report to union bodies. Gradually those stewards came to
act as representatives when day to day issues arose especially in
the munitions factories and in the overall war effort in 1914-
18. By 1917 their power was at its zenith, official TUC
leadership was unable to endorse strike action and besides
taking direct unconstitutional action, the stewards began to
campaign for peace and opposed conscription. They were
supported by ILP leaders such as Ramsay MacDonald and
Philip Snowden. During the Depression of the 1920s and
1930s their role was limited by the danger of victimisation, but
since the onset of post-war full employment there has been a
tremendous rise in their number and influence. Today there
are about 300,000 shop stewards,[11] about a third of these in

the engineering industry, which represents 30 per cent of all industrial output. In the 1960s their numbers increased rapidly because of increasing government intervention in collective bargaining and the frustration felt on the shopfloor at the support often given by national union leaderships to this degree of state intervention.

It also became the policy of some unions, notably the Transport and General Workers Union, which is the largest single union with a current membership of two million, deliberately to give positive support to the downward shift in bargaining levels.[12] To some extent the T&GWU wanted to avoid government-imposed controls and to deal with opportunities at individual factories to exploit productivity deals and any other loopholes or agreed flexibilities made necessary by successive national incomes policies: but there was also a conviction that shopfloor bargaining was a better and more democratic way of settling wage levels than central bargaining.

It is impossible for the Labour movement to continue ignoring this dichotomy between the Labour Party and the Trade Union Congress. The centralist tendency of the Labour Party carries the seeds of conflict with a decentralised trade union movement and the fundamental lesson of Labour's 1979 electoral defeat is that this issue must be faced. It is little use wistfully recalling the past with its strong trade union leaders, the era of Arthur Deakin, or of 'Caron's law' in the AUEW. The trade unions are very unlikely to reverse the decentralist trend or to agree to vest much authority in the TUC itself. If this is the case, there is an obvious contradiction in the Labour Party, still pursuing a centralist incomes policy with its norms, flat rate increases and detailed procedures. Logically there is a need to define a new decentralised form of incomes policy which matches the realities of the negotiating structure specifically in the private sector.

' It is also very apparent that the Co-operative Movement feels that the centralist tradition within the Labour Party has ensured that the Party is less receptive to their underlying philosophical concepts. In particular, the inability to see the potential of state incentives for an expansion of industrial co-operatives as an alternative to state ownership has been a source of immense dissatisfaction. The 10 million consumer co-operators, in addition to the more committed 12,000 members of the Co-operative Party, are a substantial potentially sympathetic electoral target for socialists. They probably represent a more naturally receptive audience in terms of underlying attitudes than those many trade unionists who are not co-operators.

A growing number of people identify with the theme of decentralisation and there are strong electoral, as well as philosophical, arguments against re-emphasising the centralist tradition of the Labour Party. The expanding ecological movement has strong decentralist elements within its arguments, as have the campaigns of the various minority groups which gain from the depth of feeling within a locality on a particular issue rather than relying on overall national support. If the Labour Party refuses to reassess its centralist tradition and its continued support for the trend towards greater corporatism then there is good evidence that the electorate as a whole, dissatisfied with many of the practical consequences of the workings of the centralised state, will vote against it, even though they may be attracted to the justice and humanity of socialism. Many people appear already to feel that remote bureaucracies are as hostile to their needs as privated vested interests used to be.

It is necessary to distinguish these criticisms. Some represent a passing mood or are symptomatic of a general frustration directed against our overall national economic decline. Others are serious criticisms of the existing structure of government. However, it is too easy to lapse into generalised condemnation of the state and to avoid facing the disadvantages of some decentralised structures. The case in favour of the network and scale of existing British state institutions is that they attempt to meet specific demands made over the years by the electorate. It can be argued with some justice that they have been established as a direct response to democratic pressures, and are a mechanism for trying to implement democratic government. Democracy, corporatists will argue, is enhanced by involving non-elected but representative persons, as well as the elected, in the decision-making process. Power and influence is thereby dispersed, so the state is able to establish more support for the implementation of its policies. The growth of corporatism in Britain may have helped our success in meeting the challenge of the last fifty years without the social unrest experienced by other countries. It is true that, broadly speaking, the welfare state and in particular the National Health Service and some of the nationalised industries, have been approved by the electorate and successive governments. Even the much-criticised 'quasi-autonomous non-governmental organisations', Quangos, have proved their usefulness and are easier to decry than to abolish.

Though these arguments present a case for the retention of corporatist elements in more or less their present form they are mostly far too complacent. Corporatism is rarely as democratic as its proponents argue. Superficially it appears to be democratic that interest groups should be represented at all levels of government and that powerful institutions such as the TUC and CBI are able to make their views known. As an extension of democracy it is unobjectionable; but it is not acceptable that it should replace democracy or that so much of the dialogue should be held in private. In consulting interest groups it is necessary to take into account how representative they are and to what extent their spokesmen are democratically elected and accountable. It is also necessary to guard against giving the formal interest groups exclusive access. It is difficult to ensure plurality when opinions are dispersed and hard to assemble. Powerful groups are often given weight, and some-times a veto, to the detriment of less organised groups and the public good. Employers often find it easier to obtain a hearing than employees. Individual firms or local authorities are either large enough for their case to be heard or they can join forces and make representations to government as a coherent group far more easily than wage or salary earners. Small business has remained unorganised and uninfluential com-pared with big business: it lacks both the finance and the personal contacts to be able to lobby government as effectively. The homeless and other vulnerable minorities are completely unorganised and are represented only because of the efforts of small protest groups and the campaigning charities. The contrast in strength where, for example, a ratepayer's association or a suburban action group speaks out against having a community project such as a hostel for alcoholics located in its area, is obvious. Producers' organisations organise more easily than groups of consumers and have the necessary finance to research issues and present a case well.

The advocates of interest group democracy make an unspoken assumption that the groups themselves are internally democratic, but often this is not so. Some trade unions have an active democratic structure electing their officials and holding ballots of the membership on policy; others have very little internal democracy. Many interest groups have undemocratic constitutions and a structure which makes no provision for the whole membership to be involved or consulted so the active members have an influence and express views which are not representative of their real support. Where the active members hold minority views the distorted power of their representation can be serious. This is not to criticise activism, since it reflects desirable political commitment, but merely illustrates that the corporate form of representation falls short of the democratic claims so often made for it. If, as is fairly certain, many of our political activities must take place through interest groups then far more effort should be put into helping the groups to be more fully accountable to their members and for members to take a more active interest in what is being done in their name. Publicity is an important check on the unrepresentative exercise of influence. The balloting of members is another way of checking the validity of the representation and is an extension of democracy. Financial support from the state for ballots should be made available on request to all organisations that have a democratic structure, not just to trade unions. Funding should come from an independent commission answerable to parliament not to government, and therefore not capable of being associated with controversial governmental legislation. This form of specific state aid is not open to the objection to general funding, that it will help ossify existing political structures and make them less responsive to their membership and to changes in public support.

Western countries are founded on a belief in parliamentary democracy but periodic general elections offer insufficient opportunity to involve an educated and sophisticated public which is aware of the problems of a complex, mixed-economy industrialised society. New legislation passed by parliament each year has grown rapidly since the First World War.[13] It has changed too in character, from being rather general to dealing with specific and detailed questions and we are no longer governed solely by laws passed by the Westminster parliament. Our membership of the European Community carries with it a mass of Community regulations and directives. The framing of legislation has shifted from the House of Commons to discussions between the civil service and interest groups in London and Brussels. Politicians and politics have always been subject to satire and caricature as an antidote to their power and influence but the trivialisation of debate, stemming from a sterile adversary relationship and the growth of opposition for its own sake, contrast strikingly with the increasing complexity of the issues to be decided. The extent to which in practice the political parties work together for the national interest is frequently hidden from the public by an unacknowledged conspiracy between politicians, who prefer to retain the myth of adversaries in parliament and who mask the corporatism within Whitehall.

Involvement of the state has also been stimulated by large multinational organisations. Now British industry is dominated by a small number of companies controlled by a small number of men whose allegiance may well be to the main Board situated in another country. The concentrated power of industry through mergers and takeovers is demonstrated by the fact that in 1950 the top 100 companies in Britain produced about 20 per cent of our national output. By 1973 they produced 46 per cent and by 1980 this figure had risen to over 60 per cent.[14] This same trend can be observed among financial institutions: the number of clearing banks fell through amalgamation from eleven in 1960 to five in 1980. In education and health many local small schools and hospitals have been closed. In 1960 there were 29,289 schools: this had fallen to 28,352 in 1977. In 1959 there were 3,027 hospitals: by

1978 this had fallen to 2,592. White-collar workers have been unionised, specialised lobby groups have sprung up and abbreviations such as NUT, BMA, RSPCA and NEDC have passed into such common usage that newspapers or newsreaders use them without spelling out their full title. The state sector in Britain has been progressively enlarged until, of the Western democracies, only Austria has a proportionately larger state industrial sector. The British public service is now the largest in the European Community, as a percentage of population, with one public servant for every ten citizens. The nearest Community country in this respect is Germany, with one civil servant for sixteen citizens. These figures are for public servants and do not include the nationalised industries and public corporations.

Obviously, corporatism is reinforced and deeply influenced by the attitudes of those who work within the civil service, but great care should be taken in defining the relationship of the civil service to society generally. In administering the complex of state services and state industries, Ministries and civil servants have a statutory duty placed on them to consult parliament and interested groups, but for the most part, the civil service consults interest groups in private. Its relationship with parliament is a public one but parliament often lacks the authority and the expertise to probe effectively. Discussing the role of interest groups concerned with education under a Labour and a Conservative Secretary of State for Education, Professor Kogan has written: 'neither Crosland nor Boyle would have thought to move very far without consulting Sir William Alexander, Secretary to the Association of Education Committees, Sir Ronald Gould, Secretary to the National Union of Teachers, and their counterparts in the other local authority and teachers' organisations . . . Such officials as William Alexander constitute a powerful, perhaps the most powerful, entity within the educational service for a longer period than any Minister or Permanent Secretary.'[15]

This requirement to consult interest groups has given rise to another manifestation of corporatism, the network of advisory bodies, consumer groups, regulatory agencies and semi-independent organisations such as the University Grants

Committee, all of which enter into a client relationship with the state. By January 1980 there were 489 bodies in this group, accounting for expenditure of £5,800 million in 1978-9 and employing 217,000 staff. Advisory bodies numbered 1,561 and cost their sponsor bodies, which were usually government departments, £13 million. There are different tribunal systems each containing many individual tribunals as well as some constituted on an ad hoc basis, such as the 2,000 National Insurance Local Tribunals set up each year. The question is whether tribunals are effective in controlling routine administration as it affects the citizen in a way parliament can never hope to be. An approximate count revealed that there were 67 'tribunal systems' with administrative costs in 1978-9 of £30 million. These figures do not, however, include the nationalised industries or the National Health Service. In 1978-9 the Health Service had 900,000 employees and cost £7,000 million. The nationalised industries employed 1,000,000 and had a turnover of nearly £24,000 million. A further unwelcome aspect of corporatism is the number of top jobs at the disposal of Ministers and civil servants. The Department of Health and Social Security, for instance, had 3,100 appointments at its discretion in 1980 while the Department of Employment had 650.[16]

There is a corporatist tendency to stress the need for secrecy to safeguard citizens' rights generally, but to be shockingly insensitive to a particular or individual case. If we are to develop a more responsive form of political activity all our institutions will need to become more accountable and their size will need to be reduced, for the larger an institution the less democratic and the more bureaucratically top-heavy it is likely to be. Clearly institutions must range from the small school to the giant coal industry, but we need a new, more vigilant approach to guard against the tendency for the upper levels of any institution gradually to accumulate power at the expense of lower levels. Each of the three major concentrations of power within the state, the civil service, the trade unions and large-scale industry, whether in private or state hands, will need to adopt a more open attitude to information if power is to be effectively controlled. It is not the paranoid spectre of a civil servant actively misleading or obstructing Ministers which is worrying, but rather that ever-growing civil service power and influence has not been countered by a matching growth in democratic checks and controls. Opening up civil service advice by introducing more short-term outside advisers, allowing decision-making to be subjected to greater public and parliamentary scrutiny and insisting on a more highly developed system of answerability is all feasible. So is a radical Freedom of Information Act and so are reforms of administrative law to protect individual citizen rights.

Decentralisation is not without disadvantages nor will it be easy to achieve. For example, the decentralisation of the trade unions to meet the demands of shopfloor workers who were dissatisfied with the policies of a remote union leadership, has diminished the authority of the trade union leader and, along with his authority, that of the TUC. No longer can the TUC guarantee the support of individual trade unions, let alone a majority of trade unionists in negotiations over government policy, particularly over incomes policies. This means that any TUC-government or -CBI dialogue must be more realistic in its aims and objectives. The dialogue, though useful, must reflect the limitations imposed by the structure of its constituent participants. The CBI is also unable to deliver the management of many of its individual companies. The importance of industrial democracy is that it realises that changes in attitudes do not come simply through changes in ownership but only through real worker participation at the factory floor. The First World War and subsequent history has shown that trade union power is something which the state cannot ignore; to that extent the corporatist trend was irresistible, but the way that the state has sought to come to grips with trade union power through a dialogue between the TUC and CBI is no longer enough. The dialogue must increasingly now take place between management and trade unionists at the factory floor. This is why industrial democracy is so essential for it provides the framework for such dialogue and it reflects the realities of decentralised industrial bargaining.

Decentralising power in any society means that co-ordination of that society becomes more difficult, since no group easily sees the need to safeguard legitimate national interests. Part of the attraction of the new society which has evolved in Britain is its loss of deference and authoritarianism so the state now finds it harder to coerce groups or force them to work together. A decentralised society needs therefore to develop a counterbalancing sense of interdependence where, instead of an identification with the state first and then to the community, one starts with the community and then relates that responsibility to the nation. Hitherto the state has feared the creation of a mass of non-accountable, self-interested factions and has consciously condemned the sectional interests that community identification has produced. The task now, having clung far too long to a dominant role for the state, is to build up through democratic involvement a sense of community in order to rediscover a responsibility from the individual to the state.

There has been an underlying confusion about the nature of democracy that has justified the corporatist trend of the past. The virtue of democracy is that though its processes involve delay and have a definable cost it is a decisive mechanism. The issue for decision is put to the vote and the majority view then prevails. Corporatism with its emphasis on consensus, consultation and committee decision-making carries both the delay in decision-making and the costs of democracy but lacks its decisiveness. Corporatism is a recipe for choosing the lowest common denominator, for the stifling of initiative and innovation. By its very nature it plays safe, it follows the cautious, timid and indecisive path. It is a recipe for drift and decay and it is no accident that it is the corporatist trend which has coincided with Britain's decline. Britain cannot be revived unless corporatism is rejected and democracy allowed to flourish in its place.

4

The Social Democratic Tradition

Social democracy is part of the development of European socialism. Not only are most European socialists called Social Democrats, but particularly in the late 1950s and early 1960s they began to develop a distinctive character within the Socialist International.

The British Labour Party, which has always avoided being labelled a social democratic party, convened the first post-war meeting of socialists in London in March 1945. It was a time of great optimism for socialism in Europe. Julius Braunthal, the historian of the International, and a former Secretary General, wrote: 'It seemed as though a conference to discuss the re-establishment of the International could hardly have met under more hopeful auguries. For the first time in history, the working class had entered the scene as a decisive factor in world policy . . . while the fundamental split in the International Labour movement had not yet been overcome, in most of Europe, as in France, Italy and Czechoslovakia and all other Eastern European countries, socialist parties were co-operating with communist parties in joint action alliances or coalition governments. An International, based on the power and influence of the European socialist parties, was for the first time in a position to become a true power capable of direct influence over world policy.'[1]

It was not long after the May 1946 Conference at Clacton, however, before fundamental differences began to appear between those Eastern European socialists, by no means all of them, who supported their countries' increasingly close relationship with the Soviet Union, and the socialist parties of Western Europe. It was not therefore possible for a united International to be re-founded: instead, the parties decided to set up a small secretariat in London – The Socialist Information and Liaison Office (SILO) – to exchange information and organise periodic discussions, meetings and conferences on the international situation. This was staffed by the British Labour Party. Another international socialist conference – this time in Bournemouth in 1946 – failed to make progress towards re-uniting Eastern and Western European socialist parties. Many Socialists – including British Labour Party members – still tended to believe the wartime propaganda line that all Germans were Nazis, and the conference could not bring itself to make a decision to admit the German socialists.

The decision to admit the Germans, taken at the next international socialist conference, at Zurich in June 1947, marked the beginning of the important role the SPD was to play in European socialism. The other watershed in post-war European socialist politics was marked by Stalin's decision, in September 1947, to revive the Communist International as the 'Cominform', with a clear intention to oppose and be hostile towards the democratic socialist parties of Western Europe. The decision, implemented at a secret meeting in Poland, established the Cominform as an instrument of Stalin's foreign policy: the meeting was attended by the Soviet and East European governing communist parties, but only two Western European communist parties – those of France and Italy – were invited. As Braunthal comments: 'to those communist parties who had not been invited it came as much as a surprise as it did to the rest of the world'.[2] This was certainly not the old Communist International. The politics of European socialism were now inextricably caught up in the geopolitics of the Soviet Union. That same year the United States launched the Marshall Plan to rebuild Europe, strongly influenced by Ernest Bevin, the British Foreign Secretary. The basic outlines of the Cold War were already drawn. The Marshall Plan as such was never conceived as anti-communist; indeed, communist states were eligible to take part in it, and the Soviet Foreign Minister, Molotov, attended a conference in Paris in June to discuss the implementation of the Plan; but Stalin concluded that it was all part of a United States' policy against the Soviet Union, withdrew Molotov from Paris, and embarked on his cold war phase, harnessing communist parties to that basic purpose.

The Cominform was to be the instrument of Stalin's policy, and from that moment onwards, the Soviet Union presented the problem as one of the two opposing 'camps'; the democratic, peace-loving Soviet Union and its friends, on the one hand, facing, on the other, the imperialist United States, bent on the economic and political 'enslavement' of the world, beginning with Western Europe. Soviet propaganda portrayed the socialist parties of Western Europe as 'masks' behind which the evil forces of imperialism did their dirty work. Communist parties like those of France and Italy which had, during and immediately after the war, co-operated with the socialists in the tasks of resistance and reconstruction, now found themselves having to denounce their former colleagues as traitors, and, in carrying out the orders of the Cominform, organising largely political strikes. The socialists, in their turn, became alarmed at what they saw as increasing Soviet interest in exerting influence, or even control or domination, in Western Europe, disguised as national movements seeking improvements in working-class living and working conditions. In Britain the Communist Party began active opposition to the Labour government during 1947.

Simultaneously, Stalin began to move against the socialists who were in coalition with communists in the Eastern European governments. Two hundred socialist leaders in Poland were arrested in 1947, and the following year 82,000 of the Polish Socialist Party's members were purged. In 1948, following a series of manoeuvres and ruses – involving the publication of a false statement that the social democrats had agreed to an amalgamation with the Communist Party – the Social Democratic Party of Hungary was swallowed up into the Communist Party. In Czechoslovakia in February 1948, after disputes in government between the communist ministers and those from other parties, the communists seized power and formed their own government, the socialists were 'fused' with the communists, and elections were held with only communists and social democrats taking part: 214 communists out of 300 deputies were elected; a few weeks later, by mid-1948, the social democrats had been absorbed into the Communist Party and Czechoslovakia, too, had passed through the complete process of Stalinisation. For socialists the Prague coup marked a watershed; few disagreed that Stalin's desire for expansionism and control now represented a grave danger for the whole of Western Europe. Ernest Bevin, robust trade unionist first and Labour politician second, never had any doubts. On 4 April 1949, twelve countries signed the NATO pact; it received the full backing of European socialists, including many on the Left of the British Labour Party. In 1948 European socialists had to concern themselves with what differentiated themselves from the European Communist Parties. They faced, in the words of a 1948 International Socialist Conference resolution, 'the problem of defending democracy'. And in June 1948 the Socialist International defined what it meant by political democracy: 'The parties represented at this conference are opposed to the one-party state and all systems of government based upon it. They are of the opinion that a system of political democracy must combine in itself a recognition of the pre-eminence of the individual which is to be guaranteed by the following freedoms: Freedom of thought, opinion and speech; security in law and protection against interference by other individuals; . . . equality before the law and protection against political tampering with the machinery of justice; unimpeded freedom and guarantees of rights in elections; the right to an opposition; the political and lawful equality of all citizens, irrespective of class, race or sex.'[3]

The Socialist International as such was not formally reconstituted until the Frankfurt Congress of June 1951. 'The Frankfurt Declaration' – the 'Declaration of Aims and Tasks of Democratic Socialism' – stands with the Communist Manifesto of 1848 and the Inaugural Address of the First International of 1864 as fundamental documents in the history of the International.[4] The Declaration was drawn up after weeks of work by member parties and represented, in a way the earlier declaration had not, a clear distillation of the views of the socialist movement as a whole. The Declaration said, 'socialism aims to liberate the peoples from dependence on a minority which owns or controls the means of production. It aims to put economic power in the hands of the people as a whole and to create a community in which free men work together as equals.' At the same time, however, the Declaration insisted on the importance of freedom: 'without freedom there can be no socialism. Socialism can be achieved only through democracy. Democracy can be fully realised only through socialism.' The Declaration also made the point that, despite Marxist doctrine, the advent of socialism was not 'inevitable': 'it demands a personal contribution from all its followers'. But such a contribution did not have to be along narrowly or dogmatically defined lines. The Preamble makes the point, in Article 11: whether socialists build their faith on Marxist or other methods of analysing society, whether they are inspired by religious or humanitarian principles, they all strive for the same goal – a system of social justice, better living, freedom and world peace. These were the beliefs and doctrines which shaped all the European socialist parties whether they were referred to as social democrats, democratic socialists, Labour, or by any other name, in the period following the Second World War.

In a number of countries European socialists held power for long periods. When it lost the 1976 election, the Social Democratic Party in Sweden had been in government for forty-four years. Although there was some unease among some Swedish voters about what they consider to be the semi-'corporate state' established by the social democrats, there can be no doubt about the achievements of that Party. Sweden developed a far greater degree of perceived fairness among wage-earners, and measures such as comprehensive occupational retraining schemes, and the planned provision of housing helped to reduce differentials among manual workers and to lessen resistance to technological innovation. The highly centralised system of Swedish wage-bargaining, successful for many years, encountered serious problems only in the winter pay-round of 1979-80. Yet interestingly Swedish socialism has never been dominated by the debate about the nationalisation of private industry as British socialism has. When the Swedish socialists lost power 95 per cent of all industry was still in private hands. Facing recession it has been its non-socialist government successor which has had to take large sections of industry into public ownership.

The Swedish Social Democratic Party has taken an active role in the Socialist International. Under successive social democratic governments Sweden increased her aid to the Third World. In 1977-8 Sweden fulfilled her target of devoting 1 per cent of her GNP to development assistance, and was one of only three countries which reached the 0·7 per cent target set by the International Development Strategy in 1975. Sweden has refused to join either NATO or the Warsaw Pact, and has been closely involved in international work on disarmament and in supporting UN peace-keeping efforts; but at the same time Swedish social democrats believe in maintaining strong defences and over many years they have spent more per head on arms than any other West European country.

Another highly successful Socialist Party is that of Austria. It has consistently gained over half of the country's votes and its active membership includes nearly a tenth of the total population. Originally strongly anti-clerical, and with a basic programme drawn up in 1926 when a Right-wing coup was a serious possibility, the Austrian socialists met in Vienna in 1958 and adopted unanimously a major reformulation of principles under the New Programme. They then made it clear that theirs was not only the party of the 'working class' narrowly defined, but the party of 'all working people'. On nationalisation they said it should be considered when it was in the 'national interest'.

Part of the secret of the Austrian Socialist Party's success has been the popular and charismatic figure of Chancellor Kreisky. Active in the Socialist International, and a strong advocate of better relations between Europe and the Third World, Kreisky has been particularly effective in encouraging dialogue between Israel and the Arab World. Yasser Arafat, leader of the Palestine Liberation Organisation, took part in discussions with socialist leaders at a party leaders' conference of the

Socialist International held in Vienna, under Kreisky's auspices, in February 1980.

If the Swedish or Austrian parties had, by the 1960s, become virtually the 'natural parties of government' of their respective countries, the same cannot be said of the British Labour Party or the German SPD. The SPD is the oldest and best-known social democratic party in Europe, and its role in the development of democratic socialism has been extremely important. But in the immediate aftermath of the Second World War it had failed to develop as a dynamic party and, under the leadership of Kurt Schumacher, a survivor from Weimar days, had begun to decay. 'The SPD had begun to display the bureaucratisation and ageing that had been so marked in Weimar,' one British scholar noted.[5] When Schumacher died in 1952, 'the organisation and programmatic symbols of the party were still intact, but they were decaying from within. Membership had fallen steeply since 1948 and the parliamentary party was becoming the most influential organ of party decision.'[6] After its second electoral defeat, in 1953, efforts to change the party accelerated. These efforts took place against the background of a strong upsurge in Christian Democrat party support and organisation, and where the German Democratic Republic, and its claims to be socialist, were constantly before the German public as a permanent and damaging source of confusion between Marxist-Leninist bureaucratic socialism and the democratic socialism of the International.

In 1956 the Communist Party was banned in the Federal Republic. This was the background to the special party conference called by the SPD at Bad Godesberg in 1959, at which a completely new 'Basic Programme' for the party was adopted. There the old aim of nationalisation of the economy was abandoned. 'Free competition and free initiative for the employer' were to become 'important elements in Social Democratic economic policy': while 'the private ownership of the means of production has a claim to be protected and promoted, so long as it does not hinder the setting up of a just social order.' This was fully in line with the Frankfurt Declaration, which stated that one of the aims of democratic socialism was 'effective democratic control of the economy'. The co-operative ownership of the means of production was, however, recognised as a 'legitimate form of public control'. Economic and social change, it was argued, had not been taken into account, and a major re-statement of party principles was therefore necessary. Marx was effectively dropped. Thus the SPD became what some observers have termed a 'Volkspartei', in other words a party aiming to bring together as many voters as possible rather than to be the expression of one class. The attainment of government became the main objective of the party. Its emphasis was laid not on 'agitation or extra-parliamentary activity, but rather governing, research and expertise and a pragmatic – some would say technocratic – approach to the problems of the day'.[7] By 1966 the SPD had entered government as part of the 'Grand Coalition' and after the federal election of 1969 Willy Brandt became Chancellor, at the head of an SPD/liberal (FDP) coalition. The new programme seemed to have brought about an SPD breakthrough to parts of the electorate which the party had never previously reached – the Catholic working-class, rural voters in general and the female vote. But the Young Socialists rebelled against the new programme, causing difficulties in the party for Brandt, who also faced calls for a tough line against the Young Socialists, right up to the time he resigned as Chancellor in May 1974. But since then the new programme has, by and large, been accepted and supported by the membership and October 1980 saw another electoral victory for Chancellor Schmidt with the continuation of the SPD-FDP coalition – though it was the FDP who gained the most electoral support.

Very similar processes have gone on in the Dutch Labour Party. In 1946 the Labour Party had replaced the old Social Democratic Workers Party (SDAP) – partly in order to deal with the religious problem in Dutch politics, by broadening its appeal – but it, too, felt the need – also in 1959 – to embark on a redefinition of its basic objectives. Here too it was the acceptance of the mixed economy and the abandonment of a formal revolutionary social position which provided the real significance of the change. The Dutch Labour Party (PvdA) then became a pragmatic party of government, not afraid of entering government in coalition with others. But divisions in the party came to a head in 1970, when some people left and formed the new 'Democratic Socialists '70' Party. In 1973-7 under proportional representation it was possible for the parties of the Left and Centre to combine in a coalition under a Socialist Prime Minister pursuing policies which were often more radical than those pursued by the British Labour government. This is particularly so in relation to the Third World where the Dutch socialist position is the most radical and enlightened of any other European socialist party.

Most of the major European socialist parties have, formally as well as in practice, accepted the mixed economy. Only in Britain, since the failure of Hugh Gaitskell's formal attempt, following the election defeat of 1959, to get the Labour Party to amend Clause 4 (see Chapter 2, the Decentralist Tradition), has there been real tension between the constitutional commitment in Clause 4 to common ownership of the means of production, distribution and exchange, and Labour's behaviour to the private sector when in office. How important is this tension? Why did Hugh Gaitskell feel it necessary to embark on this struggle at all when so many of his friends advised him against doing so? The whole controversy was deeply emotional and, as his biographer has written, shrouded with biblical terminology with warnings against tampering with Tablets of Stone, touching the Ark of the Covenant and bothering about the 39 Articles, so much so that Gaitskell said he 'wished he led a political party and not a religious movement'.[8] In the aftermath of the defeat over changing Clause 4 in the Constitution even Gaitskell admitted that if he had foreseen the kind of opposition he would never have raised the issue. He did so because he knew, and many others knew too, that the reputation of wanting to nationalise everything was damaging the party with the electorate. In the 1960s it was possible to believe that nationalisation was dead as an issue, buried by the emphasis on technology and the search for economic growth and that the statement adopted by the 1960 Labour Conference had succeeded in shifting the emphasis away from 100 per cent nationalisation and in emphasising other aims. However, as so often in Labour history emotive issues keep reappearing. The 'idolators' on the Left, as the defenders of Clause 4 were called, recognised that this was an issue on which they could rally the party activists and particularly in the wake of the electoral defeats in 1970 and again in 1979 this issue was used as a lever in the inner power struggle as much as to attack the whole concept of the mixed economy. If it could be said that the issue was only a problem in Opposition it could no doubt be shrugged off but there is now considerable evidence that it is a running problem for Labour governments in office. The stark fact has to be faced that a considerable body of influential people in terms of policy formation in the British Labour Party are not content to adopt a pragmatic case by case attitude to state ownership. It is an exaggeration to claim that the controversy over state ownership has been a dominant factor in Britain's economic decline but it has been a contributing factor. The refusal of the Labour Party to face the need for a fundamental reassessment of attitudes, such as took place for the SPD at Bad Godesberg the same year as the Clause 4 controversy, has meant the Labour Party cannot claim and does not wish to claim, that it is a Social Democratic Party. It prides itself on being instead a Democratic Socialist party. In fact in post-war European socialism the two terms have been until recently widely regarded as interchangeable. The Campaign for Democratic Socialism, which played an important part at the grass roots in overturning the 1960 Labour Conference decision for unilateralism, 'was originally conceived by some of the younger Labour candidates who had written to support Gaitskell over Clause Four'.[9] Yet slowly as European socialists became the governing party and demonstrated that their rejection of Marxism and their less ideological approach to the mixed economy was successful in Sweden, Austria, Germany and Holland, a Social Democrat became a description not just of a socialist but of a socialist who worked constructively within the framework of a mixed economy, not against the framework of the mixed economy, as is the more prevalent attitude in Britain within the Labour Party.

Within the British Labour Party it is acceptable to defend the mixed economy but not to espouse it. The dominant attitude is one of resigned acceptance and 'true socialism' is still assessed against the yardstick of support for nationalisation. Just as the labelling of Left and Right within the Labour Party, though often having little justification, is very hard to change, so it now appears that democratic socialist is no longer an interchangeable term with social democrat. After an initial reluctance to stop using the term democratic socialist, I am now clear that it means little within the ideological mix within the Labour Party, for everyone from every position in the spectrum claims it as his or her own. It is now time for those in Britain who wish to identify with the form of socialism successfully practised by other European socialists boldly to proclaim their adherence to the traditions of social democracy and wear openly the label of being a social democrat. I hope it will enable those of us who claim to be radical socialists to shed the press label of being 'Right wing', given to us just because we oppose the policies of bureaucratic centralism labelled 'Left wing'. For any socialist to be labelled Right wing is a damaging term, for it challenges the general identification of socialism with the Left and Conservatism with the Right. Similarly to be called a moderate is to imply a lack of radicalism, commitment and passion. Social Democracy is not a consensus, watered down form of socialism. It has a record in Europe of pioneering socialist policies of welfare reform which have redistributed wealth and power, but it has not yet identified with decentralisation.

The best working definition of social democracy is that of Leszek Kolakowski: 'the trouble with the social democratic idea is that it does not stock and does not sell any of the exciting ideological commodities which various totalitarian movements – Communists, fascists or leftists – offer dream-hungry youth. It is no ultimate solution for all human misery and misfortunes. It has no prescription for the total salvation of mankind. It cannot promise the firework of the last revolution to settle definitely all conflicts and struggles. It invented no miraculous devices to bring about the perfect unity of man and universal brotherhood. It believes in no final victory over evil.

'It requires, in addition to commitment to a number of

66

basic values, hard knowledge and rational calculation, since we need to be aware of and to investigate as exactly as possible, the historical and economic conditions in which these values are to be implemented. It is an obstinate will to erode by inches the conditions which produce avoidable suffering, oppression, hunger, wars, racial and national hatred, insatiable greed and vindictive envy.'[10]

It is the obstinate will to erode by inches which contrasts so sharply with the passionate will to jump by miles that reflects the divide between the realists and the idealists, the achievers and the dreamers. Most social democratic parties in Europe can point to a record of practical achievement which neither of the British Labour governments of the 1960s or 1970s could match – of specific welfare measures and economic success which have directly benefited the poorest people in their countries.

What Kolakowski describes is an approach. It is not a soft, middle of the road, flabby consensus, but a hard-headed realistic assessment of what is obtainable within the democratic constraints that are imposed on any government. It is an approach built neither on dreams nor on dogmas. In every social democratic country the social democrats have strong links with trade unionists. The politicians see themselves as speaking for the views of trade unionists but there is not the same tendency to an exclusive relationship which is detectable in Britain. The relationship with the Trade Unions as organis-ations are close but not all pervasive.

As Paterson and Campbell have pointed out[11] some political scientists have attempted to define labour parties, as opposed to social democratic parties, by the closeness of their relations with the trade union movement: social democratic parties, in contradistinction to labour parties, are friendly to labour but do not have direct trade union affiliation. But the Dutch Labour Party adopted its name in 1945 when it ceased to have direct union affiliation, and only the British Labour Party retains direct affiliation and organic links with trade unions. Most social democratic parties began as 'labour parties' but have loosened the organic connection. In Belgium the Workers' Party was largely responsible for the creation of a strong labour movement after the war; but while the General Federation of Labour of Belgium is socialist-led it contains many other elements besides socialists and while it generally works closely with, and supports, the socialist Party, it has at times been harshly critical of it. In Germany, too, the Weimar period saw close relations between the SPD and the trade union movement, but those who helped set up the reconstructed trade union movement after the war – who included a number of SPD leaders including the present leader of the SPD in parliament, Herbert Wehner – ensured that the trade union confederation, the DGB, should not take on a party political affiliation. The SPD rejected a proposal that it should become a German Labour Party in 1945. As in Belgium, relations have in practice been good and close, but in Germany the unions do not financially underwrite the SPD as the British unions do with the British Labour Party, neither is there the type of close institutional involvement which takes place in the bodies of the Labour Party. In late 1980 following the re-election of the SPD/FPD coalition tensions occurred between the two coalition partners because the unions, backed by the SPD but opposed by the FPD, wanted tougher measures to ensure worker participation in industry, particularly in the coal and steel industries. In France and Italy, meanwhile, the Communist party has dominated the largest trade union confederation, while in both countries social democrats, socialists, Christians and the extreme Left have competed for control of other confederations and unions. David Hine has contrasted the French and Italian pattern of labour movement with the British, in which 'the potential for inter-union conflict is very great, but in which formal commitment to the ideology of labour-movement unity prevents an organisational rupture at confederal level'. The TUC is not politically linked – but this is a formality to cover the position of those unions not affiliated to the Labour Party. It does not stop the TUC working on future policy with the Labour Party through a body called the Liaison Committee.

The question must arise as to whether the 'formal commitment' to unity in the labour movement is sustainable. The Labour Party and the trade union movement have different jobs to do – the one may work closely with the other, but for both the disadvantages of too close an organic relationship can be considerable. The defects of the one may be visited upon the other: at the moment the argument that the British Labour Party is run by the trade unions is a criticism of the Labour Party, but there could equally come a time when trade union members might be critical of the trade union movement's close relations with a future Labour government. The fact is – as the continental parties have recognised – that the interests of a broadly-based socialist party and those of the trade union movement do not always coincide as in the past. That Britain remains the only country in Europe to retain such close organic links is something which should be re-examined. If state funding for political parties was to be introduced that of itself would help to change the relationship from one of dependence to one of interdependence, and this would be highly desirable.

There has been little public concern in Sweden, Austria, Germany, Holland or Denmark when the social democrats have been in power that the government is controlled by or in any sense dominated by the trade unions or that the trade union leaders have an overwhelming position of influence. Labour governments in Britain have in contrast frequently been subjected to this charge. It often has little justification but at times the exclusiveness of the relationship has been justly criticised. It has also damaged the trade unions, for their primary relationship has become increasingly with the Labour Party to the detriment of their relationship with the CBI and with any Conservative government. It is a worrying aspect of the Labour Party's decline in membership and in organisational efficiency that this has thrust the Party into an ever closer financial relationship with the trade unions, fortifying a recent trend towards trade union dominance. It is essential that a socialist party that hopes to win the support of all sections of society should have a measure of financial independence so that it is never wholly dependent on trade union support. It is no part of socialism to identify itself only with the interests of the trade union movement particularly when a growing number of trade unionists vote Conservative. The present

69

danger is that the Labour Party will identify increasingly with trade unions and the political leaders of the trade unions and less with individual trade unionists. This trend towards an isolation from the grass roots is another aspect of centralisation and corporatism and is part of the explanation for the decline in the Labour Party membership and votes in successive elections. Emphasising the approach of the social democratic parties is the only way to rebuild a wider electoral appeal for the Labour Party. Narrowing the appeal, reinforcing the financial and political links with trade unions as opposed to trade unionists, is likely only to speed the decline in the Labour Party's fortunes. The Labour Party's refusal to recognise the mood which wants to give every member the vote on crucial issues, the Labour Party's reluctance to move away from delegated democracy to a more genuine participatory democracy, is against the trend of social democratic parties in Europe and against the trend of public opinion. It is a profoundly conservative response, the response of a Party that will not face the future, will not contemplate the equivalent of an SPD Bad Godesberg conference. It is a response heavily influenced by those trade unionists who resist the introduction of ballots in their own union and fear that their supporting one member one vote for the Labour Party will carry implications for their own union's procedures. Some trade unions want delegated democracy to continue in the Labour Party for the same reason, and these support GMC decision-making and the introduction of mandatory re-selection. Some also want the trade union block vote to exert an increased influence in the Party, which is why they voted, unsuccessfully, at the 1980 Conference for the NEC to be solely responsible for the Manifesto in an attempt to remove the joint responsibility of the NEC and Cabinet or Shadow Cabinet; and it is why they have voted for an electoral college, with the block vote, which includes Conservative and Communist levy payers, for the first time being able to influence the election of the Party Leader and Prime Minister. The Labour Party, unlike the German SPD which had a clear Marxist philosophy prior to the Bad Godesberg decisions, has a less defined ideology, summed up in the saying 'Socialism is what the Labour Party does', and this makes it harder to grapple with a decisive redirection of policy. The Labour Party is facing the 1980s with the old recipes of 1945: more nationalisation, more state control, more centralisation. The problems of the 1980s are very different from the challenge of recovery from the effects of the Second World War. The task now for socialists in Britain is to develop a new approach, drawing on two traditions, decentralised socialism and social democracy; to develop a new political force in Britain which can hold public opinion for a sustained period of government. Socialist values and attitudes will only bear fruit in Britain, as in Continental Europe, with a sustained period of over ten years of socialist government.

PART TWO
The Pursuit of Equality

5

Inequality

The Beveridge Report, published at the end of the Second World War, contained radical proposals which aimed at eradicating want. This was to be done primarily through a comprehensive system of social insurance benefits, the introduction of non-contributory and non-means-tested allowances for children, with some means-tested benefits to fill a few gaps, and with the provision of health services free of charge. By the 1960s it was commonly assumed that full employment and the apparent implementation of the Report had substantially alleviated poverty. However, careful research work soon showed this assumption to be wrong: poverty had not been eradicated by Beveridge. It became possible to identify sectors of poverty[1] where the social security system was proving inadequate to cope with the scale of the problem.

Neither has the record proved to have been very much better on the redistribution of wealth in the post-war period, with massive inequalities remaining largely because they have been buttressed by structural and institutional resistance within society. In a recent detailed and thorough study of poverty and inequality[2] it is argued that these two are linked, since the minority who hold wealth determine the level of the income of the majority and when wealth holders are squeezed they ensure that a corresponding squeeze is put on other people's incomes.

This argument is of course only one factor in the continuation of inequality. If one broadly accepts that wealth holding is related to unearned income not only does this represent only about 5 per cent of total income but the wealth holders are rarely crucial decision makers or as great an influence as tax payers in the middle range of incomes. Nor can it be credibly argued that it is just the capitalist systems in the world that have failed to distribute incomes and wealth fairly: there has been a similar failure in authoritarian communist countries and authoritarian socialist countries. It used to be felt that the key to fairer income distribution lay in economic growth. But while economic growth produces a buoyant climate of well-being in which it is easier to ensure that some people's incomes increase relatively slower than others, that very same buoyant climate is one which often induces inertia in grappling with income distribution because most people are benefiting. Paradoxically it is in periods of low economic growth that the climate of opinion is more opposed to marked inequalities of income, and yet the resistance to income redistribution is then greatest as people hold hard to what they have. The market economy, in as much as it can be separated from the capitalist economy, is also criticised as impeding redistribution but the controlled planned economies have if anything a no better record on redistribution and certainly a worse record on overall economic prosperity.

The harsh fact is that there is no one set of circumstances which will guarantee a more equal income distribution with an increasing level of general prosperity. Britain has never had a socialist government coinciding with a period of sustained economic growth so we do not know whether this combination would produce income redistribution, but it remains the most likely combination for success. The danger in the present argument within British socialism about inequality is that in a climate of despair it is easy to forget that there is very considerable resistance within the Labour movement to change in income distribution. The trade union commitment to free collective bargaining works against any centralised income redistribution: decentralised bargaining by different unions representing different crafts and skills perpetuates and often increases differentials. Resistance to paying much higher child benefit does not just come from Conservatives; it is very strong within the trade union movement and amongst traditional Labour voters; and it is these people, who form the bulk of the population, who are the electoral target of all the political parties. The strength of the pressure from pensioners who vote for increases in the pension benefit level, is very strong. Pressures of this kind influence decisions which run counter to the factual basis of assessing need and real social priority for non voters such as children and the mentally handicapped.

The debate about inequality is about more than the distribution of wealth and income alone, though those issues remain central for any socialist wishing to reduce inequality. The facts about how wealth and income are distributed are themselves difficult to find and to agree on. Considerable methodological difficulties arise in trying to measure their present distribution, and it would be misleading to claim that any one set of figures show the 'true' position. The change in distribution over time is especially fraught with problems of measurement because of changes in official statistics and the inadequacy of information. The most recent information about Britain is summarised in Table 1.

TABLE 5.1. Cumulative (percentage) shares of personal wealth 1960-75[3]

	Great Britain			
Group	1960	1965	1970	1975
Top 1%	38·2	33·0	29·0	23·2
Top 5%	64·3	58·5	56·3	46·5
Top 10%	76·7	73·3	70·1	62·4
Bottom 90%	23·3	26·7	29·9	37·6

These figures show that the shares of the richest groups have fallen since 1960 but that this movement towards redistribution has not been marked, neither does it show any sign of accelerating. The reasons for the falling share of the top 1 per cent has not been the imposition of increased capital taxation by Labour governments but has been due to the slump in the market for shares and the erosion of the value of assets, apart from property, through inflation.[4] It remains a fair conclusion that inherited wealth is still responsible for a substantial degree of inequality and that large-scale inheritances still pay relatively little tax. The Vestey affair in 1980 is merely the tip of a very large iceberg.

It is apparent when analysing the inequality of incomes over time that a similar modest trend has reduced the extent of inequality but that, as with the distribution of wealth, great inequalities in the distribution of income remain (see Table 2).

TABLE 5.2. Cumulative distribution of personal income after tax, 1949 to 1977-8[5]

	Great Britain							
	1949	1959	1963	1967	1972-1973	1973-1974	1974-1975	1977-1978
Top 1%	6·4	5·3	5·2	4·9	4·4	4·5	4·0	3·9
Top 5%	17·7	15·8	15·7	14·8	14·2	14·3	13·7	13·7
Top 10%	27·1	25·2	25·2	24·3	23·6	23·6	23·2	23·3
Top 40%	64·1	65·0	64·7	63·5	63·8	63·5	63·6	64·2
Top 70%	85·4	88·7	88·2	88·0	87·8	87·2	87·2	87·4
Bottom 30%	14·6	11·2	11·8	12·0	12·3	12·8	12·8	12·6

It is noticeable that the small amount of redistribution which did occur over the period largely failed to help the very poorest, the bottom 30 per cent, and helped only the middle income groups at the expense of the very high earning groups. The lack of redistribution is also remarkable, given that, throughout the period, a progressive tax system with increasingly higher rates was in force. The UK tax system seems progressive, since marginal rates of tax are higher than the average, but the effect of inflation in the 1970s was to bring more low earners into the tax net during the long period when the tax allowances were not index-linked. The failure to raise tax allowances, the increase in indirect taxation and the small rises in universal benefits in the 1970s created the 'poverty trap', a social scandal whereby many families with children were better off not working, as can be seen in Table 3. It is worth examining the poverty trap for the period of two governments 1978-80. Of course many of the trends were inherited from the previous Labour government so the criticism of the disincentive effect and the inflationary effect have to be shared by both governments. But the result of every step that the new Conservative government has taken in the field of tax and social security benefits has been to exacerbate the poverty trap.

The salutary conclusion is that a family with four children has more spending power if the father earns £45 a week than if he earns £85 and in every case the spending power gain from extra earnings is less two years later. The poverty trap is primarily due to inadequate child support and the poorest paid, particularly those with children, are paying much more in tax today than ever before.

The impact of tax on the potential Labour Party voter is a recent phenomenon and one which carries immense electoral implications. In 1945 redistribution of income through tax was a popular policy and even in 1955 the average married male manual worker paid no income tax. But by 1967 he was paying the standard rate on his marginal earnings and by 1974 nearly half of his income was taxed at the full rate, a factor which is particularly important if the taxpayer does not enjoy the tax advantages of owner-occupation. The effects of fiscal drag, where people are pulled progressively into paying tax, account[6] for the political resistance to paying tax but it has also contributed to poverty for it has created a group where actual increases in poverty took place in the 1970s. This is shown clearly in the relationship between wages and the level of income at which supplementary benefit becomes payable.

The other alarming feature of the poverty trap is the extent to which it triggers inflationary wage pressures. Between May

TABLE 5.3. The poverty trap, May 1980 compared with November 1978[7]

	NWSP from GWE of			Extra NWSP from GWE of £85 compared with NWSP from GWE of £45	Implied marginal tax rates
	£ 45	£ 65	£ 85	£	%
Single					
person: Nov. 78	25	37	49	24	40
May 80	27	36	49	22	45
Married					
couple: Nov. 78	32	41	53	21	48
May 80	36	43	53	17	58
Couple + 2					
children: Nov. 78	44	49	59	15	63
May 80	54	52	60	6	85
Couple + 4					
children: Nov. 78	58	61	65	7	83
May 80	71	71	69	−2	105

NWSP = net weekly spending power defined as gross weekly earnings less tax, national insurance contributions, rates, rent and work expenses, plus child benefit and means-tested benefits. Housing costs are based on the averages for local authority accommodation, and work expenses are assumed to be £2.10 in 1978 and £3.00 in 1980.

GWE = gross weekly earnings.

All figures rounded.

Assumes that the local authorities do not grant free school meals to families with gross incomes above Family Income Supplement (FIS) level.

TABLE 5.4. Potential effects of the poverty trap on wage inflation, May 1979 to May 1980, current prices[8]

	(a) NWSP from GWE of £55 in May 1979	(b) NWSP equal to 122% of (a)	(c) GWE needed to produce (b) in May 1980	(d) Rate of increase in GWE needed to produce (c)
	£	£	£	%
Single person	32.21	39.30	70	27
Married couple	37.01	45.15	70	27
Couple + 1 child	41.11	50.15	72	31
Couple + 2 children	46.78	57.07	77	40
Couple + 3 children	52.63	64.21	83	51
Couple + 4 children	60.01	73.21	95	73

Assumes that the local authorities do not grant free school meals to familes with gross incomes above FIS level.

1979 and May 1980 prices rose by 22 per cent so that in order for net weekly spending power to be maintained over the year a person's gross weekly earnings of £55, which was just over 60 per cent of average male earnings, had to rise from between 27 per cent to 73 per cent; the larger the family the greater the wage increase. See Table 4.

To understand the nature of poverty it is necessary to isolate those groups which are most susceptible to poverty. Table 5 shows that the poverty is still widespread. Successive govern-

TABLE 5.5. Percentage of families with incomes[9]

| | 1976 | |
	At SB level or below	above SB but within 20%
elderly single people	46	20
elderly couple	21	24
single adult	11	3
couple without children	3	2
couple with children	5	7
one-parent family	48	4
Total	15	8

ments have adapted Beveridge, so instead of being the exception means-testing has become widespread, and ad hoc changes have brought about a system which is insensitive to the demands of some of the groups experiencing the worst poverty. Instead of using objective criteria for fixing benefit levels political choices are being made about who deserves extra benefit often quite unrelated to measured need.

The post-war period has seen several important demo-graphic changes develop which have contributed to an additional commitment placed on society. It is not often sufficiently appreciated how substantial a shift in expenditure priorities towards meeting these changes was achieved by the 1974-9 Labour government in terms of the relative value of the pension and the extension of disability benefits. By 1976 there were 2 million more pensioners living on Supplementary Benefit than in 1966.[10] The number of people eligible for disability benefit is also increasing, quite apart from the widening of the criteria of eligibility. In both cases the reason is that advances in medical science have made it possible for people to live longer. A hundred years ago a boy at birth could have expected to live to 41 years and a girl to 45. Today a boy can expect to live to 69 years and a girl to 75. This amazing transformation of life expectancy has been brought about by many factors, but a significant though unquantifiable factor has been a conscious decision by society to divert money and skill to preserving human life. However, although child care, for example, has improved dramatically, the transformation of life expectancy does not persist throughout a person's life. A man who had reached the age of 50 in 1841, could have expected to live for just over another 20 years more; but by 1972 a man aged 50 could expect to live for over 23 years more, despite the vast improvements in health care in that time. The change lies in the primary causes of death – from being TB and pneumonia to the modern killers, cancer and coronary heart disease. While there was a 19 per cent increase in the population aged 65 and over between 1965 to 1975, it is projected that the increase will be 5 per cent from 1975 to 1985, and 1 per cent from 1985 to 1995. But this slowing down in the increase of people of pensionable age will be matched by a very significant increase in the projected growth in people living over the age of 75: from a 16 per cent increase in 1965-75 to a projected 21 per cent increase in 1975-85, dropping to 2 per cent in 1985-95. For those living over the age of 85, a 16 per cent projected increase in 1975-85 is followed by a projected 24 per cent increase in 1985-95. Throughout the 1980s demographic changes will bring great pressure to bear on health and personal social services budgets to meet the increased costs of caring for an ageing population. The major challenge to the sensible development of social policy will be in adjusting to these demographic trends and relating cash provision with care provision, a particularly difficult match when public expenditure is being cut back and when increased care costs will fall on the health authorities' and local author- ities' budgets. In a period of high unemployment there is the additional need to ensure a degree of equality between workers in secure well-paid jobs and those who are employed only intermittently or who face long periods of unemployment.

Another trend is that the number of one-parent families doubled between 1966-76. As a result the system of Supplementary Benefits, which Beveridge saw as being a safety-net only, has had to cope with providing for the needs of an increasing number of pensioners and young children. Furthermore, it was hoped by Beveridge that incomes from employment would be sufficient to support a one-child family, but this has not proved to be the case and the need has arisen for a state scheme which caters for those families in poverty even when the wage-earner is in full-time employment. The low level of 'take-up' for means-tested benefits has also meant that poverty has continued even where relief is theoretically available. Low take-up has been especially persistent among those groups most at risk, the elderly, and the large family.[11] The overall rise in the levels of unemployment in the 1960s and 1970s has increased poverty among those of working age, and has placed a heavier tax burden on the working population. Public expenditure constraints over the last five years have meant that social security, health, social services and housing budgets have all grown more slowly than was desirable in terms of proven need and restraining their growth has had a disproportionate effect on the poor. In addition the large increases in charges for services which usually went hand in hand with expenditure reductions have hit many on low incomes who do not enjoy statutory exemption. The Labour government of 1974-9 sought to protect spending on the social services but they still suffered when considered against the adverse demographic trends and the increased demands on child support services. Though social security expenditure increased during this period in real terms, as a proportion of public expenditure and as a proportion of Gross Domestic Product, the largest increases took place in the early years of the government when the economy was declining. Spending was relatively static towards the end of 1978 and the beginning of 1979 when the economy was growing more rapidly and this interesting discovery has prompted one author to write: 'whether, given this performance, it is true that redistribution can only take place when there is economic growth must be in some doubt' and that, 'in aggregate, to have achieved a shift to

TABLE 5.6. Unemployment and poverty[13]

Weeks worked in year*	% of families with annual incomes	
	SB level or below	above SB but within 40%
48 or more	1	1
27 to 47	4	20
1 to 26	22	25
0	71	11

* Male heads of household in labour force, aged 21-64, self-employed excluded – figures relate to 1975.

social security at a time when real incomes were static or declining was a major achievement.'[12]

The link between unemployment and poverty is very strong, as Table 6 shows. It is staggering that under the 1980 Social Security (No. 2) Act the government should have introduced a 5 per cent cut in benefits on the grounds that they are tax free, yet unemployment, sickness and invalidity benefit are the only national insurance benefits below the tax threshold; so the 5 per cent cut applies to all the claimants despite the fact that only some will have other income which is taxed. It is one of the most dishonest arguments for introducing a change in social policy that has ever been put forward. The possible abolition of the Earnings Related Supplement means that more people would become reliant on means-tested Supplementary Benefit and this would further undermine any incentive to make voluntary savings.

Policies to generate more employment are fundamental to preventing poverty. What is now required, as is argued in Chapter 8 on Industrial Policy, is a programme for guaranteeing some form of employment training or job opportunity scheme such as was being developed under the Labour government in 1978-9. A job opportunity scheme for young people is certainly feasible, but it is the growth in the long term unemployment figures which is becoming ever more serious. Studies have shown that the longer an individual remains unemployed the less likely he or she is to be employable and the greater the risk of that person drifting out of the labour market with an income supplemented from time to time from the irregular twilight world of the black economy. The need for retraining is acute among middle-aged manual workers who are not catered for by the majority of schemes aimed at school-leavers and the young.

Another crucial aspect of employment policy in preventing poverty is to increase and make more secure the employment of married women, since the proportion of families in poverty is closely related to the mother's earnings. The two-income family is becoming more important. Social policy should be designed to make it easier for those mothers who wish to work by making better provision for the under-fives in poor communities for nursery education, pre-school play groups and child minding. Because many women work insufficient hours to qualify for unemployment pay the loss of their jobs does not feature in the unemployment figures but the loss of income for the family can be an important factor in pushing the family into poverty.

Social policies in the area of child care have been ambivalent: cutting the subsidy for school meals is effectively to cut child benefit. This link was recognised in 1945 when the government justified its introduction of family allowance at 25 pence, instead of the 40 pence recommended by Beveridge, by promising to provide meals and milk free in schools. It is arguable whether central government should make any changes in the school meal subsidy but to do so without substantially increasing child benefit as an offset is part of the general incoherence of current social policy. We are not prepared as an act of social policy to give – as some countries do – financial support for a parent to stay at home with the child, but equally we do not make it easy for the child to be cared for if the parent goes out to work. Whether children can attend day nurseries depends on where they live, but nursery provision is still a low priority in many local authority areas.

The playgroup movement, which was the most encouraging development in the 1970s, has not yet been linked as sufficiently as it can be, with existing primary schools and with surplus educational buildings, nor are we yet giving proper priority to improving the standard of child minders. A redistribution of resources to create better and more flexible provision for the under-fives in deprived areas would help both to reduce poverty and to give a needed head start for children who begin with a handicap under the present system of education. It could do much over a couple of decades to help break down class rigidities within education.

Another area of social policy that needs changing is sickness benefit, since here the case for taxing the benefit is strong and there are obvious anomalies stemming from the coverage of the sick pay scheme. Unfortunately, from the proposals put forward by the government in 1980 we could see greater inequalities resulting. In office jobs and the public service most employees receive full pay when sick, in outdoor work, manufacturing and the private sector very many fewer workers have full sick pay cover. The government's proposals would only heighten the distinction. They are afraid to introduce a statutory earnings related sick pay scheme and propose instead a statutory sick pay minimum income. Abolishing earnings related supplement and having flat rate sick pay would result in the inequalities in sickness that we saw before the Second World War. Far better than to introduce such a damaging combination of measures would be just to tax short term sickness benefit.

Low pay is also a major cause of poverty, although most of those with the lowest hourly earnings have few dependants, or are one of two earners in the family. This applies especially to married women, who are not among the poorest in terms of income relative to needs. In 1975 only one-fifth of workers in the lowest 10 per cent of wages were in the lowest 10 per cent of all income recipients. Many of the lowly paid who are not in the lowest 10 per cent of earners are very badly paid in relation to the work they do, but this finding does suggest that measures directed at low pay are not sufficient to cure poverty. The effect of successive income policies, aiming to give a larger percentage rise to the low paid, is discussed in Chapter 7 but these policies have not had any marked effect on differentials and have not increased the percentage share of the lowest paid groups' incomes.

Minimum wages legislation, attractive though it is, would eliminate working poverty only if it was pitched at a level that ensured that large families would secure incomes equal to the poverty line. This would be very expensive and would need to be accompanied by substantial extra revenue and a tax system which discriminated more against the single person and in favour of families with children. Setting minimum wage levels could also be self-defeating through its effect on inflation and unemployment, though the extent of this is uncertain. Experience in the United States has tended to show that the imposition of minimum wages, and increases in their rates, have led to sharp rises in wage levels in low wage industries but that substantial and persistent unemployment was created.[14]

No cause for optimism is afforded by the evidence of the British equivalent of the minimum wage, the wages councils sector. The councils have largely failed to fulfil their original purpose of protecting workers in those industries in which trade unions are not strong and in which very low wages have been prevalent. In November 1978, of the minimum rates for typical adult grades, only 4 of the 42 councils set rates exceeding £40 a week, while 24 had adult minimum rates of less than £35 a week. These wage levels compare unfavourably with the then Supplementary Benefit level of £43.60 (plus average rent) for a two-child family. In 1970 the major industrial councils accounted for 33 per cent of all low paid manual men and 34·2 per cent of low paid non-manual men, but by 1977 these proportions had risen to 42·2 per cent and 44·5 per cent. At best wages councils only protect the most vulnerable workers and even here they may fail because of underpayment of the minimum rates by employers.[15] The most successful aspects of government intervention in the area of low pay have been the Equal Pay Act and the Sex Discrimination Act. Equal Pay legislation largely explains the fact that the average hourly wage of full-time women relative to men rose by 15 per cent over the years 1973-6.[16]

The pessimistic conclusion that can be drawn from this brief survey of government intervention is that most policies have not worked. Low pay is associated with a low level of skills and a weak bargaining position of the trade unions representing these workers. Their bargaining position and relative wage levels are likely to be changed substantially only if the skills of the low paid are dramatically improved. Increasing skills, rather than spending scarce resources on higher rates of benefit will help such workers more over the course of their working life and will be more cost-effective for the Exchequer. As long as a large proportion of the poor depend on social security as their main source of income social policy must continue to be centred on improving the rates of benefits.

Means-tested benefits have an average take-up which is estimated to be only 75 per cent. The major need is to lift people off means-tested benefits by raising the levels of basic benefits. There are a large number of reasons why the present social security and taxation systems are in need of radical change. The level of many benefits has been too low and as a result poverty, defined as hardship, has not been eradicated, especially among families. Existing policies contribute to the growth of the 'black' economy by encouraging moonlighting, tax evasion and fiddling. The national insurance and supplementary benefit systems do not complement each other, as Beveridge hoped, and in recent years the number and composition of those on supplementary benefit has changed and now puts a large burden on the system. The number of unemployed people on supplementary benefit has increased dramatically and has added very greatly to administration costs, while the overlap between taxation and the provision of benefits has increased the number of wage earners facing the 'poverty trap'.

The most immediate goal must be a dramatic rise in the level of child benefit, which should be fixed at 5½ per cent of average gross male industrial earnings. At November 1980 prices this would be £6.30 a child. There is also a strong case for an infant care allowance. The abolition of child poverty should be the overriding social priority for the 1980s. It will be expensive but a similar quantum leap was made as a result of the 1974 General Election commitment to increase the old age pension. Though children do not have votes families do, and presented with a mixture of commitment and concern such a reordering of immediate social priorities ought to be able to become more popular than hitherto. Politicians have for years been afraid of the electoral consequences of increasing family allowances, now called child benefit. The objective case is incontrovertible for a switch of money towards cash for child poverty and more care provision for the elderly where the demographic changes are posing real problems for community care budgets.

Greater reliance on means-tests, of which there were 41 in August 1980, has created problems of complexity and overlap: they are costly to administer and recipients often feel stigmatised. Supplementary benefit costs 3-3½ times as much to administer as the non-means-tested national insurance, while the means-tested Family Income Supplement costs about 2½ times as much to administer as family allowances.[17] The use of discretionary payments within the supplementary benefit system has also grown and, although necessary, such payments are costly to administer and are not always regarded as being equitable by claimants. The complexity of the taxation and social security systems have contributed very greatly to increases in the numbers of civil servants; for instance, from 1965 to 1977 the numbers employed by the Inland Revenue, Customs and Excise, Health and Social Security and Employment Departments rose by 72 per cent.[18] Administration adds about 11 per cent to the costs of benefits paid out, with administration costs being especially high in the case of some local authority means-tested benefits. The Meade Committee noted that: 'if the costs of administering supplementary benefit, as a percentage of benefits paid out, had been equal to those of administering National Insurance benefits, there would have been a saving of administrative costs of £123 million in 1975 – sufficient to have paid for the implementation of the full child benefit scheme as originally envisaged'.[19]

Overall the income maintenance system is now regarded with a good deal of cynicism by claimants, administrators and by the general public. A costly bureaucracy has been created to disburse large sums of public money and it cannot even be argued that any substantial reduction of poverty has resulted. A variety of reforms to the system can be suggested, ranging from the uprating of benefits to proposals designed to integrate the tax and welfare systems. A minimal strategy, merely to improve the existing system, would be to alter the workings of means-tests in order to increase the rate of take-up of benefits and to reduce the unpleasant tensions felt by claimants and social security officers. The amount of administrative discretion over supplementary benefit could be reduced, greater publicity could be given to the availability of benefits, and combined assessment schemes for benefits could be used to reduce administrative costs. There is some scope for changes of this nature but at best such changes are unlikely either to reduce costs substantially or to remove the stigma attached to the claiming of means-tested benefits. In addition, changes of this nature are also likely to produce further complications such as the intensification of the poverty trap or an increase in the length of forms.[20] In recent years the take-up of supplementary benefit and family income supplement has greatly improved and the problem of disincentives is now greater than that of take-up.

Other, more far-reaching, policy options are, however, open – although it should be admitted that they are likely to involve either increased costs for higher benefits or considerable administrative changes for the Inland Revenue and the Department of Health and Social Security. Changes of a more radical nature cannot take place rapidly or even within the lifetime of one parliament and will require a degree of cross-party consensus, such as was achieved over the original Beveridge proposals, on a long-term strategy to help the poor. This consensus will be difficult to achieve but if we are to take seriously the needs of the poorest of our society the political parties must recognise the need to compromise and, as was done successfully in 1975 over the new state pensions legislation, plan together for the future. Achieving a synthesis of views in social policy is a constructive task for Parliamentary Select Committees.

The major options which are feasible are threefold: we can

either drastically increase the levels of basic benefits, or replace the present social security and taxation systems by a reverse income tax, or move to a system of tax credits. The first strategy would aim to raise social insurance benefits to provide a guaranteed minimum income and to extend insurance to groups which at present rely on supplementary benefit. Further, a small degree of co-ordination of taxation and social security could also be achieved by raising the tax threshold to at least the supplementary benefit level. These changes could be undertaken entirely within the existing government institutions and would reduce the costs of administration by lifting groups of claimants off means-tested benefits. Take-up of benefits would also be increased by a reduction in means-testing and the poverty trap would be eased by a reduced dependence on Family Income Supplement. However, this strategy would involve a reform of the contribution conditions of the social insurance system and would necessitate a large increase in spending on universal benefits. Reform of the contributory nature of national insurance is long overdue and a number of feasible options exist for its replacement by a social security tax[21] but the main objection to the raising of universal benefits is that this is likely to be very costly, even after taking into account possible savings through the reduction of means-testing. These increased costs could be financed by the reduction or removal of tax relief for married couples or on mortgage interest payments. The strategy remains perfectly feasible and could be achieved given the political will; but it is possible that administrative reforms such as the introduction of a Reverse Income Tax, might be equally viable and less costly.

A tax credit scheme which was once seen as solving many problems is now less popular. It would replace personal tax allowances and family allowances by tax credits and any excess tax credit over tax due would be paid to the claimant. All national insurance benefits would become taxable, with everyone having to file a tax return, although those receiving only supplementary benefit would still be catered for by a separate system. Tax credits would increase the workload of the Inland Revenue and it is unlikely that this would be offset by administrative savings in the provision of supplementary benefits since many benefits would still need to be provided. Depending on the level at which the poverty line is fixed some supplementary benefit claimants would be raised above supplementary benefit levels, and the problem of take-up would be solved since payments would be automatic and the system would be simpler both to administer and to understand. Many of the existing means-tests would remain and with them a poverty trap – since supplementary benefit would be retained for many one-parent families and many of the unemployed. Like the strategy relying on increased rates of benefits, the tax credits scheme is difficult to cost, but a tentative estimate, for 1978, was that an increase in social security payments of £5,000 million was not unrealistic.

Reverse income tax would pay benefits, equivalent to seven-tenths of the deficit, to individuals whose incomes fell below a poverty line. Unemployment benefit, supplementary benefit, retirement pensions and sickness benefits would be replaced, along with employees' national insurance contributions. Entitlement to reverse taxes would be calculated at the end of the financial year, with those in urgent need being able to receive cash by instalment payment. The reverse income tax would involve the Inland Revenue processing a tax return for every tax unit in the country and to a certain extent it would be responsible for the extra function of administering means-tests for families requiring immediate assistance. Alternatively, this function could remain with a much smaller Supplementary Benefits Commission. With reverse income tax a poverty trap would remain high because of high marginal tax rates, although marginal tax rates could be tapered to minimise the poverty trap. The income tax system would also lose much of its capacity as a tool of macro-economic management if short term changes in Pay As You Earn are ruled out as likely to impose hardship on the poor. The extent of the poverty trap which would remain would depend on the level of benefits set and benefit levels would have to be very carefully constructed to maintain incentives. Tax changes, for the purpose of economic management, could be balanced by changes in the level of benefits for the poor or by differential tax rates for different categories of taxpayer. Computerisation of the PAYE system offers the possibility of fully implementing a reverse income tax by 1986/87 since the increase in the number of tax-paying units required by a reverse income tax will be able to be dealt with more economically by computer than by the present manual system.

A further aspect of computerisation is that it will allow a switch to self-assessment of income tax liability with a saving of administrative costs, although an increase in costs in terms of time and money will have to be borne by employers and taxpayers. It is very difficult to put precise estimates of costs and savings on a proposal of this nature, but some indication of possible savings is shown by the fact that there are four times as many Inland Revenue employees per 100,000 taxpayers in Britain compared with the United States, where self-assessment operates. Self-assessment would have a number of advantages such as allowing income from self-employment to be taxed on a current year basis, instead of a year in arrears. It would also allow for the collection not only of income tax but also of tax on short-term social security benefits, a local income tax and a wealth tax integrated with local authority rates. The Inland Revenue has identified four objections with regard to self-assessment. The first is that 'a large amount of work which the Inland Revenue now does for you for free, would be transferred from us to the taxpayer.'[22] This is a valid objection, but if the social security system is integrated with the tax system the administrative savings will be much larger than those concerned purely with the Inland Revenue. The Department of Health and Social Security could be reduced in size and many of the unpleasant aspects of means-tests could be eradicated. The filing of annual tax returns, as undertaken by citizens in many other countries, does not seem to be an excessively large price to pay for these savings.

'Secondly, you would have to give up the luxury of a cumulative system, whereby every time a Chancellor reduces the taxes, or for that matter, increases them, the change is made as fast as we can do it within the year, or, if you are unemployed and want a repayment, you can get it in the year.'[23] The Inland Revenue is justified in making this objection but this ignores the fact that a number of other countries have shown that a variety of measures can be used to reduce these ill effects. It is incorrect to argue that a country must have either a cumulative or a non-cumulative system since a variety of intermediate options exist. If a non-cumulative system is adopted some provision will continue to be needed for short term claimants to obtain cash when in hardship.

'Thirdly, you would have to accept that the [Inland] Revenue would have to be given powers, sanctions to enforce compliance, and in the [United] States these are automatic, swift and severe, and they would have to be the same here.'[24] This suggestion sounds draconian but would merely bring Britain into line with other Western countries and would only increase the powers of the Inland Revenue to the same level as those possessed by Customs and Excise in respect of VAT. Safeguards could be built into the system to prevent abuse of these enhanced powers, which it should be noted would be far from being morally wrong or terrifying since the Inland Revenue would be enforcing a law that had been properly passed in parliament and already applies to social security claimants.

'Perhaps a fourth point is that you would probably have to reconcile yourself, even so, to a tax leakage of somewhere in the region of 5%.'[25] This figure of 5 per cent is admitted to be approximate but even so it compares favourably with other Inland Revenue estimates of the extent of the black economy as it now exists. In March 1979 Sir William Pile, Chairman of the Board of Inland Revenue, estimated that as much as £11 billion of incomes per annum is escaping paying income tax, an amount equivalent to 7·5 per cent of the gross domestic product.[26] More recently the Central Statistical Office has estimated that the 'hidden economy' is equivalent to 3·5 per cent of national income, not all of which will be accounted for by tax evasion.[27]

Tax evasion under a system of self-assessment may also be countered by a variety of measures. In the United States, for example, after all returns have been checked by a computer for purely arithmetical errors, a small sample is chosen for intensive audit. Because this sample is heavily weighted towards taxpayers who are more likely to evade tax – i.e. those with some non-wage or salary income, or with total incomes above a certain level – the deterrent to evasion is fairly effective: those with incomes of $50,000 or more a year, for example, are statistically liable to be audited in two years out of three. These audits are extremely thorough, involving the scrutiny of bank statements and a demand for detailed documentary evidence of all relevant transactions, and have a high chance of unearthing cases of evasion. Actual prosecutions for making false returns are not numerous in relation to the total number of taxpayers, approximately 1,400 in the United States in 1974-5; but they are far more numerous than in Britain, where there were only ten prosecutions in the same year. Being highly publicised and often resulting in jail sentences, they seem effective as a deterrent in the United States and would be effective here in Britain as well.

It will be rightly argued that many of these changes in the direction of tax policy will be worthless unless accompanied by more financial resources. What is not recognised sufficiently is the narrowness of our traditional tax base. Comparative evidence from other countries shows we are not paying relatively too much tax or relatively loading too much on to income tax, for the contributions of income and payroll taxes are about the average of most European countries. Where Britain is out of line is that though the total sum collected in tax is about the same as in other countries we have much higher marginal tax rates on average earnings which are then offset by very large allowances. The allowance which causes the greatest inequity between individuals is mortgage relief, which ensures that the house purchaser is given a marked preference in relation to the rent payer. The sums of money involved in tax allowances are very large. The tax reliefs on mortgage interest, life assurance premiums and pension schemes reduced the yield of income tax by £2·4 billion in 1979-80. If an employer's contribution to pension funds was paid as income and then taxed the income tax yield would have been increased by around £1 billion in 1979-80. It will be difficult to abolish or reduce the present system of allowances and exemptions but having reduced the high marginal tax rates there is an overwhelming case for adjusting downwards the allowances and exemptions which grew up in a period of unrealistically high marginal rates. It could produce immediate extra revenue for raising child benefit in advance of the long overdue major restructuring of the tax system and the introduction of a specific wealth tax.

Tax reform will meet massive institutional resistance; it will require a resolute Chancellor, and a readiness to act decisively and early in the life of a new government. The Commissioners of Inland Revenue have run an independent fiefdom for too long and they will almost certainly block and play for time. Above all it needs to carry the support of all party opinion in parliament. Reform cannot be subject to constant chopping and changing and it will also be considerably influenced by the way in which the computerisation of the Inland Revenue is structured. This ought to be the subject of detailed parliamentary scrutiny, for the decisions that are made in 1981 will affect the structure of tax for the next two decades and therefore the social policy and issue of inequality in society throughout that period.

It is impossible to construct a strategy for the reduction of inequalities without analysing the pressures which inhibit the freedom of any socialist government that wants to redistribute wealth. It is in many ways a diversion to concentrate only on the pressure of the very wealthy or of top management. Those pressures do exist, and have influenced Labour governments as well as Conservative governments, but it is an illusion to pretend that they have been the dominant or even a very influential force on Labour governments. They are influenced by the resistance to paying tax among their own voters, as are Conservatve governments influenced more by middle income taxpayers. The way through these often conflicting pressures can only lie in the democratic process of publishing the facts, arguing for the priorities which the facts support and constantly challenging vested interests wherever they are. It means ensuring that the debate about inequality does not centre only on income but also on access to services: and that the debate on the provision of basic services – those available to all as part of the social wage – is not just a question of simply looking at money quantities without also taking into account how that money is allocated and the quality of the services.

The quantity of services has become a vested interest too: it provides jobs, and with the public service unions naturally concerned about this aspect as well as wage rates, it is important that their pressure is counterbalanced by pressure over quality. If the quality of services falls then resistance to paying taxes and rates will rise among the very people for whom the services could provide a measure of real improvement in their overall standard of living. The debate about the social wage should be at the forefront of socialism but too often it has been seen as the championing of more services and more jobs at the cost of a deterioration in quality. The quality and size of the social wage must be safeguarded, with more public resources being used to improve efficiency and industrial relations in a sector in which some manual grades are paid very low wages.

The only way of achieving a more equitable distribution of income in a democracy is to secure a greater awareness by the mass of the population of the facts about poverty, and by greater diffusion of wealth-holding. The cost for the social security system of an effective anti-poverty strategy will be very great and the taxes necessary to provide for such social security will be very high. Unless more people can feel secure and satisfied by their present and future standard of living they will resist paying such tax levels. Additional incomes from a share in profits and the security afforded by an ownership of assets is still the prerogative of the few. What is needed is to widen the definition of standard of living from a comparison of income to a concept that embraces asset-holding, whether in terms of home ownership, secure rented accommodation, shares or savings, and security, with the ability to benefit fully in our society from access to a good education service and health service – and to have con-fidence in the financial and care provision available in old age, sickness or disablement. It is this wider concept of the social wage, where the taxpayer sees his or her standard of living in broader terms than the after tax figure on the wage slip, that will cause the voter's resistance to paying tax to alleviate the poverty of others to be moderated. For the democratic, decentralising socialist, nationalisation is neither a necessary nor a sufficient condition for social change of this kind: reliance must be placed on changing people's attitudes, on promoting industrial democracy, and on industrial co-operatives, wider share ownership and, above all, wider home ownership.

There has been no greater determining factor in wealth creation in post-war Britain than home ownership. The overall achievement of Labour governments in the area of housing policy has been judged as fairly good[28] by those who have not hesitated to criticise other areas of social policy. But in political terms all the evidence shows that the lack of an attractive policy to counter Conservative manifesto promises to sell council houses at preferential terms helped to reduce support for the Labour Party among skilled workers in the 1979 General Election. This was particularly marked in new towns, where the percentage of voters affected by such a promise was far higher than in the average constituencies. Radical reforms of housing were promised by the Housing Review initiated by Anthony Crosland in 1974 but hopes of reform were dashed by the disappointingly timid 1977 Housing Green Paper[29]. Housing policy is split inevitably between local government, whose task is to respond adequately to social changes and to anticipate and take account of the aspirations of council tenants, and central government, which is responsible for the tax and social security framework which affects the housing policy of every local authority. The Labour Party has been fairly criticised, as a 'narrow preoccupation with the traditional issue of the level of council house rents blinded it to the growing impact of owner-occupation on the distribution of wealth – an issue now taken up by the political right.'[30]

The only radical way forward is to treat housing and tax reform as part of a comprehensive package designed to end the massive distortions and inequalities produced by government subsidisation of owner-occupation and by the damaging shift of financial resources into house purchase and the trading up of house prices. Since the Second World War housing has come to represent by far the best investment and hedge against inflation, and as such it has seriously distorted the pattern of investment. From 1946 to 1978 retail prices increased 7 times, house prices 12½ times and industrial shares only 5 times, with the share of personal wealth held in land and dwellings doubling from 1960 to 1974 and the proportion held in company shares falling by half.[31] Part of this shift can be explained by the replacement of personal shareholding by institutional shareholding and by the low profitability of industry, but it is an alarming fact, in terms of an industrial nation's priorities, that 90 per cent of net personal savings in Britain – compared with 60 per cent in the USA – flow into pension funds, life insurance and owner-occupied housing – all of which enjoy favourable tax treatment.[32] The disproportionate flow of funds into the building societies reduces the funds available to industry, forcing companies to borrow from the commercial banks, increasing interest rates and raising the money supply. Over-investment in owner-occupied housing, especially by the wealthy as a consequence of tax advantages, has helped to bid up the price of housing and as an indirect result has helped to reduce labour mobility, with this process being subsidised by government tax policies. In 1978 direct subsidies from central and local government to the housing revenue accounts of the local authorities totalled £1·6 billion, mortgage interest relief cost a further £1·1 billion and the relief on capital gains on owner-occupied houses cost £1·5 billion. The size of the total, £5½ billion is hard to justify given the adverse macro-economic consequences of subsidies to housing. It should also be borne in mind that a reduction in the level of subsidy would allow either a substantial fall in income tax, with £1·0 billion being equivalent to a 2p reduction in the basic rate of income tax,[33] or it would allow necessary public expenditure priorities to be protected.

Reform of the tax treatment of housing should be guided by two aims: firstly, to reduce the amount of investment in housing as a whole by tax neutrality between housing and the rest of the economy; secondly, to achieve equal tax treatment for different kinds of housing in order to prevent distortions and cross-subsidisation within the housing sector. The aim is not to reduce the level of provision of housing since it is clear that a large number of families are still inadequately housed. A reduction in government subsidies to owner-occupiers will allow a freeing of resources to provide housing for the inner cities and for those in greatest housing need, instead of the present wasteful subsidisation of those social groups which already enjoy high incomes and a good standard of housing. Two methods of altering the tax treatment of housing have been suggested with these two aims in mind.[34] The re-introduction of tax on the imputed income derived from home ownership which as Schedule A was abandoned in 1963. This tax treated the ownership of a house as a form of consumption rather than as an investment; it would be administratively feasible to reintroduce if considered as part of the reforms of the rating system as recommended by the Layfield Committee.[35] The tax deductability of mortgage payments would be retained in order that a person with a mortgage equal in value to their house would have no tax to pay. The tax would have the consequence that all existing owners would suffer a tax loss and a capital loss although the effects of this could be eased by a phased introduction of the new tax, allowing house prices to adjust gradually. An alternative to the re-introduction of the tax would be to end or phase out mortgage interest relief either by maintaining the £25,000 ceiling in money terms and allowing it to fall in real terms or by restricting tax relief to the basic rate of tax.[36] The former would allow a gradual lowering of house prices, would be administratively simple and would lead to the ending of interest relief if inflation persisted. The second possibility would allow interest to be paid net of tax and would simplify the operation of tax relief and mortgage subsidies and would also be the means for a phasing out of interest relief.[37]

Both sets of reforms would increase the cost of housing to owner-occupiers and in order to prevent cross-subsidisation within the housing market it would be necessary to alter the cost of housing to council tenants. This would not necessarily imply that the general level of council house rents would have to rise, as the return on local authority housing is already high relative to that obtaining in the owner-occupied sector,[38] but it would involve for some tenants sharp increases that would have to be phased in and even so would cause some distress. Any changes in the method of taxing housing would necessitate the introduction of a new social security benefit to take account of housing costs. A new social security benefit could be made administratively simpler if it was introduced in conjunction with national rent pooling for council properties, to offset certain of the differences among councils due to the age of buildings. A unified housing benefit, as advocated by the Supplementary Benefits Commission,[39] would improve incentives, reduce the poverty trap and would reduce the staff of supplementary benefits offices by 2,000 or more. This is the area of prime responsibility for government. It is primarily for local government to improve the position and rights of council tenants by giving more choice of dwelling, improving the rights of tenants in relation to the arbitrary powers of housing managers and by encouraging experiments in democratic control of decisions affecting the provision of housing.[40] Central government can create the basic legislative framework but its implementation is for local government. The socialist case for helping first time house purchasers by preferential lending terms and tax treatment has already been accepted in principle, but the schemes have always been overtaken by inflation and lending restriction particularly affecting local authorities. There is a need to improve access to credit for those young families with low incomes who are unable to obtain mortgages from the building societies. A possibility is to set up a public mortgage agency, linked to the expansion of local authority mortgage schemes.

These wider issues of housing and housing finance should concern every socialist and form part of a strategy which welcomes the wish of many families to own their own house but seeks to treat fairly those who are council tenants or who prefer to live in private rented accommodation. Housing should be seen in the context of the whole economy. In the name of justice and in the pursuit of equality we have no alternative but to take radical steps to reform housing, and these steps are bound to offend large sections of the population which have benefited from past distortions. 'Unless Labour breaks with its defensive housing policy of the past it will not be able to prevent the shift to welfare housing, keep taxes down and preserve the social wage.'[41] Yet central government must be very cautious about interfering with a local authority's freedom to develop its own housing policy. A council that wants to sell its stock of council houses, providing it is not adding to the homeless, should be allowed to do so even if central government feels the local authority is acting unwisely. Similarly a council that refuses to sell its stock of council houses should have the freedom to do so, even if central government thinks the council should sell. Central government should lay down tough criteria to phase out distorting financial subsidies, to prevent creating or adding to homelessness and should intervene if these criteria are not applied; for these are issues affecting national housing finance and overall social policy. But however well intentioned, detailed direction from Whitehall runs flatly against the essential democratic freedoms of successful local government. On balance socialist policies will be better sustained by accepting the swings and roundabouts of local government democracy than by trying to overrule local freedom by central government interference with an overall very dubious social return, for the principle of autonomy once ceded means a Conservative government also inhibits the differing priorities of socialist local authorities.

Apart from housing, other methods of diffusing the pattern of wealth-holding and gradually changing existing patterns of ownership need to be considered. The role of co-operatives and industrial democracy are discussed in Chapters 11 and 12 though they are likely to change our society only gradually. In the United Kingdom share-ownership is estimated to cover 4 per cent of the adult population.[42] Stocks and shares can be both a source of income and of capital growth and socialists cannot ignore the need for a wider distribution just because this means associating with capitalism. At present employee share-holding schemes which have the potential to widen distribution have made little impact. One of the largest of the schemes, that of ICI, has involved 85,000 employees, only 40 per cent of whom have retained their shares over the seven years in which the scheme has been in operation. The amount of profits distributed to employees has been small and the stock, with normal voting rights, has made up only a very small percentage of the total stock, so that employees have not gained any real say in determining the policies of the company. In the Barclays Bank scheme the amount available for distribution is just 4 per cent of consolidated profit before tax, subject to profits exceeding 15 per cent of issued share capital. In Boots 2 per cent of UK profits are distributed as shares and 7 per cent as a cash bonus. At present about fifty schemes are in operation and about 150 are being vetted by the Inland Revenue. In only one firm, Kalamazoo business machines, has a scheme resulted in workers having a majority stake; in this case being due to the Quaker principles of the original owners. Schemes of this sort are unlikely to have much impact on the distribution of wealth or on the level of motivation of employees and do not by themselves constitute a strategy for radical change. In the USA the proportion of employee shareholding as a percentage of shareholding in individual firms has not risen above 25 per cent in the past twenty-five years due to labour turnover and retirement leading to the selling of shares. Companies have also found that small amounts of shareholding does not increase the interest of employees in their firm since the level of profits is still felt to be determined by factors outside their control. In the British schemes dividends are not paid for five years and employees do not regard themselves as shareholders during this period. The schemes apply mostly to white collar workers and the amount of profits distributed is so small that it does not increase motivation.

The TUC does not favour workers being given shares in their own companies and would prefer companies to pay a fixed proportion of profits into a national fund from which dividends would be paid out. In 1974 the TUC stated that employee 'schemes do not provide any real control over the managerial decisions. Even if shares were distributed and carried voting rights this would have to be on a fairly massive scale before any real control were vested in the workers as shareholders.' The TUC also sees shareholding as undermining collective bargaining and as capable of setting workers against each other where only some workers hold shares. But shareholding is not just connected to ownership, it is also a source of assets and if inequality is to be reduced asset holding must become more widely spread. Shareholding schemes are a limited step forward, particularly in very large firms that cannot be split into co-operatives, and where industrial democracy has less impact, such schemes are one of the ways the workforce can feel involved in the success of their company, but they are not a radical step forward in changing industrial ownership. They can be useful during a period of wage restraint in ensuring that the restraint does not just increase the distributed profits of the firm. Shareholding schemes could be negotiated by which £1 foregone in the wage packet could ensure £1 of shares. A direct say for workers in how the share capital from this type of share issue was used would be more radical in that it would not only extend shareholding to the bulk of the workforce but give them a more obvious say in the handling of this money than if they were just a small element of the company shareholders. In common with other schemes, it would take a substantial period before any real degree of ownership was transferred to the workforce. An extension of such a scheme would be to legislate for a proportion of profits in all companies to be transferred to a fund to be administered by the workforce. The fund could be used to pay cash bonuses, for social purposes or used to purchase shares in the enterprise which employs them. Unlike the present system of collective bargaining, the aim would be to redistribute current income and affect the long term distribution of income and wealth. Unlike the TUC scheme for a national fund, administration would be decentralised and there would remain the option of trans-ferring shares to individual workers. This would be less remote and more likely to ensure the involvement of the workforce and capture its enthusiasm. A national scheme would be viewed by many with suspicion as putting the fruits of their labour outside their control. The performance of the industrial company would influence the speed at which ownership could be changed since the level of company profits and the need to preserve investment would set limits on the amount of profits to be set aside in each year. Existing shareholders would need to be confident that their earnings potential was not to be adversely affected if they were to retain their investment and the Government could allow for this by 'a progressive series of cuts in company taxation, with the emphasis preferably on reducing or eliminating the employers' national insurance surcharge – the "job tax". That way industry's re-investable income would be increased and employment would be encouraged by reducing unit labour costs.'[43]

In evaluating social and economic policies it is also useful to study sociological evidence on the class structure and rates of social mobility, as well as to look at poverty and inequality. The evidence shows that Britain is still far from being an 'open' society in which everyone has a roughly equal chance of attaining higher education and well-paid jobs, and that social mobility between the classes has not substantially increased over the last thirty years. The expansion of education since the Second World War has helped increase the chances of working-class children moving into higher social classes but in a truly mobile society the amount of upward mobility would be very much greater than it is at present.[44]

Geographical inequality is another aspect which needs careful analysis: initially much of the statistical work concen-trated on regional inequalities in the distribution of health and educational resources, and the worst regions were often also found to be those with older declining industries with the highest levels of persistent unemployment. More recently the focus of attention has concentrated on identifying smaller areas of geographical need and poverty. The evidence had been accumulating for some years, but it was not until the 1970s and specifically in 1977 that the severity of the problems in the inner cities were first tackled with a substantial, though still inadequate, allocation of resources.

The riots in the St Ann's district of Bristol in April 1980 dramatised the problems again of the inner-city areas. All of Britain's major cities have their St Ann's: areas such as Handsworth in Birmingham, the Highfields district of Leicester, Moss Side in Manchester or Brixton in London. They all share roughly the same characteristics, they are areas which knew their heyday at the turn of the century, and where the housing and other social structures are often old and dilapidated. What were large homes for Edwardian households have now often become overcrowded tenement buildings occupied by old inhabitants lacking the will or the means to move to the suburbs, together with immigrants such as the Irish, Asians and West Indians, and some who positively choose the inner city – including middle class people who, in some London inner-city areas, are returning the Victorian and Edwardian mansions to single-family occupation and are bringing in the phenomenon known as gentrification. But generally speaking inner-city areas are marked out by a number of pronounced demographic characteristics: the population is concentrated in the young and old age-groups, relatively few households are owner-occupied, families are larger, and more likely to consist of only one resident parent, than is the average for the country as a whole, and there is a distinct lack of skilled or qualified people.

Teachers often do not want to live in these areas and dislike the prospect of travelling long distances to get to school; and even if they do travel they are isolated from a community where they do not live. Doctors and social workers face the same problem. The inner-city areas have the highest percentage of lock-up surgeries; the family doctors often live outside the area and use deputising medical services to cover at night and at weekends.

More importantly, these are areas of declining population and declining job opportunities for those who remain. Ever since the last war inner-city authorities, particularly in London, have made it part of their policy to reduce 'overcrowding' by encouraging people and employers to move out to new towns and expanding areas for London such as Peterborough, Harlow, or Crawley. As a result, many working class families who previously lived in crowded or otherwise inadequate accommodation in Inner London have been able to enjoy newer, more modern housing, a healthier environment and better schools, hospitals and recreational facilities. The demographic characteristics of the suburbs and new towns are almost the exact opposite of the inner-city pattern: families are smaller, a higher proportion of the population lives in family units, more are aged 20-40 than are very old or very young, very few are immigrants and many are owner-occupiers. Most importantly, there is relatively little unemployment.

In the inner-city areas, by contrast, there is high unemployment, heavily concentrated among school-leavers and, above all, among black school-leavers. This is the section of the population where post-war social policy has been least successful. There are two major issues to be faced: the whole process whereby deprived inner-city areas are formed; and the race relations' dimension. The polarisation in society between the inner city and the suburbs is as dangerous as any of the divisions facing society. It is a division which mirrors the political polarisation which has increased so much under the Prime Ministership of Mrs Thatcher. In the May 1979 election the Conservatives appealed to the values which some of the skilled workers and the upwardly mobile of the suburbs hold dear and did spectacularly well in outer-city affluent working class areas such as Basildon, Billericay and Dagenham. Conversely, Labour did particularly well in the inner-city areas, and there is some evidence to suggest that otherwise 'lukewarm' Labour voters were more likely to turn out actually to vote Labour if, other things being equal, they were members of minority ethnic groups rather than white. The 'haves' in contemporary Britain are not so much the top-hatted plutocrats so beloved in Labour mythology, but rather those families whose parents are both working and who can afford to run one or two cars, take foreign holidays and buy the clothes, furniture and gadgets advertised on commercial television; the 'have-nots' are those for whom the products and life-style extolled by the commercial television are visible and desirable and yet out of reach. The deprived in the inner city like unemployed young blacks are not a revolutionary sub-proletariat but people who want access to the material benefits of our society and who want to gain society's esteem and respect. Existing social and racial tensions are being exacerbated by a government which tells the successful that their success is the product of their own 'initiative' and proceeds to reward them even further by cutting their taxes and releasing them from some of the burdens of financially supporting those less well-off than themselves.

Such a polarisation could have devastating consequences for the future cohesion of British society. The electoral challenge for socialism is not just to ease these tensions and reverse the polarisation but, as a prior condition to being able to do so, to win back the allegiance of those skilled workers who have been won over to the Conservative Party by their belief, which is certainly not without foundation, that Labour is the party which embraces, and wants to enlarge, an interfering and wasteful bureaucracy, and is committed to a taxation system which penalises them for working overtime or for being skilled craftsmen.

The practical and immediate task is the physical one of redeveloping the inner-city areas, restoring to them industrial life, and reversing their descent into the status of ghettos which house the unwanted and those on the margins of society. Money will of course be needed, but simply setting up undemocratic Inner City Development Corporations, as the Conservative government has done, will of itself solve nothing. These new Corporations may be able to cut through the stultifying bureaucracy that has allowed wasteland to proliferate, they may pioneer new projects designed to rejuvenate the housing in such areas and to attract employers back, but they will fail unless they can re-create what is all too rare now in the inner cities – genuine neighbourhoods where people of different classes and backgrounds can live harmoniously together – and this will require the co-operation of local people and the involvement of the local authorities who view the Corporations with suspicion. Inner-city areas have an attraction for some people, and with the very high cost of commuting caused by the ever increasing public transport fares, more and more suburban dwellers might be persuaded to return to the inner city. The Corporations deserve to be given a chance, and the inner city needs positive discrimination over resources. It is sad that some socialists are uneasy over any form of selectivity, even geographical, and are reluctant to endorse any form of social provision which is not universal in its application. There was immense resistance from many trade unionists and socialist politicians in London to the 1975 attempt to reallocate hospital resources from London to the provinces. The resistance was institutional and linked to the hospitals but it would have been easier to overcome if there had been decisions to increase resources for community care in London. The level of community care in London has for years been well below that of community care in other places which have very poor hospital services. The reallocation of resources to the mentally handicapped and mentally ill from the acute hospitals started in 1975. This has been resisted, however, by a combination of the powerful acute hospital lobby and weak Ministers and members of Health Authorities afraid to challenge the vested interests of hospital consultants and the health service trade unions. Although it is not necessarily implied in the notion of special assistance to special groups that such assistance should be at the expense of others, many still react strongly against what they see as the creation of 'privileged groups among the under-privileged'. These people find great difficulty still in accepting the thinking which lay behind the first Race Relations Act of 1965 and was later embodied in the Race Relations Act 1976 and the Equal Opportunities Act setting up the Equal Opportunities Commission to deal with discrimination against women.

It is a mistake to say that coloured people, for instance, only suffer the problems suffered by all people of lower socio-economic groups; if the demographic data dealing with the coloured population in Britain is examined, it soon becomes apparent that numerous characteristics of that population, including its occupational and residential patterns, can only be explained by reference to the fact of colour. The notion of 'special treatment', therefore, needs to be replaced by the concept of compensation for deprived minority groups. Lord Scarman pointed out in his Minority Rights Group lecture in 1977 that dilemmas could arise when the rights of the individual are put at risk in the interests of a disadvantaged group. But the notion of the disadvantaged group needs to be seen as an essential concept in a plural society which aims to alleviate poverty, pursue greater equality and to bring the exercise of genuine personal freedom within the reach of the largest possible number of its citizens.

6

Economic Policy

In post-war British politics no subject has been more obsessively discussed than how to achieve economic growth. One of the country's leading economists, Sir Roy Harrod, summed it up correctly when he wrote in 1965, 'economic growth is the grand objective. It is the aim of economic policy as a whole'.[1] As successive governments have failed to achieve sustained economic growth, they have been deserted by a disillusioned electorate ready to turn in despair to an opposition espousing a carefully packaged and electorally attractive set of seemingly new policies for achieving a higher standard of living, more jobs, and a better balance in Britain's international trading figures. It is the combination of poor economic growth and inflation which makes the British experience unique; few other countries have faced a similar economic and political cycle. What is also unique is the extent of the political differences over the economy. Britain at the start of the 1980s faces yet another period of polarised debate over economic policy.

The Conservative government came to office in 1979 committed to a complete overturning of the economic policies of the previous thirty years. Its rejection of Keynesian demand-management and its total belief in monetarism led the Conservatives, at a time of world recession, to start immediately to reduce public expenditure, rule out an incomes policy and increase inflation by raising VAT. They believed that a strict control of the money supply – which some monetarist commentators soon criticised as being too tight – with high

111

interest rates, would ensure, together with the unfettered impact of market forces, an eventual reduction in inflation. The consequences in terms of unemployment, industrial bankruptcies, closures and cutbacks were known to be formidable, but the extent of the damage to Britain's industrial base was judged to be tolerable. Yet one of the consequences which soon became apparent was the distortion and downgrading of other aspects of economic management which began, in turn, not only to discredit the valid case for keeping control of the money supply, but also to shake the belief of some people that a mixed economy could ever again generate economic growth. In the 1970s the monetarism of the Right began to emerge to challenge the Keynesian consensus and so did the so-called 'alternative strategy' of the Left.

The alternative strategy, a mix of protectionism and state intervention, is advocated, predictably, by those centralist socialists who have never reconciled themselves to the virtues of a thriving private sector within the mixed economy. What is more worrying is that it is becoming also the refuge of others who have been driven to despair by the failure of past policies and are tempted by the argument that everything else has been tried. It is necessary, first, to convince all democratic socialists that support for the success of the mixed economy is essential, that it is still possible to achieve a measure of economic growth even against the background of the lower world economic growth over the next decade and that it is only possible to do so within the framework of the mixed economy. It is hard to do this when the advocates of monetarism and the alternative strategy are linked together in an unholy alliance to propagate the belief that all else has failed as the ultimate justification of their differing viewpoints, and when ever higher unemployment figures sour the atmosphere and make rational debate very difficult.

Since the Second World War British economic policies have been adopted against a background of economic decline not found among our major economic competitors. This has been due in part to the severe problems of the legacy left by two World Wars and to the accompanying dismantlement of the Empire, which would have faced any model of the British economy. But it also reflects the nature of British politics. Alternating Labour and Conservative governments have sought, particularly over the last decade, to repeal the policies of their predecessors in the belief that this would deal with the fundamental problems facing the economy. In some policy areas the symbolic issues of importance to the party faithful of both the major parties have come to be elevated well beyond reason. The commitments and attitudes adopted in opposition, combined with the volatility of the money markets, have contributed to the major economic mistakes made in the early years of the life of most new governments. The Labour government's refusal to devalue in 1964, something clearly envisaged by Reginald Maudling if the Conservatives had been returned, bedevilled the possibility of achieving planned economic growth in 1964 and 1965; a Labour government in office after thirteen years of opposition and facing the necessity of another election because the majority was only five, sadly lacked the confidence and authority to devalue in order to pursue economic growth. The same excuse could not be used when, in July 1966, deflationary measures were taken even though there was a large parliamentary majority. In 1970 and 1971 the industrial relations' legislation, the decision to wind up the Prices and Incomes Board and the Industrial Reorganisation Corporation, destroyed all feeling of a continuity of economic purpose across the parties. The 'market forces', 'stainless steel' approach, characterised by the Selsdon Park pre-election conference held by Conservative strategists, helped to destroy any chance of a sensible partnership between the TUC and the new Conservative government. In 1974 and 1975 the new Labour government inherited indexation commitments which it felt it could not break and which made a major contribution to inflation; this was then compounded by agreeing to high public sector pay settlements. It can be claimed in the Labour government's defence that in 1974 it was a minority government that had to face another election soon, and that the public mood after the miners' strike was very unsettled. It took, however, until the summer of 1975, after the EEC referendum had been held, before the government grappled with the spiralling inflation rate which by then

113

was frighteningly near 27 per cent. But it was in opposition that the Labour Party had committed itself to the view that rising wages had little to do with inflation and this still hung round their neck in the first year of government. An albatross of unreality.

In 1979 inflation was already rising, but the new Conservative government, again partly because of unrealistic attitudes adopted in Opposition, decided unwisely virtually to double VAT. This was a consequence of their unwise pledges to cut direct tax and it was done despite party spokesmen having denied throughout the election campaign that an increase in VAT would be the result. But it was this decision, like the Heath government's decision to index, which was the decisive factor in doubling inflation by the middle of 1980.

Some people believe that a solution to this political yo-yo effect in the immediate aftermath of elections is to reform the electoral system. They suggest introducing a form of proportional representation in order to establish a number of smaller parties in the House of Commons to moderate between the polarised policies of the two main parties. The wider political arguments for proportional representation are considered in Chapter 14 on the Constitution. In terms of making difficult and possibly unpopular economic decisions, however, there is no guarantee that a coalition across small parties, as opposed to the present coalition within the political parties, would strengthen the ability of any government to take difficult economic decisions. Whether or not electoral reform will ever be introduced, a greater political realisation is needed that the growth of the economy and the creation of wealth and, indeed, the very survival of Britain as a major industrial power, depend on a considerable continuity of economic policy across administrations.

This does not automatically lead to a form of corporatism, which carries its own institutional lethargy. The parties can and will still disagree about many aspects of economic policy – such as, for instance, the question of the distribution of wealth – but the structure of the nation's economic life cannot be switched and changed with the rapidity of the past without weakening the country's ability to compete in world markets or to serve the domestic market. For example, whatever the detailed criticisms about the management of the British steel industry since the war, no one can seriously question that the endless political uncertainty and debate about its structure has been a major debilitating factor contributing to its decline. 'It is high time the political parties sorted out the difference between the things which as a nation we can afford to disagree about and the things which we cannot.'[2] Perhaps this is a utopian hope, since it is precisely our economic decline which has contributed to the polarisation.

It is hard to escape the conclusion that the British economy has suffered uniquely from this peculiarly polarised debate existing in Britain between the two governing parties about the relative roles of private and public enterprise. It is an oversimplification to trace all the swings of economic policy to this debate, but it has had a corrosive effect on the creation, in many sectors of the economy, of a working partnership between the private and public sector. While the debate has ranged between the extremes of Left and Right, the consensus that has emerged and has been labelled 'welfare capitalism' has itself made fatal compromises, eroding the virtues of both the private and state economy. Instead of recognising that within the mixed economy the private sector and public sector, providing public services, need to be treated in different ways, there has been a tendency to meet the criticism from the extremes in a way which militates against any such differentiation. The non-commercial public sector has been expected to adopt many of the disciplines and attitudes of the private sector, to present its accounts in terms of a largely bogus profitability, to charge so-called market prices for services and to create market forces or pretend that they exist where they do not. The private sector has for its part been expected to take on many of the disciplines that the state applies to the public sector, their pricing structure and profit ratios have been subjected to detailed control, their employment practices expected to be modelled on the state sector and their salary and wage levels held down with an expectation that they will provide the same job security and pension entitlements as the public sector.

The most damning criticism of the socialist 'revisionist' case is in this area. They have tried to amalgamate the public and private sector while at the same time advocating the merits of a mixed economy. They have tried to have the best of both sectors by refusing to face the political difficulties of admitting that there are necessary differences between the sectors, and that one of these differences is that profits are the motive force of the private sector but that in the public sector these can conflict with the concept of public service. Fault can also be found with liberal conservatives who, while criticising the 'unacceptable face of capitalism', have listened too much to the interests of property, insurance and the stock market and have not given enough attention to the interest of producers, and particularly to that of the manufacturing exporter. They have, too, been reluctant to defend the public sector against their own Right wing, and have acquiesced in unfair criticism of the virtue of public services and necessary state involvement. The strengths and virtues of the mixed economy and much of its dynamism come from a sensitive understanding of the extent to which an amalgamation of public and private sector attitudes and policies is tolerable and a readiness to sense the point at which amalgamation destroys the dynamics of the system itself: when curbing profits really does limit investment, or when squeezing prices reaches the point when it does limit expansion, or when a movement towards average wages and job security impairs innovation and risk-taking and contributes to low productivity and inefficiency.

Britain has, unlike most of its Western European competitors, lurched between expansion and recession, between wage inflation and statutory freeze, between unrealistically high sterling exchange rates and precipitous falls in the value of the currency, and from the peaks and troughs of industrial investment to periods of intense property investment and speculation. It has a stock market where, compared with other countries, there is a uniquely high priority given to paying large annual dividends at the expense of capital growth, and a financial sector which will not lend long.

Over all these years it has also had a running dispute over the need for new industrial relations' legislation and both of the governing parties have swung with the pendulum of public opinion and fashionable comment as to the priority to be given to legislative control of the trade unions. Immense quantities of legislative time and political capital were expended on this issue in the 1960s and 1970s. Legislation has been introduced, bitterly fought, then repealed or replaced, with very little net benefit to anyone. If a fraction of this ministerial, opposition, parliamentary and departmental effort had been put instead into fashioning and promoting agreement over industrial relations, with the steady introduction of industrial democracy by negotiation, it could only have had a far greater effect on reducing industrial disruption and increasing productivity.

The condition for making the mixed economy work is the preservation of the degree of flexibility that allows for a swift market response to continuing changes in the world economy. There are those on both the extremes of British politics to whom a degree of consensus between the major parties on the policies which are adopted to reduce our economic problems is an anathema. They are content for the periodic lurches to Left and Right to continue unchecked. They know what to do. Doubt for them is a stranger, for dogma and doctrine provide their certainty.

The essence of the decentralist socialist case is that no one economic policy can be pursued in isolation without distorting the other policies. It is a recognition in politics of an approach that is central to the behavioural sciences with their emphasis on inter-reaction and inter-relationships. Such an approach is not an argument for the status quo for tolerating current levels of economic inequality, or for being less concerned about the existing maldistribution of resources.

Any economic policy should be judged against a background in Britain of persistent class divisions and the widespread existence of poverty. Class divisions in Britain remain pronounced though it is less certain that they are more extreme than in most other Western countries and we need more comparative evidence. The difficult task of changing attitudes is best tackled by a variety of policies and the problems could be resolved quicker if we were able to achieve greater

117

economic growth. The advocacy of low or zero growth as an alternative may appeal to conservationists but offers little hope for the poor and unemployed. Britain like other Western countries will have to adapt in future to a lower economic growth if we are to redistribute wealth within the world, quite apart from consciously deciding at times that the environmental and social price of a particular high growth policy within Britain is unacceptable. Even as conventional a study as former President Carter's Global 2000 Report[3] suggests that current economic methods such as those used in agricultural production will have catastrophic consequences if they are pursued for another twenty years.

There is a major difference between adapting to low growth and adopting a low growth strategy as the most desirable course within present day Britain. Priorities for public spending are difficult enough when the need is to divide an expanding, albeit slowly expanding, national income. If in deciding where to put additional finance the question of where to reduce spending in order to cover that finance is also introduced, the arguments become fiercer and harsh choices are more likely to be avoided in favour of the status quo. A serious attempt to face these choices has been attempted by some socialists who fiercely reject the low growth argument, warning that: 'The middle-class obsession with certain aspects of the environment must not be allowed to divert attention from more serious allocation problems. These include, first, the distribution of income, both internationally and within countries. They also include major problems such as those of education, housing, health services, and working conditions, and in the poorer countries they even include even more basic ingredients of life.'[4]

The thrust of this argument is correct. Economic growth is necessary to improve Britain's housing stock, to provide jobs for an increasing workforce, to provide for job enrichment, and to relieve the tedium of assembly line production. We will not be able to do this without greater resources. But it is unfair to criticise the low growth strategy just because its advocates are largely middle class. Many movements for desirable social reform have been spearheaded by middle-class activists. The

118

environmentalists have serious arguments for challenging the automatic assumption that all economic growth is desirable. The sensible ones are now increasingly arguing the limits or counter effects of high economic growth rather than the desirability of low growth. They carry more conviction as they concentrate on those aspects of economic growth that produce specific and quantifiable damage to society, and pursue a selective growth strategy. This is the path for socialists who see the environment in the widest context of bad housing as well as of open cast mining and who worry about the values of a harsh, materialistic and market-dominated society.

It is understandable why some socialists have come to reject economic growth as they have become disillusioned by the acquisitive values of affluent society, disheartened by the rapacious nature of a growth-orientated society with its emphasis on materialism, competition and money. In the past the emphasis of the revisionists on economic growth was not accompanied by a sufficient awareness of the degradation of values that would accompany growth and it was wrong to imply that more growth could of itself satisfy all the needs of our society. Growth increases the amount of resources at our disposal. Some of these resources can create greater freedom, but unless the society in which growth develops can also develop different attitudes to counter those associated with growth, it can create a divisively competitive and harshly acquisitive society.

In as much as one of the motivating forces of most people is to improve the standard of living of themselves and their families, we are seeing that people strive not just for a high salary, but also for prestige goods, unusual furniture, antiques, rare books and china. People want interesting creative jobs, they seek rural peace, even remoteness and seclusion, and these are all trends which increase with affluence. In some senses the rarity value is self-defeating if large numbers of people seek the same ends, for the appeal is related to its uniqueness, its exclusivity. Individual acquisition in these terms cannot satisfy everyone's needs and so the nation, city, town or village is driven to make collective provision and this is more equitable and allows more people to achieve their goals.

119

However, this cannot satisfy everyone; the quest for exclusivity is one that simply cannot be satisfied, and we need to acknowledge that this tension will not disappear, 'to the extent that the mismatch between current expectations and resources is qualitative rather than quantitive, the restraint necessary would be not patience but stoicism, acceptance and social co-operation – qualities that are out of key with our culture of individualistic advance.'[5] Stoicism does not mean resigned pessimism, but realism and a readiness to relish diversity. The change in attitude that is needed is to moderate the abrasiveness and starkness of the ethos of the individual so that we seek harmony, by extolling the ethos of community, not by advocating the destruction of individualism or by compelling collectivism but by recognising the value of co-operation. We need to work together, not on the basis of perfect equality but on the basis of searching for equality – something that cannot be achieved in a society riddled with inequalities.

The growth record of the British economy in the last decade has been very poor, both when compared with what has been achieved by other EEC countries and when compared with our immediate post-war record.[6] It is likely that in the 1980s growth will be even more difficult to achieve, given that world trade is growing far more slowly than in the 1960s and the 1970s. World trade in manufactures, of crucial importance for the British economy, is estimated to grow by 2-7 per cent per annum in the 1980s compared with an average for the 1960s of 9 per cent. A 1 per cent growth in world trade adds about a quarter per cent to British national output, so it is of the greatest significance for our rate of growth that the world economy will be sluggish: 'even on the most hopeful assumptions, the world trade environment suggests that growth in the economy will be much harder to achieve in the 1980s than it was in the 1960s.'[7]

In this situation the export-orientated manufacturing industries will find it progressively more difficult to export and will face increasing competition from imports. The implications for employment if manufacturing industry faces a difficult world market situation are very serious since Britain, in common with other industrialised countries, still depends on the manufacturing sector to provide over a third of total employment. In the 1950s and 1960s shortages of skilled workers constituted a bottleneck and impeded growth, whereas in the 1980s the situation is very different as the number of people of working age is increasing rapidly and, with more women in employment, the proportion of the age group seeking work is increasing. In the early 1980s the workforce is likely to grow by 0·5-0·8 per cent per annum and, assuming an estimate of productivity rising by 1-1½ per cent per annum, then output will need to grow by 2-2½ per cent per annum just to produce a gradual reduction in unemployment.[8] These estimates are subject to a wide margin of error; the estimate of the rise in productivity may, for instance, be too optimistic. They indicate, however, the scale of the problem of providing sufficient jobs for an expanding workforce which will require a level of growth above that which has been achieved in recent years.

There is, in addition, the further problem presented by new technology bringing a serious mismatch between the available jobs in new industries and the old skills or a total lack of skills. The disparities between regional rates of unemployment could increase dramatically with the industrial north, Scotland and Northern Ireland declining and falling further behind the relatively more prosperous southern England, where it seems likely that many of the new industries will be located. Youth and inner city unemployment could rise even further and threaten a generation with long periods of enforced stagnation and consequential alienation.

Job sharing schemes and reductions in working hours could help to reduce unemployment provided they are introduced in a way which keeps British unit costs broadly in line with those of our major competitors. This proviso is crucial. Job sharing and other such techniques provide an answer only if people are willing to accept lower real incomes in return for fewer hours of work. The trouble is that by and large people are not willing to accept this and it will require a major effort to persuade people to do so and to agree that this is a technique which must be used to ease unemployment.

Steady growth will remain necessary to provide, and pay for, full-time secure jobs for all those seeking work. If a period of a high rate of growth can be achieved the service industries will increase their share of total employment; this should not be decried for it is an inevitable trend. Jobs in manufacturing can possibly increase if investment in new plant and machinery is sufficient to offset the reduction of jobs implicit in the introduction of new technology. The manufacturing sector must, above all, ensure that it is competitive in world markets; only this will guarantee steady employment and earn foreign exchange to pay for our imports. At present the service industries, including government and defence, provide about 69 per cent of employment, while manufacturing employs 31 per cent. The numbers employed in manufacturing have fallen by 17 per cent or nearly 1½ million in the last fifteen years, and serious unemployment cannot be avoided if this rate of rundown continues. The service industries, such as retailing and administration, owe their ability to provide jobs to the continued existence of a healthy manufacturing sector, while the ability of the government to provide jobs in education, health and the social services also depends to a large extent on the revenues generated by industry.

In the United States, where the concept of a post-industrial society has been under discussion for longer than in Britain, manufacturing industry has increased its productivity and been able to compete in world markets, having moved into new technological growth products more successfully than in Britain. Manufacturing industry in Britain is a large and important sector of the economy, earning 50 per cent of our total foreign exchange and constituting 60 per cent of our exports of goods and services. Britain's share of world trade in manufactures fell from 24·6 per cent in 1950 to below 9 per cent in 1974. Since then it has stabilised at a level of 9-10 per cent and this represents a real achievement. At the beginning of the 1980s, with a world economic recession and Britain appearing to be worst hit, the prospect is that our share of world markets will decline even further; this possibility is strengthened by some disturbing evidence that the 'technology component' of United Kingdom exports is not as high as that of the United States, Japan and West Germany and that

Britain's performance has been weak in rapidly growing, high technology markets.

Import penetration of British markets has shown a long-term tendency to increase which, in part, reflects the post-war liberalisation of trade and an increase in the division of labour on a world scale. Similar trends towards an increasing dependence on imports can be observed in all developed countries, but in the case of the United Kingdom this process has gone much further, and has increased more rapidly than in all other developed countries except Italy (see Table 1).

TABLE 6.1   Import penetration of manufactured goods into the UK and other industrialised countries 1969-74[9]

Country	Manufactured imports as a % of the domestic market		
	1969	1974	% change 1969-74
United Kingdom	10·2	16·7	63·7
Germany	13·4	11·8	−11·9
Italy	15·2	20·1	32·2
France	12·1	14·3	18·2
United States	3·7	4·7	27·0
Japan	3·1 (1970)	3·7	19·4

In the United Kingdom imports met 17 per cent of total demand in 1970 for manufactures, but by 1979 imports had risen to 26 per cent, while this trend has shown an alarming acceleration with imports of finished manufactures rising by 20 per cent in 1978-9.

Our growing dependence on imports has not been due to Britain being 'flooded' by cheap goods from the low wage developing countries or the newly industrialising countries. In

123

TABLE 6.2 United Kingdom imports as a proportion of GNP – 1975 constant prices[10]

| | Percentage | | | | | | |
	1973	1974	1975	1976	1977	1978	1979
Food, beverages & tobacco	4·3	4·2	4·3	4·2	4·2	4·0	4·0
Basic materials	2·8	2·4	2·1	2·5	2·4	2·4	2·5
Minerals, fuels & lubricants	4·6	4·9	4·1	4·1	3·4	3·2	3·1
Semi-manufac- tured goods	5·9	6·4	5·7	6·0	6·2	6·6	7·5
Finished manu- factured goods	7·2	7·4	7·1	7·3	8·3	8·6	10·5
Total	24·8	25·3	23·3	24·1	24·5	24·8	27·6

1979 there was a £2.1 billion surplus in our balance of trade with the low wage developing countries and a surplus on manufacturing goods of £1.2 billion in trade with South Korea, Taiwan and Mexico. Our manufacturing deficit is with the EEC and Japan, a trend that reveals the type of goods that we are making and the growing technological gap between Britain and the other industrial countries.

We have done better in trading with the European Community since joining it than we have with the rest of the world. Exports increased by 350 per cent to the EEC in the first seven years as opposed to an increase of 200 per cent elsewhere. Before entry to the EEC our trade balance with EEC countries was deteriorating and now the trade deficit is narrowing markedly in real terms. The increase in UK oil exports to the EEC is speeding the improvement but even excluding oil the eight other member states in 1980 were providing 39 per cent of the total market for British exporters. Britain's export growth in the 1970s was rapid, with the proportion of GDP being exported rising from one-quarter in the mid 1970s to one third by 1980. This was a major achievement but while the value of exports rose by 334 per cent between 1970-8, the value of imports rose by 458 per cent to more than counterbalance it.

In the 1970s manufacturing industry was also subjected to an unprecedented profits' squeeze, which was both a cause and a consequence of the declining ability to compete internationally and one of the more serious effects of the successive prices and incomes policies operated during that period (see Table 3).

In the early 1980s overall profitability figures are only likely to be maintained by the build-up of profits from North Sea oil. The challenge will be to achieve the right combination of

TABLE 6.3   (Post-tax real) rate of return on trading assets of industrial and commercial companies*[11]

	%
1970	4·4
1971	5·1
1972	4·9
1973	6·1
1974	4·3
1975	3·6
1976	3·8
1977	4·2
1978	4·5
1979	3·5

* Excluding their North Sea activities.

channelling North Sea profits into productive investment in manufacturing industry at home and investment in overseas assets rather than into home consumption. North Sea oil introduces a major new factor in the handling of the British economy and its significance can hardly be overestimated. It has direct effect on those who work in or have invested in the oil and gas fields, it spreads out from them into the offshore industries and above all it provides the British government throughout the 1980s with substantial revenues from taxes and royalties. Oil exports will make a major contribution to the balance of payments; but that does not mean, as some have argued, that the expanding oil contribution must be offset by a decreasing contribution from manufactured products. Some of the balance of payments benefit will and should flow out again so as to increase Britain's foreign currency income when the oil income declines; some of the balance of payments benefit could and should be spent increasing our imports of raw materials and semi-manufactured goods so as to make it easier to expand economic activity within the UK and boost the level of manufactured goods.

There is no case for accepting the view that other countries who import our oil must export more to us and therefore boost our import bill, or that our net exports of other goods will have to fall by an equivalent amount if we are to keep the same target for our balance of payments.[12] According to this view, we can allow the size of the manufacturing sector to shrink and we should reinvest virtually all the profits from oil abroad, producing a restructuring of the economy due to the effects of oil and a high exchange rate. The problem with this analysis is that it offers little help in reducing unemployment in the industrial sector in the short to medium term and simply assumes both that a restructuring of the economy can create sufficient new jobs outside the manufacturing sector, and that Britain will be competitive in new industries when the flow of oil dries up. It would be wrong to argue that North Sea oil does not entail a restructuring of the economy, but what is very damaging is the extent to which oil is contributing to keeping the exchange rate at a level which is destroying the country's manufacturing sector. Even if interest rates are the major influence on the exchange rate, we shall have to cope with the oil factor when interest rates fall in line with those of other countries. If oil revenues were used to remove the balance of payments constraint facing the government they would allow the economy to be reflated through investment in key sectors of industry that have been identified as core industries that must be maintained, through higher public spending in selected areas which have a high employment content, through reducing insurance contributions to encourage employers to retain their labour force, and through tax reductions to ease the burden on those least able to bear it, which would also stimulate the economy through increased spending power. If we were to increase our import bill, this would decrease our balance of payments surplus, but would also allow the exchange rate to fall, which should increase the competitiveness of British industry. In 1980 the trade weighted index was near to 80 after a sustained rise in the exchange rate. In the autumn of 1977 within the Labour government I was arguing that the trade weighted index should be kept around 62. The handling of the exchange rate has been wrong ever since 1978.

What is needed is a balance of policies, a mix in the allocation of oil revenue. There is a need to assert, however, that the prime objective is to preserve our industrial base if Britain is to continue as a manufacturing nation. To rely only on income from overseas investment would be to make the British economy deeply vulnerable to external events beyond our control. While some revenue could be invested abroad and achieve a good return, we must reinvest the major portion of the profits from oil in Britain rather than abroad. Additionally a tougher oil depletion policy, which is advocated in Chapter 9 on Energy Policy, would decrease the rate of extraction of the oil and spread the revenues over a longer period. This would prevent the distorting effects that would accompany a few years of massive revenues, much of which would find its way not into industrial regeneration but into consumer spending. This is why there are important psychological arguments for devising a special Oil Fund so as to achieve at least a theoretical separation of oil revenues from the normal revenues available to government, rather than putting oil revenues directly into the Treasury. In practice, of course, all revenue is effectively within the control of the Exchequer, but the case for treating oil revenues differently is that not only are they 'one-off' revenues coming from a finite resource, but all experience shows that if we treat revenues in the normal way as we did with North Sea gas we shall do what the Dutch Government did: use the revenues for short-to-medium term economic management and leave behind a legacy of industrial decline. A special Fund will not guarantee that the revenue will be prudently used, but it at least will ensure that governments are held specifically accountable and the pressure is maintained to increase investment in manufacturing.

Manufacturing investment has been at a level very much lower than in other countries for some time; gross fixed capital formation per head in manufacturing 1970-4 was £240 in the UK compared with £450 in Germany, £540 in France and £740 in the USA.[13] As a result, in part, of low investment, the rate of productivity growth has declined from its long-term trend rate of 2·5 per cent per annum, 1950-73, to 0·7 per cent per annum, 1974-80, a level which is well below that of the rest of the EEC which was on average in 1974-80 2·5 per cent. The prolonged recession of the 1970s, with low or negative growth since 1973, did not have the consequence of controlling the rate of inflation. The decade witnessed a succession of increasingly severe policy measures designed to control inflation with a cycle of stop-go reducing business confidence and investment. The performance of the British economy in the 1970s was described in 1978 by some Cambridge economists in the following terms: 'Events have so far confirmed our worst fears. Manufacturing production is barely higher than 7 years ago, while the volume of imports of finished manufactures over the same period has risen two-and-a-half fold; unemployment has risen from 600,000 to nearly 1,500,000 – a figure that would not have been believed 10 years ago. Inflation is now at about the same rate as it was in 1970-71.'[14]

There is every indication that the adverse trends of profitability, investment, employment and competitiveness are not temporary phenomena and that they are likely to continue and worsen unless new economic policies are produced. Other economists deny that the rapid growth in imports of manufactures in the 1970s should cause alarm since, they argue, the increase reflects the Kennedy Round of tariff reductions and the tariff changes and stimulus of EEC entry, and that it is wrong to extrapolate from the trends of this exceptional period.[15] Some part of the very large increase in imports has been due to the reduction of tariffs in the 1970s but this does not adequately account for the size of the increase in import penetration in Britain as compared with other countries.

The maintenance of the exchange rate at an unrealistically high level, due to government policies and North Sea oil, has reduced profitability and pushed our trade in manufactures into deficit. One measure of the effect of the exchange rate is that in 1980 export prices were 15 per cent higher relative to world prices than the average post-war level and were 25 per cent higher than after the devaluations of 1967 and 1976. The build-up of production of oil to self-sufficiency has obscured the growing non-oil deficit and has allowed the problem of declining British competitiveness to be avoided rather than faced. The worldwide depression since 1974 has also allowed policy-makers to regard our prospects as a consequence of depression in other countries. But our loss of output and growth has been much more severe than in most other countries, with our level of manufacturing output in 1977 being only 5 per cent greater than in 1970, while in OECD countries as a whole output was up 26 per cent.[16]

Two or even three decades of relative economic decline in Britain have reduced our ability to compete in international and domestic markets to such an extent that it is understandable that there should be a search for drastic and dramatic remedies. Economic historians have pointed out that a relative economic decline is difficult to halt since it produces a vicious cycle of low profits, low investment, and hence an inability to compete in new markets. There is a clear need to break into this cycle and turn it around, to lay a firm foundation for long-term growth with balanced policies. Self-sustaining growth has been achieved by several countries in the post-war period, notably by Japan, France and West Germany and it is difficult to see why Britain should not be able to do likewise.

For several years two main schools of thought in Britain have been offering rival versions of what they regard as the necessary drastic action. The 'protectionist' school is identified with the Cambridge Economic Policy Group (CEPG) which has drawn attention to the rapid rise in imports of manufactures and to the consequences for Britain's manufacturing base and standard of living if this process is not checked. The 'international monetarist' school, whose theories are propounded in this country by the London Business School, sees control of monetary variables as being of paramount importance in achieving the necessary conditions for growth. This school attaches importance to the reduction of inflation. The 1979 Conservative government adopted the 'international monetarist' doctrine though not all of its practical policies and gave it a dogmatic, insensitive and ruthlessly capitalistic image. In a somewhat similar way the so-called Left of the Labour Party have adopted the theology of 'protectionist' doctrine but not all of its practical policies and have tended to turn ideas that need serious consideration into a crude, chauvinistic 'siege' economy.

Many other combinations of democratic policies exist besides those of the 'protectionist' group and of the 'monetarists'. It is a fallacy that there are no other alternatives and that they represent a straight choice. These policies are, however, challengingly different from the conventional policies of the last thirty years and at least seek to go to the roots of Britain's economic problems. They therefore deserve serious consideration. The strands of a fresher, tougher and more realistic approach can with benefit be garnered from them both.

The Cambridge group is Keynesian in outlook and consequently its members stress demand-side factors as largely determining the level of output of the economy. They argue that if a large proportion of national income is spent on goods from abroad there will be a lack of effective demand for British goods and industry will suffer accordingly. The economy cannot be expanded rapidly to help industry because with an over-valued exchange rate it will run into a balance of payments constraint due to higher imports. Paradoxically, industry either faces a lack of demand in a slump or else it is undermined in a boom by imports capturing markets, with the stop-go cycle hindering long-term planning and invest-ment. Industry, particularly the exporting sector, has been unprofitable and as a result it has been starved of funds for investment.

The Cambridge remedy is to impose a uniform tariff on imports of manufactures in order progressively to cut back their share of British markets, while maintaining their total volume in order to avoid or reduce the likelihood of retaliation from other countries. Controls would be accompanied by devaluation to boost exports and by a strong anti-trust policy to increase competition.

The case for some kind of import restriction – if this did not provoke retaliation against British exports – is very strong, since the predictions of most forecasters, and not just the CEPG, show that unemployment is likely to increase greatly in the early 1980s. When Britain has negotiated import restric-tions, as has been done, for example, bilaterally with Japan over cars and television sets and multilaterally with the newly industrialising countries over textiles, it has had a beneficial effect on the levels of output and employment in this country. British industry could, with a more protected home market, also gain a level of profitability that might result in more investment in new technology. The CEPG argue that product-ivity would also increase with new investment and by eliminating short-time working and working below capacity. Inflation need not increase through more expensive imports since, firstly, the government can offset this source of inflationary pressure by cutting VAT and, secondly, higher growth will allow real income to rise and will reduce trade union demands for higher money wages. Some, however, believe that an incomes policy would be a necessary accompaniment. The Cambridge economists also cite the evidence of economic history in showing that import controls helped the economies of the USA and continental Europe to industrialise in the late nineteenth century and helped Japan throughout the twentieth century.

Critics of the CEPG make the case that a large number of factors other than import penetration explain the decline of British industry and that import controls, by reducing competition, will make these factors worse. They point to the existence of poor management, a lack of incentives, outdated bargaining procedures and a resistance to the use of new technology on the part of managers and workers. These factors have undoubtedly been important, and it is unlikely that the CEPG would deny this, but they argue that new initiatives to retrain workers or introduce new technology can only be taken when the economy is expanding and more resources are being made available to undertake the necessary social reforms. It is characteristic of the Cambridge approach that they neglect supply-side factors and attach little importance to the stimulus of competition. The size and scope of the tariffs envisaged by the CEPG have been criticised as being unprecedented in a Western country and as being likely to cause substantial retaliation following the contravention of GATT and EEC rules that their adoption would involve. The CEPG advocate the imposition in 1981 of a 15 per cent tariff on imports of services, 20 per cent on semi-manufactures and 30 per cent on finished manufactures, with these figures being raised by 1990 to 36 per cent, 48 per cent and 72 per cent respectively. They also make the politically unrealistic assumption (given the potential life-time of the 1979 Conservative Government until mid-1984) that Britain's membership of the EEC will end by 1981 and that the EEC's external tariff is applied against United Kingdom exports and that due to retaliation the volume of exports is reduced by 3 per cent in 1981, and by 5 per cent after 1982. One of the most crucial assumptions by the Cambridge group is that inflation will not be increased by import-competing industries raising their prices since, they argue, pricing behaviour will continue to be based on costs plus a standard mark up.

'This claim is controversial. A priori, it does appear likely that some import-competing sectors would react with relief by putting up prices that had been squeezed by international competition. The CEPG appear to envisage rather different pricing behaviour in export and import competing sectors. They do not see export prices as determined in part by the pricing of competing products in international markets. Home prices, however, are unaffected by the price of competing imports. No satisfactory explanation of this assymetry has been provided.'[17]

The CEPG also underestimate the potential effects of a gradual devaluation which, if accompanied by an incomes policy, would allow a similar shift to profits as would be produced under import controls.

The major criticism of import controls is, however, that they are likely to start off an international trade war. Many other OECD governments are under similar pressures to be protectionist and, with the exception of Norway, they lack our indigenous energy resources. Protectionism already exists in the US and the pressure to introduce more is mounting. With the US economy relatively less dependent on exports they risk fewer retaliatory consequences if they adopt protectionist measures and many who are close to the US Congress believe they would match measure for measure any unilateral protectionism from fellow OECD countries.

The Cambridge estimations of the extent of retaliation are optimistic and highly suspect and certainly do not offer sufficient assurances for any British government to commit itself lightly to such a policy. Experience in Britain has already shown that the imposition of import controls would be met by opposition from other Western countries. The 15 per cent surcharge on imports of manufactures and semi-manufactures, imposed by the Labour government on coming into office in October 1964 was in breach of both GATT and EFTA Treaties and within a month the government had given private assurances that it would be reduced. It was cut to 10 per cent in April 1965 and ended in November 1966, having had little effect, since importers believed that it would be temporary and absorbed the charge themselves rather than lose their share of the British market.[18] Retaliation will come also not just from the West. In 1980 action by Britain against Indonesian textiles provoked damaging counteraction and is a sign of what to expect if Britain adopts unilateral protection. Retaliation is also likely to be greater than that envisaged by the CEPG since the volume of manufactures imported by the UK will fall and the imports of semi-manufacture will rise. Although the total of imports will remain constant the nature of these imports is crucial in determining the extent of devaluation. The CEPG also fail to mention that import controls would involve setting up a new bureaucracy to administer what would be an increasingly complex system.

The extent of opposition to a more widespread system of controls in the 1980s would be greater than that faced in 1964, when protectionism was more acceptable and when Britain was not a member of the EEC. However, it is worth noticing that in the 1970s, despite the Kennedy and Tokyo rounds of tariff reductions, there has been a trend towards a greater proportion of world trade being managed as a reaction to the 1973 rise in oil prices. It has been found that between 1974 and 1979 the proportion of world trade in manufactures which was managed by the market economies rose from 13 per cent to 21 per cent while the proportion of total trade which was managed rose from 40 per cent to 46 per cent.[19] It should be noted that this increase has largely been due to the adoption of a more protectionist stance by the developing countries and that retaliation would be greater for an oil-rich developed country such as Britain. Despite these objections it will continue to be argued that the potential benefits of a restrictive approach to imports would outweigh those defects and it remains difficult to fault the Cambridge contention that industry has been tightly squeezed over the last decade and that action is needed to restore profitability and international competitiveness.

The monetarist policies of the Conservative government aim at a less direct solution to this problem by way of forcing companies to cut labour costs and rationalise their capacity. A shift to profits is envisaged by a reform of labour markets, and new enterprise is to be encouraged by lower taxes and a reduction in 'crowding out' due to the existence of a large public sector. This strategy is in direct contrast to the CEPG strategy in assuming that industry can survive a further squeeze and that it will in fact be strengthened by this combination of policies. Unlike the CEPG, it is explicitly non-Keynesian in seeking to manipulate monetary variables and in believing that this is sufficient to create the conditions for growth. At the heart of Conservative government policies is the belief that the state sector of the economy is both too large and inefficient and that the level of public spending is too high. The case against the growth of public spending is that it has diverted labour into the public sector and away from manufacturing industry, thus reducing the capacity to produce the marketed goods needed for exports, investment and consumption. This process required that an additional tax burden be placed on industry and workers, and this reduced incentives and helped exacerbate inflation, with wage rates in private industry being driven up by the increased demand generated by the public sector.

The second major theoretical attack on the level of public expenditure is that adopted by the 'international monetarists'. A clear statement of the manner in which the Conservative government believes that reductions in public spending will help the economy was given by the Chief Secretary to the Treasury: 'The reduction in public expenditure plans below those of the previous Administration will, over the medium term, allow a lower rate of monetary growth than would otherwise have been the case. This will be reflected in a lower rate of inflation, for a number of reasons, especially that the exchange rate will be higher than otherwise and pressure of demand lower. Any loss of output will be temporary. Both the lower level of interest rates that should accompany this process and the slower rate of inflation itself will increase private sector demand and output.'[20]

Any rational discussion of public expenditure is fraught by problems of definition. Following a re-definition in 1977, public spending now includes the capital expenditure of public corporations. There is also a rather arbitrary dividing line between expenditure and revenue. When child benefits were switched from an allowance to an expenditure item, public expenditure increased by 1½ per cent by 1978-9. International comparisons are also suspect for similar reasons, since different countries have different kinds of services accounted for by public spending. In Britain public spending as a proportion of GNP rose by 4 per cent following the introduction of the NHS and the transfer of health spending to the NHS, a purely accounting change that did not have any implications for the possibility of achieving growth. With all these qualifications, international comparisons do not show that the United Kingdom has a high level of public expenditure relative to GDP among Western countries. In 1977 the government's current public expenditures as a percentage of GDP was 36 per cent, which was lower than that of France (39 per cent), West Germany (39 per cent), Norway (43 per cent) and the Netherlands (49 per cent).

A further crucial distinction is that it is important to divide public spending into that part which represents spending on buildings or manpower, and that part which represents a transfer of income from one part of the community to another. It is only the first category of spending which makes a claim on the nation's real resources and as Table 4 shows this proportion of spending has fallen as a percentage of GDP.[21]

It is misleading to compare total public spending and GDP

TABLE 6.4 Ratios of public expenditure to GDP at market prices

	Total public expenditure including debt interest	General government expenditure on goods and services
	%	%
1973-4	41·5	24·5
1974-5	46·5	26·0
1975-6	46·5	27·0
1976-7	45·0	25·5
1977-8	41·0	23·5
1978-9	42·5	23·0
1979-80 (estimated)	42·0	23·0

since the former contains transfers of income while the latter does not, so the division of total public spending by GDP will exaggerate the size of the public sector relative to GDP.[22]

The reductions in public expenditure in the late 1970s fell disproportionately on public sector investment, that part of public sector spending which adherents of the 'crowding out' hypothesis are most anxious to see reduced. The reductions made between 1976 and 1979 fell on capital expenditure to the tune of £5 billion, while current expenditure on goods and services was reduced by £3 billion below what it would otherwise have been. The result has been that the public sector investment in 1978-80 was more than 20 per cent below its level in 1975-6 in real terms. The diversion of labour out of the public sector can only have any real significance when the economy is at or near full employment level. It is therefore difficult to see why this strategy has been adopted so enthusiastically by the 1979 Conservative government just at a time of rising unemployment, and why little attempt has been made to phase its impact to relate to a possible upturn in the economy.

Yet throughout the 1970s the size of the public sector has been subect to growing criticism. There has been a rise in the numbers working in the public sector but: 'Much of the rise in employment in the public sector was among women – mainly married women – who had not worked in manufacturing and who would not have got jobs in manufacturing had they not found employment in the public sector. In fact, the main effect of a slower rise in employment in the public sector would have been a higher unemployment rate and – among married women – a lower participation rate in the labour force. This would have represented a much greater waste of resources than the high level of public expenditure which was so often a target for the charge of wastefulness. No evidence suggests that the output of manufacturing industry has been held back by a general shortage of labour . . . '[23]

The monetarist objection to high public spending is that lower public spending will reduce the size of the Public Sector Borrowing Requirement (PSBR) and will reduce the rate of growth of monetary variables and, eventually, inflation. This long and complex argument depends on certain assumptions being made about the relationships between each of the stages of the argument. For instance, it can be questioned whether lower public spending will actually reduce the size of the PSBR if the lower spending pushes the economy into a depression in which tax receipts fall and social security payments to the unemployed rise. The relationship between increased spending and increased borrowing varies according to the form the spending takes, but some estimates suggest that about half of any increase in public spending will be self-financing.[24] The link between the PSBR public spending and GDP is complex, but it remains broadly true that higher government spending, if it leads to higher growth, can reduce the PSBR. The Treasury itself has estimated that a 2 per cent rise in GDP reduces the PSBR by one half per cent.

More government stock will need to be sold to finance that proportion of public spending not financed by tax receipts or borrowing from the banking system. That inflates the money supply and will force up interest rates, making private sector investment borrowing unattractive. High interest rates also attract funds from abroad, driving up the exchange rate and adding an element of uncertainty to the level of the exchange rate. These effects do take place but: 'It is not enough to show that some crowding out exists; opponents of fiscal expansion have to show that it cancels out the whole impact of the expansionary action. This is clearly untrue . . . cuts in public spending in Britain in recent years have led to net reductions in total output. Increases have led to expansion not only of the public but also of the private sector.'[25]

In recent years the PSBR has varied widely, especially in the wake of the 1973 rise in oil prices. However, the PSBR as a proportion of GDP has not shown a long-run tendency to increase and the real value of debt owed by the government has not risen since the Second World War. It is meaningless propaganda at a time of high inflation simply to quote the size of the national debt without adjusting the figures for inflation. Since 1975 the size of the PSBR, compared to GDP, has fallen greatly, a factor which shows that the policies of cuts have helped to push the economy into recession. (See Table 5.)

Opinion in the 'City', which is mainly that of the bankers

TABLE 6.5   The PSBR 1963-78[26]

Year	£m	PSBR/ % GDP
1963	842	3·1
1964	989	3·4
1965	1,205	3·9
1966	963	2·9
1967	1,863	5·3
1968	1,117	3·0
1969	−449	−1·1
1970	−14	0·0
1971	1,361	2·8
1972	2,034	3·7
1973	4,195	6·6
1974	6,372	8·6
1975	10,520	11·4
1976	9,188	8·4
1977	5,925	4·8
1978	8,344	5·9
1979	12,564	7·7

and brokers rather than the industrialists, has developed a slightly hysterical attitude towards the PSBR as the one important financial measure. It can be argued with conviction that it is not the only crucial sign of economic health or sickness. Attitudes to the PSBR have become increasingly founded more on a dogmatic dislike of the state sector than on any coherent appraisal of economic policy. The point has been made regarding the size of the government deficit in 1975-6 that, 'much opinion in the City and abroad was so busy shaking its head and pursing its lips over the size of Britain's

PSBR that it entirely failed to notice that in more successful countries the general government deficit . . . was larger, as a percentage of GDP or GNP, than in Britain. In Germany, for example, it was 6%, in 1975, and in Japan 7%, compared with a figure of 5% for Britain. Whatever else might be said about Britain's public sector deficit, it could hardly be regarded – as the City was inclined to regard it – as the sole source of the nation's troubles.'[27]

The monetarist revival of the 1970s has focused attention on the control of monetary variables as a means of reducing inflation and under the Conservative government the policy of controlling the money supply has been elevated into the supreme goal of policy-making. There remain, however, serious doubts as to the reliability of sterling M3 as an indicator of the tightness of credit in the economy since M3 – which is bank lending to all other sectors – does not constitute a measure of the liquidity of public and private institutions. In particular, in a period when large inflows of capital are taking place which British banks can use to increase their lending to UK residents, M3 does not accurately reflect liquidity as these inflows are excluded from sterling M3. While such large ambiguities exist, it is extremely foolish for any government to adopt one measure of money supply as its target and to stick rigidly to the limits laid down for it. This charge is especially serious in view of the fact that evidence for a strict correlation between the money supply and the inflation rate is remarkably poor: 'The cycles in the growth rates in the two official measures of the money supply do not seem to correlate particularly well, either with each other or with the cycle in inflation.'[28]

The cycle in M1 growth lags behind the cycle in inflation while change in M3 only gives an approximate correlation with inflation if a two-year lag is incorporated. The rapid expansion of M3 in 1972-3 is thus held to have accounted for the acceleration in inflation in 1974-5, but this theory does not adequately account for inflation during 1970-2, since the modest growth in M3 in 1967-8 was insufficient to cause a rapid acceleration in inflation. The link between the PSBR and M3 is also problematical since there is an inverse relationship between these two variables for the period between 1972 and 1978. In Britain, with a highly developed financial sector, no single monetary indicator can accurately represent the ease or tightness of credit as financial institutions have been able to overcome controls placed on them by the government. As has been pointed out, 'the linkages between the financial and real sectors of the economy are not well understood. Given the limited state of knowledge and the fact that financial variables which may be of importance are not highly correlated over short or over long periods of time, we doubt if it is sound policy to treat one particular bundle of financial assets as the ultimate form of money and grand regulator of the economic situation.'[29]

No government can ignore the need to control the money supply, but any government should be prepared to learn from experience rather than theory which are the variables that are most necessary to control, and any government should recognise that, given the imperfect state of economic knowledge, rigid and dogmatic adherence to keeping only one variable under control is too risky a policy. The same fundamental lesson can be applied to other aspects of policy, controlling inflation through a prices and incomes policy and to maintaining the level of public expenditure. The natural scientist operating within all the limitations of behavioural science would never seek such certainties or apply remedies with such single-minded determination. One of the tragedies of much post-war economic practice is its rigidity, its search for solutions, its inability to learn from experience and to operate for any sustained period a mix of policies. The 1979 Conservative government, far from being pragmatists as some claim them to be, adopted new economic theories with all the uncritical fervour of the convert. At least the Left who adopt the alternative strategy have never wished to be associated with pragmatism; they have always had the inner certainty of knowing what must be done and want to impose it.

It is wrong and mistaken to abandon all policies of the last thirty years and to attempt an economic 'experiment', whether from the 'protectionist' or the 'monetarist' viewpoint. There is no evidence to support the view that such a drastic switch of policy at a time when Britain's economic position is extremely weak will do anything but further debilitate the economy. Past policies have failed to deliver the same levels of economic growth as many of the economies of other Western countries, but we have nevertheless maintained – at least until recently – reasonably full employment and, in the majority of post-war years, an annual improvement in people's standard of living. The failure of our economy has not been because the analysis of what was wrong was essentially flawed or because anyone lacked the economic tools to implement the correct policies. Analysis of the last few decades shows rather that failure in most cases was because the economic policies were applied too late and with a timidity and reluctance to initiate sustainable change against the resistance of individuals and institutions. Any economic strategy aiming at a revival of the British economy should be accompanied by changes in the operations of our powerful financial institutions and of the markets for investment finance. The stark alternatives of the protectionists and the monetarists aim at macro-economic variables and neglect the scope for reforms of micro-economic markets and institutions in order to improve resource allocation. The low level of industrial investment in the British economy and the age structure of our industrial plant and machinery clearly place our industry at a competitive disadvantage when it is compared to Western Europe, Japan and the United States. In addressing itself to the major problems facing British industry the Wilson Committee,[30] set up to review the functioning of financial institutions, stated that: 'A higher level of worthwhile private investment will only be achieved if a number of conditions are satisfied. First, managements will have to have the incentive to seek out viable projects and, in appropriate cases, to maintain their existing operations. Secondly, there will have to be changes in attitude on the part of both managements and employees about making the most efficient use of existing financial assets. Thirdly, finance of the right type, price and maturity must be available.' The problem of the provision of finance for industry was regarded as not being one of a shortage of funds, for the Wilson Committee noted: 'we have received no evidence of any general shortage of finance for industry at prevailing rates of interest and levels of demand, and with present perceptions of the risks involved in real investment. Industry has not felt that it has been held back by an inability to obtain external funds provided it was prepared to pay the price asked.' This view was qualified by saying that the existing financial mechanisms 'seem to have a degree of difficulty in meeting the demands of small, especially new, firms', and that the dominance of financial markets by cautious portfolio managers of pension funds and life assurance funds has served to inhibit investment in high-risk areas. It can be argued that there is no shortage of investment funds and instead there is a shortage of worthwhile projects in Britain, with a high enough rate of return. This neglects the important point that the supply of funds must be of the 'right type, price and maturity' in order that potential investment projects will be regarded as being economically viable.

The commercial banks in Britain lend money to industry for shorter periods than do banks in Japan and in the EEC and they attach more stringent borrowing conditions to the loans. A result has been that investment is curtailed by the need to repay interest on loans in a short period, before a project has begun to generate a return on the investment. Businessmen are reluctant to consider long-term investments, when faced with short-term loans, or large investments when banks are unwilling to advance a large proportion of the cost of a project. A cautious and unenterprising attitude is instilled which, in part, serves to justify cautious lending policies by the banks. This is in marked contrast to the confidence shown by European businessmen and the institutions from which they borrow.

There is a need in Britain to foster a set of attitudes which accepts risk-taking by entrepreneurs and by financial institutions. For socialists this means recognising that a market economy is founded on a readiness to take risks, which can bring also high rewards. This is not to advocate or extol unfettered capitalism. The City – which advocates the un-inhibited operation of the market system for everyone else – was extremely reluctant to see its rigours applied to its own secondary banking system in the early 1970s. No depositors

143

with any of those banks lost their deposits – the banks concerned being rescued by the lifeboat fund operated at the request of the Bank of England. Sir Leslie Murphy who supported the operation, which was mounted to sustain the integrity and credit of the City, has commented that, 'it is an odd result that those who received higher interest rates on their deposits because of the lower security involved in depositing with a secondary bank were not penalised when those banks got into difficulties. The City is, it seems, not always in favour of the unfettered operation of market forces.' What is needed is a better balance. A role for government is in trying to encourage less restrictive lending policies by the commercial banks in order to help to stimulate industrial investment and risk-taking and to break into the vicious downward cycle of confidence-sapping economic decline. A limit should be reimposed on the total of bank lending, in order to prevent bank credit financing consumption of imports, and the government should make it clear that an increasing proportion of the total is to be used to finance productive investment. The banks could also be persuaded to increase the length of loans, from the present low average level of three years to the continental level of five years or more. To meet these needs the banks will require an increasing proportion of personal savings to be deposited with them instead of with the building societies and to do so the banks should be allowed to offer more attractive terms to depositors. It will not be easy to achieve these changes since radical reforms are perceived as being more difficult during an economic decline and caution is preferred to risk-taking. There is a need to establish a totally new concept of mixed private and publicly funded investment facility to channel oil company and government North Sea oil revenues into productive investments in the United Kingdom. At present too much of the revenues of the oil companies goes abroad and government revenues have been used to finance tax cuts and could well be used to stimulate consumption of imported manufactures. The management of the fund being mixed would make it more entrepreneurial, since it is vital that it is a risk-taking investment facility. The existing financial institutions, such as the pension funds and life assurance funds, could lend a proportion of their funds to such a new investment institution and would receive in return a guaranteed minimum rate of return to equal that for gilt edged stock. This could encourage the trade unions to be less conservative in the investment decisions of their own pension funds. Finance could be offered by the investment bank at a variety of interest rates and it would be expected that, as the note of dissent to the Wilson Committee Report noted, 'the ability to offer finance on favourable terms would have a major effect on the number of new projects being put forward.'

The fact that sensible economic policies have been applied for too short a period to achieve results has been due in particular to the discontinuity between governments which started most markedly with the change of government in 1970. Since then a succession of ideologically-motivated governments has ensured little or no economic continuity other than that forced on them after a period in office by the realities of a world economy. The exchange rate in particular has for long periods been too high and has been instrumental in undermining our manufacturing base.

It is clear that the 1980s show every sign of continuing this trend. Instead of there being a gradual depreciation of sterling, a high exchange rate will be maintained under the influence of high interest rates and the possession of North Sea oil, and it will severely damage industry. Selective import controls will be necessary where penetration is having damaging effects and support is likely to grow within the EEC for a more detailed policy for managing trade – or, as it is called by the French, more 'orderly marketing arrangements'. If severe import penetration takes place, the already high unemployment figures risk reaching levels which would not be tolerated by other Community countries. We should use our membership of the EEC to negotiate specific import restrictions: if Britain could demonstrate that real disruption was occurring, some arrangement might even be negotiated for intra-Community trade. Unilaterally introduced controls, however, should be a last desperate remedy. Before they were to be instigated there should be seen to have been serious international negotiations in a genuine attempt to reach agreement. Presenting our

145

trading partners in the EEC and GATT with a *fait accompli* would incur the same hostility as we encountered in 1964 by our EFTA partners. To argue that Britain can easily act alone is dangerously chauvinistic and unrealistic. In any serious negotiation a readiness to act unilaterally in the last resort has to be a negotiating counter but it has to be used with skill and understanding. Unilateral protectionism would receive a very hostile reception from our Community partners if they assumed it was merely a prelude to our withdrawing from the European Community or if we appeared to care little for our obligations to other nations under GATT or under our membership of the IMF.

Above all, Britain's economic policy needs to be approached with a greater intellectual humility and political sensitivity, a willingness to learn from our past mistakes. A position of economic weakness nationally and internationally is not a time either to espouse an economic ideology hostile to the working of the mixed economy – which would be seen by a significant section of those who work within our economy as being harmful to achieving the goals of full employment and a rising standard of living – or to adopt a policy which cannot be made broadly tolerable to all who work in the public sector, to management and to unions. To pretend that any British government can impose its will in economic issues on important sections of the national community or international economic institutions without any serious counter-balancing consequences is fundamentally to misunderstand the limitations of democracy within Britain and the interdependence of the world economy.

7

Incomes Policy

The history of the last thirty-five years suggests that full employment, reasonable price stability and free collective bargaining are mutually incompatible. All governments which aspire to economic growth have tended at various times to concentrate on incomes policy and to challenge the principle of free collective bargaining, but they have rarely followed a consistent line. It is impossible to challenge the corporatist trend of the past while endorsing the centralising trend of post-war incomes policies and, as has been argued in Chapter 3, on corporatism, the issue of decentralisation within the trade union movement cannot be ignored by socialist politicians when they come to grapple with the problem of influencing free collective bargaining.

All the policies that have been tried have failed in a number of respects: they have not substantially held down wage inflation except in the short run; they have not reduced the problem of low pay; and they have not markedly improved industrial relations. These failings can be attributed to lack of flexibility, to inability to take account of 'special cases', and to neglect of grass roots' pressure. The policies, though initially often popular, have not been regarded as fair in practice, particularly those that started with cut-off anomalies and were then increasingly circumvented. As a result, trade unions have not been able to restrain their members' demands, even though opinion polls may still have been indicating popular support. Moreover, when the results are retrospectively assessed over a five-year period and all the economic consequences are

147

averaged out, including what happens when the policy ceases to operate, it is clear that the real economic effect is open to question. The problem is that no one can calculate the effect of what would have happened if there had been no incomes policy. There are some who argue for a statutory policy and claim that only if the full weight of parliament is brought to bear can there be sufficient democratic authority to maintain the policy. But this is to ignore changes in the structure of British society and the patterns of wage bargaining that call for a more flexible, decentralised approach.

Governments have generally felt that, if they can be confident that wages will rise within certain percentage limits, they can more easily plan for a higher overall level of demand in the economy without risking a high rate of inflation or damaging the balance of payments. 'The need for incomes policy arises when it appears that a tolerable degree of price stability cannot be achieved by reducing the level of demand, or can be achieved only at an unacceptably high cost in terms of unemployment, loss of real output, and interference with growth. Hence, incomes policy is often presented as a means of improving the trade-off between unemployment and price stability.'[1] Governments have tried, therefore, to show workers that the lower the earnings figure in its economic projections then the higher will be the growth and employment figures that the government can aim for without failing to contain inflation and the balance of payments deficit.

This has been the thinking behind the policies worked out by the social democratic governments of Scandinavia, the Federal Republic of Germany, and Austria, with fiscal policies and incomes policies being linked in various ways. Some have involved a form of social contract which is agreed by the national trade union organisations, the employers' federations and the government.[2] The unions have agreed to limit wages in return for government action to secure full employment and certain social benefits. For instance, in Norway in 1975 the unions agreed to accept only 80 per cent compensation for the rise in the cost of living over the previous year, with only 30 per cent out of the 80 per cent being taken in wage rises and the remainder in increased family allowances, income tax cuts, pension rises and a price freeze.[3] A similar policy was achieved in Ireland in August 1979 with a 15-month pay deal. The package was made up of separate agreements on pay, taxation and employment, with the pay policy being agreed between the Irish Confederation of Trade Unions and the employers, but with the implementation of each policy closely linked to the observance of the other two.[4] These policies have been very successful, both in securing social goals and in containing inflation. 'For more than a decade after 1956, the Swedish system of centralised wage bargaining . . . constituted an important element in the realisation of the policy goals of minimal unemployment, moderate price inflation, rapid growth of productivity, and rising real income, and greater equality of income distribution, especially through the provision of pension benefits and health insurance. In Norway, incomes policy based on similarly centralised bargaining, but with direct participation by the government in the process, enabled the authorities to keep the rate of unemployment generally below the European average and to secure steady and rapid economic growth.'[5]

One reason for Britain's failure to achieve a similar success is our different institutional framework. In Scandinavia, the national trade union organisations, the equivalents of the TUC, have authority vested in them by their constituent unions to negotiate with the government and employers and they have the power to deliver their side of the bargain by limiting wage increases. This is not so in Britain, where the TUC is weak and unable to control strong unions such as the miners or engineers and where individual unions are unable to control shop-floor organisations of their own members. The Donovan Commission found that in the 1960s the level of effective decision-making moved downwards from the national trade union officers to committees of shop stewards, a trend caused by comparatively full employment, which enhanced the ability of the shop-floor to demand increases, and by increasing shop-floor frustration with the acquiescence of the unions in incomes policies. The rise of shop-floor power created a dual system of industrial relations, with national wage agreements being supplemented by local pay rises.

Some unions responded to this by formally decentralising.

It is interesting that the Donovan report stated that 'it is often wide of the mark to describe shop stewards as trouble-makers . . . Quite commonly they are supporters of order exercising a restraining influence on their members.'[6] Four major changes took place within the unions in the 1970s: a movement from national level to lower level bargaining, changes in the scope of lower-level bargaining, an increase in lay involvement on negotiating bodies and the extension, or introduction, of reference-back procedures. An example of lower-level bargaining was the withdrawal of the T&GWU from the Road Haulage Wages Council in December 1975. Other examples were the Liverpool Dockers' secession from national negotiations in 1967, and the Confederation of Shipbuilders and Engineering Union's withdrawal in 1971. This movement has also been influenced by companies either leaving an employers' association and/or withdrawing from industry-wide negotiations. Metal Box withdrew from the Tin Box Joint Industrial Committee (JIC) in 1969 and 1970 and moved to individual factory bargaining. Cadbury-Schweppes left a JIC in 1968 and introduced plant bargaining. A change in the scope of lowest level bargaining was of greater significance and represented what Donovan called the 'two-system pattern', where national negotiations set minimum rates and hours and substantial increases are obtained at the local level via productivity deals. T&GWU annual reports increasingly show the union's involvement in productivity deals. By 1975 the scope of discussions at National Joint Industrial Committee level was considerably reduced and over 50 per cent of all wage increases were obtained at the local level.

Devolved bargaining has also produced a marked change in the structure of the T&GWU, largely because, if the union had sought to retain the involvement of full-time officials in local bargaining, a large increase in the number of officials would have been needed. The number of full-time officials declined from 530 to 485 between 1968 and 1975, while the ratio of members to senior shop stewards and conveners fell from 637:1 in 1965 to 433:1 in 1975. There is also evidence that shop stewards were replaced less often and hence numbers of full-time and senior stewards rose. Obviously more local bargaining will lead to increasing involvement by lay unionists, as a result of increases both in the number of local negotiating bodies and in the scope of local discussions. However, there has also been an increase in lay involvement in bodies above the local level.

In the Scandinavian countries there are fewer unions and all the major negotiations take place at the same time of the year, the synchro-pay day; it is, therefore, easier for the national union bodies to achieve agreement from the individual unions, since the latter do not have to worry that other unions will achieve higher settlements in the current pay round. The Scandinavians have in consequence to some extent avoided the leapfrogging that is endemic in Britain. But in the 1970s, when world inflation rates rose and Scandinavia was particularly vulnerable to oil price increases, the system of centralised wage bargaining began to break down; it may be that the success of the past was possible because of sustained growth and low inflation and that a centralised incomes policy cannot withstand the strains imposed by world economic recession and high inflation. Although British trade unions have a far more decentralised structure than do the Scandinavian, successive British governments have attempted to instigate a very similar pattern of centralised incomes policies. National norms have been either agreed with a reluctant TUC or imposed on them and, in most cases, later abandoned as being either unrealistic or too inflexible to withstand growing pressure from the shop-floor or the challenge of a major union.

The most successful period of prices and incomes' policy was from 1940 to 1945, when Ernest Bevin, as Minister of Labour, introduced a statutory policy which resulted in the only redistributive five-year period in British history. The problem of continually rising prices was foreseen even then in the 1944 White Paper *Employment Policy*, which stated that, 'Action taken by the Government to maintain expenditure will be fruitless unless wages and prices are kept reasonably stable'. Sir Stafford Cripps in 1948-9 had a policy which simply asked for moderation, and for those two years it worked, but it was undermined by the growing power of shop stewards and by devaluation in September 1949 and the Korean War in June 1950. Moreover, as prices began to rise faster than wages it lost the appearance of equity which had been so carefully preserved during the war years. Interestingly, Aubrey Jones argues that, 'the 1948 White Paper had shown little awareness of the fact that shop stewards in the factory were moving out of the control of the national trade union leaders.'[7]

The next attempt was by Harold Macmillan when, as Chancellor of the Exchequer in 1956, he set a 'plateau' for public sector prices but with direct control of wages. Then, in August 1957, Peter Thorneycroft set up the Council on Prices, Productivity and Incomes to create a greater awareness of the need to limit rises in prices and wages. On 25 July 1961 the then Chancellor, Selwyn Lloyd, announced a 'wage pause' for government employees, later extended to workers covered by Wages Councils; it was not backed by statute and existing commitments were honoured. The pause ended on 1 April 1962 when the National Economic Development Council was set up.

In 1962-3 a 'voluntary restriction' was set of 2-2·5 per cent and then 3-3·5 per cent. This allowed exceptions for high productivity, labour mobility and certain adjustments found to be in the national interest. In November 1962 a National Incomes Commission was founded to set future targets. In 1965-6 a new Labour government evolved a voluntary 3-3·5 per cent policy with the same exceptions but with an additional provision for low pay, and set up a Prices and Incomes Commission, later to become a statutory Board. This was followed in July 1966 by a compulsory six months' 'freeze'. In 1967-8 the 'zero norm' was introduced, and a voluntary policy adopted, though the government retained powers of delay. The exceptions were for productivity, low pay, labour mobility and adjustments in the national interest. By 1969 a 3·5 per cent ceiling on rises in exceptional cases was permitted. In 1969-70 a 2·5-4·5 per cent 'voluntary band' was agreed, but there were no statutory powers, for example, to delay wage rises, and wage levels soon began to exceed the limits. In 1971-2 the 'n-1 formula' was a voluntary guideline, but it was imposed by the government on its own employees. In the private sector, however, free collective bargaining pushed wages far ahead in advance of productivity, and unit costs rose. In 1972-3 there was a statutory freeze, no exceptions were allowed; this was followed in 1973 by the 'one pound plus 4 per cent formula' and a '12-month rule'. This was again a compulsory policy, the only exception being for moves to equal pay and for settlements deferred by the freeze. In 1973-4, a system of 7 per cent or '£2.35 flat rate plus threshold payments' was introduced as a compulsory scheme. It had a 1 per cent margin to deal with pay structures. Genuine productivity schemes and payments for unsocial hours were the only exceptions allowed. The productivity element was a deliberate loophole to cope with the miners, but because of bad handling and more by accident than design, a major confrontation followed, leading to the 1974 election defeat.

In 1974-5 inflation soared, fed by the threshold payments provision that the new Labour government had inherited. This compensation for price changes between the main settlements was an inbuilt escalator and, as a result of the social contract, exceptions were allowed for low pay and equal pay, which in turn led to large increases for nurses under the Halsbury award and for teachers under the Houghton award. In the summer of 1975, with inflation running at 27 per cent, a '£6 maximum' with some exceptions for low pay and equal pay was agreed, together with a 12-month rule; there was no statutory back-up on wages, though a statutory price restraint introduced by the previous government had been maintained. In 1976 a 5 per cent policy with a minimum of £2.50 and a maximum of £4.00 was again agreed with the TUC, but no exceptions were allowed. In 1977 a 10 per cent maximum with exceptions for productivity was introduced and, though not agreed by the TUC, it was acquiesced in, though in the early stages it did involve the government withstanding industrial action from the firemen.

All these policies have been challenged by workers in profitable industries demanding a share of those profits. In 1977 Ford workers achieved an 11 per cent settlement which, with other provisions, was well above the government's 10 per cent maximum and very nearly broke the whole policy. In 1978 it was again Ford who, with a 27 per cent settlement, not only substantially broke the then attempt to agree a 5 per cent pay guideline, but was also the test case which led to the parliamentary rejection of government sanctions, to the abandonment of the pay policy and the famous 'winter of discontent' in January and February 1979 which led, in turn, to the fall of the Labour government in May 1979.

This is a sombre tale, and before embarking on the same course again, it is very necessary to analyse objectively the record of incomes policies in affecting the economy and to see if there are lessons for the future.

Successive British incomes policies have in fact failed to achieve the social goals that have been for many their chief purpose. They have, notably, not affected the hoped-for redistribution of income in favour of the lower-paid. The spread of differentials has not been substantially narrowed by the flat rate policies of 1973-4 and 1975-7, except at the very top of the incomes spread. A certain amount of caution is necessary in drawing any conclusions about the effects of policies on differentials, since not all the information is available, but the evidence shows that what slight narrowing in differentials did take place between 1970 and 1977 was not confined to the periods of flat-rate policies. It is noticeable that, during the period of the Labour government's £6 per week policy, there was no movement in favour of the lower-paid. Much larger changes occurred between April 1976 and April 1977 when a percentage policy was in operation. Stages II and III of the Conservative government's policy between April 1973 and April 1974, which were only partly flat-rate policies, appear to have had as much redistributive effect as other pay policy periods.

Figures available for the top 1 per cent of men in full-time employment show that there was a substantial narrowing of the gap between the top percentile and the median between 1970 and 1976, but that this took place between 1970 and 1974 and was actually reversed under the Labour government between April 1975 and April 1976 – a period during which the Stage I policy permitted in theory no increases for those earning over £8,500. These results are disappointing, but they can probably be explained by the considerable potential for evasion through promotions, job changes and circumvention of the limits.

Differentials can also be studied by looking at the wages structure within companies. These figures show long periods when differentials stayed fairly constant followed by short periods of narrowing. In engineering a large compression took place between June 1974 and June 1975, the period of the original social contract, which was effectively a period of free collective bargaining when compared to later policies. A further narrowing did take place during the year of the £6 policy but this was not as great as the previous movement. None of the policies of the 1960s had very much effect. On shipbuilding a National Institute of Economic and Social Research study said that, 'There is certainly no evidence therefore that the skill differential in shipbuilding has been eroded at an industry-wide level during periods of incomes policy.'[8]

Differentials have been decreasing over the last twenty years in manufacturing industry, but there is further evidence that this has not been a result of incomes policies but a reflection of the influence of long-term changes in the labour market and the rate of inflation. A study by the University of Aberdeen concluded that, 'the narrowing [of differentials] was under way well before the most recent incomes policies, so that the explanation of this significant development must be sought elsewhere.'[9] Another study found that the narrowing of differentials had occurred because of rapid inflation and equal pay legislation. A National Institute study of 1978 concluded that, 'we can find little evidence, apart from the highest income groups, that there has been a strong compression of pay brought about directly by incomes policies.'[10] A 1976 study came to the surprising conclusion that after the policies of 1972-4 the restoration of free collective bargaining reduced differentials further instead of returning them to their pre-policy level.[11] The problem of low pay and the poverty trap on this evidence is not likely to be solved through the marginal changes that a pay policy can make, but will require major reforms of the taxation and benefits system and a resolute commitment to redistributive patterns within such reforms.

It is also arguable that all policies have failed to limit wages in the long term, because catching up takes place after the end of a policy. A recent major study concluded that, 'whilst some incomes policies have reduced the rate of wage inflation during the period in which they operated, this reduction has only been temporary. Wage increases in the period immediately following the ending of the policies were higher than they would otherwise have been, and these increases match losses incurred during the operation of the incomes policy.'[12] And a series of econometric tests carried out by the Department of Employment for the period 1951-69 found that the 1965 Labour policy had some effect in its first two years, but that in the next two years pay rose by about the same amount that it would have done without the policy.[13] Some people would argue, however, that anything can be proved with econometrics, and the 1967 devaluation, which allowed inflation to be 'imported', may have affected the econometric model used. The net effect of incomes policy in the 1960s was merely to alter the timing of the onset of inflation, though it should not be forgotten that in some circumstances such an influence can be very important, as it was after the 1973 oil price rise. Overall, it has been claimed that the effects of all the policies up to 1972 had been 'derisory' and that 'incomes policies have repeatedly failed to achieve any of their . . . stated objectives'.[14]

The first major issue to resolve in the 1980s is the extent to which any prices and incomes policy, as opposed to general tax and social security policy, should contribute to a redistribution of income. There is a strong case, in the light of the evidence, for leaving redistribution to tax and social security policy. Only if the economic circumstances were so bad that incomes needed to fall in real terms would there be a case for attempting a redistributive formula, and even then there are grounds for believing that the tax and social security system is a better vehicle for protecting the low paid. The redistributive argument is often used to justify an incomes policy, but there is very little hard evidence for the assertion that free collective bargaining itself produces low pay. It is impossible to ignore the record of the Wages Council in perpetuating low pay, or the appalling situation of the unskilled employees of central and local government. In equity there is a strong case for a formula that seeks to allocate more to the lowest paid than the market economy will allow, but this needs to be negotiated since it will be resisted if it is imposed, and will eventually undermine the other more worthwhile benefits of an agreed pay policy. Statutory minimum wage legislation phased in, as was done for equal pay, may help, and could be imposed, but the difficulties are considerable. They are considered in the context of an anti-poverty strategy in Chapter 5 on Inequality.

One of the keys to developing an agreed long term incomes policy is to accept that a greater measure of decentralisation is inevitable and that past failures have been due to excessive centralisation. The issue underlying the centralised or decentralised argument is very basic: should wages relate to the task the employee does or to the ability of the employer to pay? In theory, the most socialist wages policy and the one which should lead to a more equal wage distribution is one which relates to the nature of the work. This pattern could emerge in centrally controlled economies and broadly does, even though they also retain very considerable pay differentials. But in a mixed economy the issue is far more complicated. If the profitable company which can easily pay more has its wage levels controlled or influenced to a level below that which it could pay, it merely increases its profitability. As a consequence, those who want free collective bargaining point to the inconsistencies of interference in wages. The centralised Left, who most frequently argue for no interference, often square their socialist conscience by saying that until the state owns all the means of production there is no alternative to playing the market game. Although this position is escapist and patently absurd, it is nevertheless used to counter the charge that there is nothing socialist about free collective bargaining. The danger of the centralised approach to all these issues is that its very strength – its across-the-board nature, its apparent fairness, its ease of implementation – contains the seeds of its own destruction: an inability to discriminate and adapt flexibly to circumstances, the creation of anomalies, and the possibility of circumvention which will threaten its overall credibility.

The question of how to handle profits during a period of incomes restraint is a substantive issue. So far the only way it has been tackled is by calls for dividend restraint – which only postpones an eventual pay-out to shareholders. It is interesting how, in the commercial state industries, wage claims are increasingly related to arguments about profitability, rather than focusing on the nature of the task. Trade unionists are often the strongest advocates of nationalised industries adopting a pricing structure which produces profit, since it is easier for them to argue for higher wages against a profit than against a loss. One of the stresses to which the prices and incomes policies of 1975-9 eventually succumbed was the ability of many sections of the private sector to pay high wage claims and their readiness to do so either of their own volition or under industrial pressure. Ford was only the most publicised case, no doubt because it always comes early in the pay round, but also because the car industry is seen to be a pace-setter. Where were Ford's profits to go if not in wages or benefits to the Ford workers? How, if Ford could offer both to pay higher wages and to keep within the Prices Code, could one justify depriving Ford workers of the benefits of the company's commercial success? The same was also being argued for British Oxygen, for the oil tanker drivers, and many other private companies. This issue must be tackled as part of a credible long-term policy for prices and incomes.

There is also the vexed problem of productivity. If wage increases are related to productivity increases, or wages to levels of productivity, then one has the problem of high wages or big wage increases in sectors such as petrochemicals, where productivity is very high because the process is very capital intensive, or in sectors where increases in productivity can be very big because of technical progress. This can easily produce enormous discrepancies in the wages of people doing very similar kinds of jobs, dependent only on the area in which they work. Centrally imposed flat-rate or percentage increases may last a year or more at a time of economic crisis, but the real need is for a policy which operates before an economic crisis occurs, and stops the crisis from happening. The first essential in the private sector and in the public commercial sector, such as NEB companies and some industries like steel, ship-building and aerospace, must be a readiness by unions and employers to negotiate within the particular parameters of profit and productivity that relate to the specific firm. This will mean more realistic bargaining in some private sector indus-tries than hitherto and a greater readiness by trade unions and employers to face up to market realities. Yet even if this is achieved and the average wage increase for the private sector does not put unit costs above what can be justified in the market place there is likely to be a very wide difference in wage increases. The evidence is that these wide differences add significantly to pressure for higher increases in other sectors where they cannot be so justified. So in countries like the Federal Republic of Germany and Austria, employers and trade unions have come together in a loose arrangement with the government to concert the general guidelines within which free collective bargaining will take place.

Such a concertation procedure accepts in very general terms that people are going to be paid for what they do and that the profitability or losses of the company will determine wage levels, but argues that a nationally-agreed margin for manoeuvre in wage bargaining helps control national inflation. It could be linked to a vetting and scrutiny procedure similar to that operated for productivity deals at one stage by the Prices and Incomes Board. Yet some firms' profitability will allow for wage increases considerably in excess of the agreed margin for manoeuvre. If the firm pays up, the national margin is widened and a drift upwards in wage levels will soon follow. The value of concerting nationally is that it is a way of neutralising or dampening down this otherwise very wide margin of wage negotiations.

Yet some way is needed of ensuring that the worker in the profitable concern shares in its success, and sees any excess profits used creatively and constructively for the good of the firm, and its future work prospects as well as improving working conditions and fringe benefits. It is here that a measure of genuine industrial democracy is so crucial, so that the workpeople are involved in decisions about the reinvestment of wage increases foregone because of national wage guidelines. This is much more realistic than a national investment fund which would be remote from the workers on a particular shop floor. Trade unionists cannot be expected to support a wages policy if they feel that their restraint simply provides higher dividends for shareholders. Unless they see a wages policy in the broad framework of an acceptable industrial and social policy for their particular workplace, not just for the nation as a whole, they will act as exploiters of market forces. It has been a major failure in all prices and incomes policies that have ever operated in the UK that they have not really grappled with this problem. To last, any incomes policy must relate to the individual and the individual firm; it must cover investment in the particular industry and the effect on jobs and conditions of service for employees. The government may decide to intervene to control key prices as part of their contribution to creating the climate for concertation, but the distortion effect on the market needs to be carefully weighed and the extent and scope of the intervention must be agreed as part of the concertation process. Past national prices policies, like incomes policies, have been far too centralised. An overall percentage price ceiling can result in bankruptcies or lack of investment, particularly when world commodity prices are rising fast. The powers and structure of the Price Commission as they stood in 1979 were a better compromise with all the conflicting pressures.

The hardest question, particularly for those who wish to rely on a voluntary policy, is the extent to which sanctions should be used. Arbitrary power is disliked and if any sanctions are to be used for any period, then some form of appeal machinery is essential. But it is necessary to be able to challenge price increases or dividend distribution by a company which has exceeded a pay ceiling voluntarily agreed by unions and management, even where the particular company was not directly party to the agreement. Similarly, the government's role as purchaser should be able to take account of breaches of the pay guideline. It can be argued that these are not statutory sanctions in the conventional sense; but the devotees of free collective bargaining on the Left and Right oppose them, seeing a precedent for introducing statutory wage curbs on employees: if there cannot be agreement, then the case for statutory control may have to be faced. Recent Labour governments have been virtually committed to never introducing a statutory policy, which has the effect of gravely weakening their bargaining power in trying to establish a voluntary policy. Yet it is hard to see why parliament should not intervene if negotiations fail; democratic imposition is far preferable to the arbitrary use of executive power for which there is no formal legislative authority. But voluntary agreement, such as has been negotiated in Austria and the Federal Republic of Germany, is far preferable.

The dilemma in those parts of the public sector that are financed by consumers through price tariffs is well illustrated in the understandable wish of gas workers to benefit from the huge profits of their industry, and by the water workers who want to be compared with those key public service supply workers in the gas and electricity industries. Yet to what extent can we accept ability to pay as the only criterion that should dictate wage levels? How do we compare gas workers' wages with those of the miners, traditionally high industrial earners? Society needs both gas and coal, and the profitability of the industries depends on accounting conventions, subsidy policies and other factors in a managed energy market – to say nothing of decisions made by the OPEC cartel – as well as on efficiency and productivity. The tripartite structure of government, National Coal Board and mining unions being involved in a planning agreement forum, where wages are discussed but not negotiated, along with investment and conditions of work, is a good augury for the future and a valuable manifestation of industrial democracy where the particular unions do not wish to be represented formally on the National Coal Board.

If a margin for manoeuvre in the consultation process for the private sector is inevitable, why, it will be argued, should this not cover the public sector as well? It probably can cover the price-linked public sector, but in the purely public service sector, where the service is financed by central taxation or rates, free collective bargaining cannot involve arguments relating to profitability, and here even productivity is hard to assess. Comparability in the public service sector means a guarantee that the public service employee will not fall behind the movement in earnings in the private sector and the commercial public sector. Provided it is honestly and objectively applied and takes account of such factors as fringe benefits, it should not lead to the leap frogging and inflationary pressure that it has generated in the past. The plethora of public sector pay arrangements that have operated in the past cannot continue. The Armed Forces Pay Review Body, Doctors and Dentists Review Body, Top Salaries Review Body, Civil Service Pay Research Unit, and other ad hoc bodies – all need to be brought together into a single Comparability Commission. Without such a safety valve, workers in areas where profits are not measurable will seek to demonstrate their indispensability by industrial action, as health and local government employees did in 1979.

A prices, investment and incomes policy must not be asked to bear the strain of acting as short-term manipulator of the economy, for this will discredit it in the long term. It needs to start out with the objective of being sustainable over the minimum time scale of a four to five year parliament. This requires a new understanding of the limitations as well as the potential of such policies. It means that trade unionists in the private sector must have access to a level of information about profitability and investment that is not at present widely available, and that collective bargaining must take place in a wider context of the firm's future than at present. This will benefit from the introduction of industrial democracy, in the context of which it should be possible to achieve a trade union commitment to concertation and to establishing national wage guidelines. Trade unions in the public services would have to represent their members' interests less in direct negotiation with employers and more in marshalling their evidence to a Comparability Commission. The safeguard that they would be able to offer their members is that their incomes would move with the overall movement of incomes and be directly influenced by free collective bargaining in the private sector. In 1979 the public sector trade unions thought their interests were best served by breaking free from an incomes policy which at least attempted to cover both public and private sectors. In 1980 after a year of free-for-all the government began to apply a purely public sector pay policy. Again, as in 1962, a Conservative government was attempting to operate a discriminatory incomes policy, with restraint in the public sector. But all past experience shows that the social price of this type of incomes policy is a growing discontent as the public sector falls behind the private, and that such a one-sided policy is no longer compatible with the industrial strength of the public services, whose power to disrupt society is now very strong. One of the tragedies of the 1979 'winter of discontent' was that the establishment, in the Clegg Commission, of comparability machinery for the public sector, which was eventually the basis for a return to work, had actually been offered to the relevant trade unions by the government in the November 1978 renegotiated package.

Public service trade unions do not share the view of many commentators that the Clegg Commission gave inflationary awards; in some sectors they felt the awards were not generous enough, and they are becoming more hostile to the concept of comparability. True comparability will allow both private and public sector working conditions and fringe benefits to be compared. If any of these are improved by negotiation, with profitable companies coming up against the ceiling of any overall nationally-agreed margin for manoeuvre over incomes, then this will be taken into account and reflected back in public sector wage awards, but where public sector conditions and fringe benefits are in advance of those of the comparable private sector they will not be able to obtain much improvement. Such a combination of bargaining within agreed limits for the private sector and comparability for the public sector based on realistic criteria reflects the pattern, if not the exact formulation, that was emerging by November 1978. The government was then within a hair's-breadth of agreeing the crucial fourth year for a flexible prices and incomes policy. The offer was of comparability for the public sector, an extra weighting for the low paid and flexible arrangements to cover productivity, skill shortages and other marginal improvements. The offer was not 5 per cent, but between 8 and 9 per cent, which with drift would have had an out-turn nearer 12 per cent. Inflation was 8 per cent when, in October 1978, negotiations restarted over the 5 per cent limit which had been rejected by the TUC and Labour Party Conference. The renegotiated package, itself the result of a three-year learning process, was lost by one vote in the TUC General Council on 14 November 1978. Yet even had it been won by one vote, the crucial will to make an agreement stick was missing. The two key figures in the trade union movement who had helped to make the 1975 agreement work, Jack Jones and Hugh Scanlon, were retiring and it was the public service unions, like NUPE, that were setting the pace. By 1980 most trade union leaders knew that failure to reach agreement in 1978 had worked against the interests of their members. They faced the introduction for 1980-1 of a pay policy of 6 per cent for the public sector, which was designed to cut living standards, as inflation was running at 16 per cent and was unlikely to fall to single figures before the end of the pay round.

The social consequences, with unemployment steadily rising and likely to stay high through the middle 1980s, demonstrate yet again all the problems of abandoning the search for an incomes policy. A clear commitment by all political parties to try to establish an agreed framework is urgently needed: 'It is not only that each party in turn has abolished the institutions of its predecessor, so that none of the bodies set up during the past two decades – the National Incomes Commission, the National Board for Prices and Incomes, or the Pay Board – had a chance to establish itself. In addition, each party in turn has changed sides on this matter, opposing income policy when out of power and adopting it when in power.'[15]

A new policy will require a more realistic and specific framework than previous generalised social contract agreements. It must accept that the pace of wage movements cannot be fixed centrally, but must reflect, at least initially, market realities in the private sector and a disaggregated wage bargaining pattern. It will also need to be concerned with prices and dividends, with limits being agreed with the consent of the trade unions and employers' organisations. A one-sided bargain which limited only wages and not other sources of income would be seen as unfair and merely as a way of forcing one group to bear the brunt of the struggle against inflation. In accepting that past prices policies have been over-centralised, based on either a freeze or an inflexible set of criteria for price rises, it must be recognised that a flexible price policy needs to be supplemented by a competition policy which limits the powers of monopolies to pass on price rises to a captive market. The virtual absence of serious anti-trust and monopoly legislation in Britain is in marked contrast to the powers that exist and are being extended in the USA and that were introduced by a social democratic government in Sweden.

Any incomes policy should also be supplemented by an active employment and rehousing policy to enable the labour market to work more efficiently. For instance, skill shortages in certain areas of the country have been responsible for bidding up wages, while unemployed labour with suitable skills has existed in other areas. If in this process other occupations demand wage rises to maintain some past pay relationship, then general inflation occurs, relative wages do not change rapidly and shortages of labour tend to persist.

A decentralised incomes policy cannot be expected to halt wage inflation in its tracks, since it would not attempt to freeze wages or rigidly to contain all wage rises within a certain percentage figure. However, it would offer a better chance of eventually keeping inflation under control than would a series of ad hoc, centralised policies that eventually collapse and allow inflation to rise again until other draconian measures are adopted. And it should reduce the need for trade unions to demand large rises to compensate for inflation in advance, which has contributed to previous inflationary spirals.

A decentralised policy that relies on a mixture of market forces, controls and comparability should be able to be maintained by successive governments of whatever party. A socialist government's approach would temper market forces and agree social goals with the trade unions, in the realisation that the pure free market alternative was likely to protect against both inflation and unemployment. A Conservative government would tend to place a greater faith in the working of market forces and give less weight to the trade unions, hoping that market disciplines would prevail and would tolerate higher levels of unemployment. Yet all governments would at least be rejecting the stop-go policies of the past and recognising that curing inflation by deflation has serious medium-term effects which in their turn have dangerous implications for our longer-term industrial strength.

Monetarist deflation has brought inflation down from its 1980 peak of nearly 22 per cent. Large firms that were semi-monopolists were able to pass on higher wage costs, whereas small firms who could not were then pressed by large firms for payment, with the alternative of bankruptcy. Large firms also secured loans at more favourable rates than small firms, so that the credit squeeze was not impartial in its effects. Most companies reduced investment before they laid off workers or refused to pay wage claims, since they were generally reluctant to interrupt production as a result of a strike, knowing that they could lose markets and that their extra capacity would no longer be needed. Making workers unemployed hitherto has been an option that tended to be considered only as a last resort: most firms conceded wage demands before laying off skilled workers since they knew that there would be difficulties in recruiting those workers back once the economy picked up. But as the economic prospects in the 1980s worsen more firms will be ready to shed labour.

The economy is dominated by large firms able to secure finance from banks, to finance claims themselves, or to pass on cost increases. It is likely that the 1980s free-market squeeze will take a long time to bring inflation down below that of our major industrial competitors; and the medium-term effects on industry are likely to be drastic. The challenge for politicians of all parties is not to ignore in opposition the lessons of government and not to reject the need for an incomes policy. What must be developed is a policy for incomes, investment, prices, profit and productivity which is geared to the actual working of a mixed economy and realistic enough to be sustainable over a number of years.

PART THREE

The Mixed Economy

8

Industrial Policy

Britain's industrial decline will be a dominant issue throughout the 1980s. Designing an industrial strategy which will arrest the decline and provide a base for future expansion will require flair, imagination and a major shift in attitudes towards co-operation in industry. One thing is certain; co-operation will not be achieved on the basis of the simplistic polarised dogma of the Conservative government, with their animus against the public sector and their belief that there is no useful role for the state in stimulating industrial activity. But neither will it be achieved by replacing the present dogma by an equal, but opposite, animus against the private sector and a belief that only state intervention can stimulate industrial activity. Such a swing of political opinion and government decision-making in the 1980s would be an unmitigated disaster from which Britain's present industrial decline might never recover.

In 1968 the Washington-based Brookings Institution, in an analysis of the British economy, highlighted the slow rate of economic growth and poor productivity in comparison with other countries. If anything, the report was too sanguine; the decline continued over the next twelve years. In 1980 when they produced a new study, *Britain's Economic Performance*, the Institution's researchers concluded more strongly that the economic difficulties derived from poor productivity, the origins of which lay deep in the country's social system. The authors believe that our productivity problem needs to be tackled by improving industrial relations and increasing industrial incentives. It is difficult, but essential, for politicians to absorb the research findings of such studies and start to make policy on the basis of similar research and facts. The central focus must be the failure of managers and workers to trust each other and to co-operate effectively, together with the apparent inability in Britain to develop a commercially-orientated social climate within industry.

In the post-war development of an industrial strategy for Britain the obsessive debate about the role of the state – privatisation versus state nationalisation – has been destructive and damaging. The debate cannot, however, be ignored, and therefore the role of state intervention in the 1980s is discussed in these chapters at some length, with examples of the newer forms of intervention in BNOC, ICL and pharmaceuticals. But it is fundamental that interventionism is not allowed to become the dominant thrust of an industrial strategy or its marginal benefits exaggerated. Far greater importance must be given to creating changes in attitude in industry rather than embarking again on a state nationalisation programme on the scale of 1945-51. The centralised-corporatist incomes policies of the past must now be rejected in favour of a more modest, and, one hopes, more sustainable decentralised approach, where commercial realities in the market sector of industry are not obscured by overall national norms and centrally imposed pay rigidities.

It may be too harsh a criticism, but one of the country's foremost scientists, Sir Alan Cottrell, in the 25th Fawley Foundation Lecture in November 1979, attacked successive governments for choosing to play God with industry: 'in the Conservative government, to take but one example, there were the crazy directives given to British Rail in 1972. The order in June was *economize*, by saving £15m a year. By July it had changed to to *keep fares steady*, even if this meant losing money! But September brought more golden fruit: a new policy, *spend* as much as possible! That is the policy, not of Marx, but of the Marx Brothers. The Labour government were not to be outdone in commercial ineptitude, however. Thus by the mid-1970s we had Mr Benn blithely bestowing taxpayers' money on commercially hopeless private firms, to convert them into commercially hopeless workers' co-operatives, on the curious principle that the way to mend a broken-down car is simply to change its owner.

'But these are minor examples. Much more serious was the overall effect of frenetic governmental actions on industry generally: of stifling success by various financial and other controls; and of propping up failure by handouts from the public purse. The industrial policies of the governments in the 1970s thus ended up as a "reverse-carrot-and-stick" policy. Stick for the winners and carrot for the losers. This was one of the ways in which the actions of government undermined British industry; by destroying incentive.'[1]

How important is incentive? There has been a strange reluctance to consider the disincentive effect of the 'poverty trap' where tax acts harshly on people who receive a low wage for a full week's work, and puts them only just above the level for claiming a variety of means-tested benefits. The debate has concentrated instead only on the disincentive effect of taxation on the middle to higher incomes. It is absurd to deny that incentive is a source of motivation; but it is not the only motivation, and not always even the most important motivation. There are real problems relating to our present tax structure, particularly for the low wage earner and at the level of middle management in motivating someone to move or undertake more responsibilities. There are problems, too, associated with low profitability and the general dampening down of the adventurous and innovative spirit which cannot be dismissed as of no consequence. The levels of tax have to be fixed to take account of how people behave as well as according to criteria of social justice. Politicians need to approach the subject with a greater readiness to initiate research, to take note of comparative evidence from other countries, and generally to act on evidence not prejudice.

In developing a distinctive approach to British industry best suited to the British political and cultural tradition, we cannot expect to mirror exactly either Japanese-French commercial *dirigisme* or German-American benign *laissez-faire*, for the UK industrial base is different from either that of Japan, France, West Germany or the USA. We do not necessarily need the

171

same tax system in terms of rates or allowances, though the extent to which British management at quite low levels is able to claim fringe benefits, with company cars and special allowances, is unique. Nor do we need the same profit ratios, but if profitability is to be restored to increase investment, it must be accompanied by a review of corporation tax, which has virtually ceased to exist as a revenue-raising tax, and a review of corporate tax. What Britain cannot ignore is that our industrial strength depends on our ability to compete and sell our goods in world markets. We must learn from the experience of France and Germany and start to put a far greater emphasis on winning markets than hitherto and on recognising throughout British society the commercial and competitive imperatives on which our prosperity depends. This does not mean an emphasis on unrestrained market forces. The two decades of low economic growth before 1973 were wasted years; and even then our growth rates were sluggish by comparison with those of other countries. Intervention by governments is taking place in the wake of a world recession in most countries, and is increasing in all countries in the European Community, even in West Germany, and in the USA the government intervenes to help Chrysler and Lockheed.

What government must learn, however, is to judge when to intervene and when not to intervene, on the basis of a disciplined, scientific and thoughtful approach, not on the basis of dogma, doctrine or prejudice. Improving our commercial orientation must come from a change in attitude and this can in part come from an extension of industrial democracy, and where possible from industrial co-operatives. It will not be enough to improve industrial relations in the conventional sense, for this will not of itself achieve the orientation of the whole workforce towards the market place or a basic understanding of the need to compete commercially. Britain also requires a greater emphasis on the application of science and technology, on good management, the encouragement of small business with the recognition of its importance to the economy and a readiness to respond more rapidly to changing technologies. It means economic policies aimed at steady even if modest economic growth and increasing the demand for industrial goods supported by increased industrial investment. Above all, what is required is the development of an industrial policy which can be operated over a sustained period with the reasonable hope that it will not be chopped and changed about. Within a stable but market-orientated climate there is undoubted scope for more government intervention: for a new state-funded investment facility, for the National Enterprise Board to diversify and put in risk capital in support of high technology, and support regional policy in association with Regional Development Agencies. There is also a case for much tougher monopoly legislation. One of the effects of the corporatist trend has been to allow a steady increase in monopoly provisions and to pay too little attention to trust busting, and generally to accommodate too easily to the monopolies within the mixed economy.

The problem facing those who merely advocate a further extension of state monopoly nationalisation is that it is widely realised that past experience of most nationalised concerns has been that it no longer commands immediate uncritical support, even among Labour activists, let alone among Labour voters. Some nationalised industries have done well, particularly those which provide predominantly a service to the public. British Gas has a good record, and so now, after five years of much needed sustained investment, has the National Coal Board. Germany, Belgium and France all subsidise their coal industry far more than British governments do and we are still doctrinally hesitant to do the same. British Railways have struggled against inadequate investment and the failure to produce an integrated transport policy. It is inescapable that any rail network will need a public subsidy; such a subsidy can be justified on energy, environmental and social grounds and we should stop being so defensive about the need for and the desirability of a rail subsidy where again other member states in the European Community see it as inevitable and right to provide large subsidies.

It is in the commercial sector that nationalisation has a much poorer record. Essentially it has suffered from ill-considered governmental intervention in support of regional industrial policies, as well as a poor commercial orientation and a political reluctance to face up to the need for faster adjustment in the face of very stiff international competition. The record of British Steel is depressing, despite every allowance for the distortion of its performance by its critics. British Shipbuilders faced a dramatic decline in the world market for ships on being nationalised but have made a reasonably good start in rationalising wage rates and in improving productivity. With Defence contracts playing such an important role the shipbuilding industry is bound, whether in private or public ownership, to have an interlocking relationship with government, and denationalising the profitable warship-building yards is no answer to the industry's difficulties. The case for state involvement in the ship repair yards was always dubious; they are probably best left to operate within the private sector, particularly since the government already has the four large naval dockyards. The argument for the nationalisation of British Aerospace was that the state was a major purchaser, it had a continuing close interest because of Defence, and on projects like the European Airbus other governments were playing a leading role in their national industries. In this industry the introduction of mixed finance between public and private investment need not necessarily be a bad policy and there is little justification for the automatic assumption that it must be wholly government financed and owned. The same argument may apply to British Airways – although their financial difficulties are such that few would wish to purchase private equity at a time when airlines all over the world are facing economic difficulties.

Two central themes of an interventionist industrial strategy for the 1980s must be to revive the historic commitment to developing an integrated transport policy and an overall energy policy. The absence of such policies is a major omission in pursuing a coherent industrial strategy and there is no evidence that putting the major emphasis on state ownership has contributed to the development of integration; some would argue that it has actively impeded progress by constructing powerful obstructive monopolies. In an attempt to remedy the criticisms of nationalised industries which are widespread, and to try and produce a single dramatic solution,

174

Tony Benn, sensing the need to produce new ideas, advocated that junior Ministers should become the chairmen of national-ised boards. As so often with this sort of idea, it has some superficial attractions; it appears more democratic, more likely to ensure that a government's policies are carried out. Yet apart from being a further move towards greater central-isation of power within the Whitehall bureaucracy it carries with it a mass of problems and inconsistencies. The effect would be that the board of a nationalised industry, instead of managing its own industry, being answerable only for major policy decisions to its Secretary of State and through him or her to parliament, would find itself merged with the Executive. A junior Minister, since the Secretary of State would not have the time to be so closely involved, would by the very act of accepting the Chairman's role, be accepting responsibility for all board decisions, and could not avoid taking that responsi-bility on to the floor of the House of Commons and into the Committee rooms of the House of Commons to answer questions on the most detailed issues affecting the industry. Since a Minister only exercises responsibility as part of a system of collective Cabinet responsibility, even more detailed board decision-making than at present would be dragged not only into Whitehall, but into the collective ministerial decision-making process, resulting in considerable delay. It also runs against the trend of much criticism from politicians of the quality and professionalism of the top management of British industry and the considerable scepticism about the role of part-time Chairmen or non-executive directors and the wish instead to promote higher standards of full-time professional management. Many of the nationalised industries are among the largest industrial organisations in the country. It is hard to see the wisdom of their day to day management becoming the direct responsibility of a Minister.

There is considerable disillusionment about the practical working of the nationalised industries under the model arrangements conceived by Herbert Morrison, but the disad-vantages which he foresaw of their day-to-day management being subject to detailed ministerial and parliamentary scrutiny are even more real today, as their complexity has increased.

There are two possible evolutions of the Morrison model. Firstly, to try to split the nationalised industries such as railways, coal, gas and electricity into smaller management units. The other is to bring in alternative sources of finance, not through equity shares but through public bonds. Ending the dogmatic polarity between privatisation and nationalisation is an essential national interest and an acceptance of some degree of mixed financing might help. It would also help to make a clearer distinction between the public sector which operates commercially – British Aerospace, British Airways, British Steel and British Shipbuilders – and those which provide a service – British Rail, British Gas, the Electricity Boards and the National Coal Board.

The Labour Party is already pledged to repeal all the legislation introduced by the Conservatives to bring private equity capital into the public sector, whereas adaptation of this legislation could be a more sensible course. If state industries have a mixed source of finance they may become accepted as politically neutral and be given the necessary stability by all governments to concentrate on producing higher standards of service and becoming more efficient.

The main concentration of the minds of Ministers and parliament should be on the techniques for developing an integrated policy in the two areas of major public service covered by nationalised industries: transport and energy. A more effective role for Ministers is essential in all the areas of transport and energy but it is unrealistic to believe that the mere act of legislating for the nationalisation of the ports, road haulage or buses, of the nuclear power industry or North Sea Oil will integrate policy in these areas.

Pricing is the key to an effective integration of policy in relation to rail and road transport for industry, or to car, rail and bus for passengers. In transport the need is for an investment strategy, and a tax and pricing structure which balances the economic, social and environmental costs, and the advantages and disadvantages of an integrated transport system. There is a need for rationalisation between rail, air, ship and road transport and for a socially sensitive policy for rural and urban transportation.

The issues are extremely complex and cannot be resolved by concentrating on ownership. In transport central government is not always the dominating presence. The role of local government, particularly in the major cities, is in many respects more influential than that of central government. Private decision in terms of the motor car ensures that no policy wholly based on state intervention can carry conviction. The more policy is developed within the context of the regions rather than centrally the more likely it is to serve local needs and adapt to local circumstances. This is a task which could be overseen by the regional assemblies advocated in Chapter 17 as part of the reform of the constitution.

The pseudo competition between gas and electricity with different showrooms, different policies and incoherent pricing policy militates against any integrated energy policy. Energy policy is influenced substantially by the OPEC cartel fixing oil prices, so to talk about about market forces and market prices in the energy field is grossly misleading, and has worked against the rational wish for consumer choice.

A further problem is the organisation of the electricity supply industry. The case for regional all-purpose electricity boards along the lines of the proven and efficiently run Board in Scotland, would be worth a fresh appraisal for England and Wales, now that the government in 1980 has rejected the Plowden Report's recommendation for reorganising the electricity supply industry on a more centralised pattern.

The development of natural gas, the home conversion programme, and the transition from town gas was helped by a centralised British Gas organisation. But there is a case for examining the establishment of autonomous Regional Gas Boards for the future, when the gas industry starts adapting to the situation which will exist in the early part of the next century. Then, as North Sea Gas declines, while we will not return to the old pattern of small town gas plants, area synthetic gas plants will have to be developed, initially making up for, and eventually replacing, natural gas. There is at least a strong argument for considering afresh greater regional autonomy in the future.

Slowly over the next few decades, driven by cost and anxiety about availability, a much more diverse energy supply situation will be developing, with householders investing in solar power, wind power and even, where available, water power as additional energy sources for the future. Rationalising energy prices against these trends with the need for a far more active conservation strategy and the need to encourage the use of the most efficient energy source will present major conceptual as well as practical difficulties for central, regional and local government.

Conservation is still not seen within central government as a source of energy. Government has a decision-making structure which absorbs easily a multi-million pound decision to build an individual power station, but has as yet no mechanism to offset the value of such an investment to increase electricity supply with a range of smaller investment decisions in conservation – which cumulatively should add up to a multi-million pound programme to reduce the demand for electricity. Investing in conservation would also provide a major source of employment in the 1980s when unemployment is certain to be distressingly high. Yet also there is a necessity for a steady ordering programme for new power stations in order to maintain a viable industry for the future. A pricing structure which discourages the use, particularly in daytime, of electricity as a source of heating would, for example, have to be sensitive enough to allow for the situation where the householder or industry has no access to the preferred alternative of gas or coal. A pricing structure for industry is also needed which encourages the use of coal but which discourages the use of gas except for those industries where gas is essential. It is also important that a pricing structure ensures that Britain's industries' energy costs are certainly no higher and preferably lower than the international average, so as to help reduce manufacturing unit costs in comparison with those of our main industrial competitors. This is an area where industry can be helped without breaching international trading agreements and where other countries are already doing far more than Britain.

The amazing complexity of developing an integrated transport and energy policy, is one which has as yet been barely touched on by successive governments, bogged down by detail and dogma. Indecisive and incoherent, this lack of integration represents government at its worst. In both energy and transport, the believers in market forces, if they are honest, soon discover that there is not a true market, and that playing around with privatisation and talking about beating monopoly power are irrelevant. The task of national government, and in some of these areas also the European Community, is to try to bring different strands of policy together into an integrated whole. In some senses the continuing debate in the last few decades over nationalisation has been an excuse to avoid grappling, in energy and transport, with the much harder task of developing an integrated policy. Clarifying the different roles and the different techniques of managing and controlling the private market-dominated industrial sector and the public service-dominated industrial sector is the essential prelude to achieving greater coherence.

Coherence also demands that politicians accept an even more formidable discipline: they should be very reluctant to implement structural industrial changes which appear to have no long-term hope of being accepted, and will only be reversed. That is not to exclude imposing structural changes against the view of an official opposition party, or of vested interests, but to shift the onus of proof for making such a change in a way that gives a far higher priority to ensuring continuity than has been done hitherto.

For some, on both the Right and the Left, this will be the hardest discipline of all to accept. It will be argued that this is a prescription for 'middle-of-the-road', consensus politics and that the same arguments could thus be applied in education, health and social policy. To some extent this objection is valid, but it is also true that in the areas of social policy in post-war Britain there has been a greater degree of continuity across governments, particularly over the last decade, than there has been over industrial policy. Yet it is our industrial success which determines the national wealth which alone can support, extend and improve our education, health and social services. We cannot continue to conduct ill-judged political experiments with our industrial strategy, whether by taking non-intervention by the state to an extreme or state interventionist policies to an extreme. Our industrial base is crumbling, and far faster than in other comparable countries. We can best alleviate this, not by violent shifts of policy, but by the steady, firm and resolute application of a variety of policies directed towards modernisation and greater efficiency. We cannot afford to spend the 1980s with major industries like ship-building, aerospace, aero engines, air, road and sea transport, gas and oil, oscillating between private and public ownership.

The trend towards industrial discontinuity as an article of political faith was started by the Conservative government of 1970, the yo-yo effect has continued ever since and the 1980s promise to be worse. Automatic repeal of the legislation of previous governments besides being very disruptive and negative when it is accompanied by threats to renationalise without compensation, is also wrong. Politicians out of government would be wise to pause, consider carefully all aspects of industry, and nearer the election decide what should be the overall strategy. Politicians should also consider whether attitudinal change is more important than structural change. A measured response over reversing privatisation and extending state ownership if combined with a radical commitment to introduce industrial democracy is a more credible programme, also with a better chance of acceptance. There are strong grounds for believing, as is argued in the chapters on industrial democracy and co-operation, that emphasising a change of attitudes would bring a far better return in terms of socialist objectives than emphasising structural changes. It would help to increase awareness of the need for increased productivity, improved industrial relations, and add to the commercial orientation of industry, which is so essential to increase national wealth.

Planning is another aspect of an industrial strategy which can contribute to attitudinal changes. The saddest aspect of policy development in Britain has been the decline over the last fifteen years in the politicians' confidence and belief in the potential contribution that planning can make to the development of an industrial strategy. Planning is not just concerned with obtaining an information base, though this is an essential prerequisite. It is also concerned with anticipating trends and taking action to prevent or mitigate situations which may be foreseeable, and then trying to develop policy which is not just reactive but ahead of its time. If new products are developed at the start of the world recession they can alleviate some of the worst consequences in terms of unemployment and industrial decline.

The arguments for Ministers having a personal policy advisory team as well as a political advisory team are developed in Chapter 13 on Parliamentary Government. Such a team will have little effect, however, unless politicians can also be convinced of the need to restore planning to an important position at both political and bureaucratic level, in the European Community, Whitehall and local government. There is no contradiction in deploying the case for greater decentralisation and at the same time arguing for more highly developed centralised planning; the two run logically in harness. Sensible decision-making necessitates a careful assessment of the right level at which decisions should be made, and in a decentralised system it is even more necessary to establish links so that information and experience are carried back from a wide spread of decision points.

The European Community, and in particular the Commission, has a modest planning role on broad international strategic issues covering monetary policy, forward trading patterns, industrial adjustment, agricultural balance and energy self-sufficiency. The Commission often fails to cover these areas adequately because the European Community has allowed itself to become deluged in the detail of harmonisation and of policy implementation. The Community has commissioned over the years many valuable medium- to longer-term reports which contain interesting ideas and projections, but the systematic monitoring of national states performance towards agreed goals is still in its early stages. What is needed is not one-off reports or a collection of remote academic statistics, but information related to the decision-makers' needs. This should be put together in a tougher, simpler and more political planning system which works for the President of the Commission and reports direct to the Committee of

Permanent Representatives, and through them to the various Councils of Ministers. This does not necessitate the acquisition of any new powers by the Commission; what it requires is a greater readiness of member states to submit to Commission scrutiny. For example, West Germany should accept retrospective analysis conducted for the Council of Ministers as to why in 1979-80 that country failed to keep within the oil consumption figures previously agreed at European Council meetings; the extent to which the overshoot was preventable by government action in Germany or Commission action in Brussels; and the extent to which the excess consumption was actually the result of greater economic activity than had been predicted and whether such economic growth had been of overall benefit to the Community.

A powerful rationalising factor internationally is the exposure of an argument, with all the facts, to public scrutiny; and an important aspect of planning is its readiness to analyse past mistakes in order to learn for the future. In most respects the European Commission is much more open with information than Whitehall, and a well-informed press has so far done a better job of scrutinising the Commission than has the European Assembly. The fear now, with the directly elected Assembly, is that under democratic pressure the Community and the Commission will become weighed down by detail which would be best left to national governments, and that, as with the Westminster parliament, the civil service mentality within the Commission will suck in information and decision-making in order to cope with day-to-day political pressures, questions and debates and, once sucked in, there it will stay, never to be returned. The Assembly is in danger of being the stimulus for a growth in the Commission.

The centrifugal forces of a bureaucracy are given greater strength when they are linked to democratic answerability. It will require a sustained effort to avoid this happening to the European Community. The climate of opinion in most other European Community countries is more receptive than it is in Britain to the concept of planning and even to interventionism by government. In the European Community at present the use of subsidies in Germany, France, Italy and Belgium is quite widespread, with increasing reliance on state aid in many areas of the new technologies of telecommunications, microchips and robots. In France the National Plan has been given perhaps too much of the credit for their industrial revival, but it has been of some value, and planning has helped to maintain continuity in Italy despite its uncertain political history; even West Germany, hitherto hostile to planning because of its identification with state control in East Germany, has changed its position over the last few years, and the case for planning is put now much more strongly within the SPD.

In Britain, the ghosts of past failure are still strong; the collapse of the National Plan, the slow dismembering of the Department of Economic Affairs, still arouse painful memories. But if the Labour government in 1964 had devalued and put growth as its priority policy, its whole planning initiative might have been a success. The 1974-9 Labour government tried to develop planning through the sector working parties as part of a less ambitious overall industrial strategy developed within the framework of the National Economic Development Organisation. Some valuable work was done but the structure, by concentrating on ensuring sectoral representation, tended to encourage a fragmented approach to planning, with a high degree of special pleading.

Another aspect of industrial planning is retraining and the upgrading and updating of skills. In many European countries this has been given a far higher priority than in Britain. In Sweden 2 per cent of the workforce is being retrained at any one time; in Britain the same proportion would mean retraining 400,000 people. In West Germany nine out of ten school leavers are trained for two years or more in a professional skill of their choice, whereas in Britain nearly half our school leavers get no further training or education at all. We have an appalling record, and our reluctance to introduce educational maintenance allowances to encourage children to continue with educational training beyond the age of sixteen simply demonstrates our lack of commitment. Imaginative policies towards employment planning are more important in the long term than many of the changes relating to structure, for without skilled employees no company, private or public, can compete.

The British record in this sphere is lamentable, falling far below that achieved elsewhere in Europe, and it is symptomatic of our preoccupation with much less crucial factors that this failing has rarely been discussed by civil servants or by politicians. Britain has not attempted wide-ranging employment planning since the National Plan and more recently under the last Labour government when policies were adopted more as a reaction to rising unemployment than as a conscious attempt to plan and to make the best use of the workforce. Industrial decline in Britain is related to our inadequate and outmoded educational and training systems, which have failed to produce skilled workers in sufficient numbers and with the right kind of skills. Education and training are also important, in a wider political perspective, in helping to break down class barriers, to create a more socially mobile population and in educating workers for a wider democracy in which they will be better equipped to participate more fully in decisions which affect them most directly. The acquisition of skills, especially by those from poor backgrounds who are at present badly served by the education system, can help in reducing social tensions arising from unemployment among ethnic minorities, inner-city youth and in easing the transition to new technology.

Training and retraining will need heavy investment by future governments in order not only to contribute to economic growth but as a socially just measure to allow manual workers to share in the benefits of new technology. The immediate, short-term challenge can be judged by the fact that the proportion of manual jobs is projected to decline below 50 per cent by 1985 from the 1978 level of 56 per cent. A recent report, *Education, Training and Industrial Performance*, came to the alarming conclusion that: 'the delivery of training in the UK has two major weaknesses. The first is the concentration on initial training at the expense of upgrading and retraining later in life. Secondly, training is concentrated on a relatively narrow range of jobs, for reasons which are as much to do with tradition and collective bargaining as with the intrinsic needs of the occupation. Women and unskilled workers suffer particularly. As a result of these two factors, the system of training is rigid, conservative and slow to respond to new industrial requirements.'[2]

The report went on to note that as many as 15 per cent of young people leave school with no formal qualifications and that nearly two-thirds of young people leave school at the age of sixteen and do not go into full-time further education. A Manpower Services Commission study found that Britain's performance contrasted badly with that of other members of the EEC and that Britain has the lowest proportion of young people in industrial training or full-time vocational training within the EEC, with the deficiency being marked between Britain and our major industrial competitors in Europe.[3] The Finniston Report made suggestions for policy changes and noted 'that by the late 1980s a serious shortfall is likely in the supply of new engineers relative to the continuing high demands from employers.'[4] A significant fall in the numbers taking apprenticeships and other kinds of formal training within industry has also taken place in recent years, with a decline from 450,000 (or 5·6 per cent of the industrial workforce) in 1968 to 240,000 (3·6 per cent) in 1980.

It is to the credit of the last Labour government that employment and training schemes were given an enhanced role during a period of severe financial restraints. A wide series of measures sought to protect jobs and to retrain workers, with the emphasis being on job preservation rather than on training and job creation. The Temporary Employment Subsidy saved over 400,000 jobs between 1975 and 1978 and the Young Employment Subsidy and the Small Firms Employment Subsidy saved several thousand more jobs from 1977 to 1979. The government increased training opportunities for adults sixfold from 1971 to 1977 and the most important of these schemes, the Youth Opportunities Programme, had catered for 203,000 young people by July 1980.[5]

The employment subsidies had a very direct social benefit and they have been found to be a cost-effective solution to rising unemployment. It has been found that the amount of revenue lost through lower tax collection and the increase in social security payments by the government when a worker becomes unemployed, is equal to 89-105 per cent of average male earnings in manufacturing industry for a single man and 89-96 per cent for a married man with two children. Therefore subsidies of up to 90 per cent of the average industrial wage are likely to reduce the budget deficit.[6]

It is a task of central government to develop a comprehensive programme of retraining and job protection, integrating these two aspects to avoid the indefinite protection of jobs which are in uncompetitive industries. Retraining should be encouraged by the adoption of training boards which will estimate future labour needs in the expanding industries and which will be allowed attractive rates of pay to workers undergoing re-training. We should aim to provide training for those young people – a majority of young people – who at present leave school with meagre qualifications.

The 1974 Labour Party Manifesto gave prominence to formal planning agreements between unions, management and government, but what was underestimated was that without agreement they would never have much chance to take root. Initially planning agreements were advocated as part of a serious attempt to plan an industrial strategy on the lines of experience in France and Italy, but they became identified as another way of achieving state ownership, and were presented as such by some politicians. Rather than being seen as planning aids they became politically highly contro-versial and were in consequence virtually boycotted by private industry. Chrysler was the only private firm to agree to introduce one, and that was as part of a deal to win state financial support. For five years the Labour government achieved virtually nothing over the implementation of planning agreements, and then it accepted a commitment to introduce them in statutory form, though what was envisaged was not explained in the 1979 Election Manifesto.

The French in their planning machinery have relied on persuasion and have not compelled even the very few recalci-trant private firms. A credible approach would be to build on the statutory disclosure of information for companies employing 100 or more workers which is suggested as part of the proposed industrial democracy legislation. There would be a code of conduct and that could specify the details of the simple information required and the way in which it should be provided for computer tabulation by government, as well as the type of information needed for the workforce. Companies who employed 2,000 or more could quite reasonably be asked to provide more detail for government since they are already judged to be in a different category of importance and would be covered by the suggested statutory obligation over employee board representation.

A further category of companies required to give more detailed planning information would be any accepting government financial support. It is reasonable for these companies to accept a more formal agreement with the government, to give full recognition to trade unions and to participate fully in patterns of industrial democracy.

National planning can also benefit from using the information available through public ownership or by virtue of a government shareholding. The state is able thereby to secure access to sensitive information which in other companies would be held back as commercially secret. This particularly applies to identifying the scope and extent of transfer pricing and the way some multinationals avoid paying their proper amounts of UK tax. There undoubtedly is a specific multinational problem over transfer pricing as there is in the resistance of multinationals to complying with regional planning by threatening to invest in another country. Trying to limit the power of manipulation of the multinational company is very hard; it certainly cannot be constrained by national legislation. With common EEC company laws and tougher Community legislation it should be possible to insulate the Community from some of the abuses of multinational power, but it will require a stronger push from national governments than it has received hitherto, and in Britain, because of ambivalence over the EEC and any extension of the Commission's powers Labour governments have never taken a particularly strong line. There is immense scope for a well thought-out socialist initiative in this area: the Socialist Group within the European Assembly could use the Assembly's investigative powers to question companies operating in member states and then, in close co-operation with the European trade union movement,

187

question companies operating in member states and then, in close co-operation with the European trade union movement, could put pressure on the governments of member states. A Commissioner could be given multinational companies as a prime area of responsibility, and work across all the conventional Commissioner portfolios. There would then be a possibility of developing a Community policy with the backing of the Council of Ministers and full Commission authority. The crucial area for government is in setting the most beneficial economic climate for industry. A major truism over any industrial policy is how marginal is the beneficial effect of government action. Yet even if government can exert only a minor influence it should not be disparaged merely because it is minor, for cumulatively every positive development adds up. The danger comes from pretending that government action can have a major impact and from the disproportionate effect of ill-judged and damaging action.

9

Energy Policy

Over the last fifty years, oil supply in the world in general has increased fairly steadily at the rate of about 5½ per cent per year, and the price of oil – until 1973 – remained stable and well below the cost of most other sources of energy. As a consequence the economies of both the industrial and the developing countries came to depend heavily on oil. At a time of recession and unemployment in the West it is easy to forget the impact of oil price rises on the economies of poorer countries: to give one example, in 1973 Costa Rica had to sell 24 kilograms of bananas to buy a barrel of oil, yet by 1980 the Costa Ricans had to sell 260 kilos of bananas to buy the same barrel of oil.

The pre-1973 price stability relied heavily not only on a readiness to invest in exploration and development but also on an assumption that very large oil fields with recoverable reserves greater than 5,000 million barrels would continue to be discovered. Yet – and it is a sobering thought – no field of this size has been discovered in the last ten years. It is no longer possible to rely on a rapid increase in the rate of discovery of smaller fields to meet growth in production. Furthermore, the amount of oil capable of being extracted from known fields is also not as much as was at one stage hoped; the main Ghawar field in Saudi Arabia is the most obvious example; previously it had been hoped to recover 47 per cent of the reserves, but this estimate has now been revised down to 33 per cent. Since it is one of the world's largest oil fields, the impact on world supplies is considerable, reducing known reserves by 70,000 million barrels: an amount more than the total of Iran's proven reserves. If the Saudi Arabians invested more it would be technically feasible for them to produce 16 million barrels a day, as opposed to their 1980 rates of production of around 9 million barrels a day, but they know and fear that heavy investment would bring inflationary pressures working through and affecting the social and political stability of the country. Throughout the 1980s Saudi Arabia will be the crucial oil producing country; the fact that the Saudis show no interest in developing their full oil production potential has the most serious consequences for world energy supply.

The Iranian revolution of 1979 brought forward policy changes of even more fundamental long term importance than the four-fold price increase of 1973. The Organisation of Petroleum Exporting Countries (OPEC) discovered that falls in production could be so managed that price increases could cover the lost production without any fall in revenues. In addition, the revolution in Iran set in motion a series of processes which are changing the depletion policies of Saudi Arabia and Kuwait, and probably mark the end of the era of ever-increasing oil production. Governments and oil companies now work on the assumption that the amount of oil produced each year through the 1980s is unlikely to rise above the peak level of 1978, and could well be less. There is a haunting fear in the West – dramatically highlighted in late 1980 by the Gulf War between Iraq and Iran – that at any time in the 1980s there could be a precipitous fall in world oil output. But it is not just the West who have fears, for the US action to freeze all Iranian assets in 1979 only confirmed the fears of the surplus oil producers that their investment overseas was not as safe as they had always been assured.

The year 1980 marked a major stage in the maturity of OPEC, following a decade in which its members steadily established their independence. The threshold of independence for price fixing came in 1973-4, while the threshold for production independence was 1979. The threshold for market independence has not yet come, but an interesting pointer was the decision of Venezuela and Mexico in 1980 to make preferential marketing and price arrangements with poorer countries in their region. The need is for negotiations between OECD, OPEC and the Third World, relating energy policies to the world economy. A critical passage in the Brandt Report says that: 'The result of increasing borrowing in the 1970s has been a rapid growth of the indebtedness of developing countries. Their combined debts rose from $70 billion at the end of 1970 to an estimated $300 billion at the end of 1979. Much of it was concentrated in a relatively small number of middle-income countries. The greater role of private commercial lending was reflected in an increasing share of short-term debt at interest rates which have recently risen steeply. Unless oil-importing countries are to check their imports and growth in the 1980s it is clear that their debts will have to increase further. Between 1980 and 1985 as much as $300-500 billion may have to be added to developing countries' debts if their financial needs are to be met – provided the funds can be found.

'We face, therefore, not merely one, but several crises: the crisis of relentless inflation and increasing energy costs, the crisis of dwindling energy availability, the crisis resulting from mounting financial requirements, and the crisis posed by constraints on world trade and on the growth of export earnings to meet increased debt service commitments. Taken together, they threaten the whole structure of our political, industrial and financial institutions, unless we move urgently and adequately to deal with the basic causes.

'As an immediate step, we recommend that the various international institutions begin immediately to study and articulate the range of likely debts and debt servicing problems as they emerge, particularly in the various categories of developing countries, and the likelihood of existing private and public institutions being able to meet these needs. In this connection it is important to consider the relative roles in the recycling process of the private banking system of the developed countries, multilateral financial institutions, jointly shared guarantees by developed countries and capital surplus oil exporters, and direct lending by the oil-producing countries themselves.'[1]

The world must adapt itself now to living with less oil. Such an adaptation will have profound implications for the automatic expectation in the Western industrialised countries of continuous economic growth. OPEC countries will ensure that their oil revenues are not undercut by a fall in the value of the dollar and will set their price against the average movement in value of a sample of currencies. The growing sensitivity of OPEC to the fears of Third World countries that they will be priced out of the international oil market will, in the 1980s, mean that many more individual OPEC countries will follow Venezuela and Mexico and develop a supply strategy for protecting the oil demands of the Third World. As they do this the pool available for the Western industrialised countries will almost certainly contract. With governments of the consuming nations negotiating more and more supply contracts and barter arrangements direct with OPEC governments we could see a ruthless price competition between Western oil companies for a preferential share of a smaller pool of market priced oil. An inadequate response has emerged from successive economic summit meetings of the United States, France, Germany, Britain, Japan, Italy and Canada, in OECD and the EEC. National targets for reducing demand have been adopted and the case at least in theory for government interventionism has been accepted. Yet government involvement in the struggle to restrain the demand for oil in particular and energy in general is, as yet, in its infancy.

Britain is among the countries which have subscribed to national target figures which have in fact been fulfilled without difficulty by switching oil-fired power stations to coal. Others, such as the Federal Republic of Germany, have accepted higher target figures, but particularly given their higher economic growth, have then not reached the targets, so that the whole exercise is in grave danger of being devalued. The fact is that the West has continued to turn a deaf ear to the Saudi warnings and has not taken even remotely strong enough action to reduce internal energy demand. The United States is by far the worst offender in terms of excessive energy demand. The Americans' heavy reliance on imported oil will make them worryingly vulnerable throughout the 1980s, despite the fact that they are now deploying technological capacity and shifting resources into coal and alternative energy sources in such a way as to make very substantial reductions in oil demand by the 1990s.

The likeliest outcome in the early 1980s is that world oil demand will be restrained by economic recession in the West. It may be that we will achieve through recession a sufficient fall in demand to avoid major shortages of supply. The danger on the supply side will come when and if there is a world economic upturn. The critical period is likely to come in the middle-to-late 1980s rather than in the middle 1990s, in other words before the Americans have had time to harness their immense coal reserves and nuclear potential to reduce their dependence on oil. In the United States around 40-45 per cent of oil is consumed as petrol, as against 20-25 per cent in Europe, so the scope for dramatic reductions is immense. The scope in Europe is less dramatic but much more can be done.

It is impossible to be certain of any prediction in the energy field. Future demand in any country is very difficult to forecast correctly, and supply is subject to almost as many varying factors. All one can do is to apply commonsense in evaluating different forecasts. A justified criticism of worldwide energy decisions is that investment has hitherto gone into increasing supply while investment to curb demand has been a minor consideration. All forecasts for future energy demand depend critically on projected economic growth. At present at least, no country has developed policies which allow for economic growth without consuming more energy, though fortunately there are signs of the development of an economic growth profile which is not so energy-demanding as in the past. All governments have to work on existing assumptions about the present relationship between growth and energy demand. A comparison of energy projections to 1985[2] analysed 78 energy studies published since 1973. It revealed huge discrepancies, with vastly different estimates, for example, of indigenous oil supply in Canada, estimates for nuclear power, indigenous gas supply in Europe and net OECD gas imports. At least this comparison of past estimates gives a basis for evaluating the future, but even with profound scepticism about the validity of the forward projections the facts force the conclusion that price increases and other measures have not yet produced extra indigenous energy production or the conservation some expected in different OECD countries. Yet economic growth has been well below forecast and because of this no major energy shortage has so far developed, though for a few months following the Iranian revolution the West felt there was an energy shortage because of some scaremongering and the US petrol rationing. There is little evidence that the economic growth forecasts have been depressed because of the failure of indigenous production and conservation of energy, or that this relationship is self regulating through market forces. All the evidence points to a failure of the industrialised West to act decisively enough in the early 1980s either substantially to increase indigenous energy production or to improve conservation.

In consequence if economic growth returns in the mid-1980s it is likely to provoke – in some countries at least – acute energy shortages. Against such a background there is no escape from the logic of needing to increase world coal production, develop nuclear power and take strongly interventionist action to promote conservation over the next decade if we are to be able to expand our economies and reverse the present recession. On the assumption that OPEC's depletion policy does not allow a precipitate fall and that there is no dramatic fall in production because of revolution or instability in the major oil producing countries, the world may stagger through the 1980s poised on a knife-edge of energy supply. All the major industrialised countries, both OECD and COMECON, have concluded that they must reduce energy demand, rapidly reduce their dependence on oil and increase energy supply from non-oil resources by extensive new programmes covering coal, gas, nuclear power, and conservation and the development of alternative sources of oil. There is likely to be an increased demand for OPEC oil from the COMECON countries, and the non oil producing, least developed countries will have to rely on increased oil supplies if they are to have any economic growth over the next two decades.

The argument for giving a higher priority to conservation

does not come only from the ecologists and environmentalists. It is also justified on grounds of cost effectiveness.
At the start of the 1980s the British government has the
distinction of having invested less in energy conservation than
any other government in the European Community. We have
over 6 million houses without insulated lofts, 7 million homes
with no cavity insulation. We are still not giving anywhere near
enough priority to home insulation itself, something which is
capable of creating more jobs, pound for pound of investment,
than almost any other job creation scheme – and yet has a
proven medium-term return on capital invested. We commit
thousands of millions of pounds to the building of nuclear
power generation stations but will not back combined heat-
and-power generation. We still vacillate over the capital
investment for building the Severn barrage. We are reluctant
to question the ever-increasing size of power stations and
economies claimed for them over a period of time. We fail to
grasp the potential for decentralising and diversifying our
energy supply pattern for the future. We tend still to be too
dismissive of the useful contribution to be made from
alternative sources of energy, particularly from wind and solar
power.

Britain is very rich in coal reserves. We should continue the
expanding investment programme, started in 1974, while
doing everything possible to increase production. The Conservative government in 1980 showed a dogmatic reluctance to
subsidise coking coal, a measure necessary to maintain
production from marginal coal fields in areas where the
National Coal Board's manpower planning needed the planned
rundown of pits based on agreement through the Tripartite
procedure established with the industry. West Germany,
Belgium and France give substantial subsidies to their coal
industry, yet the British government reiterates old-fashioned
doctrines of non-interference and the need to reflect market
forces, ignoring the extent to which energy is a managed
market. Britain's very large coal reserves should be exploited
to the full; but even if we meet the most optimistic forward coal
projection from our own indigenous production of 175-185
million tons by the year 2000, it will be impossible, given the

consumption of coal by the existing coal-fired power stations and the planned use of industrial coal, to produce enough coal to cover the nuclear power stations that will need to be replaced before the end of the century. We should continue with some of our smaller coal-fired stations in urban areas, introduce the new fluidised bed coal-burn technology, and link them to combined heat and power schemes. But there are limits to the pace at which this can be introduced. Any such schemes will encounter consumer resistance anywhere other than in new towns because of the amount of pavement work and disruption involved, and because householders will fear that hot water supplies will be outside their own control. The switch out of oil-fired power stations must continue; this too adds to the demand for coal.

Even with the most pessimistic forecast of economic growth to the end of the century, it is impossible to see how coal and conservation can meet all the likely needs for electricity power generation. A proportion of nuclear-generated electricity is necessary, objectively, under any criteria, even taking account of different forecasts about renewable energy and likely electricity generation demand figures for the future. Another factor is that as we cease to be self-sufficient in oil and gas we shall need to use our coal production to fill the energy gap that will follow their decline, something which is certain to come in the early part of the next century. It will be prudent, therefore, for us to cut our dependence on oil imports to the maximum possible extent and have a mix of energy supply sources, never being dependent on one source, either coal or nuclear.

It is therefore inevitable that, despite our relatively rich supplies of coal, gas and oil, Britain will have a continuing need for nuclear-power stations. It will be necessary over the next few years to maintain a minimum build rate despite falling energy demand, simply in order to allow the nuclear industry to survive, to develop its existing technology and to pioneer newer technologies such as the commercial prototype fast breeder reactor, possibly at Dounreay. Balanced argument about these difficult choices is not helped by false claims and by presenting the nuclear option as the sole determinant of our energy future. The public seems to view the prospect of a continued programme of coal and nuclear electricity generating stations with a fair degree of understanding and support. There is, however, considerable ambivalence in public opinion: a Gallup poll can show that 45 per cent believe that Britain should increase nuclear power generation and only 17 per cent believe Britain should stop generating nuclear power, yet 42 per cent would oppose a nuclear power station in their own area, with only 16 per cent supporting it, and 24 per cent, though not actually opposing it, feeling anxious at the prospect. Open public debate in Britain has helped to counter ill-informed criticism and public opinion in Britain, though concerned about nuclear issues, has not become as hostile or frustrated as the movement of opinion in other Western industrialised countries. Yet public opinion could easily switch and the anxiety generated by the prospect of building the American-designed Pressure Water Reactor (PWR) could provide the trigger. Britain started with a Magnox reactor in 1956, and was one of the world's leaders: the building of the stations was initially a source of national pride. The Atomic Energy Authority is a respected national body with a long record of enlightened public service which has attracted scientists of very high repute. Successive governments since 1974 have shown a greater degree of openness in publishing information and encouraging open debate in this area than in many other cases of government, and there is fairly good accountability to parliament on all matters relating to safety. The decision to hold a major enquiry into the reprocessing of nuclear waste at Windscale was a watershed in the acceptance by government of the public's right to deploy a case against a nuclear development in principle and for the arguments to be openly weighed. All these are praiseworthy factors, but genuine environmental and social concerns remain.

Anxiety about the safety of nuclear power is frequently raised by people buffeted by the arguments of the zealots on either side of the debate. The basic facts are that all material is composed of free elements; the basic unit of any element is the atom. The atoms of the heavy elements uranium and plutonium can, under certain conditions, break into two lighter atoms described as fission products, and in these circumstances, an emission of radiation and a release of energy is produced. This is the basic source of the energy released in nuclear power reactors and in nuclear weapons. Radiation, however, is a natural phenomenon. Many naturally-occurring substances produce background radiation and it is estimated that the man-made source of radiation – X-ray machines, radioactive isotopes in industry, hospitals and research establishments as well as nuclear power stations – contribute only about one-hundredth of the dose from natural background radiation. This helps to put the issue of radiation into perspective, but it does not answer those who ask what will happen if things go wrong.

The non-expert in the midst of a highly charged and partisan debate has to rely on the judgment of someone he or she respects. Lord Flowers, FRS, an objective scientist with a balanced concern for the environment, as the Chairman of the Standing Royal Commission on the Environment, is prepared both realistically to face our energy needs and to examine the safety factors. He says: 'it is fair to say of the commercial reactors at present operating that at worst, megawatt for megawatt, the nuclear industry is safer than the coal industry, and is probably much safer. It is true that there may exist the very improbable event in which a large fraction of the radioactive content is released, but even allowing for the worst interpretation that can be put upon the resulting chain of events the most likely outcome would be a few hundred deaths from various forms of cancer, and serious evacuation and clean-up problems for perhaps 30 miles downwind, with an outside chance that it might be ten times worse. Disastrous, certainly, but not out of all proportion to what an industrial nation has to face from many other of its activities or from natural causes; about as bad as a very severe earthquake or hurricane, but not so probable. Thus, a nuclear programme should not be regarded as unacceptable as far as the safety of its reactors is concerned, especially as safety in design is continually improving.'[3]

These comments cover only the safety of existing thermal reactors burning natural or lightly enriched uranium. Britain, a country which has no workable natural uranium deposits, has, not unreasonably, wished to reduce her dependence on other countries' uranium, and has therefore researched the fast breeder reactor in which plutonium is bred and burnt in a way which increases by a factor of about 50 the energy available from uranium. In reply to those who ask whether this can be done safely, Lord Flowers's view is that 'there are respects in which a fast reactor is safer than some kinds of thermal reactor'.[4] We know from experience of the Prototype Fast Reactor at Dounreay in Scotland that it is extremely stable in normal operation. The fast reactor is cooled by low pressure liquid sodium which can absorb large amounts of heat without boiling, in contrast, for example, to the high pressure water coolant of light water reactors.

The Windscale enquiry dealt with nuclear waste disposal, in many ways the area of controversy over nuclear power which gives rise to the most genuine concerns. Are we entitled to produce radioactive waste for future generations? Can it be made safe? At last, a method has been devised called vitrification, whereby the toxic radioactive material is bedded in glass blocks and then buried deep below the surface of the earth. But no one can doubt that this aspect of the nuclear power programme has been sadly neglected. Lord Flowers warns, 'one may feel optimistic, as I do, that a solution will eventually be found for the disposal of nuclear wastes, although expert opinion is that it will take many years of painstaking research before one can be sufficiently sure. The systematic methods of safety assessment as applied to reactors and other industrial plants have yet to be adapted to geological formations over immense periods of time. We seem to have our priorities wrong here. The same engineers who rightly insist that you cannot establish the safety of a reactor without actually building it, have apparently been willing to contemplate the disposal of wastes for centuries to come on the basis of little more than rudimentary calculations. Until we know at least in principle how nuclear wastes can be disposed of there is bound to be serious public disquiet about the large-scale development of nuclear power.' This is a fair criticism though the neglect of the past is being corrected now by considerable new investment at Windscale.

The vexed question of the plutonium cycle will be examined in a full public enquiry on whether a commercial prototype fast breeder reactor should be built. One hopes this will be done with the same care as the reprocessing of waste was examined at the Windscale enquiry. 'Plutonium is a substance which has a particularly unpleasant collection of characteristics, being extremely toxic when inhaled in microscopic quantities and extremely explosive when assembled a few kilograms at a time.'[5]

The spread of plutonium to countries seeking to become nuclear weapon states raises legitimate fears, the seizure of plutonium by terrorists, the danger of a madman using a deliberate accounting error in the plutonium records to hold the country to ransom over a theoretical loss of plutonium, are all possibilities which need to be considered seriously. The checks and safeguards which have been introduced all need to be examined, and even if it is decided that in the course of an enquiry some evidence must, for security reasons, be given in private, it is essential that the public be satisfied that all aspects of the cycle have been scrupulously examined. The recent report of the International Nuclear Fuel Cycle Evaluation Study, INFCE, provides a much-needed element of international agreement as to what now needs to be done to safeguard plutonium and enriched uranium. Without strict safeguards there are grave dangers for the proliferation of nuclear weapons.[6]

An internationally-agreed plutonium storage scheme is urgently needed, as well as schemes for fuel management which limit the number of countries which will handle plutonium and provide safeguards for the safe transport of nuclear fuel. It is argued by some that Britain should, in this field as in so many others, make a unilateral decision to withdraw from this activity and not continue building thermal nuclear reactors. Others argue we should not develop fast breeder reactors. Moral, economic, technical and environmental arguments are conscientiously and genuinely advanced. It is, however, now certain from the INFCE report that other countries, including the United States, which have until now held back, will continue to develop nuclear power, for the report concludes that 'nuclear energy is expected to increase its role in meeting the world's energy needs and can and should be widely available to that end; that effective measures can and should be taken to meet the specific needs of developing countries in the peaceful uses of nuclear energy; and that effective measures can and should be taken to minimise the danger of the proliferation of nuclear weapons without jeopardising energy supplies or the development of nuclear energy for peaceful purposes.'[7]

One of the crucial determinants of the size of the nuclear programme in the Western industrialised countries will be its heavy capital cost and the relative economies, as against the cost of coal; and here again estimates vary greatly. The developing nations are, by contrast, most concerned about the supply of oil. Even so, they will not accept unilateral measures by countries which have nuclear power plants to refuse them uranium supplies or nuclear technology. They prize their sovereignty as much as we do. We cannot reintroduce a new form of colonialism under the guise of genuine fears about the proliferation of nuclear weapons. The developing countries want the industrialised countries to develop nuclear power, even if they themselves are limited by financial and technical constraints from developing nuclear power – it could ease their fears about the oil supplies on which they, with their less sophisticated infrastructures, critically depend. All the COMECON countries are developing nuclear power, and so are the countries of the European Community and France in particular. In Austria, as a result of a referendum, a completed nuclear power station lies unused. In Sweden, after years of divisive debate, a referendum gave a respite: it rejected an alternative that called for no nuclear power, but signalled the end of nuclear energy by the year 2010. In West Germany there has been public disquiet but the major political parties are all committed to a nuclear power programme and the argument, as in Britain, is mainly about its size and the rate of expansion.

For those who positively want low or no economic growth the case for a ban on nuclear power has at least an inner logic. But for those who want to see economic expansion in Britain, faster economic growth, and whose environmental concerns embrace such issues as overcrowded slum housing conditions, Victorian hospitals and inner city squalor, the issue is not so simple. Despite genuine worries about nuclear waste disposal, nuclear safety and nuclear weapon proliferation, there is little escape from the logic of continuing with a nuclear power programme while doing everything possible to maintain its excellent safety record. But where the environmentalists are clearly right is that generating electricity by nuclear fission is not the most desirable way of producing electricity and there should therefore be no over-commitment to nuclear stations and no massive switch into nuclear generation but rather the maximum possible use of coal-fired and pumped storage. In continuing with nuclear power because of energy demand projections, we must remember that nuclear waste and the half life of uranium ensures that we are leaving behind a dubious legacy for future generations. The sooner an alternative technology – biomass fusion, possibly solar photo voltaics – is available, the better. The contribution that alternative sources of energy can make is building up. New technologies, such as solar photo voltaics, produce direct current which, when converted to alternating current, could allow for the large-scale separation of hydrogen and open up the whole field of hydrogen technology. We must therefore avoid becoming so linked into nuclear energy that we deploy insufficient resources into those areas which might allow the world to pull back from, and then out of, nuclear energy.

It is acknowledged by everyone concerned that any major new decision in the nuclear field – such as a decision to opt for a Pressure Water Reactor or a commercial fast breeder reactor – cannot be made without a major public enquiry to examine the issue of principle. There are good grounds for doubting whether Britain can develop simultaneously three reactor designs, and this is the best argument for abandoning the PWR and concentrating on solving the remaining problems with the British designed Advance Gas-cooled Reactor which is the safest design. If we had difficulties with the AGR we could buy off the shelf the German PWR. Advancing the date of the fast breeder reactor enquiry would avoid delay. International co-operation over fast breeder technology before the enquiry will be difficult to establish and we must guard against losing our technological lead because of our usual hesitancy to exploit our own research and development. Despite extra cost of land lines – since the fast breeder reactor is some way off being a commercial proposition – the government should propose to site any commercial fast breeder at Dounreay, where there is public acceptance, and ask the Atomic Energy Authority (AEA), with its proven safety record , to take prime responsibility for the project. These two decisions would do much to allay fears and help speed up the public enquiry. Britain's industrial future depends on her ability to remain in the forefront of technology. Through indecision we have lost our once leading position over thermal nuclear reactors, and we must not let the same thing happen over fast breeder technology. This issue is quite unrelated to the pace at which we should proceed with nuclear power generation. Using advanced technology, trying to cut energy costs, and ensuring energy self-sufficiency are of vital concern for an industrial nation. To carry conviction when espousing a steady nuclear power programme the government must also be seen to be cutting demand, and genuinely exploring alternative sources of energy such as solar, wave and wind power. No one can look at energy prospects for the next ten years with anything other than deep concern, but even over the next twenty to thirty years there is no one single decision or strategy which holds the key to ensuring energy supply. Britain like the rest of the world needs a balanced programme not relying unduly on any one source of energy but seeking some security in a diversity of sources.

With all the public concentration on nuclear power and oil it is easy to forget the crucial role that natural gas has played and will increasingly play in expanding world energy resources. Between 1955 and 1977 natural gas production increased worldwide nearly five-fold so that by 1977 natural gas was supplying nearly 20 per cent of world energy demand compared to 45 per cent for oil and 30 per cent for coal. Natural gas now constitutes about 40 per cent of the world's total hydrocarbon reserves with an estimated life of about forty-seven years. The other striking fact is that proven gas reserves have doubled over the last decade, and even the most conservative estimates show a doubling of world gas output by the end of the century. This will be achieved by a substantial increase in the world trade of gas despite the fact that since the revolution, Iran, with 15 per cent of world reserves, has reduced its export potential.

In 1978 only 10 per cent of the world gas output was traded internationally compared with 48 per cent of crude oil. Of that gas 85 per cent was transported by pipeline. By 1985 world trade in gas will double and liquid natural gas (LNG) will play an important part in this expansion, rising from 1 per cent to 4 per cent of world production by 1985, Algeria providing over half, and Indonesia, Brunei and Malaysia most of the rest. The Soviet Union in Siberia has the largest gas reserves of any country and could greatly expand its output if it decided to invest heavily, but it is likely that most of the gas will be kept for home consumption. All the indications for the future are that the high cost of LNG, both in liquefaction plants and in sea transport, and the high cost of long-distance pipelines, will not be so great restraining factors as in the past, and that a rapid increase in international trade is inevitable. But if there was one major LNG tanker accident this would have as profound an impact on LNG forward planning as the Three Mile Island nuclear power station incident has had on forward nuclear power planning. The proportion of gas flared worldwide dropped from 11·5 per cent in 1976 to 8·8 per cent in 1978, but this is a high percentage of world gas output and represents a large pool of recoverable energy. For the present it looks as if LNG costs will be lower than synthetic natural gas (SNG), but since producer-countries are likely to raise prices it is hard to predict how long this situation will continue.

It is against this international background that British energy policy affecting gas, oil, coal, nuclear power, conservation and alternative sources of energy needs to be assessed. Despite occasional criticism from private enterprise dogmatists it is an incontrovertible fact that the record of British Gas bears favourable comparison with that of any undertaking in any country in the world. They have switched 14 million consumers to natural gas over ten years; and built up production to a peak level in 1979 equivalent to one million barrels of oil per day. Demand for gas in the UK now outstrips supply. It is a resource which must be carefully husbanded and there can be no case whatever for exporting surplus Southern Basin gas to the continent. With the possibility of storing gas underground or in old oil wells we should take every opportunity of spinning out our own indigenous natural gas supplies. The case for investing in an extensive network of gas gathering pipelines has been accepted, as has the use of the powers available for restricting flaring. The discovery in 1965 of commercial quantities on the UK Continental Shelf and their exploitation have been of immense help to the British economy, something easily overlooked now in the debate over oil policy: in 1977, a very difficult year for the economy as a whole, the contribution of North Sea gas to the balance of payments was about £2½ billion, or about 2¼ per cent of GNP. Without natural gas the effects of the 1973 oil price rise would have been crippling. Using its monopoly purchasing power British Gas has bargained toughly with the oil companies and held down consumer gas prices.

Shrinking reserves and growing demand in Western Europe have shown the wisdom of husbanding our own reserves. The Netherlands, the main supplier of gas to West Germany, France, Italy and Belgium, have now reached a plateau and their gas will begin to decline in the mid-1980s; now belatedly, they are developing a conservation policy. The strategic importance of gas pipelines is easily overlooked. Before the revolution Iran was supplying the Soviet Union, and provinces such as Georgia suffered acute gas shortages in the aftermath of the revolution. Then the complicated swap arrangements planned for the IGAT II pipeline, whereby the Soviet Union was to be supplying Europe, was cancelled. The delay in developing Iranian gas supplies means that there will be a gap in European gas supplies which will have to be filled by LNG, which could be expensive. The EEC countries burned in 1977 the same amount of gas in power stations as the whole of the gas sold in the United Kingdom in the same year. Yet two thirds of that gas was wasted in the conversion process and

205

ended up heating the air and rivers. It is no wonder that West Germany, France and the Soviet Union are keen to expand their nuclear programmes so quickly.

Having analysed the world oil situation, the oil depletion policy of the OPEC countries, coal, nuclear power and the world gas market, we can better consider the elements of a British oil policy. Without considering the global situation it is impossible to judge the conflicting arguments which relate to a sensible UK oil depletion policy for the 1980s. The issue is: should we export light North Sea oil during the projected peak production period in 1982-7? In other words should we export oil over and above the amount which covers the cost of importing the necessary OPEC heavy oil for which our refineries are still geared, which is what is meant by self-sufficiency in oil, and is something Britain first reached in 1980. Successive British governments have underestimated Britain's oil reserves. There is much more oil available in the North Sea than has hitherto been acknowledged, but it will be in small fields made economic because of the high price of oil. Exploration is of the utmost importance, as it is through this activity that we shall be able to ascertain the extent of our reserves. The private oil companies have always been reluctant to drill the more marginal prospects until the environment, whether it be oil price increases or government concessions, make it worthwhile. In early 1979 it was calculated that well over a third of the UKCS blocks had not been drilled at all while over a half had only one to three exploration wells. For those companies earning taxable profits (for Petroleum Revenue Tax and Corporation Tax) on the UKCS it is worth noting that the taxpayer will effectively subsidise exploration drilling to the tune of 86-87 per cent. The government should tighten the minimum work programme they impose on companies in all future rounds. The need is to develop all oil fields which are economic in the national as well as purely commercial sense. The object of a national depletion policy, in the most simple terms, must be to prolong self-sufficiency for the longest amount of time possible, while at the same time being so designed that in the event of severe production cut-backs elsewhere in the world or, indeed, in the UKCS, for example, by a pipeline fracture, additional production can be brought on stream quickly. In short the government should aim for the maximum productive capacity while tailoring actual production to meet the national needs. Against all the uncertainties of world oil supply it would be gravely damaging for the national interest to export oil in the 1980s over and above what we currently export under the definition of self-sufficiency. Though Britain in the 1980s will be one of the world's top ten oil producers our output will represent under 3 per cent of world output. The effect of Britain's oil policy on the world will be only marginal, but no less important for being marginal, particularly within the context of our membership of the European Community. It is, however, for its impact on the British economy over the next twenty years that oil is so fundamental. The use to which it is put is of the utmost significance for Britain's future, since it offers nothing less than an opportunity to revive our country.

The decision now is whether we should sell the net potential exportable surplus in the middle 1980s, but it is hard to predict for certain what this figure will be. Development delays, the lack of water drive in reservoirs, and geological problems, in addition to gas flaring restrictions could all cut the surplus down. The main Departments in Whitehall are divided and ambivalent about future oil depletion policy. The Treasury is reluctant to see Britain forego substantial revenues which it argues would be available to regenerate the British economy in the middle 1980s, at a time when the world economic recession would still be depressing our ability to expand or even hold the current 35 per cent of GNP we commit to world trade. The Foreign Office as usual hovers irresolutely, wanting self-sufficiency for as long as possible on overall strategic grounds, yet responding to the argument that the UK has a responsibility to set an example to the OPEC countries by not adopting a tough depletion policy. It hopes that if Britain expands its production then it will be easier to persuade OPEC, and particularly Saudi Arabia, to relax their present depletion stance for the crucial ten-year period ahead. The Foreign Office is also tempted to go along with the argument of our Community partners, particularly the Federal

Republic of Germany, who feel that the UK has a responsibility to maximise production so as to export oil to them and protect Europe's economy from any supply shortages resulting from the OPEC countries' depletion policy.

In 1978 and 1979 I argued as Foreign Secretary for a much tougher depletion policy against the then complacent view endorsed by the Department of Energy that there was little room for reducing the production profile. The detailed economic implications of a depletion policy are discussed in Chapter 9 in relation to economic policy. Most oil companies argue against a depletion policy and for taking advantage of present world oil prices. They might have a better case if we were still living in the 1970s when it was not at all clear that prices in the oil market would continuously rise. It is easy to forget that we were so uncertain about future world prices in relation to North Sea oil's high production costs that, even after the 1973 oil price rise, we were still trying to negotiate with our EEC partners a minimum selling price for North Sea oil. This was finally rejected in 1975 during the so-called renegotiations and no longer has any relevance. Analysts are divided about future oil price increases in excess of world inflation rates. If the shale oils and tar sands in the US are developed quickly, if conservation proceeds faster than some predict, then some time in the 1980s OPEC could lose its cartel influence on oil price, and price would be determined more by true economic forces rather than by political forces. The price of oil might cease to increase in real terms, and if some producers responded by increasing production there could be a decline in absolute terms. It is very difficult to predict future oil prices but this fact is not sufficient justification for allowing the oil companies to produce as much oil as they can now in the hope of selling while oil prices are high. The European Community wish for maximum North Sea oil production in the 1980s would have more justification if they had been prepared in the early 1970s to make a commitment to a minimum selling price. Even if it had then been above world prices, they would have had the certainty of supply.

In 1978-9 the trend of world oil prices was such as to convince many, both in industry and in government, that the

OPEC countries would so manage the market that there would be for at least the next five years an ever-increasing real price for British oil which would easily cover the high costs of extraction from the North Sea. Oil fields hitherto regarded as too small to exploit and with only marginal economic returns are becoming profitable and it seems clear that this trend will continue. Against such a fairly predictable future, to sell excess oil in the 1980s, and then to pay for it in the 1990s would, even on short term Treasury revenue considerations, be a very unattractive proposition. Exporting surplus oil in the 1980s would also ensure that the oil-generated pressures increasing the exchange rate – already one of the most serious economic problems we face – would be stepped up and would lead to an even more unrealistic exchange rate in relation to our industrial competitiveness.

There is no sound economic case for believing that an injection of extra revenue in the mid-1980s will be critical to our industrial recovery. All the signs are that Britain's industrial recovery will take some time, and certainly needs to go beyond the decade of the 1980s, so that keeping a steady 5 per cent of GNP as a contribution from the North Sea into the 1990s is of more benefit than a spurt of perhaps 6-7 per cent at its peak in the mid-1980s. Our fundamental industrial weakness makes it vital that investment be sustained into the 1990s. As to the wider international argument, potentially the strongest, all the available evidence leads to the conclusion that the OPEC countries' depletion policy is based on national self-interest and will not be even marginally influenced by the depletion policy of the UK. In as much as their depletion policy may be modified, the important influences would be a feeling that the US, and to a lesser extent Europe, not only understands their regional problem but is dealing responsibly with their major political concern – Palestine – as well as arguments of self-interest relating to world economic activity. Within Europe it is true that, if the European Community is to mean anything, all the member states have a wider responsibility going beyond mere national self-interest: the existing preferential supply agreement to EEC countries in a supply crisis recognises this responsibility. For similar reasons we agreed, during the supply agreement to EEC countries in a supply crisis recognises this responsibility. For similar reasons we agreed, during the supply shortage following the Iranian crisis, to relax our North Sea flaring restrictions to increase oil supply – but it was ironic that one of the results was that our own supply situation became tighter than that of many of our EEC partners, with North Sea oil purchased by a German company being resold on the spot market at a far higher price. But Britain has accepted that in fixing the price for North Sea oil we should not be a market leader and successive governments have instructed BNOC to act responsibly in view of the fact that increased revenues do not offset the adverse effect of a depressed world economy as a result of high oil prices on our exports.

Given the present world situation, if Britain were to increase her oil exports to the Community instead of spinning out our own self-sufficiency, the net effect is likely to be that other member states would relax their determination to switch out of oil-fired or gas-fired power stations, buy less LNG and go slower over introducing nuclear power. There is no evidence that an increase in UK oil exports is vital to maintain current economic growth rates within the EEC. The case for a specific European oil policy is in dealing with a supply shortage in Europe but Britain can have a tough depletion policy and still contribute to protecting our Community partners from a dramatic fall in oil supplies. It is by developing a strategic surge reserve capacity that we can contribute to the Community in a crisis, not by exporting surplus oil now, nor by relaxing a tight depletion policy before any such shortages appear.

The political decision which overrides all these economic and technical arguments about a tough depletion policy remains the compelling strategic argument. It is the very case which Winston Churchill made when, as Chancellor of the Exchequer, he took a government financial stake in British Petroleum between the World Wars, in order to safeguard oil supplies for the Royal Navy. No prudent nation will forego for the future the ability to be self-sufficient in energy. Energy is as crucial to our survival as our defence forces. Maintaining self-sufficiency in oil for as long as possible, flattening the hump in oil production in the 1980s and controlling oil exports must now become a national policy. Yet just as our defence policy cannot be framed solely in terms of a narrow national self-interest, or be buffeted by polarised party politics, so we cannot develop an oil and energy policy within a wholly national framework or without some cross-Party continuity.

Slowly we are starting to develop some understanding between the Parties over the exploitation of North Sea oil –and not before time. The first two licensing rounds in the North Sea were concerned with exploration for gas, and oil was only discovered in the Montrose field in 1965 and then in the Forties field in 1970 during the Third Round. In 1971-2 the then Conservative government went ahead with a large Fourth Round of licensing with Brent being discovered in 1971. The Public Accounts Committee of the House of Commons, chaired by Edmund Dell, issued a report in 1973 which was unusually critical for such an all-Party body, of the then Conservative government's tax arrangements. The new Labour government in 1974, with Edmund Dell as a Treasury Minister, acted swiftly to meet the major criticism of the Public Accounts Committee. The Oil Taxation Act in 1975 was introduced, establishing new tax laws affecting the UK Continental Shelf, and a new tax, the Petroleum Revenue Tax. The Petroleum and Submarine Pipeline Act in 1975 gave British government powerful controls over all UKCS activity and control over the rate of development. It also provided for the establishment of the British National Oil Corporation, BNOC, an example of effective state intervention, giving the state the power it needed over a critical sector of the economy. It was a classic case for public ownership being in the best interests of the nation.

The powers of BNOC under the Act were to explore for, produce and refine petroleum, to store, distribute and buy and sell petroleum, to act as an adviser to the government on petroleum matters, to carry out research and development and to operate abroad. The net effect of the two acts was to increase and safeguard the public's share of North Sea oil revenue and greatly enhance government control over offshore activities. Majority state participation as originally conceived involved the purchase for value of 51 per cent of all equity interests in the North Sea, and for this purpose the National Oil Account was devised to handle the very large revenues which would have to pass through BNOC's accounts. Since the Labour Government had already pledged that they would make the companies 'financially no better and no worse off' this could have involved a bizarre financial transaction, with all the positive cash flow from the oil produced, less the tax due flowing back from BNOC's accounts in order to pay for the 51 per cent at value. Such a mechanism would have meant at times of economic crisis a further burden on the balance of payments, and so a different way of achieving the same end was devised whereby negotiated agreements with the oil companies gave BNOC a formal position on the licence, membership of the company operating agreements and the right to attend operating committees, the right to information and the option to purchase 51 per cent of all the oil at 'market prices'. In some cases the companies were given the right to re-acquire oil where they could show it was needed for their own activities within the UK but the government retained the right to stop this if they felt it to be in the national interest. For the expenditure of no capital the long term British national interest in the UKCS was safeguarded.

This was perhaps the single most successful example of the assertion of the British national interest since the Second World War and an excellent example of wise state intervention. BNOC also took over the equity holdings of the National Coal Board in the North Sea and their small staff, and soon after that, the Labour government was able to acquire the North Sea oil assets of the Burmah Oil Company, which was agreed because of the company's financial difficulties. In a single decisive step this gave BNOC a much firmer basis for expansion and very considerable expertise in the Thistle field. This transaction was separate from the earlier financial rescue operation launched by the Bank of England to help Burmah, which led to the acquisition by the Bank of England of a substantial shareholding in British Petroleum. Despite the political controversy over the creation of BNOC as a state oil company, in 1975, within a year of its creation, it had become a powerful force in the North Sea. By early 1980 it had established itself as a major oil company. It had equity interests in five producing gas and oil fields, in four oil fields under development and in 77 licences representing some 150 blocks. It had established its operating capability being the operator for three oil fields, one in production, one under development, and one still in the appraisal stage. The real market value of its oil and gas fields, ignoring conventional accounting methods, was probably near £2 billion. The Corporation was the single largest trader of UKCS oil, handling over a million barrels a day, representing well over half of the nation's total oil requirements. This oil was acquired through equity, purchases from third party, government royalty and participation rights. It had been involved in 90 exploration and appraisal wells, nearly one third of the total effort on the UKCS. It had an expert staff of 1,400, had earned the respect of the major oil companies and after some cosmetic and a few doctrinal changes by the new Conservative government there was no major figure in the UK oil industry who believed that BNOC should be abolished. Dogmatically the new Conservative government within a few months of taking office in the summer of 1979 told British Petroleum that they could buy BNOC lock, stock and barrel for £1 billion. Then realising in part its folly the government switched policy and said that they would split BNOC into two, sell equity shares in the production and development side but retain full government control of the trading side. Then in October 1980 they again switched policy and announced that they would keep BNOC intact and under government control. So as to cover their embarrassment and placate their supporters the equivalent of 'Granny Bonds' were to be issued as window-dressing to cover the continuation of BNOC unchanged.

More worrying was the decision to take power by legislation to enable the public to have a direct equity stake in BNOC. This should be resisted not on grounds of partisan party politics but because, if BNOC changes its character and becomes a company with public equity stock capable of being purchased on the stock market, it opens up the whole legal question of past participation agreements, risks the agreements being challenged in the courts after the equity stocks have been issued and also makes it more credible for the European Commission to challenge British sovereignty over the oil in the UK Continental Shelf. If BNOC does not get caught up in partisan arguments over privatisation or nationalisation it should be able to continue effectively unchanged to the benefit of the whole nation. But this means the government allowing BNOC to invest its revenues to develop new fields, like Clyde, as it feels is commercially prudent, and to retain its development team. It is absurd to put BNOC's investment and development programme at risk because of a wish to use its revenues to reduce the PSBR, prejudicing the oil needs of the 1990s. The basis exists for a long term energy policy but it can only be maintained across successive governments if there is more recognition of the need for give and take between the political parties. It is sad that those financial commentators who supported the selling off or the break-up of BNOC are those who also urge Labour governments to moderate schemes for the nationalisation of various industries so as to achieve the much needed industrial stability that every sensible person knows is necessary. They would carry more conviction if they used the same arguments over the doctrinaire attitude of Mrs Thatcher to the privatisation of BNOC. Large parts of the City of London have been self-interested in pursuing partisan politics for too long.

BNOC provides, as a result of its unique structure and operation, a major safeguard for the maintenance of the British legal position within the European Community, over our right to exercise full control over the UKCS. BNOC is not a monopoly. It has established working partnerships with the major international oil companies, is highly profitable, has the prospect of earning very substantial revenues, has a substantial positive cash flow through the National Oil Account and has helped to ensure a high percentage of orders for the UK Offshore industries. The Conservative government can claim the right to make changes in BNOC. Some of these decisions carry no serious implications for the future – such as the decision to legislate for a change in the National Oil Account and to end BNOC's exemption from PRT – while others, though doctrinal in origin and regrettable, can easily be reversed – such as stopping BNOC's representatives from sitting on the operating committees of fields where they do not have an equity interest. Though for the 7th Round the government has said BNOC must sit on all operating committees which relate to production when a field is commercial and is under development. The other decision was to stop what was virtually a right of first refusal on trading between licensees on oil properties and the ending of the position in the 7th Round of Licensing, where previously in 5th and 6th Rounds, BNOC had to have 51 per cent of all the awards in the round and had the right to apply for 100 per cent licences.

It is estimated by 1982 BNOC will probably be handling 1 million barrels a day comprising 15 per cent equity, 20 per cent royalty and 65 per cent participation and will be operating as a major international oil company. With the introduction of Bond holding it was to be hoped that at least all political constraint to its development had been removed and that it would be able to acquire any new equity holdings it commercially wished, apply for any new licences and form any partnerships with other public sector enterprises or oil companies it wanted, raise its own capital on international markets, operate abroad as a public enterprise which other governments can trust to operate fairly. A move downstream from crude to product trading, into refining, specialised and chemical manufacture and specialist engineering allows BNOC to be involved in the gas gathering system through its access to over 60 per cent of the total liquids to be produced. BNOC must in addition keep throughout a sense of public responsibility in terms of depletion policy, exploration policy, research, development and trading. If this is done then there will be a chance of a period of sustained continuity of policy across governments in relation to the basic structure of developing North Sea oil in the best interests of Britain. In 1974 the case for the compulsory state acquisition of all operations in the North Sea was rightly rejected by a new Labour government despite some unrealistic doctrinal commitments made in Opposition. In 1981, the case against reverting all operations in the North Sea to the free market economy and private

215

ownership might be accepted by the Conservative government despite similarly unrealistic doctrinal commitments made in Opposition. If this happens, the Labour Party in Opposition must not commit itself again to overall nationalisation of the North Sea.

There will be a sensible case for changes to be made in licensing policy, tax policy, depletion policy, in exploration policy and in the way in which BNOC is able to operate, and a wise socialist will develop a strategy in all these areas. The case for nationalisation will, however, remain hard to justify. Unlike in 1974, in 1984 there will be self-sufficiency in oil so that it will be harder to argue against nationalisation on the grounds that we could not achieve self-sufficiency quickly if international oil companies pull out of the North Sea. This was a real risk in 1974 when the oil price was still low in comparison to the costs of North Sea production. By 1984 the UK priority will be to use every means to maintain UK self-sufficiency of oil into the next century by exploiting a large number of small oil fields hitherto thought to be uneconomic. It will be necessary to keep the interest of all the oil companies in operating marginal oil fields and using their expertise to bring all possible oil ashore. Building up BNOC will be an essential element in this strategy, but with a period of even two or three years, let alone five or six years, of uncertainty about what is to happen to the commercial environment for the North Sea there would be a great risk of returning by default in the early 1990s to a position of being an oil importer again. This would incur a balance of payments cost, but would above all mean that we could once again become strategically vulnerable to shortages of supply from a downturn or collapse in world production. Socialists must cease to believe that the only way of ensuring economic advance is to reproduce the old patterns of state nationalisation. The essential power having been taken there is a need for stability in the North Sea oil industry.

The fundamental issue, however, is how tough the government's depletion policy will be, and to what extent the government will challenge the oil industry when it bleats about interference with its natural production levels. It is not sufficient, however, for the government to use its power to limit the oil equity production of BNOC (which in 1983 could be just under 200,000 barrels a day) and also the smaller production of British Gas (probably under 35,000 barrels a day). This is production directly under government control, which, by negotiation with its partners, could be reduced to balance high depletion during years still affected by past commitments over depletion policy given to private industry. The need is to announce the flattening of the 1980s' production curve. What is needed is ministerial boldness to cut through the inertia of differing Departmental priorities. The assurances rightly given by Eric Varley as Secretary of State for Energy should not be used as an excuse or for inaction or irresolution over a tough depletion policy. There is considerable scope for reducing production by more than 10-20 per cent even within the terms of these assurances, but it is also possible to negotiate a deal with the private industry which will meet their legitimate concerns but also allow no excess production over that which Britain needs to maintain self-sufficiency. The government's commitment to the EEC to export additionally in 1985 at least 100,000 barrels a day should be a maximum figure, not a minimum.

The oil industry is highly sophisticated. The realists within it know they have had a stable, fair deal from successive British governments. They know that apart from the direct controls in the Petroleum and Submarine Pipe-Lines Act, the government can deploy, given the will, damaging and disruptive indirect controls, such as the restricting of all flaring, the cutting back of exploration and the delaying of development, which, if indiscriminately applied, would harm their interests. The industry knows it has more to gain from negotiation than from sticking to the letter of past assurances, and that the balance of power rests with the government. The political question is: will a Conservative government, for whom non-intervention in private industry has been elevated to the status of theology, be prepared to tell the oil industry that it would use these powers if it did not negotiate a sensible depletion policy? It would be possible to negotiate an arrangement which safeguards the capital investment position of the smaller oil companies

who cannot easily spread their cash flow and which puts the
burden for delayed production on the largest oil companies,
including BNOC, who can well afford the delay in revenues
and can easily cover their investment. The large companies
will also know that the cost of delay will almost certainly be
more than covered by increased revenues – it might even be
worth the government's while to guarantee any possible loss.
Such a negotiation would not reduce oil companies' confidence
in investing in the North Sea (though this traditional 'canard'
might well be used by the oil companies). Real rates of return
have risen sharply in recent years and will continue to do so.
The oil companies know that circumstances have changed
dramatically since the 'Varley Assurances' were given. They
know too that they have been given more consistent consideration by the UK government than by any other oil producing
country in the world. Indeed, time and again we attempt as a
country to be absurdly and unrealistically 'fair' in our trading
arrangements. The Whitehall bureaucracy and Ministers
making the final decisions are far too sensitive to the special
pleading of vested interests. A little more ruthlessness would
not go amiss in putting more backbone into Britain's industrial
revival.

We need more self-confidence and assertiveness, and there
is no more important place to start than with a tough oil
depletion policy. Few issues are more vital to our future: oil
kept in the ground is the economic seedcorn for Britain's
recovery in the 1990s. Rapidly lifting North Sea oil in 1982 and
1983 might soften the impact of the austerity and savage
unemployment of 1980 and 1981. It could produce an income
tax concession on the eve of an election, a boom reminiscent
of the pre-election consumer booms of the Conservative
governments of the 1950s. But that would be at the expense of
our future prosperity, and would result in the destruction of
Britain's only chance of economic recovery. It is time to warn
the country that North Sea oil policy should be a dominant
issue at the next election, for how a future government handles
the nation's most precious natural asset should concern
everyone – there will be no room for dogma or doctrine, for
partisan electoral politics. Any political party that seeks to

advocate such a course, that seeks to bribe or hoodwink the electorate may make a profound misjudgment of the serious mood of the nation as they face the realities of Britain's future.

10

State Intervention

State intervention in industry has become highly controversial. It is neither a universal panacea nor the ultimate solution to all our industrial difficulties. Wisely chosen, intervention can give important marginal help. There has been a tendency only to focus public attention on the extravagant, like Concorde, the loss makers like British Leyland, forgetting what an appalling state it was in when the government felt obliged to step in, and the disappointing results in the fragmented nuclear industry. It is not generally appreciated that the extension of state influence, knowledge and power into key sectors of industry has, over the past decade, led to some important and successful innovations. Successful interventions have taken place over computers in relation to ICL, and in pharmaceuticals through the Voluntary Price Restraint System – an arrangement which could with advantage be buttressed by a state interest in a United Kingdom pharmaceutical company operating commercially. These flexible approaches need to be highlighted in order to demonstrate the complexity of intervention in these areas, as well as the facts over the potential benefits that are available from arrangements which differ from monopoly state ownership and the traditional pattern of state nationalisation of whole industries. They represent other ways – and, demonstrably, far more effective ways – of achieving social control and social responsibility. State involvement with the computer industry has been a successful policy, sustained across successive governments for sixteen years – something almost unique in post-war British

220

experience. Not only does it illustrate the importance of our membership of the European Community in developing any strategy; it has also brought home to us the extent to which other European governments help their industries. In addition, many of the techniques and strategies used for the computer industry could be similarly applied to other industries, and in particular to the new technologies. The history is highlighted in more detail here than for other examples because of the particular importance of dragging British industry into the age of micro-electronics.

The governments of the USA, Japan, France, Germany and Great Britain have each realised that computers are an all-pervasive and strategically vital technology. Each country has worked out a special interrelationship between its government and its information technology industry. The relationship in the United States developed in the way it did as a result of the vast size of the single US domestic market, the ready acceptance of change by its citizens, and the existence of a virtual war economy during the period of the build-up of the industry between the mid-1940s and the early 1970s. The relationship in Japan grew out of the selection of the information technology industry as one of the industries for regeneration by the Japanese government, and out of the very structure of Japanese society, which welds national and industrial policies into a single weapon of economic warfare. Our society and economic structures are so different from those of the USA and Japan that we cannot hope to transfer their pattern of industry/government relations to Britain. But we can study these interrelationships, and, in the cases of France and Germany in particular, compare them to what has developed so far in the United Kingdom.

The world computer market today is dominated by the US industry, with the Japanese about to issue a formidable challenge to that domination. However, much of the early pioneering work in computer development was done in Europe before the Second World War. During that war, little computer development work was carried out in Europe, while in the United States the war effort was responsible for the development of ENIAC to compute ballistic tables and

EDVAC, which was developed by the University of Pennsylvania for the US Army Ordnance Department. Meanwhile, IBM, realised the important potential of electronic digital computers outside the sphere of government, and had delivered its first general-purpose computer, the IBM 604, in 1948. After the war, work began to be done in Britain, France and Germany on computer developments but it was mainly confined to academic and governmental areas of operation. In the United States, however, the combined effects of their large market, a ready acceptance of new ideas, highly skilled marketing and high clerical costs meant that the electronic computer was readily accepted by the business and industrial world. By 1959 there were 550 systems operational in Western Europe and 3,810 in the USA. By 1961 these figures had grown to 1,600 and 7,550 respectively.

In many areas of business life in the early 1960s in Europe, the computer was thought of as a passing fad, an expensive executive status symbol that would have little lasting effect on business operation or management style. The governments of France, Germany and Britain, however, had already begun to realise that it would be a serious error of strategy to allow their countries' computer requirements to be supplied entirely from outside their national borders. Their own experience had already shown them that the computer would become the focal point of all successful large organisations and that foreign control of such an important area of the economy could have serious political disadvantages. As a consequence, the governments of all three countries decided as a matter of policy to create a viable, native computer industry of their own, whilst permitting the dominant US industry to operate within their borders much as it had done before.

In 1959 the two principal data processing companies in Britain, British Tabulating Machines (Hollerith) and Powers-Samas merged to form International Computers and Tabulators Limited (ICT). They did this to meet the challenges of the rapidly growing computer business in the restricted UK market. The merger did not, however, resolve the problem of the shortage of computer expertise. In 1961 computer engineers and designers of the General Electric Company Ltd,

Great Britain, joined ICT; in July 1962 the Commercial Computer Division of EMI was added to the company and finally, in September 1963, the Commercial Computer Department of Ferranti Ltd joined the ICT Group. A parallel process of rationalisation led to the formation of English Electric Computers Ltd. In April 1963, the data processing and control systems division of English Electric and Leo Computers Limited came together as English Electric Leo Computers Limited. English Electric bought out Leo's share of the company in October 1964, and at the same time Marconi's commercial and scientific computer interests were added to the company, which was then re-named English Electric-Leo-Marconi Computers Limited. In March 1967 the name changed again to English Electric Computers, and in August of the same year Elliott Automation Computers were added to the group when Elliott Automation merged with English Electric.

In 1964 ICT introduced the first British computer to be truly commercially successful, the 1900 series. ICT knew that, with the 1900 series, they could challenge the US technical domination of the world computer market, but they also realised that they could do so only with the support of the British government. Before the 1964 election, the Labour Party realised that science and technology, hitherto subjects of little political appeal, had become both fashionable and a matter of genuine concern to the growing number of young technocrats throughout the country: this was reflected in Harold Wilson's famous Scarborough Conference speech. ICT decided to take full advantage of this development in political thinking. An executive was appointed to handle political-industrial relations and under his guidance a document was prepared with considerable care by the company which dealt in detail with the future relationship between the British company industry and the new Labour government. This document was presented at all levels of government and parliament and when, on 1 March 1965, Mr Frank Cousins, the first Minister of Technology, made a statement about the company industry, the policy he laid down reflected strongly the policy expressed in ICT's original document, saying that the government considered that it was essential that there should be a rapid increase in the use of computers and computer techniques in industry and commerce, and that there should be a flourishing British computer industry.

The British computer industry took great care to work with the growing Ministry of Technology and excellent working relationships were built up from the Chairman and the Minster downwards throughout the working levels of the Ministry and the industry. Probably for the first time, civil servants made an all-out effort to understand the workings of the industry that they were sponsoring and in the same way industry began to appreciate the pattern of behaviour that government administration imposes upon the civil service. As confidence between the two sides grew, the degree of contact expanded and became a matter of everyday procedure some-what similar to the relationship which is common in France. At no time did the close relationship between government and the industry develop to a point where the government could be said to be interfering with the day-to-day management of the company; the company had commercial freedom, it paid its staff competitive salaries, it traded as it wished and it was not subject to specific parliamentary accountability.

In a statement in the House of Commons on 21 March 1968, Tony Benn, Minister of Technology, announced that, with government backing, the commercial and scientific computer businesses of International Computers and Tabu-lators Ltd and English Electric Computers Ltd were to be brought together into one company in which the Plessey Company Ltd, a major manufacturer of telecommunications equipment, would participate. The merger was brought about through a holding company, International Computers (Holdings) Limited (IC (H)), which was constituted for the purpose. It acquired all the shares in the EE Computers, a wholly-owned subsidiary of the English Electric Company Limited. Plessey subscribed for shares in IC (H). The Minister of Technology provided up to £13.5 million by way of grants in general support for research and development expenditure and subscribed cash for 3·5 million shares of £1 each. All parties agreed that the group would be fully autonomous in all its policies and that the government would not intervene in day-to-day management.

It was clear that, if the new company, ICL, was to produce a totally new range of internationally competitive computer systems, it would require further money from government. On 3 July, Mr Christopher Chataway, the responsible Minister in the new Conservative government, made a statement in the House of Commons affirming the government's belief that the capability to develop, manufacture and market computer systems which IC(H) represented should be retained in Britain, and he announced government support of £14.2 million to maintain the momentum of ICL's Research and Development programme. On 4 July 1973, Mr Chataway made another statement to the House of Commons announcing further aid for ICL, of the launching-aid type. The government agreed to provide a further £25.8 million in support of the company's R & D programme from October 1973 until September 1976, making a total of £40 million in all. The basis for the arrangement was that no further financial assistance would be required or sought from the government after 1976. In addition to direct financial involvement with R & D, the British government introduced a policy of preferential purchasing which favoured ICL.

The objective of operating a computer procurement policy in the United Kingdom was to enable the infant computer industry to become established as a viable industry in its own right. The industry was seen to be very important in terms of its capacity to create wealth and employment in the United Kingdom. It was also an industry well suited to British skills and resources, many of the key innovations having been made in the United Kingdom. The role of the computer industry was also seen as being fundamental to the success of British industry as a whole. Total dependence on American expertise and equipment would, it was feared, severely restrict Britain's ability to seize new market opportunities or establish a lead in key areas. It also gave Britain an opportunity at that time to establish an industry which could play a vital role as a European alternative to American industrial domination.

The consequences of government interaction with industry

can only be judged in the long term by regarding the commercial success in the open market of the firm or firms concerned. ICL as a commercial entity has existed only since 1968, so that meaningful figures can only be given for the decade 1968-78, but they form a useful guide to growth. In that time turnover rose from £92 million to £509 million, overseas business from £31 million to £259 million, whilst trading profit went up from £6 million to £49 million. Little of those very considerable increases was due to inflation, because of the sharp drop in hardware costs that took place over the same period. It needs to be remembered, moreover, that during this same period the percentage of ICL's revenue coming from central government under the preferential purchasing policy dropped from some 14 per cent to some 8 per cent, whilst its overall share of the UK home market also declined by two or three per cent. The company's major growth, therefore, had come from the private sector markets outside the UK, those very sectors that could be said to be the least likely to be affected by UK government interaction with the company.

In the decade 1968-78 there is no doubt that the competitive strength of the native computer industries of Germany, Britain and France had increased significantly. However, when judging the interaction between those national computer industries and the worldwide industries under United States' control there can, equally, be no doubt that little significant improvement had been made in correcting the world economic imbalance caused by US dominance of the computer market. By 1978 CII-HB in France, Siemens in Germany and ICL realised that a new initiative was necessary from them if a new posture was to be adopted for the decade 1978-88 if they were to move towards a situation where they had at least 50 per cent shares of their own European market. They also realised that under EEC regulations preferential procurement policies had to be ended at the beginning of 1981, and that this move would be strengthened by the acceptance of the GATT code by their respective governments. Accordingly, the three companies began talks with each other to see what action they could jointly take to establish effective competition with non-

European suppliers. All parties agreed that there was a need for greater co-operative effort in a number of areas including joint lobbying of the EEC Commission, the European and National parliaments, a general promotion of the joint image of the three companies, joint co-operation on standards, joint approaches to telephone and telecommunications organisations, cross-supply of peripherals and joint bids for EEC tenders where the prospects of winning the order would be enhanced.

The representatives of the three companies agreed that while the EEC Commission had done its best to bring about a greater awareness of the need for collective action to strengthen the native European computer industry, member governments and their national industries had not done enough in this area over the past decade. The refusal of member governments to provide adequate funding had even compelled the EEC to cut back its modest four-year data processing development programme from £60 million to £11 million. The representatives of the three companies concluded that a sustained joint effort would have to be made by themselves in the lobbying and public relations' fields, as well as on the technical, commercial and marketing fronts, to demonstrate to the governments concerned the evidence of self-help so that the government would in turn give serious attention to the promotion of the needs of the information technology industry in the decade 1980-90. In this way the domination of the European market by the US information technology industry might be brought to an end.

When the new Conservative government in 1980 hesitated in giving ICL the contract for the computerisation of PAYE it was taken as an indication that for the first time in sixteen years a government might make a major change in government policy over supporting ICL. The previous decision to sell the government shareholding in ICL was political, but since the government's relations with ICL were not specifically based on a shareholding relationship, the sale could only be regretted as a bad long-term deal for the taxpayer and as an apparent lessening of involvement by the British government. But if ICL had been nationalised in 1968 it would probably have been denationalised in 1970 or at least subjected to a long period of uncertainty, and it would definitely have been de-nationalised in 1979. It has not been a radical company in terms of industrial democracy or worker involvement, except for an unusually high percentage of union membership on the part of its senior sales staff. But it is hard to point to any place where the performance of ICL would have been significantly improved if it had been state owned rather than state supported.

In late 1980 its profits shrank, it laid off 2,500 employees, and if ICL is not to decline and lose its markets to IBM, and even to CII-HB and Siemens, it is essential to develop a strategy covering not only the needs of the central government departments, but the nationalised industries and other state bodies, and to give top-level support by private industry and by local government. Within the framework of the exclusion clauses of the GATT Agreement, it is permissible for government to fund development contracts with ICL for research and development in the areas of hardware and software needed for identified applications and data bases of strategic, economic and social importance, or for key facilities. If this is done over the next two to five years, leading to prototype implementation of systems following such development work, it would be sufficient to cure ICL's problems and to ensure its continued viability as part of a sensible long-term industrial strategy. If the British government were to refuse to support such schemes on financial terms that are at least equal to those offered by other governments then the future for ICL could be less uncertain. The civil service must develop techniques for helping our own industry while operating in a way which does not openly flout international trading agreements.

The future development of the computer industry in terms of its products and services will be affected fundamentally by the activities of the telephone and telecommunications industry in relation to the network policy and activity as well as the communications protocols and standards adopted in the UK and throughout Western Europe. The government's strategy needs to ensure the closest possible co-operation with and between the industry and the British Post Office and Continental Post, Telephone and Telecommunications organisations. Public sector purchasing policy should be structured so as to ensure that while all contenders compete on an equal basis the pricing structure should require evidence and confirmation that the prices, terms, conditions and facilities offered in tender to public sector organisations in the UK are the same as those being offered to similar bodies elsewhere. Any deviation from standard practice should make a tender invalid, or should at least be taken into account in any selection process. In particular, an analysis of the adjudication should be available for scrutiny by all tenderers after awards are made. In exercising the proposed pricing structure, it should be possible to identify where free software conversion or other hidden costs or facilities are being offered. In the past, such offers have operated against the interests of British suppliers, who have not been able to match the scale of investment foreign companies have been prepared to make to gain a foothold in the British public sector. Without such minimum industrial support Britain could lose its one major British computer company, and with it sixteen years of remarkable co-operation between government and private industry sustained by successive governments.

The same types of argument apply to the new technologies such as the micro-processor industry. The National Enterprise Board is another new technique for state intervention. Its decision in 1978 to support Inmos was a reflection of the unwillingness of the private sector to put up the necessary risk capital. It was a strategic decision that Britain needed to have an expertise in this technology. It will be a tragedy if the hesitation and delay of the Conservative government in supporting Inmos means that an opportunity to catch up in a fast-moving area of technology has been lost. But at least there is now a continuity of policy. The NEB, though emasculated, has survived and is providing venture capital for high risk projects in new technologies. The Inmos project, though unenthusiastically supported, is to continue, and perhaps it will prove eventually to have been another successful and sensible example of state intervention. A previous Chairman of the National Enterprise Board, Sir Leslie Murphy, at a seminar organised by the Policy Studies Institute in 1980 made it clear that he was never prepared to acquiesce in the use of the NEB as a means of extending public ownership as an end in itself. 'True to its philosophy the NEB acquired shares only as a necessary and indispensable means of achieving its major objectives of helping individual companies to improve their industrial operations, of setting up new enterprises in advanced technology, or assisting regional development and small companies and of promoting exports. The NEB never used its funds or its financial muscle to go into the market to buy shares or buy profitable companies as an end in itself. It operated only by persuasion and never acquired shares against the wishes of the companies concerned.' This role for the NEB is a sensible, practical one and with a record of success in linking public funds to commercial disciplines and with a long-term return on capital. It is this approach to state intervention which is particularly well suited to the new scientifically based or technologically advanced industries and the decision in 1980 to launch a jointly owned company called Anglo American Venture Management is a sign that its past Chairman, Sir Arthur Knight, had convinced the Conservative government that the NEB had a role in pioneering new product development.

An industry which is dominated by multinational companies and yet where there is a strong rational case for greater state involvement is the pharmaceutical industry. The pharmaceutical industry with the NHS as its main purchaser is inevitably subject to state control. In the year 1978-9 the NHS cost £8,863 million, or 4·7 per cent of GNP. The NHS market in pharmaceuticals was £565 million, 8 per cent of total NHS expenditure. The household market in pharmaceuticals was £300 million. Since the Department of Health and Social Security is such a large purchaser of pharmaceutical products, it cannot avoid having a direct interest in the pricing policy of the industry, in which it effectively controls the profit ratios through the Voluntary Price Regulation Scheme, VPRS. Yet this is an industry which in 1980 had export sales amounting to almost £700 million; so that the industry's pricing policy abroad is not so damaged by domestic constraints as to make exporting unattractive.

There is a dilemma: as purchaser the state has an interest in low prices, but the state also has an interest in export earnings. There is inevitably a relationship between domestic and overseas prices and VPRS has balanced these two interests. A moral problem, however, which tends to be ignored, concerns the extent to which the World Health Organisation should intervene to prevent developing countries in particular paying excessive amounts for their pharmaceuticals. The major problem for national government control is how to control the practice of transfer pricing, the mechanism whereby a subsidiary of a multinational company in one country can sell the patented ingredients of a pharmaceutical product to one of their companies in another country at an excessive price. The profits through transfer pricing can be immense and very difficult to trace. There have been two very serious publicised cases in Britain involving Tetracyclin in the 1960s and Librium and Valium in the 1970s. In 1971 Roche Products Ltd were referred to the Monopolies Commission over the supply of Librium and Valium after the company had refused to pay any further repayments to the Department of Health and Social Security. The Monopolies Commission reported in 1973[1] and recommended that the price of Librium should be reduced to 40 per cent of its 1970 price. The report suggested that the element of profit in the transfer price might exceed 80 per cent. Eventually Roche, after protracted negotiations and legal proceedings being started, agreed to repay the British government and also re-entered the Voluntary Price Regulation Scheme and continued to invest and manufacture in the UK.

The report also drew attention to methods of restricting competition and concluded that as the ultimate paymaster the Department of Health and Social Security was in a position to bring some pressure to bear upon prices, and did so through the Voluntary Price Regulation Scheme, but that its influence was qualified in two important respects. In the first place it could not decide what drugs should or should not be prescribed and bought. Secondly, it drew attention to the fact that the government department with responsibility for the pharmaceutical industry as well as for the NHS could not exert its bargaining power as an independent buyer would exert it, since it had to have regard to the general prosperity of the industry, including its exports and its research programme. It is certainly true, that, despite the fact that within the NHS the DHSS is a monopoly purchaser, it has never bargained on equal terms with the monopolist sellers of drugs. This dual function for the DHSS is corporatist in concept and a separation might both cut NHS prices and make the industry more competitive in exports.

The VPRS requires any manufacturer with a reasonable level of sales to the NHS to provide detailed Annual Financial Returns to the DHSS, giving details of profits and costs. It requires departmental approval for any price rise. The price is justified not so much on what is reasonable for the specific drug but more by the overall profit position of the company. It puts immense power of discretion in the hands of a few civil servants. The degree of interference from government through VPRS is surprising given that the industry is so strongly international in character. In 1970 the ten largest manufacturers supplied 31 per cent of the world market and the four major UK companies were respectively Glaxo (16th), Wellcome (25th), Beecham (26th) and ICI (37th) in the list of the forty top pharmaceutical companies. The VPRS depends on information supplied by the companies but it is hard to check information supplied by the companies and impossible to check information held overseas. The Labour Party in May 1976 published a Working Group Report which carefully analysed the industry, and since at the time I was both the Minister of Health responsible for the industry and Chairman of the Group it had unique access to all the factual information on the industry held by the DHSS, except for what was commercially confidential. The Group realised that total nationalisation of such an international industry was out of the question, but it urged many specific changes, the most important of which were that VPRS should be opened up and placed on a statutory basis, that the Annual Financial Returns should be extended into the type of information covered by Planning Agreements such as investment intentions, industrial relations and research and development, and that there should be an investigative element, developed to confirm the accuracy of information given by companies to the government, particularly over transfer prices. The Group also gave several sound reasons why the State should take a major interest in a British pharmaceutical company.[2]

The objective case for the acquisition of a state-owned commercially run pharmaceutical company is dependent on the unique relationship of the industry to the NHS. Such a company would give the government accurate independent knowledge of the industry and it could also introduce a more effective element of competition into the industry. As the government already controls the industry's profits, there is a tendency among the multinationals to allow another company to monopolise a certain drug and introduce it first on the British market on the basis that they in turn will be given a clear run by other companies over a new drug developed by their company. Section 41 of the Medicines Act was introduced specifically to allow a company to challenge the right to exclusive manufacture within the patent life of a product if it felt it could manufacture it profitably in spite of the patent licence fee because the price being charged was so high. The power has very rarely been invoked because of a reluctance to operate against each other by the major multinational pharmaceutical companies. Although a public sector company should not need to make frequent use of the existing Section 41 of the Medicines Act it could do so, against either UK or foreign firms. Another existing power is that under Section 46, where if it is thought that a company is operating its patent in a way that is prejudicial to the NHS, it can be challenged by the government – if it can persuade a company to manufacture. Here a public sector company would respond to the request of the government because of its shareholding, whereas at present the government would have great difficulty in persuading any major multinational company to act, even if British owned.

The government could also use more easily a company within the public sector for basic long-term research, in areas of major social importance, where there is no immediate prospect of commercial success. In addition, bodies such as the Medical Research Council, universities, and hospitals

233

might find it easier to establish structural links with a public company than with a purely private company, and could choose it as the channel for the commercial development of products emerging from government-financed or academic research. A public sector company would give those who operated the VPRS access to more detailed information on production and other costs, including the all-important research and transfer price costs in the industry. Though it would be only over a limited product range, depending on the size of the public sector company, it would still give a valuable insight into the pricing structure of the industry over which the government at present exercises its controls on trust. The advantages would be primarily to the NHS not to industrial policy if the National Enterprise Board acquired a major interest – it does not have to be a controlling interest to achieve its purpose – in one major UK-owned company with an interest in pharmaceuticals. The company would operate commercially, buying and selling at home and abroad, with the same commercial freedoms in all respects as a private sector company. This was the way in which BNOC contributed to the knowledge of the oil industry in the Department of Energy, as described in Chapter 9 on Energy Policy. A state pharmaceutical company could contribute knowledge within the Department of Health and Social Security which would then influence the way in which the VPRS system operated. It would not be a 'spy' within the industry but an objective source of information of a kind which the industry is already expected to provide for government. Its purchase cannot, however, be regarded as of the highest priority. It would not justify being the first call on the money available for industrial investment because the industry is a successful exporter, and the existing control system is fairly effective.

This account shows how in computers and pharmaceuticals the state has exercised its influence and can further develop its influence with a flexible approach, mixing informal and formal involvement, controls and ownership. It is this sort of approach which should be carried into other areas and which offers a sensible non-doctrinaire approach to the essentially practical issue of exerting the national interest within the framework of internationally competitive industrial markets. It is also an approach which can protect good labour relations, promote genuine industrial democracy and also see that profits are both re-invested and returned to improve the standard of living of the workpeople.

An unresolved question for the 1980s is whether government involvement in British Leyland can ensure that the company becomes as successful as the French nationalised company, Renault. In the early 1960s Renault was in serious financial difficulties and had problems over its product range, rather like British Leyland has today. Now, at the beginning of the 1980s Renault is expanding, while most of its competitors, including British Leyland, are contracting. Whereas British Leyland in 1980 was struggling to maintain 20 per cent of the UK market share and exported only 25 per cent of its output, Renault had 40 per cent of the French market and was exporting 60 per cent of its output. The Board of the Renault holding company includes civil servants, directors and worker directors, which ensures that the government and the work-force know what is happening inside the company and disposes of the need for much of the formal presentation of forward plans and investment needs. The government appoints the head of the company, as the British government does with British Leyland, but there is a tradition of appointing from within the company. The French government's relation-ship with Renault is an example of the sort of informal working relationship in which the French specialise and which has been one of the hallmarks of ICL's relationship with government, but, crucially – as in the case of successive British governments with ICL – the French government has been prepared, though the sole shareholder in Renault, to leave the company total commercial freedom. It has been an amazing record of success, with the company generating most of its own financial needs and being free to borrow on international money markets. An answer to those who, from a socialist viewpoint, question why a nationalised company should be given freedom to operate commercially, is that Renault claims that its wages in 1980 were 17 per cent above the rates paid to workers in comparable jobs, though this has not always been the case, and that the government as shareholder has been content to accept lower profitability in order to sustain these higher wage rates. British Leyland workers ought to be encouraged to believe in a similar return: if the company starts to operate commercially and generates sufficient profits to cover its future investment programme then it too ought to be able to operate on a lower rate of distributed profit to government as the shareholder than a private company with public equity capital. Renault openly admit that if the wages and salaries they paid in 1980 had been fixed at the same level as that of their competitors in France then they would have earned an extra billion francs a year. This demonstrates that a state owned enterprise can be commercially profitable but ensure that it returns the wealth generated by its employees in above average earnings and good working conditions. This is market socialism in practice, not just in theory.

11

Co-operatives

Britain is the home of the co-operative movement but there is little public knowledge of its vitality as a world movement. The Rochdale Pioneers founded the first really successful consumers' co-operative in Britain in 1844, but co-operative productive societies have been less successful. The International Co-operative Alliance has 356 million members and over 35 per cent of these are part of the consumer movement.[1] Consumer co-operatives, with few exceptions, do not try to involve their employees in their co-operative structure but operate the normal hierarchical system, with trade unions representing the interests of employees and management representing the interests of the society and its members. The same organisational structure is adopted by the co-operative banking sector and its equivalent, the credit unions. This sector is very large internationally with 90 million members, 57,000 credit unions with a total world savings of some $40 billion. In France the Crédit Agricole is the second biggest bank in the world after the Bank of America, while the Norinchukin Bank in Japan is number fifteen in the Bankers' top 100 listing – making it larger than Barclays. In the UK the Co-op Bank's 700,000 accounts are increasing by 15 per cent a year. Over the last decade it has grown faster than any other UK bank. It is due to double in size over the next five years, but even then it is relatively small compared with the big banks: at present it is one-tenth of the size of Lloyds. The UK has 55 credit unions with 6,000[2] members and savings of around £600,000 – whereas, for example the US has 20,000 credit unions and 22 million members, Canada 6 million and West Germany 3 million members. In Britain housing co-operatives have grown rapidly in number from 60 in 1976 to over 350 in 1980 and more than 10,000 people have joined them.

For socialists in Britain the continued strength of the Co-operative Societies is of the first importance. It is a demonstration that private profit is not the only model for operating within a market-orientated mixed economy. It is a movement which enshrines not only the principles of democracy but also the sovereignty of the consumer and it could become the focus for the revival of socialist values which many yearn for. Nor should we become defeatist about its strength. The Co-op employs one-third of a million people, has 150 factories, is Britain's biggest farmer, and biggest undertaker, operates the sixth largest deposit bank and the ninth largest mutual insurance company. Through its links with the Co-op Party, the co-operative movement helps the Labour movement not only by sponsoring MPs but also by researching policies. Yet sadly this linkage is weaker than it should be. The argument for nationalising all the banks carries little conviction when socialists do little to ensure that the Co-operative Bank becomes the largest bank in the country. If every socialist who now has a private sector bank account made a switch from his or her present banking arrangements, the effect could be dramatic.

It is in the agricultural co-operatives that we see the involvement of the producer or the worker and a mix of both production and marketing, and it is to their experience that any assessment of the potential of industrial co-operatives must look. The major incentive to their formation is that they allow for the sharing of expensive machinery and the establishment of a stronger selling unit to the highly concentrated and competitive food processing industry. They are a major element in the international co-operative movement – for instance, half a dozen US agricultural co-ops are among *Fortune* Magazine's 500 largest firms. Few people in the UK are aware of the potential and there is a tendency to think of the Soviet Union when there is talk about agricultural co-operatives. But they are in fact strong in the United Kingdom. The movement here has been in existence since 1867 and since 1900 has had a central organisation responsible for advice, promotion and co-ordination. In 1977-8 agricultural and horticultural co-operatives had a turnover of £1,315 million,[3] and this is still increasing. These figures include both production and marketing; sales were about one-seventh of the UK agricultural output.

A producing co-operative in most cases appoints a full-time management and a workforce for which it pays market rates. Management is answerable to the management board elected annually by the members. A member is responsible for employing his own workforce. Thus the agricultural co-operative involves one level of producers, the farm owner, it does not attempt to involve the farm worker or the employees of the co-operative itself unless one of its members also takes on management responsibilities within the co-operative. The UK agricultural co-operatives' record of success clearly demonstrates that a democratic organisation can make difficult decisions relating to capital investment, the allocation of equipment in unpredictable weather and unpredictable market conditions, that it can market the producers' product and make quick marketing decisions in the interests of all. These are significant areas of decision-making which go well beyond the consumer co-operatives' price and product responsibilities to their consumers. But in the UK and in most western countries the experience of agricultural co-operatives does not extend to the involvement of all its work people and to resolving the potentially conflicting interests of farm workers and farm owners or managers.

The dilemma of the retail movement is that it frequently faces a choice between social responsibility and the conventional pursuit of profitability, operating as it does in an environment dominated by profitability and price competition. This is not to argue that co-operatives cannot compete, but rather that they cannot ignore the dangers implicit in sticking relentlessly to their social ideals if this means neglecting the overriding need to remain price-competitive and prove their superiority over conventional forms of business organisation. The consumer societies of Sweden and Switzerland have recently faced similar problems and are being forced to re-examine their social goals.[4] Some rationalisation of consumer co-operative is inevitable with margins being so squeezed by competition that they have to ensure some of the financial benefits of size in production and ordering. Yet they must also listen to local and regional feelings about their social role if they are to retain the sense that the co-operative movement offers more than just the right goods at the right price.

The retail societies have suffered a decline in their share of the market, from 8·7 per cent of all retailing in 1966 to 6·7 per cent in 1979 – although the share is higher in regions like Scotland where the Labour movement is stronger. Total sales in 1979 were 3·5 billion, with sales of 1·6 billion by the Co-operative Wholesale Society which is owned by the retail societies, making it Europe's largest wholesaler. The Co-op's share of packaged groceries is 16·6 per cent, not far ahead of Tesco with 14·7 per cent. Some see in these figures serious cause for concern. Membership is also falling, from 12·1 million in 1970 to 10·4 million in 1979, although the rate of decline has fallen recently. This has had the result that members' share capital is not as important as formerly and the co-ops have suffered from a lack of funds for investment. Dividends have fallen from 2·1 per cent of sales in 1969 to 1·0 per cent in 1979, which must have affected members' identi-fication.

Some of the reasons for this decline are structural and historic and are not of themselves a sign of fundamental weakness within the movement. The Co-ops have had to carry a legacy of old and inefficient stores, they have specialised in groceries to a greater extent than their competitors – 75 per cent of sales compared with Tesco's 66 per cent – and groceries is a market which is not growing rapidly and where margins are lower than with non-food lines. In addition, their average store size is small, many are located in decaying inner city areas facing depopulation, and there is a tradition that small stores in rural areas should be kept open for social reasons. If social sentiment at times is to weigh stronger than economics, then one cannot both praise democratic decision-making and baulk at its consequences.

Similarly how important in the context of economics is lack of centralisation? In 1974 the Co-op Congress resolved to decrease the number of societies to 27 by 1980 but there are still 189 societies. In Scotland there were 54 independent societies in 1980 and a dozen of these had a turnover of less than 1 million. It is argued with some justice that the consequences of this large number of independent societies is that they do not enjoy the economics of scale that other supermarket chains have enjoyed and which are so necessary in the retail business where margins are kept very tight. The Co-operative Wholesale Society, set up in 1963 to buy in bulk for the retail societies, today provides about two-thirds of their need as well as undertaking the manufacture of more items. The National Co-operative Chemists, which undertakes centralised buying, has proved to be profitable. A limited amount of central buying has already been undertaken in England, based on sixteen regional distribution centres servicing societies which account for 62 per cent of Co-op trade. It is impossible to deny that great rationalisation in this direction should help to improve efficiency and hold the share of the market, but there are limits to the benefits it can achieve and it has the obvious drawback of centralising and thereby weakening democratic control by the members.

Democracy and decentralisation go hand in hand. There is a conflict between 'efficiency', as conventionally measured in financial terms, and 'democracy', but since the profits are not being creamed off, as with Tesco, some of the Co-operative profits can and should go in paying for democracy. Debates in recent years at the Co-operative Union Congress show that the main objection to plans for centralisation – or even Co-op Great Britain, though that is a different concept and more of a rationalisation – is that it is feared that the Co-op will lose its democratic character and that initiatives will increasingly come from the national organisation rather than from members. People are right to guard the democracy of the movement and the power of local initiative. If this is eroded, the Co-op will cease to be a movement and will become merely another trading organisation. A paper presented at the 1977 Co-op Union Congress by Roger Kerinec, from the French retail

241

societies, argued that centralisation has been achieved in France and has greatly improved efficiency without reducing democracy. But before taking a massive single step into the unknown of a totally unified structure, it would be far wiser to speed progress towards the 1974 objective of 27 societies. The co-operative movement will be best served by re-emphasising a commitment to the right mix of efficiency and democracy. To go for total centralisation would be to go against the present healthy trend of questioning all past centralising measures and the growing wish for greater measures of decentralisation.

Recent research[5] has found no correlation between the size of a society and its level of profitability – except in the case of the larger societies which exhibit a weak correlation between their size and their poor trading position. Small societies have been able to retain a degree of local involvement and identification which has allowed them to remain profitable and responsive to local needs. They retain the loyalty of members which was widespread as little as ten years ago and which has waned in the larger societies. In 1979 losses and gains in membership were fairly closely associated with trading performance, with a good performance, usually by a small society, leading to a growth in membership. This suggests that amalgamations and centralisation do not necessarily create more efficient societies and that the scope for economies of scale is not great. Merger activity has slowed down as it has been realised that increase in size tends to lose the movement members.

It has been suggested that a better orientation for the Co-op would be to return to their original goal of meeting the needs of consumers which are neglected by the retail multiples. A precondition for this would be to revive the participation of members by giving local shop committees specific powers of control over their local shops. Postal ballots, already in use in Leeds, along with the provision of more information for members, could create a more aware electorate and a greater sense of loyalty. Better society newspapers, with less emphasis on conventional promotion of goods, and the provision of advice bureaux in shops could help to underline the difference between the Co-op and the high street multiples. The dividend could be brought back, with the aid of micro-electronics to save clerical costs, by way of member cards, as used in Sweden, which like a banker's card, can be inserted in a till which records the amount of purchases and computes the dividend. More staff involvement, perhaps by the formation of staff co-operatives to manage shops, could be encouraged and need not cut across the democratic control of shops by members. Some societies have already encouraged play-group co-operatives, bulk buying by groups such as old age pensioners or, as in Tower Hamlets in London, a motor repair co-operative for the use of members. There remains enormous scope for the setting up of credit unions and for the delivery, by co-op milkmen, of a wider range of goods.

Co-ops are starting to develop the concept of the social dividend and investing in their local areas to demonstrate that they have social goals which relate to the communities they serve. They should aim to provide the consumer with a distinctive service, more information about products as regards price, quality and health features than would be found in a privately-run shop. Co-op retailers in the United States have found that consumers are receptive to ideas of this kind and that new loyalties are developed.

The Co-op Bank, although it is growing rapidly and is reporting record profit figures, could also make use of its separate identity to pursue social and industrial objectives which would make it even more distinct from other banks and thereby attract more deposits from trade unions and from those many trade unionists who are largely still without bank accounts. What is needed is a revival of a spirit of co-operation in which the societies, the bank, the producer co-operative, the insurance and mortgage co-operative, the housing co-operative and the Co-operative Development Agency might all see themselves as part of a mutual self-helping co-operative.

Industrial or producer co-operatives which involve worker owners have never had the mass international and national membership of other parts of the co-operative movement, but there is recent evidence of a rapid worldwide growth in this area. The French and Italian co-operatives in particular have demonstrated a capacity to survive and prosper in economies similar to the British. Italy has some 3,000 co-operatives employing 160,000 people, mostly in communist-controlled regions such as Bologna; there are some 100 co-operatives in Demark and 40 in Switzerland. Further afield and in different circumstances, there are 2,400 in Poland, 1,000 in Hungary and some 20,000 in India.[6]

It is significant that France, which has a deep historic commitment to decentralised socialism and is still strongly influenced by the Proudhonist tradition, should have 556 producer co-operatives employing an estimated 30,000 people. The biggest, L'Association des Ouvriers en Instruments de Précision, employs 4,500 and has shown the management ability to move into the high technology area of micro-chips, industrial robots and telecommunications, although its fortunes have been mixed.[7] It is also interesting, given the present dissatisfaction within the UK construction industry and the arguments within the Labour Party about nationalisation of the industry, that over 50 per cent of the French co-operatives are in building and construction and only 14 per cent in engineering and 11 per cent in printing, the more traditional areas for industrial co-operatives. In France the building co-operatives of L'Hirondelle and L'Avenir each employ more than 1,000 workers, showing that in Britain there is considerable scope for the extension of co-operative ownership to this largely small-scale industry.

In Spain, as in France, the decentralist socialist tradition is strong. It is particularly strong at Mondragon in the Basque region where there is the most interesting development in industrial co-operatives in the world. In the last twenty-five years more than 70 co-operatives have been set up, creating more than 18,000 jobs and having a turnover of £244 million in 1979. The largest employs 3,500 people and is Spain's leading manufacturer of refrigerators, cookers and washing machines. Mondragon members earn more than they could in comparable jobs elsewhere and the older workers are retiring on two-thirds pensions, taking with them capital sums of between £20,000 and £40,000, the amount depending on length of employment and the type of job held. A Basque member is required to put at least £1,000 into the venture when he joins. On this the co-operative pays 6 per cent interest, which he can withdraw as conditions permit. Out of the co-operative's profits, at least 10 per cent must be put away into the Social Fund to finance social projects in the area chosen by the workers, 20 per cent is invested in collective reserves and the other 70 per cent is distributed among members according to a points system reflecting job status. The money is credited to each account, but cannot be withdrawn until a member leaves – or else 20 per cent may be deducted. If the co-operative makes a loss this too will be debited. There has only ever been one failure – ironically a fishery co-operative funded by the state, as a result of which workers' stakes were small. In the history of Mondragon there has only ever been one strike, at ULGOR, the largest co-operative, over the regrading of some jobs. The problem was one of size and now the group policy is to keep co-operatives below 500 jobs, although with typical good sense the Basques remain flexible on this issue.[8]

Britain has some long-standing producer co-operatives. Walsall Locks has been making locks since 1874; Equity Shoe in Leicester has been turning out ladies' footwear since 1893 and paid a bonus on wages of 20 per cent in 1977, and there are about a dozen others. A study of those that have survived from 1913 shows that their labour force is roughly the same as in 1913, and although some of them have expanded and taken over private firms the record is mixed. It has been argued that 'the only legitimate verdict on the experience of the old "cloth cap" co-ops is one of "not proven",'[9] since they have not been fully democratic, they have not sought the best management talent, and they have not had the support of the labour movement or the government. They have also had a large number of retired members, as well as institutions, holding shares, while some of the workforce are not members – all of which undermines the commitment of the worker-owners. In recent years, however, the number of industrial co-ops in Britain has grown. A hundred years ago there were only some fifteen. This grew rapidly to a peak of 109 in 1905 and then held steady around 80 to 90 until, in 1977, there were only 75. Since then there has been a dramatic increase: 148 in 1978, 162 in 1979 and more than 300 in 1980.

Yet the success of these new co-operatives has made few headlines. In contrast the press exposure given to Meriden, Kirkby Manufacturing and Engineering (KME) and the *Scottish Daily News* has given the impression that co-operatives are inherently financially unsound. The pity is that when people talk about co-ops they think of these three ventures. All three enterprises inherited very bad market positions. In the case of Meriden, action should have been taken ten years before to help the motor cycle industry, while at KME five previous owners had never been able to make a profit out of a factory built to hold 3,000 workers but having only 1,000 at the time of the takeover – hence the large overheads.[10] The *Scottish Daily News*, previously the *Scottish Daily Express*, faced the problem of virtually starting a new daily newspaper, using machinery that had lain idle for a considerable period. The co-operative lacked sufficient working capital to cover the large costs of starting production and, as a result, the co-operative lasted only from May to October 1974. There has also been strong criticism of the failure of the journalists to develop a new format for the paper. The market position of the paper was always extremely bad and it is doubtful whether the job-saving exercise could possibly have survived, even with more help from the government.[11]

At KME it is valid to say that the factory never really operated as a co-operative, since the workers never held all the equity and were consulted only sporadically. It remained under the control of the unions and was seen as primarily a job-saving operation. A Department of Industry report said that it was 'not a co-operative in the same sense that this term would be understood by the co-operative movement as a whole – communication between management and the shop floor in KME seems no better and, in some ways, worse than in most other companies'. A 1977 survey carried out by the Manchester University Business School confirms this impression and concluded that 'little change is seen in the way the factory is run and many see a reversion to traditional management and union attitudes . . . there is a lack of meetings of all sorts and a general lack of discussion.'[12] Other factors at KME hampered its chances. It was opposed by Whitehall and it paid too much for the building and stocks it inherited. It also lacked a managing director, failed to raise its prices and – perhaps the greatest problem – it kept 200 surplus workers on the payroll.

The Meriden motor cycle co-operative had considerable difficulty in making interest payments on the initial £4.2 million loan from the government which provided 85 per cent of the capital. This could have been non-voting redeemable preference shares, but instead the enterprise was set up as a trust holding all the shares so that there was no member investment and no member participation in the growth of assets when earnings were ploughed back. When it was founded in March 1975 after an 18-month occupation, the savings of the workers, and to some extent their idealism, were strained. Yet some provision could have been made for worker investment to promote commitment; as it was workers who had to accept lower wages than for comparable jobs elsewhere in Coventry.[13]

The disappointing record of these three experiments should not be taken as typical of co-operative ventures in general. Government intervention in all three cases was an example of failure to match genuine ideological enthusiasm to a hard-headed and realistic assessment of the facts. Socialists need to ensure that interventionist policies are buttressed by the evidence and are not destroyed by naivety. 'Blurring the distinction between lame duck rescue operations (however necessary) and the establishment of viable worker co-operatives merely damages the credibility of both.'[14] Hasty and ill-planned attempts to save jobs in uneconomic enterprises does not constitute a proper experiment in co-operation. Little care was taken to set up fully democratic enterprises and the lesson is 'that if workers' co-operatives are incorrectly structured they may even generate more conflict than conventional enterprise'.[15]

This view found a wider audience when the Wilson Report stated that, 'Our impression is that the well-publicised failure of some of these latter enterprises had led traditional sources of finance to approach many worthwhile co-operative projects requiring start-up capital with excessive caution. But the failures have generally been related to a basic lack of viability in the enterprise rather than to the form of organisation involved. Properly conceived small-scale co-operatives seems to us to have a potentially useful role in the economy.'[16]

The Labour Party National Executive Committee discussion document on Workers' Co-operatives contains much good sense and positive suggestions. Two clear statements in particular are worth quoting: 'The first task for Labour is to accept that bona fide co-operative enterprise is a perfectly valid and desirable form of social or common ownership' and 'We believe that the co-operative form of organisation offers a true socialist approach to economic planning and development.' Unfortunately the whole impact of the document has been distorted and spoilt by the highly controversial right-to-convert proposal, of which the Secretary of the Co-operative Party wrote that it is 'ill-considered, irrelevant, unworkable and non-co-operative'.

The proposal, in spite of some hedging, 'envisages an open-ended commitment to give to the workers the right to take-over throughout the whole of private industry'. This is wrong in principle. No private company could prosper under permanent threat of compulsory nationalisation. Co-operatives must be seen primarily as a first resort, as a positive development; not, as is too often the case, as merely a last resort. As the NEC document itself argues, in referring to voluntary conversions, 'the legacy of private enterprise failure is the worst possible one for a newly found co-operative'. It has a procedure supposedly to ensure that statutory conversion schemes are vetted by a Co-operative Development Advisory Board, but it is unlikely the Board would welcome such a task, since it would damage their positive role as the encourager and stimulator of co-operatives. The compulsory approach is justified because 'the number of purely voluntary conversions would most probably be small even given further tax advantages', but no evidence is brought forward to support this assertion. Nor is it clear how much, if any, compensation would be paid to the former owners and how businesses would be valued for this purpose.

The proposal is wrong; it will create very great uncertainty, it will not be accepted by the broad mass of co-operators, and it ought to be rejected. It is a reflection of the authoritarianism of much of the NEC's attitudes to the mixed economy, and few would support co-operation by diktat.

Equally damaging, when the co-operative sector needs help from many different quarters, is the NEC's inflexibility about the form co-operatives should take. The document states that 'equity capital, whether private or state, is ruled out, as is participation by other non-members such as consumers'; and that 'although the Mondragon co-operatives is our preferred definition, this emphasis on individual rather than collective ownership makes the model unacceptable to the working group'. This last comment seems especially dogmatic when the document itself notes that the economic record of the Mondragon group has been excellent and admired worldwide. It is also contradictory since industrial contributions and benefits are fundamental to the Mondragon system.

However, the discussion document also contains a minority proposal for an alternative and more attractive approach which would give workers in private firms a statutory right to begin a conversion procedure without government permission in certain clearly defined circumstances. The circumstances mentioned are in the event of a takeover, a proposed closure of the transfer of production to another site, and if asset stripping were taking place. The transfer mechanism advocated in the case of small firms would be for the workforce to buy the firm from the owners out of future profits and, for larger firms, by an employees' share fund with re-invested profits being used to buy up the voting stock of the company.

This approach would not have the grave disadvantages of the right-to-convert proposal. The provision for conversion would come into operation only when the existing owners had already decided to end or reduce their commitment to an enterprise and where this was likely to have severe consequences for the workforce. It would be a natural extension of the rights to employees to be consulted on matters of vital interest and it would not interfere with the management of successful businesses. The rights of shareholders would be safeguarded by the need for the workforce to match the best commercial bid for the assets of the firm.

The success of co-operatives in France and Italy and the outstanding example of Mondragon shows that many of the traditional criticisms of co-operatives have been invalidated. Critics from both the Left and the Right have argued that average citizens are not competent to run their own enterprises, the co-ops fragment working-class solidarity, and that they are bound to degenerate into capitalist firms or become a form of workers' capitalism. Miss Potter, the future Beatrice Webb, writing in 1891 expressed what was to become the consensus Labour Party viewpoint: 'The ideal . . . of a self-governing co-operative workshop . . . vanishes into an indescribable industrial phantom . . . in all cases, without a single exception outside shareholders hold the balance of power. Nor is this all; the minority of working shareholders are practically disenfranchised by the disqualification to act on the committee of management . . . So called associations of workers are constantly resolving themselves into associations of small masters . . . '[17] By 1921 the Webbs were even more strongly opposed: 'All such associations of producers that start as alternatives to the Capitalist System either fail or cease to be Democracies of producers.'[18] Derek Jones has conducted a thorough study of the statistical methods adopted by the Webbs and concludes that 'the Webbs' ideological stance impaired their objectivity and that as a result their data were misleading and inadequate.'[19] Of even greater importance is the fact that, as Oakshott argues, 'having correctly identified serious structural weaknesses in the producer co-ops of their day, the Webbs did not go on to point out that two fairly simple rule changes would be sufficient to eliminate them'.[20]

A stronger criticism is that the establishment of co-ops cannot build socialism in a market economy since, according to Ernest Mandel: 'In the present economic system, a whole series of decisions are inevitably taken at higher levels than the factory, and if these decisions are not consciously made by the working class as a whole then they will be made by other forces in society behind the workers' backs.'[21] The argument against the purist view, that only nationalisation offers the way forward through the regulation of all industrial activity, is put by Coates, arguing that: 'In the context of modern Britain, new co-operatives raise trade union self-confidence, and stimulate the demand for democratisation of public sector industries at the same time that they undermine the assumption of the inevitable rectitude of managerial prerogatives. If there is no breakthrough on the overall political plane, of course we can have no reason to imagine that the market pressures to which such co-operatives will be exposed will not succeed in eroding their limited independence and autonomy.'[22]

Other, more pragmatic, objections have come from the labour movement regarding the position of trade unions in co-ops, since it is recognised that a union role there is likely to be very different. Nationally negotiated wage rises may be foregone by trade unionists concerned about the survival of their co-operative, while the traditional bargaining role of trade unions will no longer be appropriate when factories are owned by their workers. Socialists also argue that weakened unions and rather insular groups of workers will prevent the labour movement from concerning itself with the wider issues of social equity. It will be pointed out, by critics on both the Left and the Right, that Mondragon has been successful because the co-ops grew up during the period when free trade unions were forbidden by Franco. The situation in Mondragon is indeed unique in that Spanish unions are still very weak. In Britain, however, trade union influence will remain since a large part of the economy will not be co-operative in the near future, and they can also play an important part in promoting co-operatives, as is done in Holland, where the ABC federation of Dutch trade unions, via the union-controlled Koopmans bank, are prepared to finance co-operatives.

It is very important that the trade unions do not see co-operatives as a threat. Membership of a trade union involves far more than just the negotiating situation in a particular firm; it involves representation of the worker across the whole field of industrial legislation, health and safety and national policy. In the substantial co-operative sector of the Yugoslav economy the trade unions remain active in protecting the interests of shop floor workers and in helping to make co-operative democracy function more smoothly. In Britain the Co-operative Department Agency encourages members of all industrial co-operatives to join trade unions. As the trade union movement becomes more decentralised and the wage negotiating national power of union leaders diminishes, it is in their interest to encourage the development of co-operatives. There is no need for a conflict of interests.

A further set of objections to industrial co-operatives is the pragmatic argument that they cannot be commercially viable because their democratic structure inhibits the practice of good management, the basic problem being what has been called 'living with the ambiguity of two control systems'.[23] It is argued that the rapid increase of industrial co-operatives in the UK is only a temporary phenomenon and that the historic pattern of decline is the real trend. Yet such research as there is tends to be more encouraging and certainly does not bear out many of the traditional criticisms. The life expectancy of co-operatives does not appear to be lower than that of private enterprise: indeed a 1966 report found that it was higher than that of other small firms. Technical and economic efficiency appears in Britain, France and the United States to bear favourable comparison with private enterprise.[24] Mondragon has a record of twenty years of success.

A more serious criticism is that co-operatives tend to under-invest because other more attractive investment opportunities are available, and that once they have invested and established a good return to their investment there is a reluctance to bring in new members to share that return. Reliable evidence on these issues is difficult to find but it is likely that they have been a limitation. The establishment of a co-operative requires a group of committed motivated people rather than a single capitalist entrepreneur. But there is no logical reason why, if capital should hire labour, labour should not hire capital, as capital grows ever more sceptical of the motivation and commitment of the labour force to private enterprise and as the record on industrial relations and collective bargaining in private enterprise worsens. It is not fanciful to believe, though it may come as a heresy to some, that capital will find that the motivation and commitment of labour in co-operatives make them an attractive investment. Perhaps one of the mistakes of industrial co-operatives has been to expect too much from worker-investment and a worker-stake.

It has to be accepted that it is a natural wish of some workers –maybe the majority – to spread their risk by investing their time and energy in the co-operative, but their money elsewhere. Motivation will vary but a greater emphasis can easily be given to arranging loan finance for co-operatives on commercial terms rather than relying, as a point of principle, on loans from the workers. The British labour movement has also been suspicious of workers investing their savings in the firms that employ them since, as the TUC has argued, 'this doubles the insecurity in situations such as Rolls Royce'.[25] Statements of this nature tend however to ignore the factual evidence afforded by Mondragon, where the workers have enjoyed wages superior to those prevailing in the region, complete job security and a share in profits. Further, as Oakshott argues, the initial capital stake of each worker in Mondragon, £1,000 to £2,000, 'though important enough to ensure commitment and positive motivation is . . . really quite small – not more than 1% or 2% in relation to prospective life-time earnings in the money of the late 1970s'.[26]

The central issue that must be faced is that if industrial co-operatives are to expand, and if their ethos is to influence the general industrial climate, then they will have to benefit from positive discrimination. The faint hearts will argue that all sectors of the economy should be treated the same, but all governments have discriminated in the past between the private or public sectors and when socialist governments are quite prepared to legislate for the nationalisation of whole industries, and to pay a high price in compensation, it is amazing that there has been, in relative terms, so little legislative support for industrial co-operatives. The Co-operative Development Agency Act was helpful, and it is essential that the Co-operative Development Agency get the further finance which the Act allows in September 1981, and that the Industrial Common Ownership Act funding be renewed after that. But marginal changes will not be enough. What is needed is a fiscal revolution, and introduction of a co-operative budget that takes as its central objective the promotion of industrial co-operatives and which is openly and unashamedly discriminatory. Such legislation will challenge the status quo and offend some of the vested interests that have grown used to a comfortable, almost bureaucratic, existence within the corporate state.

It is already clear that the Mondragon rule of a 3:1 salary/wage ratio is not universally applicable and that co-operatives need to have a specifically socialist motivation to include such a formula. Most must be prepared to pay the going rate for management skills to hire talent and expertise. A socialist commitment can be a source of inspiration that helps co-operatives function along democratic lines and with an enthusiasm to undertake sacrifices: 'it may very well be significant that through their development, the Mondragon co-operatives have been closely associated with socialist and nationalist ideals – a point given scant attention by some commentators'.[27] The Scott Bader Commonwealth differs from conventional co-operatives in that it is a community investment without personal investment or personal shareholding. Yet even at Scott Bader a pre-tax ratio of highest to lowest paid of 5:1 has been found to be necessary. Salary scales will therefore tend to differ and attitudes should be kept flexible.

The main reason why the number of industrial co-operatives is still so small is the inability of most groups of workers with ideas to provide sufficient capital from their own resources. If we are to see the growth of co-operatives coming from new enterprises it will be necessary to ensure that potential co-operatives enjoy at least as good an access to capital as do other small firms. The report 'The Financing of Small Firms' set out the difficult position facing small firms in attempting to obtain risk capital: 'There are two main aspects of the banks' relationships with their actual or potential small firm customers to be considered, the availability of finance and the terms on which it is offered. The banks are often alleged to be too cautious about both. Their attitude towards risk, and ability to assess it, are said to make them unnecessarily restrictive in their lending policy, particularly towards new or rapidly expanding firms. In addition the terms on which they do make facilities available are sometimes criticised as being too severe. Rates of interest around 2% higher than those charged to larger businesses appear to be fairly typical and the level of security demanded also tends to be high, with personal guarantees often being required.'[28] The position facing co-operatives is often even worse than this in that banks usually prefer the conventional form of company organisation and are sceptical of the democratic element of participation. In Mondragon this is not a problem as the Caja Laboural Popular (the Co-op bank) loans workers their initial capital stake interest free for 24 months and acts as a source of finance for established co-operatives; and in the United States co-op banks make loans totalling around £7,000 million. The Co-operative Bank in Britain lends merely £25,000 to co-ops and does not have any provision for treating them more favourably than conventional organisations. There is a strong case for financial incentives to be made available to the Co-op Bank for a special Industrial Loan Fund to invest in co-operatives at a low rate of interest and for giving all banks special treatment for co-operative loans. It has also been suggested that co-operatives should be allowed to raise initial share capital from members if this was raised in the form of shares on which an unlimited return would be paid for a specified period. Non-voting shares, as exist in Canada and the USA, could also be issued to non-members to raise outside finance and such shares could be made tradeable in order to increase their attractiveness. This kind of share would also allow trade unions and their pension funds to invest in worthy ventures instead of in land or in conventional firms. The Industrial and Provident Societies Act could be changed to make it clear that membership of a co-operative is not the same thing as shareholding in a co-operative and voting rules could be adjusted accordingly. These forms of outside finance and non-working members are not supported by all groups within the co-operative movement, and while it is important that democratic control by members should not be undermined by an overwhelming source of outside finance the need for proper financing remains paramount.

In some countries, such as Britain and the USA, co-operative law allows the residual assets of a co-operative on winding up to be distributed to shareholders in proportion to shareholdings. In other countries, such as France and Italy, this is prohibited by law and the distribution has to be made in proportion to membership. If a co-operative has some outside shareholding and if a gap develops between share values and asset values, there is a danger in the UK at present of a premature dissolution since the shareholders will want to make a capital gain at the expense of people working in the co-operative. A study of the decline of nineteenth-century producer co-ops, has found that the proportion of share capital owned by workers fell from 25 per cent in 1948 to 18 per cent in 1968. This is likely to have reduced incentives for workers, since the increase in outside shareholding will, if taken too far, gradually turn a co-op into a conventional capitalist business. The UK law should be changed to ensure that distribution on dissolution follows the pattern of member-ship and not of shareholding. It would help co-operatives if investment in co-operatives was made deductible for personal tax purposes and this would be vital if the government were to lift the tax liability from employees when given the option to buy shares from their companies. The rate of corporation tax paid by co-operatives could be further reduced relative to the rate paid by other companies. There could also be tax concessions in relation to personal tax liability on interest on co-operative shares.

Changes in company law are also needed to facilitate the conversion of small businesses to co-operatives when the owner either retires or dies. As the law stands at present, there is very little incentive for the owner to hand over his business to his employees since the employees will be subject to capital gains tax and may therefore have to sell a part of the business, thus defeating the previous employer's whole object of ensuring that the business remains intact and under the control of his previous employees. Such a transfer of owner-ship should be encouraged by the removal of the liability to capital gains tax, as part of a wider package of reforms relieving the burden of tax from the distribution of the shares of business to co-operatives. To encourage such a transfer, it is also important, as previously stressed, to have easily available loan finance.

Existing legislation is currently being examined to see if greater help can be given to ease the problems of a large company wishing to split its operations. Recent research has shown that the 1970s' merger boom did not produce more efficient companies but created unwieldy empires and reduced profit ratios. Large companies now realise that smaller units are often more viable and there is no reason why when splitting parts of a large company there should not be conversion directly into co-operatives. The first publication of the Co-operative Development Agency was about converting a company into a co-operative and this is provided for both in the Industrial and Provident Societies Acts and in the Companies Acts; but it has been discouraged by capital gains tax and capital transfer tax liability at the time of conversion. This problem has been solved to some extent by provisions in the Finance Acts of 1976 and 1978 which provide for exemption from this tax liability if a permanent trust is formed for the benefit of employees. Conversions might be further encouraged if changes were made in company law so as to create a special class of 'co-operative company' with provision for statutory indivisible reserves and if tax arrangements were unashamedly discriminatory. Many of the shareholders in such companies might take the view that community of interest and tax considerations could result in their receiving a better return on their investment than they might otherwise do. Once a number had converted, considerably more might be encouraged to do so.

If the will existed, the government could stimulate the growth of new co-operatives and the number arising through transfers. Even without government stimulus there will be by 1984 something like 500 industrial co-operatives and if a socialist government introduced a Co-operative Budget, this number could be quadrupled within the lifetime of the parliament. Expansion is not an end in itself; the pace should not damage the co-operative ideal and the integrity of the movement. No one knows what level of co-operative development would produce a macro effect on the whole economy but any expansion would produce a beneficial effect on attitudes within industry. There is no immediate likelihood of the solution favoured by Peter Jay of a single legislative switch to a workers' co-operative economy. The way forward over the next decade will be through the steady introduction of piecemeal changes[29] but the bolder approach may be not as futuristic as it at present appears if the movement towards co-operation gathers momentum and gains an aura of success, then a co-operative economy may not seem as improbable as at present. It is a far more socialist concept than a state run economy, and offers a solution to both inflation and alienation.

Proposals for the nationalisation of the construction industry have nothing to recommend them. The alternative decision to stimulate construction co-operatives, as a major initiative is, however, a practical, worthwhile proposition. Central purchasing arrangements such as have been made in Denmark, for example, for building materials, could be established. Legislation could, as in France, lay down that a percentage of all local authority contracts would have to be given to building co-operatives. If then local authorities sought to use co-operatives as well as or instead of employing direct labour, this would not only stimulate the formation of co-operatives but have a significant effect on the construction industry. There are some sectors of industry where the investment needed is too large to allow much prospect of developing co-operatives and experience suggests that the co-operative system is not best suited to large firms. For the next few decades there is going to be a significant private sector in this country made up of large firms, multinationals and small family businesses. A policy of stimulating the extension of industrial co-operatives should not aim at destroying the private sector but at so changing workers' attitudes that they will act themselves to reduce the size of the private sector.

The development of co-operatives is a move towards a decentralised society, and is a genuine third way in the polarised debate about workers and owners. What is needed is a political timetable that starts to lay the groundwork for profound changes of attitude over a period of decades, not just a five-year electoral period. Realistic market socialism is much needed, with an emphasis on efficiency and competition. A mixed economy would still exist but private industry would be balanced by co-operatives, not only by a state sector. The state sector would expand only if it was the most suitable alternative. This would allow a better balance to be struck in the dialogue between management, unions and government. Co-operative ideas would influence all three elements. Nationalisation as the only form of common ownership is clearly not attractive to voters or to many employees of nationalised industries. Measures to impose state control on industries run the risk of being regularly reversed by incoming Conservative governments. It is a repetitive, politically sterile cycle that could be broken through co-operation.

Co-operation offers the most radical and refreshing way of changing our industrial structure to gain the benefits of common ownership. To be convincing it is necessary to widen Britain's understanding of what is happening overseas. But a new political commitment must also be awakened to cherish, stimulate and encourage co-operatives. The ultimate stimulus will come not from government but from people themselves wanting to develop co-operatives. The task now is to help that wish for co-operation to find practical expression in industry up and down the country.

12

Industrial Democracy

Industrial democracy must be an essential element in any serious attempt to move towards a more decentralised democratic society. It is not surprising, therefore, that it was the ideal of workers' control that lay behind much of the debate between socialist centralists and the decentralists before the First World War, an argument which was briefly traced in Chapter 2 on the Decentralist Tradition. Nor is it anything other than inevitable that if the growing corporatism and its manifestations are rejected (see Chapter 3), the natural replacement of corporatism will be a revival of the power of parliamentary democracy and the extension of democracy into the place of work.

Centralism and corporation flourish on the mix of an Executive unchecked by Members of Parliament, on employers' organisations unable to reflect the specific views of individual companies, and trade union leaders unable fully to reflect the differing shades of the wide spectrum of views within very different unions. The arguments against corporatism do not seek to undermine 'tripartism' and the considerable value of management, unions and government reaching agreements and understandings. For industrial democracy itself is concerned with the means whereby such agreement and understanding can be reached at different levels, affecting people's working life, embracing far more than wages or salaries, or even pension or sickness benefits or health and safety arrangements. It covers the range of issues which affect the running of the country's economic and industrial affairs and the decisions of individual companies on their own economic and industrial activity. It is a considerable extension of the process of free collective bargaining, but complementary to it. Industrial democracy also seeks to do more than merely widen the subjects of discussion between management and workers, since its aim is to increase participation as of right by the workforce at all levels. Democracy means the number of workers having a say in decisions that affect them being greatly increased and the process of decision-making being seen to be openly democratic with the widespread use of secret ballots.

To be effective and radical industrial democracy needs to do much more than transfer power from managers to trade union officials or shop stewards. To succeed it needs to involve individual workers on a wide range of issues. It will be argued that this carries a cost in terms of money and slower decision-making. Some have attempted to quantify this, citing the Works Council and Co-Determination Laws in West Germany. But what also carries a cost is industrial disputes, avoidable alienation, and poor productivity stemming from boredom and lack of interest. By relying on agreement through open democratic procedures or openly agreed arbitration, industrial democracy represents consensus in the sense that democracy itself is in part a consensual process. But the essence of democracy is that it allows the majority view to prevail, so that industrial democracy does not have the limitations imposed by consensus arrangements, whereby everyone has to agree and where unrepresentative minority viewpoints can inhibit agreement, or when industrial action cannot be taken until there is an agreement. Balloting the workforce allows for a decisive decision to be taken in circumstances where the minority finds it acceptable to go along with the view of the majority.

The Bullock Report found widespread recognition for what the European Community Green Paper called a 'democratic imperative' that 'those who will be substantially affected by decisions made by social and political institutions must be involved in the making of those decisions.'[1] The Report found that in the last twenty years giant industrial enterprises have come to predominate, placing economic power in fewer hands and resulting in decision-making becoming increasingly remote from the people who will be affected by the decisions. The pace of change has also accelerated with the introduction of new technologies. In increasingly competitive world markets, managers have found that they need to be responsive to change if they are to survive. Such changes have been frequently resisted by employees and it is now more widely recognised that not only have employees a legitimate right to be involved in the taking of decisions which vitally affect the continued existence of their jobs, but that if they are not involved their resistance to change is invariably greater. The ailing economy of Britain has often been compared unfavourably with the growth record of the German economy and it has been asked whether the existence of forms of industrial democracy in West Germany has contributed to its success. It would be unwise to attribute too much to the existence of varying manifestations of industrial democracy there, but some significance should be attached to their contribution. The West German system, dating from 1950-1, has meant good industrial relations and a strong realisation of commercial realities by trade unionists, of the importance of maintaining existing markets and winning new orders.

Rising standards of education and a higher standard of living have produced less deferential workers who are unwilling to tolerate old-fashioned autocratic management methods and who feel able to participate in making decisions. Management has also realised that such workers can make a very real contribution if their energy and experience is harnessed to constructive ends. In a letter to his managing directors Sir Arnold Weinstock of GEC, where management techniques are controversial though arguably successful, admitted that 'if the skills, experience and intelligence of workers can be harnessed constructively in the operation of industry, if the attitudes of management and workers can be brought together in effective co-operation, then there would follow a great upsurge in industrial efficiency and a general atmosphere of relative satisfaction.'[2]

The argument is over how best such a harnessing can be achieved. GEC does not support legislation imposing industrial democracy but favours informational exchange. Yet it has been widely recognised by many managers in British industry that some form of industrial democracy will bring substantial benefits to all concerned. For the socialist there is the additional attraction that industrial democracy is an end in itself; the making accountable of concentrations of economic power, whether that power is found in the public or the private sectors. The fundamental question is the method to be used to introduce industrial democracy – persuasion or legislation.

The revival of interest in industrial democracy began in the 1960s; in part it reflected the direct outcome of frustrations felt by many trade unionists at the workings of various prices and incomes policies. This in turn highlighted the limitations of narrowly circumscribing the range of issues to be included in collective discussions and agreements. Yet despite various working party reports, the Labour Party's commitment in the October 1974 Election Manifesto was general: 'to introduce new legislation to help forward our plans for a radical extension of industrial democracy in both the private and public sectors.' There was no commitment to single-channel representation. No action was taken by the Labour government until it was forced to do so by the success of a Private Member's Bill sponsored by Giles Radice in 1975, providing for workers' representation. The result was the by now traditional response of all governments to radical change, to set up a Committee of Enquiry. Those who believed that industrial democracy must be introduced on the basis of trade union representation fought hard for terms of reference which would not allow the Committee to re-open what they saw as being essentially political decisions. After a Cabinet struggle they eventually did succeed in ensuring that their views were covered in the words of the terms of reference: 'Accepting the need for a radical extension of industrial democracy in the control of companies by means of representation on boards of directors, and accepting the essential role of trade union organisations in this process.'

Under the Chairmanship of Lord Bullock the Committee reported quickly and presented their report[3] in January 1977, a few months before the Labour government, in order to maintain a reasonably stable parliamentary majority, entered into an arrangement with the Liberal Party. The majority within the Committee proposed that its worker director system should apply to groups of companies and subsidiaries with 2,000 and more employees. A $2x + y$ formula would mean that shareholders and employee representatives would have equal representation and the two groups would jointly choose the 'y' group which would be an odd number smaller than 'x'. The shareholders and employee representatives would have equal rights and duties and would not be mandated delegates of their constituents. Shareholders would be left with a right to veto crucial matters such as acquisitions and sales of assets, although in future takeovers would not be allowed without the consent of the board being taken over. Employee representatives would be chosen by a method determined by a new body called a Joint Representation Committee (JRC). A union-run ballot of all employees would be held to determine whether worker directors were wanted and the scheme would only go ahead if there was a majority in favour and the vote in favour was that of more than one-third of the full-time workforce. All the unions recognised in the company would set up a JRC which would then decide how the worker directors would be chosen.

The Bullock Report was met with well-orchestrated hostility by the Confederation of British Industry. Some of it was genuine, but there was also a strong political element. The CBI, sensing an early election, was becoming daily more politicised and more closely identified than for some time with the Conservative Party. The trade unions were also shown to be split in their attitude, reflecting all their historic ambivalence over the issue. The Liberal Party was not prepared to support many of the Report's key recommendations in relation to the role of the trade unions. To have attempted to implement the Bullock Report immediately would have brought certain humiliating parliamentary defeat on the Second Reading. The Labour government responded instead by trying to achieve a sufficient measure of agreement to be able to legislate by the next year. The majority of the Cabinet, however, realised that even if the proposals were supported by parliament, legislation would need to be able to command far more widespread support in industry than was possible if the government stuck rigidly to the majority view in the Bullock Report. The suggested y component was not supported by German experience, and many were rightly sceptical of giving a decisive voice in any situation of conflicting views to the least knowledgeable and least committed members of the Board.

The Labour government's White Paper published in May 1978[4] satisfied few people, mainly because the political climate of opinion was by then heightened as an election grew closer. Differences of view in the Cabinet were covered in the White Paper by setting out both sides of the arguments on key controversial issues and avoiding reaching a firm conclusion. It proposed that the law should require employers in companies employing more than 500 people to discuss company strategy. Members of the Joint Representation Committee, JRC, under these proposals were to be given the statutory fall-back right to require the board to discuss company strategy. Members of the JRC would consist of employees of the company broadly representative of the independent trade unions in the company. If any trade union considered that the composition of the JRC was inequitable then it could appeal either to the existing Advisory Conciliation and Arbitration Service, ACAS, or to an Industrial Democracy Commission, IDC, if such a new body were to be established. The statutory obligation was to cover all major decisions affecting employees of the business before decisions were made over investment plans, mergers, takeovers, expansion or contraction of establishment and all major organisational changes. This would need a Code of Practice. If the JRC was dissatisfied by the company's failure to fulfil its obligations they were to have the right to appeal, and the suggested way of dealing with this was to use an existing body, the Central Arbitration Committee, CAS, which already had powers concerning complaints about failure to disclose information for collective bargaining purposes.

This part of the legislation was not as controversial. Much of the information, if made available to government, could have also provided the data necessary for the development of more systematic national planning. The case for reducing the number of employees from 500 to 100 for firms required to discuss company strategy is strong. Initially 500 was chosen to avoid putting a burden on small firms. But that argument is dangerous for it accepts that industrial democracy does not give a return to the employer as well as to the employees. Also 500 is a large company in many towns and cities and there is a need to involve many more smaller companies particularly in the range with 200–300 employees. Concentrating first on the statutory revealing of information and providing for discussion of company strategy, was deliberate in the hope that progress would be achieved by agreement in this area and that gradually the best existing industrial relations practice would become universal and that the worker director issue could be dealt with in a less political climate of opinion. The 1978 White Paper dealt with the worker director issue by proposing a statutory right to have representatives on the board in companies employing 2,000 or more in the UK. The statutory right was to be exercised as over company strategy by the JRC after a ballot of all the company's employees. It was proposed, however, in part to show an evolutionary approach, that a period of three to four years from the date of establishment of the JRC would elapse before the statutory right to board-level representation came into operation. This was also done because of the unresolved controversy about the single channel, not so vital in terms of discussion of company strategy, but an issue of more fundamental importance in terms of board representation.

It needs to be asked why such an obvious extension of democracy has had to wait such a long time to be implemented in Britain although it is common in other countries. An answer is that 'History suggests that movements for industrial democracy well up every so often, only to founder on the four rocks of conceptual ambiguity, trade union and official Labour ambivalence, employer hostility and rank and file apathy. Add to that unpredictable changes in the economic weather (pushing the issue down the list of priorities) and in the political climate (changes of government) and you have a recipe for repeated shipwrecks.'[5] It is hard to fault this perceptive and succinct summary. Industrial democracy will be shipwrecked again if there is not a better understanding among its proponents about the overriding need to legislate for the basic right and then let the schemes develop at differing speeds and in different ways. Democracy is an evolutionary process. A legislative framework can provide the right to participate but cannot provide the will. There must be a freedom for the workpeople most concerned to choose at all stages what, if any, pattern of industrial democracy is to apply in their place of work. It is because trade union leaders' voices favouring a rigid all-or-nothing trade union dominated solution have been loudest and have been listened to that progress has been negligible. It is perfectly understandable that they should have sought to enshrine in legislation the trade union movement's natural desire for predominance and that they have not been content for this position of predominance to emerge as an inevitable development. This insistence on what has been called the 'single channel' approach, whereby trade unionists alone would elect their representatives, underplays the fact that in the vast majority of cases the trade union voice would win acceptance as spokesman, and in only a very few situations would a workforce as a whole demonstrate its independence of the trade unions. The issue has been elevated to one of principle by powerful voices in the trade union movement. The effect has been to ensure that the introduction of industrial democracy has been dominated by an argument about the role and power of trade unions rather than by the issue of the rights and powers in a democracy of every individual at his or her place of work. Public sympathy which could perhaps have been won for the essentials of industrial democracy will not so readily be engaged for what is presented by the opponents of industrial democracy as a further entrenchment of the power of trade unions.

An extraordinary paradox is that in the main those trade unionists most in favour of free collective bargaining and who reject industrial relations legislation have been those most keen to advocate a pattern of industrial democracy by legislation which could not be either collectively negotiated or even tolerated by most employers. It is a position as illogical as it is paradoxical. The fact that the argument that industrial relations legislation is essential to reform the working of the trade unions is not advocated as part of the democratic reforms discussed in this and other chapters is not because the case has not been carefully considered: few subjects have been more discussed and have taken up more legislative time in parliament since 1966. It is because after weighing the evidence and taking account of past experience it is felt that the gains from any such legislation would be slight. A socialist government which could have considerable influence with the trade unions even while legislating for industrial democracy would hazard it all if it introduced industrial relations legislation, any gains being far outweighed by the disadvantages of a period of severely strained political relations.

It may be that some parts of the 1980 legislative package on industrial relations will be proved by experience to have merit. The proposals to encourage trade union balloting are certainly right, but they would have been likely to have commanded more support if they had been part of separate legislation to encourage balloting for all democratic organisations, whether political, trade union or charitable. After the self-inflicted though nevertheless real trauma that followed the argument and discussion over the fairly mild proposals envisaged by the Labour government in 1978 in the publication of *In Place of Strife*,[6] any socialist politician will hesitate before embarking on a similar course. The evidence is that a reforming government can achieve far more by persuasion than by legislation. The case for industrial relations legislation has always suffered from the grossly exaggerated claims that have been made about its proposed benefits. Few would deny that at times the bargaining power of trade unions has been used irresponsibly and that at times it has fed inflationary pressures. But the damage has often arisen from trade union weakness and that is as much the responsibility or fault of employers whether in the private or public sector, as of the workers. Legislation will not of itself provide employers with resolve, nor can it do much to alter the balance of power, except in the case of mass picketing which has recently emerged as an area needing control. The organisation and coverage of secondary picketing has admittedly become far more effective and this has changed the balance of power to strengthen forces outside the particular company, but it is still an open question as to whether persuading the TUC to wield its influence on the basis of agreed Codes of Conduct, which will obviously at various times be ignored, will not prove to be more effective in the longer term than the legislation introduced in 1980.

The broad general principle which argues that legislation for human behaviour has severe limitations and needs to be applied sparingly and with sensitivity has considerable weight. Yet if one accepts these arguments and supports the cogent case put forward in the Donovan Report on trade unions, it is impossible to justify imposing a form of industrial democracy favoured by some trade union leaders against the bitter resentment and hostility of employers. It is on issues like these, well demonstrated in the arguments over the effects of the 1975 trade union legislation on the freedom of the press that any politician faces a dilemma between his or her commitment to democratic liberties and the commitment to and support for the important interests of trade unionism. The trade union interest – wholly legitimately upheld by socialists in keeping with their recognition of the values of collective action – is nevertheless a sectional interest. There is no justification for allowing this interest to override the fundamental wider democratic interest of putting first the maintenance of an individual's liberty, where it does not critically affect the liberty of others, and this is what underlies the controversy over single channel representation.

The trade union movement expressed its views in a letter to the government in 1977 from the General Secretary of the TUC stating, 'The single channel of trade union representation is a central principle of the trade union movement . . . any statutory expression of collective rights must be related to the trade union movement if it is to lead to stable industrial relationships and is to be compatible with collective bargaining arrangement.' It is, however, for parliament to determine the balance of democratic rights for the citizen, not for the trade unions or for employers' organisations. Any democrat wisely accepts that legislation in this field must be related to the trade unions' concerns and to managers' concerns too, but above all it must be related to the rights of the individual citizen. In practice the trade unions will be the channel for representation in almost all cases and their nominee will be accepted by the work-force balloting in secret, and so the controversy tends to exaggerate the practical significance of the issue. Democracy hinges on principle and the arguments of principle on this issue are strong, correct, and cannot be dismissed on grounds of convenience or practicality.

The 1978 White Paper stated the problem rather than offering a solution, saying, 'there is a clear dilemma. One view is that industrial democracy should mean that every employee has a right to be directly involved in selecting representatives on the board. The other view is that any arrangement should be consistent with the established system of collective representation of employees in Britain industry.' In the co-operative movement democratic involvement of all members is the essential principle and in some trade unions this is becoming accepted practice. The member states of the European Community would never accept single channel representation and the trade unions in the member states would regard it as undemocratic. The sooner British trade unions accept this too, the easier it will be to make progress.

Trade unions cannot insulate themselves from the underlying movement within the country for democratic participation. Their resistance to balloting must be overcome and it is no part of socialism to identify itself as reluctantly democratic – preaching democracy on the basis of one person, one vote everywhere except within the Labour Party and the trade unions. In most large factories and enterprises there already exists a closed shop that is recognised by the workers and management as rightfully existing. In such cases the trade union machinery will be used for the election of its nominees as worker directors but a secret ballot of the workforce is the only way to safeguard the rights of individuals to reject the trade union nominee. Trade unionists individually have rights that have to be weighed with the right of trade unions as organisations. Where the unions are strong the trade unions are likely to resent any by-passing of their industrial relations' machinery and the system could lose the benefit of having the unions working together in the Joint Representation Committee. In the interests of industrial harmony it is also unlikely that many managers would wish to see the established forms of industrial relations upset by new structures. It is therefore extremely unlikely that there would be any wish on the part of the JRC to exercise their statutory rights to call for board representation if they felt it would provoke a challenge to the position of the trade unions. 'The JRC would have the right to determine how the employee seats on the board should be filled, but if any trade union considered that the methods or results of the system proposed was inequitable it could appeal to the IDC/ACAS. The IDC/ACAS could delay the implementation of the scheme until it was satisfied of its fairness, but could not impose a solution.'[7] In effect, no scheme for board representation could be introduced without either the agreement of the trade unions in the firm or the approval of an independent body if appealed to by a dissatisfied trade union, or any substantial homogeneous group of employees. The concept of the group is necessary to guard against the vexatious or mavericks.

It is not sufficient to confine the right to appeal to an individual union. This right for a group of employees will be controversial though very rarely exercised, but if the legislation is not to offend basic concepts of democratic rights, then it must make specific provision for a right of appeal to be extended to a substantial homogenous group of employees. This is in Britain the price that has to be paid by the trade unions if parliament decided to introduce legislation for industrial democracy. The statute should set out the criteria by which any appeal would be judged. These could cover the geographical and occupational distribution of employees in the company; and in the event of successful appeal there could also be a requirement for elections based on nominations of candidates by trade unions and by groups of at least 100 employees, whether or not they are members of trade unions. Given a firm legislative commitment on these lines it would be hard for even its more vehement critics to challenge the democratic basis of the proposals, though such a compromise

271

would be a particularly difficult one for many trade unions.

The White Paper proposal of waiting three to four years for implementation of board representation meant that any legislation would not achieve board representation within the lifetime of one parliament. Delay as a tactical judgment was understandable in 1978, for any legislation would have been coming at the tail end of the parliament.

Industrial democracy legislation to succeed should be given the highest legislative priority and introduced in the first session of a new parliament. It could then be timetabled so that within the first year of enactment JRCs should have been established, and where they invoked their statutory right, an agreed procedure for the discussion of company strategy would have been started. Within the second year of enactment board level representation should be established where the JRCs invoked their statutory right. This would then normally mean the new legislation would be fully operating within three years of the general election. This would be a very tight timetable, and given the considerable resistance to implementation that there would be within such a timetable, it would be wise to match it by taking some politically sensitive decisions to reduce the resistance from employers. There is a case for making changes in existing company law so that companies who wanted to do so could adopt the less controversial two-tier board structure with separate policy and management boards, and have their employee representatives serving on the policy board. It would be open to keep and appoint representatives to a unitary board. A policy board would, besides taking the major decisions in the company, also be responsible for promoting participation agreements throughout the Company. It would certainly be necessary to prohibit the mandating of employee representatives though encouraging them to keep in close touch with the employees and trade union.

It would also be wise to accept that parity of representation is too radical a change for the present. The 1978 White Paper proposed that while not ultimately excluding parity of representation on the board, the statutory obligation would initially be to appoint one-third of the members of the policy board.

As in the case of the unitary board, companies would be free to appoint a higher proportion of employees to the board. Though there will be considerable reluctance to accept one-third initially, the trade unionists who have served already on boards such as the NEB and BNOC know that numbers on the board are not as crucial as the ability to influence, and that this depends on the quality not just the quantity of the workers' representatives. A board which was putting every issue to the vote would soon cease to contribute constructively in any area.

These proposals will need to be argued for with trade unionists, industrialists, and above all the general public, for they are likely to be resisted on a number of grounds. Critics from the left will argue that separating policy and manage-ment boards will result in all major decisions being taken by the management board, with the policy board and its worker directors being little more than a rubber stamp. To guard against this it would be useful for the worker directors and their fellow directors to agree in advance the precise division of decision-making between the two boards. The worker directors must have financial support to develop quickly sufficient expert advice and research facilities to be able to understand and influence decisions. Some industrialists hope that industrial democracy will fade away; other industrialists have always feared that trade union bargaining would be transferred from the shop floor into the boardroom and that this would inhibit discussion and the making of decisions which were in the long term interests of the company. This danger will be reduced if it is made clear that the worker directors are not delegates of their union or workforce, although there is a vital need for worker directors to keep their electorate informed of their participation. The worker directors may also find it difficult to endorse all the decisions of their board, though at times like any democratic leaders they will be in conflict with the workforce they are representing. There is a case for all directors being given the opportunity to indicate dissent from a decision in the minutes of the meetings. But the legislation will succeed or fail on whether worker directors contribute to changing attitudes on both the shop floor and within the boardroom.

Some will decry such a package of measures as too cautious, others as forcing the pace far too quickly. Britain will soon come under pressure from the European Community to implement some form of industrial democracy. The long discussed Statute for European Companies and the Fifth Directive cannot be ignored, even by a government hostile to the whole concept. Statutory provision for workers to participate in industrial decision-making already exists in four Community countries, The Netherlands, West Germany, Belgium and Denmark. It also exists in Norway, Sweden and Austria. It has become a necessary element in the efficient and acceptable working of the mixed economy. It is an issue on which the time is overdue for decision. Few can expect to achieve a package with which they will agree, but the essential is to move from discussion of theory to legislation and then from actual experience to build on practice and later to bring in further legislation. In the nationalised industries, following the same procedures, there is scope for quicker and bolder action, since trade union membership is widespread and the government has the role of shareholder being able to dismiss and appoint the chairman. Where it represents the wish of the workforce, which is clearly the case for Post Office workers though not for mineworkers, workers could be given 50 per cent representation on the main board. The chairman would in case of deadlock be the final decision-maker and the safeguarder of the public interest.

The ambivalence of central government and the hostility of local government have not helped the movement towards industrial democracy. There has been only half-hearted implementation in the nationalised industries, the best scheme being for the Post Office in 1977, now abandoned. The corporatist tendency on this issue, as on so many others, predominates. Ministers and civil servants have tended to use the accountability to parliament of nationalised industries as an argument against introducing industrial democracy. The alliance between the Executive and the Bureaucracy manifests itself in an ability to obfuscate the issue. Both perceive a mutual interest in obstructing and circumventing existing parliamentary control of their handling of the nationalised industries, but they unashamedly invoke the notion of parliamentary control to avoid any reductions in their own powers that they feel may well come from strong employee representation on the boards. Hitherto nationalised boards have operated under the weakness that as all are appointees of the government they have no independent status. Unless the public sector gives the right to its employees to participate fully on their boards, it will mean keeping them wholly dependent on Whitehall civil servants and Ministers. Industrial democracy in the public sector is a potentially liberating force. The accountability of Ministers responsible to parliament for the industries is not an adequate reason for resisting the appointment of worker directors. To have worker directors is a right to make the industries accountable to their workers and it must apply in logic to the public sector just as much as to the private sector. Ministers will rightly retain a substantial measure of control, in the public interest, by the ability to appoint half of the boards, other than the worker directors, and will expect the Chairman to hold the balance in favour of the wider interest of consumers or of national priorities within the existing framework of parliamentary accountability.

Worker directors do not seem likely in the civil service, with its advisory role reaching up to private offices of Ministers. In theory there is no reason why civil servants should be deprived of the right to participate in civil service management decision-making. It may be possible to identify policy relating to the civil service within the Civil Service Department itself and in other areas where the civil service fulfils some of the functions of boards of directors in industry. The Board of the Inland Revenue and the Property Services Agency are boards which could have worker directors on the same basis as in nationalised industries.

The greatest problem over worker directors is likely to be encountered in their extension to local government. In local councils it would be possible to identify policy relating to local government service matters where representatives of workers could be given a proportion of seats on the relevant committee, if not in the main council chamber. The traditions of local government, however, strongly favour consultation and not direct representation of their workforce, and given the need to preserve their own democratic autonomy it might be better to let them adopt their own procedures and to exclude them from mandatory legislation.

Legislation will benefit not just from the co-operation but also from the commitment of the trade union movement, where opinion is at present deeply divided. There are some enthusiastic supporters of industrial democracy, as there are for industrial co-operatives, yet some trade unionists are still suspicious of both concepts. The trade union leadership needs to rethink its attitudes fundamentally. It could find that industrial democracy offers a new positive role, not on the basis of automatic rights but on winning democratically through the ballot the right to speak for the workforce on issues far beyond the narrow confines of free collective bargaining. Legislation for industrial democracy may have to come against the resistance of the trade union movement's leaders, but its introduction could be as substantial an extension of democracy as the introduction of the universal franchise. It represents a fundamental and far reaching reform and a major challenge to British socialism, to act in the best interests of all the workforce and of the nation.

PART FOUR

Representative Democracy

13

Parliamentary Government

Two current issues – the concern and questioning in the country about the health of British democracy, and the linked issue of the secrecy and power of the government – lies at the very heart of the debate about the direction socialism should be taking. The concern is soundly based. It is, however, paradoxical that many of those within the Labour Party who are thought to be radical because they identify themselves as Left still persist in their espousal of centralism, with its dependence on civil service decision-making; and choose to undermine the historic power of parliament by weakening the independence of MPs.

Looking at the development of parliamentary democracy over the last century it is hard to disagree with the judgment that, 'the House of Commons has steadily lost influence over the executive because of the increasing strength of the party system. In the nineteenth century, the House had dismissed governments without having to face a general election, it had sacked individual ministers and had introduced and carried bills against the government and had taken government measure and defeated or rewritten them.'[1] The size and scope of British government was relatively steady between 1790 and 1910 when parliament's power was greatest and the proportion of Gross National Product devoted to public expenditure each year averaged about 13 per cent. The growth of government has continued steadily since 1911, its expenditure never falling below 36 per cent of GNP since 1946. The numbers in government employment probably doubled between 1850

279

and 1890 at a time when the working population increased by around 40 per cent. Between 1890 and 1950 government employment increased by 1,000 per cent while the working population rose by 57 per cent. The proportion of the working population in government employment increased from 2·4 per cent in 1850 to 3·6 per cent in 1890 to 24·3 per cent in 1950.[2] The growth has accelerated very rapidly in the post-war years reaching 28·3 per cent of the workforce in 1979. Because of differing classifications it is hard to make an exact comparison with the pre-war years. Together with the increase in size of the civil service went an increase in its powers, a process encouraged by political leaders of both main parties. Ministers preferred to see the civil service hold the powers which they as Ministers could not hope to exercise physically, believing they could influence the use of those powers more easily than if they were passed to parliament.

In 1967 the Fulton Committee on the civil service was set up by a Labour government whose concern was not primarily the size or powers of the civil service but an anxiety that the generalist administrator was not able to deal with a technological society. The civil service was not then criticised as a political obstacle to the effective implementation of specifically socialist policies, but was seen rather as a technical obstacle to the technologically based policies of that government. Political criticism of the civil service began to increase after the 1970 election defeat. This criticism was triggered off by a series of published diaries and memoirs by former Ministers, revealing clashes of personality between themselves and their civil servants. The importance of Richard Crossman's diaries[3] was initially largely overshadowed by such titbits of personal information. In fact their real message is that Ministers confront an appallingly detailed workload and an amazing range of activity, and that the extent of ministerial discretion is matched only by the irrelevance of most of the supposed parliamentary controls on the Executive. It is an absurd distortion of reality that now depicts the wicked machinations of politically-motivated civil servants out to flout the direction of 'true socialism' as the reason for the failures of past Labour governments.

Yet this argument lies behind the justification for elevating the status of the Manifesto to that of a binding contract as the sole defence of the Labour Party's programme. 'Manifestoism' is a crude and narrow response to a complex problem. It is a wrong reaction, because, in seeking to increase the power of the Party, it deliberately weakens the power of parliament. The progressive devaluing of the decisions of Labour Party Conferences has occurred because party leaders have not fought those Conference resolutions with which they disagree; and the Left, either provoking a fight or sensing that their resolutions will be ignored, have not bothered to compromise in the wording. It is a cycle of mutual irresponsibility and a situation where no one gains. At least in 1960 Hugh Gaitskell thought that a Conference decision committing the Labour Party to unilateral disarmament was worth fighting. Ever since the July 1966 financial crisis measures, many socialists, whether of the Left, Right or Centre have felt a growing divorce from the economic judgment of Labour governments. The Left's lack of trust of the parliamentary leadership has led to a determination to write into the Party Manifesto detailed policies worked out in Opposition. In addition, a suspicion of the civil servants' ability to circumvent the Manifesto has led to demands that unforeseen arguments advanced by civil servants should not even be considered, and that the advice of expert bodies familiar with the detailed consequences, as well as the difficulties of implementation, should be set aside. It has also led to some people insisting that a Labour Cabinet or Minister should be bound hand and foot to deliver a Manifesto commitment without regard to any changing circumstances. Constitutional changes have been proposed designed to give inner party democracy an unprecedented dominance over parliamentary democracy. At its most extreme it would make Labour Cabinets delegates of Annual Conferences. Parliamentary democracy would not survive such an imposition. Undoubtedly some of those outside parliament who are pushing in this direction do not wish it to survive but, sadly, there are some Members of Parliament who, though they do believe in parliamentary democracy, are going along with this trend either out of weakness or ambition, or through

281

insufficient awareness of where the trend is leading and of its dangers.

Over 200 years ago, Edmund Burke, a whig, defined the issue which is still relevant to the debate today. He represented Bristol in parliament for only six years, from 1774 to 1780. He had an authoritarian and hierarchical view of society and did not have much interest in a modern participatory society, but his views cannot be disparaged merely because he may not have been the most sensitive representative of the views of the mere 5,000 Bristoleans who were eligible to vote for an MP. His classic case for representative democracy was that, 'it ought to be the happiness and glory of a representative to live in the strictest union, the closest correspondence and the most unreserved communication with his constituents. Their wishes ought to have great weight with him: their opinion high respect: their business unremitted attention. It is his duty to sacrifice his repose, his pleasure, his satisfaction, to theirs – and above all, ever and in all cases, to prefer their interest to his own. But his unbiased opinion, his mature judgements, his enlightened conscience, he ought not to sacrifice to you, to any man or to any set of men living . . . Your representative owes you not his industry only, but his judgement: and he betrays, instead of serving you, if he sacrifices it to your opinion.'[4]

Burke's advocacy of representative government was not hostile to political parties. He maintained long before the parties had reached their present dominance that party government was the best government, and gave a famous definition of a political party as 'a body of men united, for promoting by their joint endeavours the national interest upon some particular principle on which they are all agreed'. The issue he addressed was whether an MP should be a mandated delegate of the party. There is no more fundamental issue in British politics. Some in the Labour Party now claim they want to ensure that, as they describe it, the whole Party takes power when Labour wins an election. This sounds superficially democratic and they argue that what they advocate is not contrary to parliamentary democracy and that what they are putting forward should not lead anyone to argue that their proposed system replaces parliamentary democracy. They are correct to refer to it as a system: it is a carefully constructed, interlocking arrangement. Abolition of the House of Lords, the unelected half of parliament; mandatory reselection, even of MPs whose constituency parties wish to retain them; every Labour MP to sign a pledge of support for the Manifesto: an electoral college to elect the Leader of the Party and sometimes the Prime Minister; the election of the Cabinet, as in Opposition when there are elections for the Parliamentary Committee by all MPs; minutes and votes of all meetings of the parliamentary Party to be published; and all with the aim of extending formal accountability to the movement as a whole for all decisions taken by MPs, with the implicit threat of reselection by the General Management Committee.

Similar changes to those advocated for parliamentary procedure were advocated to apply to local councillors. This provoked a formidable outcry from local councillors. The proposals were shelved but the London Labour Party wrote the Manifesto for the 1981 Greater London Council election and wants to elect the leaders of the Labour Group. The objective is clear: to pressurise MPs and councillors, rather than to compel them – since this is known to be unacceptable – to bring them ever closer to becoming delegates of the Party. It is a far-reaching change which, it is claimed, is not designed to replace parliamentary or local government democracy; yet its effect would be that every time an MP or a councillor faced the choice whether to exercise his or her judgment or to follow the party line, the present balance – already weighted towards the Party – would be shifted even further. The scales would be tipped decisively to toeing the Party line. This is, of course, the object: delegated democracy would replace existing parliamentary and local democratic practice within the Labour Party.

Edmund Burke was right when he said, 'authoritative instructions, mandates issued, which the member is bound blindly and implicitly to obey, to vote and to argue for, though contrary to the clearest conviction of his judgement and conscience – these are things utterly unknown to the laws of this land and which arise from a fundamental mistake of the whole order and tenor of our Constitution.' He also said,

'Parliament is a deliberative assembly of one nation with one interest, that of the whole, where not local purposes, not local prejudices, ought to guide, but the general good, resulting from the general reason of the whole. You choose a member indeed, but when you have chosen him, he is not a member of Bristol but he is a member of Parliament.' That is not an old-fashioned élitist concept, as is sometimes claimed. Any political party is itself an élite simply because its members are activists and skilled advocates of a particular set of policies. They are seen by the apolitical majority as a narrow and powerful clique. Taking account of active members of political parties in the constituencies, on a generous estimate, no more than 25,000 people are actively involved in politics in this country.

Judging the national interest is not a matter just for Party activists to determine. The wider electorate do not consider the notion of the national interest a narrow or old-fashioned concept. A radical change was made with the introduction of the referendum to determine the destiny of the country within or outside the European Community in 1975. It was designed on a divisive but vital issue to reach beyond party politics and to attempt to judge the national mood. The use of national referenda in Northern Ireland in 1972 and over devolution in 1979 was justified on the grounds that a constitutional change was being considered. The Left's hesitation to adopt referenda more widely reflects that on some issues, such as the abolition of the death penalty or trade union reform, a national referendum would produce results which they would not favour. In law, the use of referenda has not challenged parliamentary democracy to the extent that in all cases the referenda were explicitly made dependent on parliament's final decision; and in fact, in the case of the referendum over Scottish devolution, parliament decided that an arithmetical majority on a low poll was insufficient to justify major constitutional change. Originally the referenda were portrayed as an extension of democratic choice, but from the beginning there were those who warned that their use would favour the conservative, no-change attitude in society and would reduce the ability of parliament to judge the national interest, sometimes against the trend of public opinion. Certainly the move towards referenda runs counter to the trend towards delegated democracy, though this has not prevented some socialists from advocating both, without an attempt to explain the contradictions. On constitutional issues referenda provide a protection against governments elected by a minority of the population forcing through fundamental legislation, and are therefore a safeguard; but they should be used sparingly for other political issues. They can only represent a snapshot of public opinion which changes rapidly on many subjects. On constitutional issues the knowledge that there has to be a referendum is a discipline for the government actively to seek out a consensus.

Another way of extending democracy is to give tenants greater participation and involvement in the running of their housing estates or blocks of flats. Greater participation and involvement of parents in the running of schools is another extension of democracy, yet both contain within them the seeds of conflict, either with the views of individual councillors or, even more, with the decisions of the Party caucus. But despite its limitations, and its possible use as a brake on radical reform, the referendum is a way of extending democracy, and its use in some States in America will doubtless increase and it may well be used on occasions by Local Authorities in the United Kingdom. But simultaneously to endorse the shift towards participatory democracy and delegated democracy, with all its authoritarian and even totalitarian overtones, is to move in opposite directions. It is a sad commentary on the present state of the Labour Party that that is exactly what it is doing, and few wish to face up to the contradiction.

Similarly, opposition to the use of secret ballots within organisations usually comes from ruling élites – who also oppose the release of information to allow for informed debate. A party which claims to be committed to an increase and extension of democratic decision-making should not resist any extension of democracy within its own ranks to give its own members the right to be involved in the taking of key decisions. This is the only legitimate way forward to extend the practice of political democracy: it is humbug to advocate greater democracy in the Labour Party and yet to flinch from the really key reform of giving voting rights to every paid-up member of the Party. One member, one vote, should choose a Prime Minister or Leader of the Party not block votes or delegates from the GMC in an arbitrarily chosen formula of an electoral college. It is wrong also to allow the sacking of an MP without giving him the chance to appeal against any decision by the GMC to the paid-up membership of the constituency Party. If the Labour Party wants to widen the franchise for choosing the leader and no longer trusts the judgment of its MPs then the only true option is to trust the judgment of every Party member.

What is right and wholly within the spirit of parliamentary democracy is for the Party decision-making process to be fully respected by Members of Parliament, who should strive to fulfil these policies bearing in mind their judgment of whether the national, overall, interest imposes any restraints on the policy. This requires any political party to approach its policy-making role on the basis of detailed information, careful thought and open debate. Money from parliament for research staff for the parliamentary spokesmen from Opposition parties needs to be increased, and, to reduce the information gap between Government and Opposition, there is a case for seconding civil servants to assist official Opposition spokesmen for a period; this would also help to improve Opposition decision-making and give its members a greater awareness of the implications and relevance of their alternative policies – something which could be crucially important to an Opposition out of power for as long as thirteen years. The decision by parliament to vote financial help for the Opposition is itself a recognition of the national interest in building-up an informed Opposition. An extension of this is to implement the finding of the Houghton Committee on State Financing for Political Parties. It concluded that a 'modest injection of state aid is the best, and perhaps the only, way of arresting the run-down of the parties, and of starting the process by which their effectiveness can be raised to an adequate level.'[5] But the level of aid must be pitched so as to strengthen Opposition political parties but not to sustain them against a decline in membership.

It is the relationships between politicians in government and civil servants which are crucial for understanding the nature of modern government. The permanent civil service, facing incoming Ministers, has initially the weapon of accumulated knowledge and expertise to set alongside what is often only a superficial knowledge or no past involvement on the part of the Minister. The civil service has a whole series of conventions about the confidentiality of government business which can ensure that Ministers take decisions outside the glare of publicity and beyond the scrutiny of the informed public. Most information available to Ministers is not made available to the general public: the criteria used by government departments even in quite routine decision-making procedures are still not published despite a worthwhile attempt by the last Labour government to make more information available. Ministers, anxious to avoid too many embarrassing questions, often shelter behind the civil service doctrine of secrecy, finding it all too easy to invoke lightly the national interest. The result is the complete absence of any informed debate. The holding back of the vital information on which government takes its decisions has contributed to the present tendency for all political parties to espouse simple ideological slogans or to take refuge in generalities. The political activists in all the political parties out in the constituencies would find it much easier to accept the abandonment or reversal of a Manifesto commitment if they could sense that the decision had been openly argued through and all the facts that had contributed to the decision made available. Nothing is more frustrating for active Party workers than to see policy commitments over-turned but to know none of the reasons. To shut interested people out of the process of decision-making is to encourage hostility to and suspicion of the system of government.

One cannot extol the merits of representative democracy without being conscious of the limits of the representatives themselves. It is fair comment that, 'A combination of thrustful and strong-minded senior civil servants, complex issues demanding both a substantial body of factual knowledge and an appreciation of the personal qualities of persons with whom the Department has to deal, and an inexperienced, indolent, ill-endowed or indecisive Minister, will sometimes lead to a situation in which a Minister dwindles to a political mouthpiece of his civil servants.'[6] The late Richard Crossman likened himself to 'a person who is suddenly certified a lunatic and put safely into this great, vast room, cut off from real life and surrounded by male and female trained nurses and attendants.'[7] The chauffeur-driven cars, the salary differential between Ministers and MPs, the cocooning and cosseting – the fact that a politician is addressed formally as 'Secretary of State' or 'Minister' – are part of the insidious bureaucratic embrace.

The most dangerous embrace of all is the growing reliance by Ministers on committee decision-making which ensures that the Whitehall view is inserted into every meeting. Far too many decisions are made collectively by Ministers and the degree of Ministeral discretion is being eroded on the seemingly unobjectionable grounds of democratic control and Departmental views. The weekly meeting of Permanent Under Secretaries which is a relatively recent development, ensures the co-ordination of attitudes. It is claimed that no decisions are made at these meetings but it is here that the co-ordinated civil service view is evolved and a sense of direction maintained. It is commonplace for Departments clandestinely to pass copies of briefs prepared for their own Ministers to other Departments, and a Department will prepare for its Minister a brief which refers to the expected position of another Minister and make it clear that his or her views are different from the views of the Department. This fosters the concept of a departmental view distinct from the Minister's viewpoint and the 'departmental' view continues across different governments. A powerful civil service, with its own ethos, can easily incorporate Ministers and drag them further away from their political party, parliament and their constituents. It is this bureaucratic embrace which a politician has most to fear. Some Ministers who serve in the Ministry of Defence 'join up' and wholly identify with one service. The Army, Air Force and Navy have developed a system of service indoctrination for their junior Ministers which can make a Parliamentary Under Secretary for the Royal Navy feel like a First Lord of the

Admiralty in the old days. Some Ministers in the Foreign Office can become so engrossed in foreign travel that they are strangers in their own country, let alone in their own party.

The civil service is not, however, a single monolithic entity. Many of the major Departments have developed over the years their own particular identity, attitudes and style which continues irrespective of which party is in power. The Ministry of Labour has a seventy-year-old tradition of emphasising conciliation and arbitration within the framework of collective bargaining. The Ministry of Health has a tradition of standing up to the British Medical Association in defence of the National Health Service that would stir the heart of all believers in the NHS. Health Department officials demonstrated this in their support in 1975 for a Labour government facing a three-month strike by hospital consultants trying to force through an 'item by service contract'. This was their constitutional duty – but it was also clear that the very idea of paying for every operation or procedure was anathema to many civil servants who supported the principles of the NHS and to many of the doctors in the Ministry who were resolute in their conviction that these payments would damage patient care and should be resisted in the longer term interest of the NHS. The free trade attitudes of the old Board of Trade still live on with a Messianic fervour in the Department of Trade's resistance to all forms of protectionism. They still champion free trade with scant regard for the change in Britain's international trading position: resist the more flexible interpretation of the various international rules and decry any covert protectionism or moves to design regulations to inhibit imports. Even measures which run no risk of retaliation and which are put forward as being in Britain's own interest are fought hard on the principle that Britain must be the purest of all nations. The Foreign and Commonwealth Office too is influenced by a small group of intelligent and single-minded people who in the negotiations to join the European Community developed a political role in influencing public opinion – sanctioned by Ministers at the time – which they now find difficult to abandon even though we have joined the EEC; they tend to adopt political attitudes of their own to the conduct of the negotiations, often in defiance of ministerial views, and brief the press independently. Yet this resistance is not party political; the evidence points to Mrs Thatcher as Prime Minister encountering the same resistance from officials in the Foreign Office as I did as Foreign Secretary when demanding a tougher negotiating stance with the EEC. The problem is that some Foreign Office officials regard their own views as according with the national interest and feel that they should let those views become known to a wider audience, in much the same way as the admirals and generals justify their independent viewpoint, invoking their wider responsibility to the security of the state.

The Ministry of Defence still continues to display many of the old attitudes of the old War Office and Admiralty – though the younger Air Force Department is markedly more flexible. The controversial reforms recommended by the Headquarters Organisation Committee in 1970 to downgrade the three service Boards were masterminded by the very able Permanent Secretary at the time, but sadly, the incoming Conservative government, supported by the Service Chiefs and the more traditional civil servants with 'single service' Departmental loyalties, decided to drop them. In effect the three Services still virtually split the Defence Budget up each year into a third for each service. They rotate the position of Chief of Defence Staff on such a strict basis that it may not even alter following the premature death of a Service Chief. The consequence is a defence strategy which is rigidly structured and based more on trade-offs between the Services than on rational choices on inter-Service priorities. The single services also maintain a direct link with defence correspondents through a press department manned, in the main, by service personnel, having a loyalty to their service as distinct from the government.

The Fulton Report's main recommendations barely touched these complex issues. They covered the recruitment and career structure of the civil service, including the merging of the Administrative and Executive classes into a single 'Administration Group'. Implementation has been slow and criticised for circumventing many of the reforms that were thought to be fundamental.[8] On secrecy, openness and civil service accountability, the Fulton Report simply advocated another enquiry. Undoubtedly the generalist bias in the civil service and the low priority given to scientific and technical expertise can be most speedily countered by outside expertise. Yet there is a long tradition of civil service hostility to outside appointments in anything other than a temporary and advisory capacity. The Diplomatic Service reluctantly acquiesce in the appointment of outsiders but only to be Ambassador to Washington or Paris and as the UK Permanent Representative to the UN. At every level there is a case for more outside appointments. Since the war no permanent secretary or deputy secretary has been brought into the civil service from outside. Yet at this level it is quite common for civil servants to leave before their retirement age of 60 or to start a job within the two year time-limit of retirement in important and influential positions in industry and the city. The fact that a former Head of the Civil Service, Sir William Armstrong, went to the Midland Bank in 1974 within a year of retirement and that the former Secretary to the Cabinet, Sir John Hunt, went in 1980 to the Banque Nationale de Paris, makes it now very hard to justify the continuation of the two-year rule on grounds of propriety. There are few important commercial or financial secrets in government to which these two civil servants were not privy. The Committee of outsiders vetting civil servants who take sensitive appointments within two years of leaving should have their powers and decisions investigated by parliament, which should either reassert criteria for the two-year limit following its erosion by prime ministers responsible for the civil service, or there should be no rule and individuals should be trusted. I refused requests from Ambassadors to take certain jobs, on one occasion putting the reasons myself in writing to Lord Diamond's Committee which upheld my decision. Criteria need to be sensibly applied because it is desirable to encourage more interchange but there is also a need to insist that senior civil servants maintain in some areas a degree of separation. This issue raises the wider question: what attitude should parliament and politicians take to administrators?

Administrators are an essential part of democracy, not a

race apart to be denigrated as 'bureaucrats'. Good administration need not be bureaucratic. The paradox is that these politicians who most criticise the civil service tend to be those who most want to legislate for and proliferate its growth. The present tension in the relationship between civil servants and politicians reflects in part the disappointment and frustration of Britain's post-war decline. Personality clashes or disagreements occur in any organisation. What is unique about the civil service is that it is almost impossible for Ministers or the civil service to sack incompetent officials or remove those whom Ministers find hold views incompatible with their own. Voluntary redundancy is available but compulsory redundancy is virtually non-existent. This is particularly serious at the most senior levels; lower down in the hierarchy it is possible to transfer an official to a departmental backwater. Yet the civil service is not slow in recommending redundancies for others and reports written by officials are bespattered with the advocacy of redundancies in British Steel, British Shipbuilders, the power generating industry and elsewhere.

Whatever the policies of Ministers' parties or the inclinations of the Ministers themselves, it is widely believed that the 'Whitehall view' tends to prevail. Why is this so? Is it the growing complexity of government? The frequency of ministerial reshuffles? Or is it – as I believe – fundamentally a question of ministerial workload, competence, confidence, courage and willpower? The constitutional position is that civil servants are crown servants employed to advise the Ministers of the Crown. Yet in practice vast numbers of decisions are made every day in which Ministers knowingly delegate the decision-making to officials. Such decisions are in some cases delegated by legislation to specific classes of officials, such as immigration officers, or inspectors at planning enquiries. Yet the tradition is still maintained that the Minister is individually responsible for every decision taken by the Department. This is not a worthless fiction, as some allege. For only if it is felt in the last analysis to be a reality will the individual civil servants feel obliged to take controversial and important policy decisions to Ministers, and thereby will ministerial accountability be upheld. This is particularly important given the fact that civil servants are intelligent, opinionated people who enjoy greater security of tenure than Ministers. Similarly, retaining the neutrality of the civil service so that different governments can be served creates a grey area between policy and practice in which civil servants are usually concerned not to impair their own ability to implement different policies. The issue of accountability to Ministers remains the most complex and important of all. It is unrealistic to believe in the absolute purity of the principle accepted by Sir Thomas Dugdale, in the famous Crichel Down case, of responsibility for the conduct of the Department. The principle is not one, however, which can be or should be totally abandoned. It is a myth, yet to some extent it is a necessary myth, if parliamentary government is to be realised. Of course twenty-four Cabinet Ministers cannot possibly control or answer for the detailed decision-making of an administrative structure that, in 1980, twelve years after the Fulton Report, employed 548,600 non-industrial servants. Ministers are not 'running the country' in the sense of taking every decision. The ultimate responsibility of Ministers simply does not provide justice for individuals, save in the most exceptional cases, and for individual cases there is an important role for accountability before the law, through developing and reviewing our existing administrative law and jurisprudence. Parliamentary scrutiny and public scrutiny should focus on a specific Minister responsible for a decision and on named civil servants responsible for decisions that are not referred to the Minister. The practice of blurring accountability by Ministers being able to retreat behind a cabinet decision, or civil servants being able to avoid responsibility by claiming it was a committee decision, should be systematically challenged by Select Committee investigation. Yet in some areas of departmental work the blurring is inevitable and there can be no real distinction. Where the area is politically sensitive then an outside political appointment should be made, for example in immigration control, private medicine in the NHS, and policy towards South Africa. The individual appointment should be justified to parliament and the person held accountable by it.

The top echelons of the civil service numbered, in 1980,

twelve years after Fulton, 42 permanent secretaries, and 158 deputy secretaries and ambassadors. The names of these senior officials and what they do was unknown to the general public and even to most Members of Parliament. While the overall civil service numbers have increased in the ten years by 7 per cent, the increase in under-secretaries and above has been 35 per cent. It is the growth in senior appointments which represents the important potential drain of talent from productive industry. These are the people who could and with a more active redundancy programme should be redeployed in any systematic attempt to reduce the size of the civil service. Yet what has happened in previous cutbacks is that cuts are applied across the board and fall on disabled doorkeepers who can find no other job, while the recent increase in under-secretaries and the top-heavy structure remains largely unchanged.

Critics of the civil service usually focus on salary levels, pension entitlements and relative job security compared with other positions. The top layer of salaries in government and state industries has been fixed, since 1971, by a Review Body chaired by Lord Boyle. This has not however insulated the issue from public comment or criticism but it is wrong to criticise the fact that civil servants are paid more than Ministers. In the past, at times when they have been advocating pay restraint, politicians have refused large salary increases. They do not need to be paid more than top civil servants to exercise control. For senior politicians to stand aside from the spiralling salary race marginally reduces the value of salary as a status symbol of power and influence and checks the belief that pay is the only reward for service. It is a healthy trend, which would be reinforced by paying Ministers very little more than MPs.

The most worrying aspect of the corporatism that has developed in Britain is the circumvention of parliament when important decisions about the future of society can be made by Ministers with little or no democratic control by parliament. Powerful groups can also bypass Ministers completely to take decisions in concert with the permanent civil service. The bypassing of parliament is most evident in two areas: industrial relations and collective bargaining. While there is a sensible reluctance on the part of many politicians to legislate in those two areas, an antipathy to legislation has become an article of faith within the Labour Party to the extent that many members now rule out any form of statutory involvement. This is worrying not only because it implies granting a special immunity to the TUC but also because it has in the past led to a transfer of decision-making in an important area of policy from parliament to the TUC and CBI, reinforcing the corporatist trend. Parliament cannot cease to be the forum for the representation of a wide variety of views and must never accept being the endorser of decisions curbing the individual rights of citizens that are taken by departments or Ministers without specific parliamentary authority. The constitutional propriety of administrative sanctions was rightly challenged by the House of Commons in 1978 over the imposition of sanctions in public purchasing policy against, in particular, Ford to secure compliance with the non-statutory incomes policy. But over thousands of smaller issues civil servants reflect, in their advice to Ministers, the consensus which emerges from their discussions with outside parties. Since many matters are connected with trade, industry, tax, social policy and international affairs, vested interests are strong or preconceptions and doctrines well entrenched, the advice to Ministers, reflecting the views of those interests, are very rarely published or separately tabulated so they can be examined independently of the Department's advice. Often the viewpoint has itself been hammered out in the matching official Cabinet Committees which have developed an identity of their own, further entrenching the move towards civil service government. The outcome is a mass of advice which is most frequently endorsed by Ministers without serious challenge. This is why the doctrine of ministerial responsibility looks jaded.

The more parliament and the public hear and see all these private arguments fully exposed before decisions have to be made, the more likely it is that ministerial decisions will reflect the wider debate. Already, where decisions are highly complex and ministerial involvement slight, but where the possibility of public or parliamentary scrutiny always exists, the civil service has a tendency to avoid from the start any policy option likely to be controversial: it may even exclude certain options, before any ministerial involvement has occurred, by saying that it might be potentially embarrassing for Ministers. Too often Ministers themselves refer issues to interdepartmental committees without any political guidance being given. Not surprisingly the result is an amorphous amalgam of conventional, safe, views always tending to the status quo. Bureaucratic procedure itself has become a source of stultification. Short-term economic considerations may be used to rule out an option which a Minister might well be prepared to fight for, despite the cost, had it been known that it was being considered. A fundamental fact which can hardly be overstressed is that in the existing system there is no substitute for ministerial activism, for intervention early in the consideration of a problem, for being sufficiently well informed to challenge the Department, tough enough to insist on using outside expertise, and for being seen to control the Department. The combination of weak Ministers and too much collective decision-making is a recipe for inaction and is the source of much of Britain's lack of drive and initiative and of its resistance to change. In the United States the tension between the President and Congress is positive, but in Britain there is a danger that there is no productive tension between the Executive and parliament, within the Executive, or between Ministers and civil servants.

The advice which eventually reaches Ministers, and on which they take their decisions, will often have already been considered by a large number of officials, and anything unorthodox or thought to be too controversial will probably have been ironed out. If there are options it will involve a choice between safe, conventional proposals. The existing structure favours but does not guarantee civil service government. It will manifest itself where there is a weakening of ministerial control of the civil service and too little public and parliamentary scrutiny of the Executive. Parliamentary scrutiny must operate a delicate balance to prevent the inhibition of thinking; and the fear of making a mistake or taking a risk which breeds a stultifying caution. It is worth giving one specific example of the way in which official committees, preparing the ground for ministerial meetings, can present an apolitical Whitehall consensus, an amalgam of Departmental interest which, once allowed to take root, can be very difficult to alter.

When the last Labour government was giving serious consideration to the options for economic and trade sanctions against South Africa the usual bureaucratic procedure was followed and a committee of officials matching a special Cabinet Sub-Committee was established. Whitehall was adamantly opposed to the application of any sanctions. The only way of ensuring that the Departmental view represented the views of the Foreign Secretary was to see the minutes of the official committee circulated to the Foreign Office participants, and to discuss with my officials their views, and even at times writing as well as approving their evidence for that committee. The issues were clearly political, and I felt the Department view needed to reflect the view of the Foreign Secretary. The debate between the diplomats and myself took place within the Department before I could have been confronted by a paper agreed by Whitehall with which I might disagree. This was thought by some officials to be a very unusual procedure, though others welcomed my intervention. Clearly time does not allow a similar pattern to be followed on every issue but there is a need for officials to come back to Ministers for political guidance in sensitive political areas of policy. Few things are more damaging to ministerial control than to hear a Minister in Cabinet refer to what 'my Department thinks . . . ' as something distinct from their own views. The Department should have a view and should challenge the ministerial view but once the Minister has decided within the Department their views constitutionally should become identical. The formal acceptance of the concept of separation is new and very corrosive of the principle of democratic ministerial control, and tends to legitimise the concept of a civil service policy as distinct from government policy. Of course civil servants have views and they should express them; their views are often correct and the Minister's wrong; retaining their expertise across governments of different parties has advantages and the case for moving to the American 'spoils system', where each Administration appoints its own civil service, is not strong enough to abandon the concept of neutral civil service; but that neutrality imposes restraints as well as bringing considerable power to civil servants.

The elected politician is not an expert, and, particularly in the early months of taking office, a new Minister will need good advice, and one hopes it will be taken. Many of the major mistakes made by government involves decisions taken in the first few months. Even after a year in office the Minister in charge will simply not have the time to master all the many subjects which require his attention. Whitehall, with some justice, argues that the early mistakes are when their influence is least and the Party's greatest.

Nothing is more nauseating than the spate of stories from ex-Cabinet Ministers about how they were thwarted by officials. A Cabinet Minister who knows his own mind, and can persuade his colleagues, can force his policies through. Any bureaucracy will resist change, but only in rare cases is that resistance politically motivated. The virtues of continuity, incorruptibility and bipartisanship which are broadly reflected within the civil service should not be decried. Any radical government will need to challenge and at times kick against the inaction of the machine. On occasion the civil service will itself put up radical proposals and some politicians are, in comparision to some civil servants, highly conservative. Permanent secretaries relish argument but most loyally support decisions once taken. Conflict between Ministers and civil servants does exist but it is no more than a reflection of the realities and difficulty of decision-making in any large organisation. The civil service has not unnaturally tended to react to the criticism of its political motivation with a cynicism about politicians and their ability to insist on their policies. This has sadly reinforced in the general public a sense of distance and alienation about the whole government process. The 'gentleman in Whitehall' is not always fairly seen as the man responsible for various planning disasters, for remote insensitive decisions and endless red tape and for wastage in the spending of public money. It is in the interests of politicians to re-establish the image of government as something in which people have a stake and which they can influence. It is not in the politicians' interest or the broad national interest to perpetuate this unfavourable image of the civil service and government generally.

But some redefinition of these different jobs is undoubtedly needed. The Labour Party, in its evidence to the Fulton Committee, had put forward the proposal that Ministers should be able to recruit personal staff to work with them as in the French *cabinet* system. It was, however, the Conservative government which in 1970 first began to include, in major Departments like the Foreign Office and the Treasury, a number of politically appointed officials working for the Secretaries of State personally. Some of them, in accordance with the fashion of time and of that government, were businessmen. When Labour returned to power in 1974 Cabinet Ministers were somewhat grudgingly allowed to appoint up to two personal advisers. Many did not, and the total of politically appointed officials never exceeded thirty. They were appointed to Departments for the duration of the Administration, the appointments automatically lapsing on the day after the following general election.

It is important to evaluate this experiment, though the role of the advisers seems to have been different in almost every case. Some took on a 'very' political role, seeing it as their duty to ensure that Manifesto policies were carried out, maintaining contact with local parties and with the Parliamentary Labour Party. Others provided Ministers with a personal confidant who knew the intimate details of the Department's business but did not have the divided loyalties of those who, while endeavouring to help the Minister, nevertheless had their own career and standing in the civil service to think about. Yet others became actively involved in the Department's work, acting as an extra pair of arms and eyes for the Minister – sometimes in this role clashing with junior Ministers. In some departments the political appointees were virtually frozen out, while in others they became part, albeit a special part, of the normal functioning of the administrative machine.

My adviser for 1977-9 in the Foreign and Commonwealth

Office went on four missions abroad that would not have had the same value if undertaken by an official. He visited Namibia to speak to all the internal nationalist leaders, visiting Ovamboland right up to the Namibian/Angolan border, which ensured an up-to-date account of a country where, for UN and other reasons, we had no diplomatic mission. He was also able to go beyond the British government's relations with the South African government by talking directly to key black African leaders. He visited the colony of Belize at a time where there was considerable tension between the Government and Opposition parties there and went to Maputo in Mozambique to talk to ZANU and improve relations at a time when ZANU felt the British government was favouring ZAPU, based in Lusaka. Finally, he went to India and Bangladesh to examine all the circumstances behind any medical examinations being conducted on women intending to emigrate to Britain and on the reasons for the long waiting-lists and delays in making appointments, something which was understandably a matter of concern.

In the Foreign Office, despite travelling commitments, the five Ministers, two special advisers and the two Parliamentary Private Secretaries used to meet once a week over lunch to discuss issues which were likely to come up at Cabinet and party politics. Issues which were frequently discussed in a party political context were the European Community, a range of African policies, and sensitive issues like the Falkland Islands, Gibraltar or Belize. The Private Secretary came to all the meetings; the Private Office were part of a team with the politicians. They managed to put their departmental loyalties into suspense for their period in the private office, and worked massive hours, but were free to criticise or suggest anything. They often felt the full brunt of the pressures and tensions that flowed through the Foreign Secretary's office but they could not have been more dedicated. It is necessary that a wider public should understand the intimacy and the confidence of most Ministers' relations with their Private Office – very well described by Barbara Castle in her Diaries.

The introduction of specialist political advisers is a valuable innovation. But it is no substitute for the more systematic development in Britain of the Continental *cabinet* system. A Minister also needs support over policy development. The Foreign Office has, like some other Ministries, a separate planning staff, set up in 1964 after the Plowden Report had highlighted the deficiencies of Foreign Office policy development saying 'Some of the most intractable international issues in which we have been involved in the last two decades could, in our view, have been handled better if their implications had been explored more fully in advance'.[9] 'It is alleged that the planning unit was quickly cobbled together in 1964 when the Foreign Office saw the proofs of the Plowden Report a month before it was made public.'[10] Whatever its origins, by 1977 the planning staff had become insufficiently independent of the Department and did not appear to be challenging the accepted wisdom from within the Department. To change the system would have necessitated a change in personnel and for the staff to work directly to myself as Foreign Secretary and not to the Department through the Permanent Secretary. This would have meant a major upheaval. For many reasons, not least that with a parliamentary majority so fragile one never knew how long the government would survive, I decided to circumvent rather than change the existing system. This was quicker and less traumatic and left everyone reasonably satisfied. In order not to engender the suspicion aroused by Denis Healey's establishment of a Programme Evaluation Group in the Ministry of Defence in the middle 1960s no formal announcement was made but, with the full co-operation of the Permanent Under-Secretary, it was arranged to transfer two people nominally to the staff of the Planning Department, a young diplomat with experience of defence policy and a young economist. These two, working closely with an existing member of that Department who had already had experience of co-ordinating work for speeches, then formed a separate policy unit working direct to myself as Foreign Secretary. At times they liaised with the Prime Minister's own policy unit and my Special Economic Adviser supervised any work involving economics.

The unit concentrated on defence issues and disarmament and also on the scope for selective import controls and their effect on the Third World and relations with the EEC and OECD. It soon developed an independent view and analysis. Its most important achievement was in challenging the accepted wisdom of the Ministry of Defence on Mutual and Balanced Force Reductions and challenging the Cabinet Secretariat on the detailed arguments over the Chevaline nuclear warhead programme. It also considered the strategic and political arguments against Trident as a possible Polaris replacement and prepared research on an alternative option to the Trident missile, the submarine-launched Tomahawk cruise missile. On none of these issues could the Foreign Office as such have made so effective a contribution. The unit was able independently to gather considerable information from the US Administration with the help of the ambassador in Washington, Peter Jay. Much of the information on Trident and on cruise missiles classified as 'Top Secret UK eyes only' in Whitehall was to be found openly in the Congressional record and amongst academics in the United States. A small expert personal policy unit is as vital for a Minister in making an informed judgment on departmental policy and advice as is the creation of a small political advisory unit. Both can work with the Department while being independent of it. Provided the units speak with the authority of the Minister through the Private Secretary there is no risk of any constitutional impropriety or unnecessary and wasteful duplication of effort, but it should be a formally accepted *Cabinet* and should not have to be constructed in this way.

Expertise is a crucial element in checking and investigating government decisions. Nowadays a single official, perhaps an able graduate in his or her early thirties, concentrates on mastering relatively small areas of the department's policy, and can deal with all policy matters affecting his or her field of responsibility, working with the main outside or non-govern- mental bodies connected with the subject, briefing Ministers and drafting replies to questions from Members of Parliament. The involvement of outside experts and of a dialogue between government and academics, which is so strong in America, is still comparatively much less developed in Britain.

No sensible person expects one Cabinet Minister effectively

to monitor everything that goes on in a Department. The very clear constitutional position which holds that Ministers are accountable to parliament, will remain a myth while very little detail of what the Department does is even known about by Members of Parliament. The decision in 1979 to establish after the initial experiment Departmental Select Committees is important, but the danger is that if they are inadequately staffed they will become dependent on and literally creatures of the Department. Given the laws and practices now governing secrecy the withholding of information can obstruct accountability to parliament yet be used as the excuse to prevent disclosure of information to the press or the public on the grounds that such a practice would diminish the accountability of Ministers to the House of Commons. It is a bogus argument: the scrutiny is all the more effective if parliament has the information on which the Ministers based their decision. So there exists a double lock on making information available. Leaks by officials to journalists often reveal far more about what is going on inside government than what is said in answer to Parliamentary Questions. As the Conservative government's ill-fated Protection of Official Information Bill demonstrated, once again, government collectively was more concerned to protect itself against leaks than to allow the public greater access to information about what those who govern are actually doing. But it is no use blaming officials. It is well in the power of government and politicians to open the system up. The fact is that successive Labour Cabinets have not had a sufficient majority within them to overthrow old prejudices and cross-party conservatism, and there has been little difference between Labour and Conservative governments. Members of Parliament, unless they specialise, are most unlikely to be able to master any but the general outlines of the subject, and, lacking expert guidance, may be unable to ask the pertinent questions. Select Committees are now appointing expert advisers but there are still considerable financial constraints on the building-up of their expertise.

However, the growth of pressure groups and activist charities, covering fields such as mental health, housing, the old, or race relations, has fortunately provided a 'counter civil service' of experts who subject every move of the government machine in their specialist field to very close scrutiny. Many of these groups have built close ties with friendly Members of Parliament. But pressure groups, even those whose scrutiny of government is consistent and independent, cannot do the job of parliament: they do not have to balance different priorities. An important task of the Select Committees is to lead an informed public discussion about what government is about to do, or has failed to do, or ought to be doing. In this area a readiness to publish more working papers prior to decision-making is very valuable. It was easier than many people thought to publish Foreign Office departmental papers and policy option papers in 1978 when the decision was taken to reveal more information. Gradually, the way government works is becoming better known. The publication of the Castle and Crossman diaries has given the general public a unique description of the work of a Cabinet Minister as seen through the eyes of those Ministers. It has also meant a greater realisation among academics and pressure groups of what goes on inside government and exactly how it works. Ex-Ministers and former political advisers have also spoken freely, in some cases at least concentrating only on past battles, but in doing so they have revealed something of how the civil service and the Cabinet system of government works. The Bingham Report on Rhodesian sanctions policy disclosed how the inner decision-making processes work when it published an internal memorandum with the circulation list at the bottom. This revealed which Ministers' Private Offices had known about the oil swap arrangement. What a further special parliamentary enquiry which the government had advocated in 1978 would have looked at, if it had not been rejected by the House of Lords, would have been why the Ministers and officials concerned did not recognise, and advise Ministers about, the important constitutional issue involved on which Ministers could be open to challenge for having condoned past illegalities. Why were the issues not presented specifically by the Ministers involved to the relevant Cabinet Sub-Committee? Another more general issue which ought still to be considered is whether a procedure of copying the minutes of a meeting to Ministers' Private Offices is a sufficient safeguard, or is part of a bureaucratic machinery which gives a blanket coverage of ministerial involvement through a mass of unread paper circulating around Whitehall.

The Cabinet Committee structure is something which successive Prime Ministers have refused to publish for no very good reason. Their membership is an important source of prime ministerial power as was shown by the existence of a small Ministerial Committee of four Ministers which under the Labour Government discussed some sensitive nuclear issues such as the Chevaline programme for improving the Polaris warhead.

The policy issues are discussed in Chapter 18. But in this context what is important is that the existence of this Committee was not known to all the Cabinet. Neither was the membership of the small economic seminars which discussed exchange rate policy and other sensitive monetary matters widely known, until it was revealed in a newspaper. This is, however, not unusual since many Prime Ministers have used unofficial groups for political discussion and have justified the practice by saying that actual decision-making remained formally with the Cabinet Sub-Committees whose membership has always been a Prime Ministerial prerogative. No formal register or details of the membership is ever circulated to parliament, although senior civil servants working in the Cabinet Office know the structure of the Cabinet Committees and the knowledge spreads out in Whitehall. There is no escaping the facts that Prime Ministers have used this freedom to ensure limited discussion as well as to reinforce their authority. There is a strong case for confining the number of Cabinet Ministers involved in issues like nuclear or exchange rate policy but no justification for not informing the Cabinet formally of the existence of all such groups, or the wider public through parliament of the membership of the formal Cabinet Sub-Committees.

Within the Labour Party there are some who have said that the Chevaline programme conflicted with the Labour Party's 1974 Manifesto pledge not to replace Polaris. It was in fact a programme to harden the existing system so that it could withstand ballistic missile explosions. There was no real security case for withholding information about the existence of the project since most informed defence commentators had been writing about the modernisation ever since it had first been decided by the Heath government – just as informed articles and books had been written for many years about oil going to Rhodesia from South Africa through Laurenço Marques at the time of the Beira Patrol.[11] But because of the feeling that there had been a government cover-up, when the issue became public through the formal Chevaline announcement by the Conservative Secretary of State for Defence in 1979, and by the revelations prior to the Bingham Report and when it was published, there was a massive public outcry. The reason was a public feeling, largely created by journalists, that they had been cheated of information – even though the facts were already fairly well known. A Select Committee on Defence should and could have been given far more details about Chevaline. The conspiracy of silence to avoid discussion about defence has only served to build up pressures within the Labour Party in favour of unilateralism and of hostility to NATO which feed on suspicion and fear. There is a price to be paid for avoiding open debate on any issue, particularly when the Labour Party goes into Opposition, when it is much harder to ensure rational informed debate. Law and order issues affect the Conservatives in much the same way, when in government they keep debate about such issues as the death penalty, corporal punishment or penal policy low key and then have to pay a price when strident demands are made to commit to hanging and flogging when they are in Opposition. The art of politics is to harness public and party opinion so that they keep broadly in step.

Paradoxically, the corporate state itself has added to the demands for greater openness because pressure groups have developed direct relationships with civil servants and have, in the course of what has become their normal work, forged a relationship with the official machine which has in turn spread knowledge about how it all works. Some of these pressure groups acquire an intimate knowledge of the work done by different officials at different levels in the departments concerned, of how their work is co-ordinated, and even of how the official machine is briefing Ministers and when Ministerial Committees will meet. Symptomatic of the corporate society is the lobbying which can be unleashed by industry, private and public, before a Cabinet or Cabinet Committee Meeting to discuss important industrial issues, or the release by the Child Poverty Action Group of a memorandum on child endowment just before key decisions are to be made. The parallel within government is the sudden arrival of telegrams from Ambassadors in European capitals to the Foreign Secretary when Britain's negotiating position in the EEC is due to be decided by Ministers. If the vested interests can be mobilised to put pressure on the decision-making, why cannot public opinion be mobilised as well?

The essential key to an effective parliamentary democracy is knowledge. Knowledge is power. The growth of corporatism has thrived on the complexity of modern life and the inability of parliament to adapt itself to grappling with that complexity by building up a countervailing expertise. Parliament's attempt to develop an independent source of knowledge and expertise has been deliberately blocked by successive Cabinets, often encouraged by the civil service. Parliament's resolve to wrestle from the political parties the power to decide when to vote has been weakened because of the rigid demarcation which many insist on retaining between Government and Opposition. Parliament has been constrained too by the rigid whipping system reinforced by the ability of the Whips to determine the membership of committees and the mechanics of voting. To some extent this is inevitable in the two-party system but one of the most welcome changes in the 1974-9 parliament was the readiness of backbench MPs to exercise their voting rights in a more independent way, while the Labour/Liberal arrangement in 1977 and 1978 showed that parliament could adapt to a situation where no party had an overall majority. It is now in the interests of democracy for parliament to insist that there should be fuller disclosure about what goes on in government, not only to its own Select Committees but also to the wider public, but this will necessitate a conflict with the Whips and traditional parliamentary leaders.

The argument about official disclosure of information quite rightly centres on demands for a legislatively-backed 'right to know'. This expresses the wish for the responsibility to be put on government to inform the public about what it is doing: yet in practice the subject has become inextricably bound up with what to government is the other side of the coin – the protection of official information from unauthorised or damaging disclosure. The debate has centred on the question of the reform of the Official Secrets Acts. The present debate about the reform of those Acts goes back to 1967 when the Labour government caused prosecutions to be brought against Jonathan Aitken and the Editor of the *Sunday Telegraph* for allegedly breaking the law in an article about the Biafran War. Both men were acquitted, but the whole episode led to the setting up of the Franks Committee on official secrecy, which recommended, in its report published in 1972, that a new Official Information Act was needed.

As a result, although successive governments did nothing, there was increasing concern both inside and outside parliament. Private Members tabled Bills and the All Party Committee on Freedom of Information built up support. Outside groups like the Outer Circle Policy Unit – which helped Clement Freud, MP produce one of the more successful Private Members' Bills – also stimulated the public argument over reform. The British section of the International Commission of Jurists, *Justice*, produced studies and draft legislation. The Labour government responded through its White Paper in 1978 which proposed, among other things, criminal sanctions for unauthorised disclosures of official information and – wrongly – made no proposal for a legally enforceable right to know. The White Paper was welcomed by nobody; it was shelved while further consultations took place and Ministers began to look seriously at the possibility of adapting Clement Freud's Bill, and they studied experience in other countries. Although a Green Paper was published in April 1979 which allowed for a statutory code of conduct, this died with the Labour government. The Conservative government attempted to introduce a retrograde Bill which included most of the civil service proposals which had been rejected a few months before by Labour Ministers. The Protection of Official Information Bill was then dropped in the face of all-party hostility in the wake of the publication of Andrew Boyle's book *Climate of Treason* and the Prime Minister's disclosure that Anthony Blunt had been a Russian spy. It suddenly became clear that if the Bill had been an Act the book might never have been published.

It is unfortunate that Ministers are even more secretive than are civil servants and hostile to parliament, even when over greater freedom of information a majority of MPs of all parties support radical change. Now that public opinion and most outside influential groups, including lawyers and consumers, also strongly favour change perhaps there will be one but there is no case for any government supporting any partial reform. It would be better to wait and allow the existing Official Secrets Act to languish unused on the statute book. It has almost reached the stage now when no Attorney General will risk bringing any prosecution under the infamous catch-all Section II.

The seriousness of the present situation in relation to official secrecy is well illustrated in a recent Fabian Tract.[12] The author cites some random examples of official suppression of information taken from press reports in December 1979: an official report with full details of the damage juggernauts cause to our roads was suppressed by the Department of Transport; eminent academics told the Social Science Research Council that the right decisions about energy might not be taken in the future without public access legislation in Britain: the full details of how children are affected by lead pollution, and smokers by the carbon monoxide content of cigarettes, were kept secret by the Department of Health: calls for the rules governing rights to welfare benefit to be published were again ignored: only public health specialists received, in the *Communicable Disease Report*, warnings and information about epidemics of infectious disease and food contamination.

The opposition to reforms comes almost exclusively from those who will be most inconvenienced by them, senior politicians and civil servants. Opposition is often couched in terms of expense, with frightening figures being produced as to the cost and numbers of civil servants needed to administer the new freedom, reminiscent of the Whitehall-inspired campaign against any serious consideration of local income tax. 'The cost of the United States FOIA in 1977 according to the official, Congressional study was a little under $26 million, about £13 million. This is a substantial sum but needs to be seen in the perspective of other government spending, for example, expenditure in 1978 of $35 million for the maintenance of Defence Department golf courses and, more pointedly, $1.5 billion for US government public relations exercises.'[13] The assumption is that once some information is released, demands will eventually be made for all information to be released. Yet, expense and inconvenience have always been a necessary accompaniment of democracy, and it is not sufficient to argue that documents will have to be sorted and classified, and arrangements will have to be made for the public's requests for information to be processed. Even if government decision-making could be only marginally improved in Britain, if the momentum towards corporatism could be checked by greater public examination of the working of government, then the limited cost would soon be recovered by more acceptable, accountable and better decision-making. Abroad, a number of countries have taken steps to create a statutory right of access to government information. In Sweden such a right has existed for over 200 years and proposed new laws are discussed by appointed commissions composed of people from a wide spectrum of backgrounds. Swedish Members of Parliament have before them the Commissions' reports, in addition to the reports of their own committee and the comments of Ministry officials, when they come to vote on the legislation. The actual interpretation and execution of Swedish law is in practice handled by independent administrative boards, and it is to strengthen the effectiveness and accountability of such bodies that the very wide provisions for disclosure of information have been devised. In Norway and Denmark, where the system is different from the Swedish one, there have been laws providing for statutory access to public information since 1970. In both countries Ministers and officials are accountable both to parliament and to the courts. In the United States, the Freedom of Information laws, which again give the citizen's statutory right to access to official documents, have been justified as being fully in accordance with the principles of the Constitution, as a device to help implement the principle that people are sovereign. France passed in 1978 a 'Law on Freedom of Access to Administrative Documents' while in the Netherlands the same year saw a 'Law on the Access to Official Information'. Internationally, among leading democratic nations, Britain is almost alone, together with the Federal Republic of Germany, in having made no formal provisions for access by the citizen to official information.

Obviously, clear guidelines will be necessary to safeguard security and other sensitive material, including information supplied to government in commercial confidence and papers relating to personnel matters or law enforcement. Yet the demands for freer information have come from such a variety of sources, and given the reception in parliament both to various Private Members Bills and to the Protection of Official Information Bill they seem to have such strong support from the House of Commons that some reform now looks inevitable. But we are unlikely given current political attitudes to move from a system of Cabinet government characterised by secrecy, a doctrine of Cabinet collective responsibility and of anonymity and protection from public controversy of civil servants to a Swedish-type system in a single step. The Labour government in 1979 – mainly because of divisions of opinion within its own ranks – put forward only tentatively the *Justice* proposal – for a general right of access to government files, in the form not of a legal right but of a code of practice to be monitored by the Ombudsman (Parliamentary Commissioner for Administration). There would be no retrospective application, and there would be no access to or involvement of the courts. But the Ombudsman would supervise the system and be able to order compliance with the Code of Conduct, and Members of Parliament would be able to exercise vigilance over the whole procedure.

The relatively cautious *Justice* proposal could, however, provide a satisfactory system if the Code of Conduct were part of an acceptance of a legislative right to know and it were put into a Regulation which would have to be subject to an affirmative vote each year. The involvement of the Parliamentary Commissioner for Administration would be buttressed by the Parliamentary Select Committee which oversees the Commissioner and which would report to the House on the working of the code. The House of Commons would have an annual debate and an opportunity to vote if the government did not progressively amend the Code in the light of experience and the comments of the Commissioner and the Select Committee.

Set up by the Labour government under the Parliamentary Commissioner Act 1967, the office of the 'Ombudsman' is designed to assist citizens who are victims of mistakes or maladministration by government departments. The Ombudsman works on complaints passed on by Members of Parliament, though when receiving a complaint direct from a member of the public the Commissioner usually passes it to the person's MP to see if the MP is prepared to ask formally for it to be investigated. In 1979, 758 complaints were received, of which 27 per cent were accepted for investigation. Usually complaints which are not accepted for investigation lay outside the scope of the Parliamentary Commissioner's powers or, rather than alleging maladministration, simply expressed disagreement with decisions reached by government departments in the exercise of discretion under, for example, planning legislation. Despite the relatively little use made of the Commissioner – only one complaint per 53,000 electors was made in 1979 – the Ombudsman has provided some extra safeguard for citizens in their dealings with the modern state bureaucracy. Its terms of reference are, however, still too narrow and access should not be restricted to use only via MPs. In the case of one small but significant group – pensioners wrongly coded for income tax purposes – the Ombudsman has scored an important victory. Provided the office is given the necessary resources to do the job properly, the Ombudsman could be a flexible but authoritative way of monitoring a Code of Conduct on Official Information. Commissioners have won the confidence of politicians and officials, while their powers and the thoroughness of their investigations – together with their constitutional link with parliament – have helped to ensure that officialdom feels the power of democratic accountability at much lower levels of administration than was ever possible before.

Privacy is another major concern which cuts across the debate about open government. So much information on individuals is now possessed by state and para-state bodies that there is apprehension about the uses to which such information might be put; and everyone is concerned that any such information is both accurate and relevant. As the state becomes more pervasive and more centralised, so such concerns become more and more critical to the relationship between the citizen and the modern state. The Committee on Data Protection, set up by the Labour government in 1976 under the chairmanship of Sir Norman Lindop, looked with great thoroughness both into the question of who is to enjoy access to data and into how the privacy of the individual could be protected. An increasing amount of data is now held, much of it on computers, about people's lives and personal charac- teristics. Nineteen pages of Appendix 6 to the Report are taken up with a list of 'computer tasks' containing information about identifiable individuals held under the authority of different legislation. The legislation permitting government depart- ments and agencies to collect such information ranges from such obvious examples as the Social Security (Pension) Act 1975 and the Census Act 1920 to the Horticulture (Special Payments) Act 1974 and the Welfare Food Order 1977. A total of fifteen different Acts of Parliament allow various categories of officials, including judges, access, in certain circumstances, to an individual's bank account.

The concept of privacy is a peculiarly difficult one to grasp. In countries like France and Germany a different emphasis – that of 'data protection' – is placed on the concept. The Committee did put forward, as a possible definition for legal purposes, the idea that: ' "Privacy" means, in relation to any data subject, his interests to determine for himself what data relating to him should be known to what other persons, and upon what terms as to the use which those persons may make

313

of those data.'[14] Not only are people worried about who holds what information about them, and particularly about how accurate it is, there is increasing concern that different computers holding records collected for different purposes might be linked up so that, for example, information given to employers in confidence for personnel record purposes might find its way into police hands or simply into the hands of other employees. In addition, lack of clear guidelines about the public's entitlement to know what is held on file about them leads, rightly and understandably, to fears that for example a prosecution, but not the subsequent acquittal, or a petition for bankruptcy but not its subsequent dismissal with costs, might find itself on official records. The Committee's recommendations would, if implemented, go a long way to reassure people. They proposed, in their report published in 1978, a Data Protection Authority to implement seven basic principles: the Authority would make rules for data users, maintain a register of all personal data users, investigate complaints and enforce compliance with the rules. A code of practice would govern the uses to which data could be put and conditions governing its disclosure. Most importantly – since fears are directed more at the prospect of an Orwellian '1984' situation developing among state agencies than in the private sector – the Committee proposed that the Data Protection Authority should not be subject to or answerable to a Minister, but rather that its members should be appointed by the Crown and subject to direct parliamentary scrutiny only, with the possibility that a Parliamentary Select Committee might supplement that function. In addition, it proposed to make the jurisdiction of the 'Ombudsman' apply to the DPA, with members of the public being able to take their complaints direct to the Commissioner while the decision of the Authority would be accountable to the courts. There is an overwhelming case for implementing these recommendations.

In one of his most perceptive essays, Henry Fairlie, one of the best post-war political journalists to work within the British parliamentary system, summarised for the politician four tasks: 'To try to reconcile the multiplicity of conflicting interests and wills which exist in any free society . . . To maintain public interest in political issues, for without such interest free government is meaningless . . . To act as a catalyst on public opinion. Eventually, and especially at moments of crisis, he may, as Bagehot demanded of him, "express the mind of the English people," but the mind is rarely clear enough to be expressed at all . . . To be the link between informed and public opinion. The two are very different.'[15] The way the Minister interacts with parliament and parliament with the Minister will determine whether or not parliamentary democracy can be revived in Britain. The role and place of Select Committees within the parliamentary system will probably be the decisive factor. That is not to argue that those Committees will of themselves resolve all the problems, or that there is any one single parliamentary, administrative or political initiative or device capable of reviving or restoring the power and influence of parliament. Select Committees do, however, have the potential to provide the varied stimulus which is needed in many areas of parliamentary government.

It is interesting to analyse the opposing forces in the argument about the introduction and extension of the powers of Select Committees. It gives some insight into what the Select Committees might contribute to parliament. The most powerful opposition comes from politicians themselves. Some politicians who have served, or who expect to serve, in government oppose them because they see them as challenging the power of the Executive: they present an obstacle to the power of the Minister to decide. Those politicians who suffer from 'manifestoism' and who believe in the supremacy of the 'mandate' or who regard decisions of party conferences as sacred, fear the power of Select Committees to erode the party basis of parliamentary decision-making, and dislike the inherently all-party nature of Select Committee recommendations. Politicians who prefer to operate on the basis of the 'grand strategy' and who are not interested in detail but delight in polemic and debate sense that Select Committees will divert attention away from the floor of the House and reduce the clash and conflict of adversary and opposition politics.

The opposition of civil servants is more diffuse. Administrators like a clear-cut, tidy, decision-making procedure: some

315

see parliament in general and Select Committees in particular as interfering with the decision-making procedure, bringing into it delays, uncertainty and irrationality. Some see Select Committees as ill-informed and their recommendations as irresponsible, something to be suffered as the price for democracy, but whose growth should be resisted and their powers curtailed. Some of the opposition comes from the House of Commons clerks themselves, who do not like the prospect of seeing their own position eroded by the introduction of specialised staff from outside the Commons.

Despite this powerful opposition – but in part because it is an opposition made up of so many different and at times contradictory strands – movement towards Select Committees has over the past fifteen years been the most successful area of parliamentary reform. Gradually they are acquiring professional specialist advisers, proper back-up facilities and are developing a political identity with an ability to arouse newspaper and public interest. They cannot hope to prosper and to acquire more powers unless they build up backbench opinion which will support them. The fundamental question is, however, yet to be resolved: will they be able to harness for themselve the voting power of parliament? Unless they are able to make this breakthrough all the academic studies and discussions about the role of Select Committees will simply be left to gather dust. It is harder to envisage, but not impossible, for parliament to do this under the two-party system.

The Home Affairs Select Committee, which looked into the reform of the 'sus' laws in 1980, made it clear that, if the government did not come forward with its own Bill to abolish 'sus' the Committee would itself produce a Bill: presumably by making use of the ten-minute rule procedure, where it could obtain overwhelming support for parliamentary time to legislate. Alternatively, it could be taken up under the procedure for Private Members' Bills.

Another vital way of harnessing the vote will come when a Select Committee challenges the government over an item of expenditure. A very sensitive mechanism is available within the existing parliamentary procedure for the control of the Executive. It has lapsed to such an extent that government has come to assume that it has the right to win on all expenditure decisions. The power of the Whips has over the decades been mobilised to guarantee the government's expenditure programme to the point of farce. The Public Accounts Committee is the most prestigious of all the Select Committees. It should be able to pick up a particular expenditure project, where it has been able to prove a scandalous cost escalation, and then reach an all-party agreement that the project should be cancelled; and it should then challenge the government either to cancel or to face a debate and vote on the cancellation. Otherwise, no matter how good the Committee's analysis, its findings will be ignored by Ministers and civil servants. The vote is the teeth of democracy in parliament. Take away the ability to put issues to the vote and there is no power.

Select Committees are already providing a far better forum for reconciling conflicting arguments and creating and catalysing public interest than the debates on the floor of the House of Commons. They have done so in complex fields such as computer technology, nuclear power policy and race relations. To the surprise of many people they have been able to investigate the highly-charged political area of the independent British nuclear deterrent, and more recently were able to conclude that the Soviet invasion of Afghanistan was defensive rather than offensive in nature. In such cases as the Musicians' Union dispute with the BBC over the planned closure of orchestras they have shown themselves able to move sensitively into complex fields such as industrial relations. The extension of Select Committee investigations into other sensitive areas is worth consideration: they could gradually replace bodies such as Royal Commissions, Special Commissions and departmental committees of inquiry. There are good grounds, for example, for scrutinising all important appointments stemming from ministerial patronage – permanent secretaries in the civil service, chairmen of nationalised industries, state-run boards, authorities and councils, and the appointment of political ambassadors. The very thought of such a development will appal many traditionalists: it would, however, tilt the balance of power between parliament and the Executive back a crucial few degrees in favour of parliament. I would have

317

liked the opportunity to go to a Select Committee to justify my appointment of Peter Jay to Washington as Ambassador.

Many of the changes advocated to revive parliamentary democracy will in themselves be of only marginal value but the cumulative effect could be considerable. It is never a good argument to criticise change because it will operate only at the margin. In a sophisticated democracy change involving a massive swing away from historic patterns and trends is very rarely the right course; changes at the margins represent important reforms if they are part of a well-thought-out series of interlocking marginal changes. The only reservation is that parliamentarians must ensure that, as they rebuild their power and influence, they do not replace bureaucratic inertia by political inertia. They must avoid creating a climate of opinion in which, for the sake of easy publicity, every mistake by the Executive is elevated to the status of a major crisis. In that case a system of government might grow up in which politicians would not be prepared to defend the need to allow for error. They would castigate civil servants for every mistake and would themselves elevate caution to being the only political virtue.

New ideas can come only from a readiness to experiment. Almost by definition, some experiments must occasionally fail. The greatest politicians have been those who have shown the ability to demonstrate that party interest never militates against national interest and that principles are not devalued by expediency. Parliamentary democracy can be the vehicle for reviving our nation, injecting hope and optimism, replacing dogma and doctrine with a practical yet imaginative future – a bolder leadership, something with which many people can identify and hold to in times of prosperity or recession, peace or war.

On this as on other issues the labelling of Left and Right within the socialist debate completely breaks down. Some so-called 'Left wing' politicians can be found rejecting a legislative right to freedom of information, wider use of Select Committees and even political advisers, some so-called 'Right wing' politicians are among the most active in championing all or some of these reforms. As is so often the case, when an issue is analysed division breaks down conventional labels and can be traced more to the divide between centralists and decentralists. The centralists, advocating or accepting corporatism in various guises, tend to want little or no change, fear the detailed scrutiny of Select Committees, resist giving to Committees the power to put their reports to the vote, and cling to keeping every issue a polarised political debate. If it is to check the Executive, parliament must not be afraid to seize back some power from the party machines. Until parliament wins back the power of the vote conceded over many decades to the Party Whip, and uses it on occasion as a body crossing the Party divide, then parliamentary democracy will continue to be unable to assert its own independence, and the present mix of corporatism, with an occasional lurch in the direction of Party dogma, will predominate.

Sentimentalists who relish the polarised debate on the floor of the House, little realising how ritualistic and unattractive it is even to political activists, will fight any such changes. The average person, whose reaction to the sound broadcasting of parliament has on occasion been very critical, will realise that there are occasions when the floor of the House should become the theatre for the nation, a forum for real debate, the centre of genuine democratic challenge and conflict. But to expect it to fulfil this role day in and day out, to fear the creation of Select Committees, to regret the wish of MPs to specialise, is to advocate a pattern of parliamentary opposition for its own sake that engenders confrontation and in its own way diminishes politics in the eyes of the public. Politicians so ready to reform everyone else have been strangely reluctant to grapple with the reform of their own institutions. It is a majority of politicians who cling to the status quo and appear unable to adapt to a modern age, and who give the predominantly false impression that they like nothing more than to exchange insults across the floor of the House of Commons – and yet who go into smoking rooms to chat and even drink together after the actual confrontation is over.

Parliament which has so many strengths, so many unwritten practices and traditions, should never be underestimated, yet, for the generation who responded to John Osborne's play, *The*

Entertainer, it can sometimes seem like a succession of continuous performances by Archie Rice in the theatre on the end of the pier – ignoring the fact that the audience has disappeared, bored and disenchanted, to read their newspapers in the sun or take the excitement from the local cinema, bingo hall or television screen. For a younger generation it can seem reminiscent of the singer's lament, 'bring on the clowns'. It is time for parliamentarians to reassert their role as the practitioners of the art of democratic free government.

14

Constitutional Reform

The present system of government in Britain is essentially Victorian in origin, though the power of the Executive in relation to parliament has increased. The system itself has remained surprisingly intact and a series of attempts at reform over the last fifteen years have all stumbled against a stubborn reluctance to contemplate fundamental change. The trend towards corporatism has been reinforced and the amount of democratic participation in the country at large has been unhealthily reduced. The result is stagnation and inertia instead of progress.

Scottish and Welsh devolution, regional government in England, proportional representation, the House of Lords, the European Assembly and membership of the European Community, and Northern Ireland, all pose genuine problems for our system of government yet the debate over these issues has never set in motion a fundamental reappraisal of the system or of the theory of British government. As in so many areas of British public life successive governments have responded to political pressures and public criticism by tactical decisions, the establishment of a Royal Commission, or Committee of Enquiry or the assumption in a Manifesto of commitments that owe more to transient moods and political prejudices than to considered or careful research and thought.

The recent history of failure over constitutional change is not just a sad saga of incompetence, prejudice and inefficiency, though all these have played a part; it is that in the absence of a theory of the state and a comprehensive view of its role and its philosophical relationship to society politicians have been buffeted by every transient pressure and have proposed piecemeal ad hoc changes which lacked both coherence and conviction.

It is interesting to note – in terms of how the cycle of constitutional change has moved over the last fifteen years – that it was reform of the House of Lords that started the process of constitutional change when a radical politician, Richard Crossman, was appointed Leader of the House of Commons. After detailed discussions between the political parties, with representatives from the House of Lords fully involved, the government published its proposals for reform in a White Paper.[1] It was in some ways a model of how to proceed. Since the issue was so central to parliament and politics it was rightly judged that it was best to consider the issue among parliamentarians and not set up an outside enquiry. Even though the government's majority was large it was wisely decided to seek all-party agreement: the proposals eventually presented were broadly acceptable to the then Opposition. The error was in not realising the widespread resistance among Labour MPs to any extension of Prime Ministerial patronage. The dialogue was confined to government and opposition spokesmen. There was no attempt to take formal evidence, no systematic consultation with other MPs. So when the parliament (No. 2) Bill, which was framed to give legislative effect to the White Paper, was presented it ran into substantial opposition from backbenchers on both sides though for different reasons. Eventually, in April 1969, after the Bill had ground on and had taken up more and more time on the floor of the House, severely curtailing other government business, the Bill was withdrawn. Many people were involved in the opposition to the proposals but it was noteworthy for the strange tactical alliance forged between two then back-bench MPs, Michael Foot, who wanted total abolition, and Enoch Powell who wanted to retain the hereditary principle. This alliance was to re-emerge over opposition to the 1972 European Communities Act and to provide the background to much of the support that the Ulster Unionists gave the minority Labour government until the censure motion in

April 1979. Both were united in their strong views about the sovereignty of parliament, the pre-eminence of the debate on the floor of the House of Commons and their romantic views of the role of backbenchers in the chamber of the House of Commons.

This combination of cross-party views and the considerable reluctance to guillotine a constitutional Bill meant that the status quo triumphed and the first major attempt at constitutional change ended in stalemate on the floor of the House of Commons. There had been 285 votes for and 135 against the Second Reading on a two-line Whip. Only 25 Labour MPs voted against and on a free vote 58 Conservatives supported the measure. Yet the Bill needed more than this; it needed an enthusiast as Leader of the House to drive the reform through. Richard Crossman had by then become Secretary of State for Health and Social Security. Writing in his diary at the time, he regretted he was no longer Leader of the House. 'I could have continued the experiment in radio broadcasting of proceedings leading up to the televising of Parliament. I could have kept going the specialist committees and the drive to get the House controlling the executive and pressing for more private business.'[2]

Personalities matter in parliament and reforms depend on a radical spirit rarely found amongst senior politicians, who are only too content to increase the power of the Executive. The demise of the Bill was a triumph for parliament, as some backbenchers claimed, but it also revealed the innate conservatism which bedevils British politics. It revealed an attitude among some backbenchers which was to haunt constitutional reform throughout the 1970s. The sovereignty of parliament became an absolute for these people. Any change posed a threat, none more so than the Treaty of Rome, which led them to oppose implacably any change in the sovereignty of Britain and particularly of parliament in relation to Britain's membership of the Community. The reforms of the Lords that were proposed in 1968 included the elimination of the hereditary principle so as to prevent any one party having a permanent majority and to allow in normal circumstances the government of the day to have a reasonable working majority. It restricted the power of the Lords to delay legislation to six months and abolished the power to withhold consent to subordinate legislation, giving only the right to ask for reconsideration. It involved a two-tier membership with a new category of 'non voting' members entitled only to speak. Existing hereditary members would continue to sit in one or other category but in future succession to a hereditary peerage would no longer carry the right to a seat in the House. The number of Bishops was to fall from 26 to 16 but the judicial functions of the Lords were to be retained.

The Labour government thought that a system of single-chamber government would not only be contrary to the practice of every other parliamentary democracy which has to legislate for a large population, but also that the case for two-chamber government in Britain had been strengthened since the end of the Second World War by the growth in the volume and complexity of legislation, the increase of the executive's activity and power, and its use of subordinate legislation. Moreover, abolition of the second chamber would subject the House of Commons to severe strain and paradoxically would result in less procedural flexibility and speed because of the need to guard against the overhasty passage of legislation.

The six-month delay period was to run across sessions of parliament, so avoiding the need for legislation to be reintroduced, and this was justified on the grounds that without it the House of Lords would be little more than a debating chamber – though the mechanism would be rarely used since the government would normally have a majority. It was described as a power of delay sufficient to cause the Commons and the government of the day to think seriously before proceeding with a proposal.

The failure of the legislation meant that over the next ten years there was little public discussion of the position of the House of Lords except that within the Labour Party the NEC established a working party and issued a statement, 'The Machinery of Government and the House of Lords', which was debated and approved by Annual Conference in 1977. It recommended a Manifesto commitment for the next election that a Labour government would abolish the House of Lords.

To preserve the constitutional safeguard against an extension of the life of the House of Commons beyond five years, it proposed that any extension should be subject to approval by a Referendum or, in time of war, by a two-thirds majority of the House of Commons. There was considerable feeling within the Labour Party about the Lords in 1977 because of their wrecking action, relying on hereditary peers to obstruct the Aircraft and Shipbuilding Industries Bill, the Dockwork Regulation Bill, the Rent (Agriculture) Bill and the Education Bill. The Labour Party study claimed that the House of Lords had not been especially valuable as a revising chamber and quoted research demonstrating that the mass of amendments were 'tidying up' amendments. The NEC felt that if there was to be a second chamber it would have to be an elected second chamber and it was feared that it could then have a legitimate right to challenge the elected House of Commons and would develop such powers. The NEC statement admitted that a case had been advanced which set out the advantages of some, if not all, members of the proposed devolved assemblies having a base in a second chamber at Westminster, but they argued against this as they argued against the suggestion that directly elected members of the European Parliament should be members of a second chamber.

In retrospect it can now be seen as unfortunate that Jim Callaghan as Prime Minister did not oppose the 1977 proposals either on the NEC or at Conference. It was wrongly assumed they were acceptable and it was – not unreasonably – resented when at the Clause V meeting between the NEC and the Cabinet in April 1979 he argued strongly against a commit-ment to abolish the Lords in the 1979 Election Manifesto. There were sound arguments against such a commitment – and Jim Callaghan was not alone in his opposition. After the election defeat this issue became the symbol of the argument that the Manifesto should in future be written by the NEC, a proposition which was lost at the 1980 Conference. It can hardly be argued that the absence of a commitment to abolish the Lords as a second chamber lost any votes and few remember that a commitment to abolish all the Lords' delaying powers was in the Manifesto. After Tony Benn's speech at the 1980 Conference, promising to abolish the Lords and to create a thousand peers to prevent the legislation being blocked, the existence or form of the second chamber has once again become an issue. Labour MPs are divided, and the Conservative government may remove some of the more absurd features of present procedure in order to be able to mount a more considered defence of the second chamber. The case for abolition of hereditary peers commands widespread support but there is little public enthusiasm for a single chamber parliament and it is not hard to see how images of the Orwellian 1984 will be deployed against the case for abolition.

There is a strong case for retaining a bicameral parliament as part of a coherent pattern of comprehensive constitutional change, and as part of a reassessment of the course to chart after the collapse of devolution in 1979. Devolution failed not on the floor of the House of Commons but through the referenda in Scotland and Wales, which were imposed on a reluctant government by backbench MPs. To analyse the roots of this failure it is necessary to go back to the political purpose which underlay the establishment in 1969 of the Royal Commission on the Constitution under the chairmanship of Lord Kilbrandon. It reported in 1973 only after the two-tier reform of local government had been pushed through parliament and the case for combining reform of central and local government had been lost. The Commission was quite clear about why it had been appointed. 'We have no doubt that the main intention behind our appointment was that we should investigate the case for transferring or developing responsibility for the exercise of government functions from Parliament and the central government to new institutions of government in the various countries and regions of the United Kingdom.'[3]

The Commission having rightly though narrowly interpreted its terms of reference soon found that during the course of its enquiry it came under pressure to report on different pressing areas of concern. With the Scottish Nationalist Party becoming a serious electoral rival to the Labour Party in Scotland, Scottish and Welsh nationalism was the urgent issue for the Labour government. Later the Commission came under pressure to pronounce quickly on English regionalism before firm decisions were made on the structure of local government. These decisions became politically necessary once it became clear that the Local Government Commission's Report proposing unitary authorities would not be implemented by the new Conservative government, for while the unitary single-tier structure called for a regional structure, retaining the counties made a regional tier arguably less important. Then Northern Ireland went to the top of the agenda for the Commission as violence in Belfast increased. Then the effects of membership of the European Community and its particular effect on the Channel Islands and the Isle of Man became an important area on which to focus. The Commission considered the position of the Lords in relation to the regions but concluded, 'In our view it would be neither practicable nor desirable for a change in the structure of Parliament to give effect to a regional policy to take the form of a change in the House of Lords. Reform of the House of Lords raises considerations extraneous to the question of regional government, and recent history shows these considerations would prevent any change in the near future; if a regional structure for Parliament were thought advantageous, therefore, it would be inadvisable to link it with the House of Lords.'[4] Given that the report was being written in the aftermath of the collapse of the proposed reform of the House of Lords the conclusion may have been an accurate political judgment, but that such an important constitutional concept could be so lightly dismissed is not easily justified and revealed the unimaginative approach adopted by the majority.

The dissenting minority report was more perceptive in its advocacy of devolution and in highlighting some of the weaknesses in the majority recommendations when it said, 'We cannot believe it is right or acceptable that the Westminster Parliament should be precluded from legislating for Scotland and Wales in a wide range of subjects (including education, housing and health) while at the same time about 100 Scottish and Welsh MPs at Westminster would have a full share of legislating in these same matters for England alone.'[5] It was this problem that was to bedevil the various legislative attempts made by the minority Labour government, and when it was debated on the floor of the House of Commons it helped to undermine the credibility of the proposals for devolution in the country as a whole. The criticism became known as the 'West Lothian question' after the Labour MP for West Lothian, Tam Dalyell, who persistently raised this question and fought devolution predominantly on it. Tam Dalyell and others considered it wrong that he, as a Scottish member for West Lothian, should be entitled to influence decisions affecting England without English members having a similar right to influence Scottish legislation. In this question many of the fundamental issues underlying devolution were encapsulated: sovereignty, separatism, over-representation, under-representation. It posed in simple terms an obvious inconsistency in the proposals, something which many felt to be a fatal flaw. It was the argument which was also used effectively by some English MPs who, though they opposed devolution for different reasons, could all combine to exploit this single issue. English MPs resented the fact that Scotland was already receiving more money per head from central government than any English region, and the fact that Scotland was over-represented to the extent of some fourteen MPs. These factors contributed to the concern particularly of the Northern group of Labour MPs, about devolution. In the crucial revolt on the guillotine motion on 22 February 1977, which effectively killed the devolution legislation in that session, the Northern group, which accounted for only 9 per cent of all Labour MPs, provided for 18 per cent of the Labour votes against 25 per cent of the Labour abstainers. There were, too, Northern members in the government who privately held considerable reservations about the legislation. What was significant was that the Northern Labour MPs, the most loyal and steady group in the Parliamentary Labour Party, actively demonstrated their concern, which became crucial when taken with the hostility of most Conservative MPs. Eventually the devolution legislation reintroduced in 1978 was enacted but only after the referendum amendment, moved by George Cunningham, a London-based Labour MP though a Scot by origin, was forced on the government by Labour backbenchers supported by the Conservatives. The amendment ensured that before the Scotland Act 1978 and Wales Act 1978 could be implemented there had to be a referendum in Scotland and Wales and an affirmative vote of at least 40 per cent of those entitled to vote, not simply a majority of those who actually voted. The referenda, as in the case of the referendum over membership of the European Community, were advisory to parliament, but if less than 40 per cent voted, an order for the repeal of the relevant Acts had to be laid before parliament.

On 1 March 1979 the referendum was held. In Wales the proposals were decisively rejected; fewer than one in eight Welsh voters turned out to support the Scotland Act, nearly 40 per cent of the voters stayed away and the margin of the 'yes' vote was 3 per cent. It was described in the *Guardian* as 'a grudging thin and meaningless consent', a significant and fair judgment from a newspaper that for all the flaws saw the Scotland Act as 'a potentially liberating force in British politics'. The referendum result meant that it was judged impossible to force through the Scotland Act. This led to the Labour government being defeated by the Scottish Nationalist Party vote on a motion of confidence while the memories of the winter of discontent were still fresh, and to the calling of the 1979 General Election with the by then almost inevitable return of a Conservative government.

There are two fundamental decisions which the country, and not just its politicians must now face. Will the issue of devolution go away? Should devolution be implemented without resolving the 'West Lothian question'? All the evidence indicates that the rise of the Scottish Nationalist Party is not a temporary phenomenon in British politics. Its rise from 1955 can be carefully traced.[6] It has waxed and waned, but each time it gathers momentum again, usually on the tide of disillusionment with the UK economy. Each time the resurgence starts, however, it does so at a higher level of support. This ratchet effect is very likely to restart some time in the 1980s. Scotland feels that it is a nation, and it is a nation, and this is the justification for treating Scotland differently from the English regions. In Westminster, characteristically, the majority feeling is that devolution is dead, yet I believe that if the issue is ignored throughout the 1980s, it will ultimately come back and challenge the unity of the United Kingdom. The 'West Lothian question' has, however, now been shown to be of importance. The record of failing to grapple with the dilemmas it raises is clear: the attempt to introduce constitutional change in the absence of some measure of cross-party support has ended in ignominious failure. It is time to learn from the past and choose a different path towards the same objective.

The key lies in re-examining the arguments in the Memorandum of Dissent to the Kilbrandon Report which took a wider and more radical view of the constitution. The minority defined four essential objectives: '(a) to reduce the present excessive burden on the institutions of central government; (b) to increase the influence on decision making of the elected representatives of the people; (c) to provide the people generally with more scope for sharing in, and influencing, government decision making at all levels; (d) to provide adequate means for the redress of individual grievances. In our view all the evidence makes it clear that it is just as important to achieve these objectives for the people in the different regions of England as for the people in Scotland and Wales.'

This is a correct judgment – though the people of Northern Ireland should also be considered, but separately, and in the context of Ireland as a whole. The essence of the minority report was to set up seven democratically elected assemblies and governments for Scotland, Wales and five English regions. The proposals were seen as reinforcing the political unity of the UK while adapting UK institutions to membership of the European Community. The minority members of the commission felt that there was very little hope for real devolution of any independent legislative power to the different nations and regions of the United Kingdom. They saw their objectives as being 'substantially to reduce the burdens on central government so that Whitehall and Westminster have the time to promote and watch over British interests in Brussels – but to do it without any significant devolution of legislative autonomy.' This was a reasonable objective but their specific proposals did not arouse much public or political support. A synthesis is required which bridges the major political obstacles to constitutional reform that can now be more clearly identified than was possible when the Kilbrandon Commission reported in 1973.

The simplest, and neatest way of resolving the 'West Lothian question' is to accept that the Westminster parliament must retain the ultimate rights over all legislation in the UK in order to satisfy the political wish to ensure the overall unity of the Kingdom. It is surprising if that is accepted, that more attention has not been given to the concept of retaining a two chamber parliament, with the membership of the Second Chamber drawn from the several countries, nations and regions of the United Kingdom. The members of the Second Chamber would be elected for Scotland, Wales and the English regions, and Assemblies in the nations and regions would operate as extensions of the Second Chamber, and under the powers of the Second Chamber. The Second Chamber or Westminster Assembly as it could be called would act as a revising Chamber only, as at present for English and Welsh legislation, but having all the powers of investigation and scrutiny at present vested in the House of Lords, which would be used in the Welsh and English regional Assemblies. The Second Chamber, in recognition of the distinctive nature of Scotland's separate legislative history, would have the primary legislative responsibility for Scotland. This responsibility would be exercised through the Scottish members of the Second Chamber who would also be members of the Scottish Assembly. The First Chamber, the House of Commons, would for Scottish legislation act as a reserve chamber, holding its existing powers but exercising them only as reserve powers, in the way the House of Lords broadly operates today in relation to the House of Commons. The term Lord and House of Lords would be abandoned for it has a connotation of privilege which can never be eradicated. The Second Chamber would be different from the present House of Lords. It would revise House of Commons legislation as at present except for Scotland; but as a Westminster Assembly it would also reflect that aspect of the nation which is a combination of nations and of English regions. Most of the special legislative provision and practice of the House of Lords would be retained and the judicial functions of the Lords would stay unchanged. There are already separate legislative powers for Scotland which are treated differently by the House of Commons through the mechanism of the Scottish Grand Committee; but, as part of a genuine legislative devolution, primary responsibility for legislation would pass to the Scottish Assembly drawing its powers from being part of the Second Chamber. In sequence, Scottish legislation would take its formal First Reading in the Second Chamber. The Second Reading and Committee stage of all Scottish Bills would be taken in the Assembly in Scotland, and probably the Third Reading. Scottish Bills would come to the House of Commons, as sometimes happens now on non-controversial Bills, after the legislation had gone through all its stages under the procedures of the Second Chamber.

The executive powers devolved to the Scottish Assembly and legislative powers as part of a Second Chamber would follow broadly the pattern of the Scotland Act 1978. It would probably be judged necessary for a Secretary of State for Scotland to be appointed to serve in the Cabinet, as was envisaged in the Scotland Act, even though the Westminster government would have transferred executive responsibility for a range of public services, and industrial powers to the devolved Assembly. It would be preferable for members of all the assemblies to be elected by proportional representation for otherwise one political party could achieve in some of them an unhealthy degree of dominance.

There is in any arrangement for devolution the potential for damaging conflict. The Scottish Nationalists could control the Scottish Assembly and might try to introduce 'creeping separatism' but the safeguard in these arrangements is that the House of Commons retains the power to reject any separatist legislation from the Assembly. Conflict is particularly dangerous with any form of legislative devolution, and the question arises what degree of freedom is sensible to minimise the possibility of conflict. Over Northern Ireland for many years the Stormont Parliament was not checked by the limited fall-back powers Westminster possessed and this contributed to the build-up of discrimination in Northern Ireland but the dominant party was not separatist but unionist. It was the fear of separatism and the feeling that the judicial powers of review and the fall-back powers of the Secretary of State for Scotland were inadequate, which helped to ensure that support for the Assembly was so grudging in the Scottish referendum. The argument used against this fear of irresponsibility was that the Assembly would behave responsibly and not enact legislation which would be deeply offensive to the Westminster parliament and damage the unity of the United Kingdom. This was a powerful argument, but it failed to convince. What is being advocated here is a change of roles whereby it is the House of Commons which would have to act responsibly and show restraint and not challenge the right of the Assembly to legislate differently from the views of the House of Commons, using the power to veto only where there were overriding reasons of national importance. This is asking a lot of any political party with a majority but the operation of reserve powers is deliberately left to understanding and practice rather than being built into the legislation. If the House of Commons is prepared to grant legislative devolution to Scotland it knows this means it cannot at the same time repeatedly flout the political judgment of an elected Assembly; only over separatism or on the rare occasion when it has a good case on merit and is probably backed by a broad section of Scottish opinion will it consider exercising its blocking power.

The extent to which a Welsh Assembly had any legislative autonomy along the lines of the Wales Act must now depend on the evolution of opinion in Wales. In the light of the 1979 referendum result it would probably be wisest to leave such a development open rather than to test the issue soon through a referendum, and let the Welsh people see the working out of all the new arrangements first in relation to the Scottish Assembly.

In the English regions there would be no likelihood of introducing any legislative devolution and the English and Welsh members attending the Second Chamber as and when they wished would tend to specialise, as do at present most members of the House of Lords, in carrying out the revising and scrutiny role for legislation covering the United Kingdom or for England and Wales. The Second Chamber would have no more than the six-month power of legislative delay envisaged in the Parliamentary (No.1) Bill and they would have no power to withhold consent to subordinate legislation.

UK members of the European Assembly would be members of the Second Chamber with full rights though they would only attend when matters of specific interest to them were being discussed. It has always been in the best interests of the European Community and the UK that there should be a serious attempt to reduce the gap between the MEP and the MP, and the case for dual membership, were it physically possible, has been a strong one. Those in the House of Commons most suspicious of European federalism should see that the most effective way of combating federal tendencies within the Community is to encourage linkage between Westminster and European MPs. All the voting members of the Second Chamber would be elected and there would be no hereditary members. There is a need for a smaller section of non-voting members being appointed on much the same lines as today to carry much of the routine work of the Second Chamber. Such a proposition might be attacked as a continuation of patronage, but this could be reduced, as in the case of the Bishops, by stipulating that the holders of certain important posts in public life would for the period they hold office be automatic members. Such posts might include, for example, the Chairman, President or General Secretaries of the CBI and TUC, the Association of County Councils, the British Medical Association, the Royal College of Nurses, the Law Society, the Institute of Mechanical Engineers – active politicians and past members of the House of Commons to provide parliamentary experience. Too large an element of appointed members would be a mistake, but there is a need to enrich the experience of the debating function of a Second Chamber by having a non-voting sector which would explicitly cover specialised interests in the country. There is a value in having some former members of the House of Commons serving in a non-voting capacity in a Second Chamber to carry out the revising role which recent research indicates has been of greater value than has been previously assumed.

The role of the Welsh Assembly and the Assemblies in the English regions would follow that envisaged in the dissenting minority report. They would not, however, take over control of the executive responsibility for the outposts of central government operating in their area. Nor would the Welsh Office, as long as there was no legislative devolution, be placed under the control of the Welsh Assembly. Control would stay with the Secretary of State for Wales and so would the Departmental Regional Offices stay under the control of the Departmental Secretary of State or Minister. But it would be necessary to establish for every English region a junior Minister with responsibility for co-ordinating Whitehall's policy for the region and answerable for the Departments to the regional Assembly executive. Regional Assemblies would not be another tier of bureaucracy, but would replace the existing Health and Water Authorities. An Assembly would also take over the consumer responsibilities from the present regional Consultative Councils for the Gas and Electricity Boards. The Scottish and regional Assemblies would have a revenue-raising capacity to conduct their operations. In part this would be a continuation of the water rate system but an additional source of revenue such as taking a part of the revenue from local income tax, a regional petrol tax or regional VAT should clearly be introduced. The Assemblies would have a scrutinising and strategic role for the development of their regions, backed up by all the powers of the Second Chamber to examine Ministers, civil servants, and outside witnesses and to call for papers. The members would operate as an Assembly within the region and as members of the Second Chamber in Westminster. It may be that at a later stage it would be found desirable, as envisaged by the minority report, for the Assemblies to take control of and responsibility for virtually all the outposts of central government. This would mean, effectively, the adoption of a federal structure of 'government for the UK, perhaps a logical development, but much would depend on the extent to which a regional identity developed under the envisaged changes. The evolutionary potential is there, as a German Foundation report contrasting North Rhine Westphalia and North West England demonstrated.

There will be great argument over the definition of the regional boundaries but there would be no intention at this early stage of changing either the boundaries or the functions of local government; though this would not exclude the more limited organic changes in the functions of some of the major cities envisaged by the last Labour government. The boundaries must coincide with existing local government boundaries. There are serious criticisms of the local government reorganisation of 1974 but to institute another upheaval at a time when local government is still absorbing the present reorganisation would be a folly, incurring considerable extra costs and further disrupting services. There is a strong case for more than the five regions envisaged by the minority report: there are at present eight standard regions in England and ten regions may be needed to reflect sensible boundaries. The far South-West needs to be a region separate from Bristol and the Southern part of England needs to be a region separate from the Greater London Council. The boundaries should be established in the light of two fundamental principles to increase regional identity and avoid change for its own sake. While not crossing existing local government boundaries, they should aim to minimise the disruption involved in amalgamating the boundaries of the existing executive authorities covering the Health, Water, Gas and Electricity boundaries and they should take into account the standard regions and existing police boundaries. It is amazing that no government has yet rationalised all the regional boundaries. Such a reform would in itself produce economies and reinforce regional and national identification which are admittedly much stronger in the peripheral regions of England than in the centre.

Constitutional change could provide the key to the vexed problem of Ireland. Fifty years ago with the partition of the island, compromise was reached which some people hoped would last. It has satisfied none of the three parties most closely involved. In the Irish Republic it is felt in the main that partition is an artificial solution, since it divides communities, divides Irishman from Irishman and, worse, has created a badly treated minority in the Protestant dominated North. It seems an affront to many people in the South that it appears that Britain, against whom they have long fought, should continue to underpin the division of Ireland. They see in the presence of British troops a modern form of colonialism. The Northern Protestants, while feeling a certain affinity with their neighbours across the border still feel British, have fought in the defence of Britain with a great deal of courage, and are set apart by their religion from what they see as the theocracy in the South. Partition allowed the Protestants a chance to remain tied to Britain and it allowed them to control what they regarded as a potential destructive element in the Catholic community. However, for the Northern Irish Protestant, partition has brought bloodshed, bitterness and suffering. The IRA campaigns have been persistent since the late 1960s and have found varying degrees of support among the Catholic population. With an open border behind them as a rest place and an escape route they have not had a feeling of being trapped which is so essential in countering urban terrorism.

British governments have been unwilling to attempt to close the border and have listened perhaps too much to military advisers. Further partition of Ireland has been ruled out under the influence of the strong and well-organised Protestant population, and, however reluctantly, Britain now finds itself sucked into direct rule. Since 1921 successive British governments have paid little attention to the social and political problems of Northern Ireland. The Westminster parliament's record in allowing injustices to persist which – if they had occurred on the mainland of Britain would never have been tolerated – was indefensible. As a consequence, the standing of Britain as a protector of human rights has suffered in the eyes of the world. Many lives have been lost and a costly security operation has had to be mounted, with British troops being withdrawn from the BAOR and rotated through Northern Ireland to try to cope with urban violence and cross-border raids of appalling savagery. The civilian population in Northern Ireland has stoically suffered. Army morale has been sorely stretched. British public opinion thankfully has shown great steadiness considering the violence, and the continued financial cost. Yet a feeling of weary disillusionment is beginning to affect many aspects of the Irish problems and, although the parallel is not exact, the pressures wax and wane for an Aden-like withdrawal. Northern Ireland cannot continue to be allowed to simmer in the background of British politics. The only bold political initiative was that launched at Sunningdale in late 1973. Any initiative must be undertaken in concert with the Irish government. There is no prospect of success if the Republic's government is excluded.

The challenge remains one of trying to satisfy the completely different aspirations of the two communities in Northern Ireland in a political climate in which populations are deeply polarised and sufficiently embittered to be not only wary of compromising with groups against whom they have taken up arms but to be often unable to conceive of compromise. Experience shows there are a large number of issues on which the two communities can work together without raising constitutional problems.

The appalling social and economic problems found in much of Belfast, Londonderry and major towns such as Newry and Portadown could yet be the factor which forces compromise. Unemployment in Northern Ireland is far higher than in any other region in the United Kingdom, the Province ranks as severely deprived when compared with much of the EEC. Both communities recognise the need to increase employment and few people would suggest that their economic problems can be solved only by constitutional changes. Both believe it is in the best interests of everyone to restore local democratic government in Northern Ireland and to ensure that it is responsive to the needs of the Province, ending the continued rule by unelected civil servants. But it is impossible to see the present deadlock being broken without a British initiative and it is time the House of Commons made it clear to the people of Northern Ireland that the current level of financial support is not something which they can take for granted.

Two major issues have so far remained unresolved: firstly, whether the six counties are to be governed from London, Dublin or Belfast and secondly, what is to be the division of powers between majority and minority, whether in Northern Ireland or in a united Ireland. The chief difficulty with the questions is that the legacy of history in Ireland is such that they are always answered with a degree of fervour that borders on obsession. The questions themselves are so phrased as to demand only a yes or no answer, with no scope being left for compromise solutions or for any real political debate to seek agreement for alternative solutions. But are these questions the best or the only way of looking at the problem, or do they restrict debate and needlessly polarise populations?

The most relevant way of stating the political problem of the status of Northern Ireland is to ask: what is the maximum amount of power that can be given to the various groups in Northern Ireland to allow them to govern themselves and to co-operate with each other and with the outside governments of London, Dublin and the European Community in Brussels? This formulation does not immediately lend itself to a simple yes or no answer, nor is it the sort of problem that can be solved unambiguously by a campaign of violence. Posing the question allows one to take account of entrenched minorities, to deal with the legitimate aspirations of the two communities and to provide for political developments in future years in what, it is hoped, will become a stable political atmosphere. Such a strategy does make substantial demands on the groups within Northern Ireland to recognise that they do not individually have the right to insist on one political structure that will alienate groups with which they disagree. For example, it becomes easier to recognise that the IRA is wrong to insist that one million Protestants turn their back on their British heritage and suddenly embrace rule from the South with its different political traditions, and that a united Ireland in this case would merely create a large and embittered minority in an economically weak Ireland: the Protestant equivalent of the IRA already exists and might well seek autonomy for six or four of the Northern counties. Unionist opinion in the North is wrong not to recognise that Catholics in the North have been given little chance to participate in decision-making in Ulster and have always been in an inferior position to the Protestants, suffering discrimination and a markedly worse economic position.

There is nothing sinister about Catholic demands for a united Ireland and a regard for Irish cultural nationalism. There is a possibility that some of these questions can be answered by policies which will not threaten the Protestant way of life and religion. For even after the shattering effects of ten years of bloody violence there remains an 'Ulster identity' common to both Catholic and Protestant which can allow political developments to occur within Ulster, given the will to compromise and abandon inflexible goals.

The existence of the EEC adds another dimension, with the needs and claims of Ulster being different from those of both mainland Britain and Southern Ireland. The wider dimension is beginning to become apparent as the three members of the European Assembly argue the case for Northern Ireland in Strasbourg, Luxembourg and Brussels. The task is to build on this European dimension which is a way of rethinking the Irish dimension. Any constitutional framework must fulfil two criteria which are not mutually exclusive: first, the majority of Protestant population must be assured that they will be given the democratic right to determine their own future, and second, the minority Catholic population must be assured that there will be no steps towards closer integration with the United Kingdom and that they will have the democratic right held open to them to move towards a united Ireland. The United Kingdom and the Republic of Ireland have now both been members of the European Community for over six years; yet at Sunningdale there had been no such period of co-operation and Community decision-making to build upon. Within the EEC, the United Kingdom and Irish governments have actively worked together, while respecting their national integrity, in many areas of economic and social life, something which was hard to envisage in 1973. Members of the European Parliament from Northern Ireland and from the Irish Republic meet in the European Assembly and discuss in detail the problem of the poorer regions of the European Community among many other political issues, on some of which they find themselves in agreement.

The message of this partnership is not that the national state is no longer a viable entity but that it is less important in an age of international co-operation, multinational corporations and the European Community than it was in the latter part of the nineteenth century when the question of Irish self-determination came to the fore. The task is to stop Protestants and Catholics still adhering to the political language and sentiments of the nineteenth century which were shown to have had such destructive consequences in the First World War. The task is to change the form of politics in Ireland from its attachment to symbols evocative of past battles or triumphs, symbols which are often designed to antagonise and which emphasise the mentality of seeking simple yes or no answers to questions which should be capable of a different, more co-operative, community orientated answer. It is no accident that Mr Enoch Powell, now the MP for Down, South, combines a passionate hostility to our membership of the European Community with constant championing of the total integration of Northern Ireland with the Westminster and Whitehall system.

Since the Unionist-dominated parliament at Stormont was abolished by the British government in 1972, Northern Ireland, with the brief exception of the period of the Executive, has been ruled directly from Westminster. The Secretary of State for Northern Ireland has been responsible for a wide variety of powers, with local councils dealing only with very minor affairs. This position has one advantage: most administration is carried out by a civil service which has retained a reputation for non-discrimination during the last ten years and which is not viewed with the same degree of suspicion as was Stormont and the old system of local administration. The minority would probably prefer the continuation of this type of administration rather than any return to Unionist-dominated and Unionist-inspired policies, since the present system ensures that both communities are treated fairly. However, the continuation of direct rule is not likely to satisfy the demand for an efficient, responsive administration, nor is it likely to offer the possibility of making any political initiatives to reconcile the two communities. The Unionist and minority communities have agreed, in a series of initiatives taken since the collapse of the Executive, that devolved government for Northern Ireland is urgently required, provided that it can secure a wide degree of support within Northern Ireland. What is needed is a sense of a feeling of movement, once engendered, which can then not just engage people's minds but also their hearts. Nothing is worse than the stale timid inertia that envelops the Northern Ireland problem. There is no parallel in content or in history but when in the spring of 1977 the Geneva Conference over Rhodesia had collapsed and there was a total policy vacuum, it seemed that there was more to risk in terms of lives being lost by sitting back and doing nothing than by taking a high risk political initiative and setting out a framework for a settlement, even to the extent of tabling a draft constitution in the Anglo-American proposals published in September 1977. What is striking, on looking back, is how similar that framework was to that which was eventually agreed in December 1979 at Lancaster House and implemented in a free and independent Zimbabwe in the spring of 1980. Yet in between, every party to the dispute attacked both the Constitution, the concept of British rule during the election period and many commentators criticised the British government for taking the initiative in tabling such detailed proposals, yet without that detailed framework and without the 2½-year discussions which preceded the agreement there would have been no peaceful settlement. The Sunningdale initiative in 1973 was both bold and imaginative. Few worthwhile agreements are ultimately secured without taking some risks. The risks of doing nothing are daily to be measured in the loss of life in Northern Ireland and in the permanent scars it is beginning to leave behind.

Whether a similar form of power-sharing Executive could be established in Northern Ireland as was tried in December 1973 must depend on discussion and negotiation. The Executive which held power for only five months operated under the most difficult possible circumstances for any such radical democratic experiment. The General Election of 28 February 1974 meant that candidates who opposed the

Sunningdale agreement, and particularly the Council of Ireland, won 11 out of the 12 seats and received over 50 per cent of the votes. On 16 May a vote in the Assembly rejecting constitutional renegotiation triggered a call for a general strike by the non-elected Ulster Workers' Council. The demand was then made by a combination of the Ulster Workers' Council's 'loyalist coalition' politicians and the various para-military organisations for early Assembly elections and, particularly in the urban areas, the effects of the industrial stoppage became severe. On 27 May, the Army eventually took control of the main petrol and oil depots but this was matched by a complete shutdown of electricity supply and on 29 May the warrants for the Executive and Administration were revoked and Northern Ireland returned to direct rule. Ever since power sharing has lacked any firm pressure behind it. In 1977 the United States promised economic aid in the event of a peaceful settlement. With the economy now so weak the establishment of an Ireland Development Fund linked to a power-sharing executive could help to persuade some people who are not totally committed. The Fund could be all-Ireland in the sense that the Irish government would be involved in developing joint projects.

Power sharing is a difficult concept to fit into democratic government which has usually relied on the balance of one elector, one vote and one member, one vote for its decision-making authority. It is too stark to see power sharing as a Cabinet containing Mrs Thatcher and Tony Benn. It was designed for a unique situation; and a determined effort should be made to revive it for there is evidence still of public support, but the auguries are not good if the issue is left to the politicians. A referendum on power sharing would be a possibility, to be followed by an election on that basis if successful, but limited to a new economic initiative.

An alternative would be to decentralise within Northern Ireland – a pattern of regional government which had boundaries which allowed part of the country to be controlled by a Catholic majority and the other, which would have to include Belfast, a Protestant majority. Both sides would fear that their people were being disenfranchised. Within Belfast some of the resistance might be lessened if as an additional safeguard for the minority Catholic population some form of two-tier government might be formed, so that some of the second tier authorities would have Catholic majorities and deal with local services. The legislative parliament for Northern Ireland would have only minimal executive powers, the members being drawn in equal numbers from the two regional tiers of government.

The danger of dividing Northern Ireland in this way is that it would for some be seen as a prelude to partition. But this would be guarded against by enacting the principle embodied in section 1 of the Constitution Act, that Northern Ireland would not cease to be a part of the United Kingdom without the consent of a majority of its people. It would, however, make it likely that at least in the predominantly Catholic region of Northern Ireland there would develop some consultation, co-operation and cross-border working if some regional structure could be established for this purpose by the government of the Republic of Ireland. It might be easier for opinion to develop constructively throughout Northern Ireland if they saw their own constitutional development separate from but coinciding with British regional constitutional development. The European Community could be encouraged to think of regional policy in Ireland in the context of Irish regions, and thereby encourage the co-operation between regions across the border with special grants from the Regional Fund. The security forces would operate in both the regions of Northern Ireland and so Protestant fears of the Catholic region becoming an IRA fiefdom would be without foundation.

Periodic referenda within the regions would determine whether either or both of the regions within Northern Ireland would participate with regions in the Republic. A referendum initially in ten years' time involving all the people of Northern Ireland would determine whether new legislation allowing for participation in a Council of Ireland with the Republic should be introduced, and further referenda should be held at ten year intervals thereafter. Such a formulation would, as at Sunningdale, allow all to retain their long-term aspirations as to the future of Northern Ireland; but the practical possibility of close co-operation between regions on either side of the border might be a less difficult threshold initially than a Council of Ireland, and would hold open the possibility of earlier movement towards wider cross-border co-operation.

The alternatives presented in 1980 by the British government lack any pressure behind them and all parties to the discussion know that if they refuse them direct rule will continue, or there will be an Assembly with no power and just talk. No scheme will succeed without a combination of financial inducement and military warning. Pulling the troops out is a crude slogan, but a recognition that the British and Irish governments expect both parties to negotiate seriously is very necessary, perhaps accompanied by a threat jointly to seal the border. Both sides to the conflict will need to recognise a need to marry democracy and fairness. The two concepts have much in common, but they are not identical. It means a degree of institutionalised tolerance which traditional political structures do not express. It is as fruitless for Unionists to clamour for 'British style democracy' as it is for Republicans to invoke 'democracy' to support their claim for a United Ireland by the argument that a majority of the population of Ireland supports such a claim. Both lines of reasoning show a contempt for the values underlying the concept of democracy and blithely ignore the fears of those who hold a differing point of view. The entire population of Northern Ireland must choose its own system of government. No solution can be imposed from London or Dublin, although both governments retain legitimate interests. Agreement can only be painfully constructed by the people of Northern Ireland themselves with a full appreciation of the legacy of 800 years. The British Cabinet cannot continue to hesitate but must put forward a proposition for the parties to negotiate over. New concepts, such as the South and North becoming members of the Commonwealth, are conceivable now that some nations are Republics and non-aligned, or the North, like Luxembourg, being a full member of the Community.

It is impossible to consider comprehensive constitutional reform without assessing the system of voting operating within the United Kingdom. Historians may highlight the way in which the problem of Northern Ireland has precipitated electoral changes which have already started to spread across the United Kingdom. The introduction of referenda started with a border poll for Northern Ireland formally announced on 24 March 1972.

It was again Northern Ireland which broke through the traditional attachment to the 'first past the post' voting system and introduced the single transferable vote in 1973 to ensure that there would be Catholic representation in the Northern Ireland Assembly. The principle of a different voting system having been conceded in one part of the United Kingdom, the long-standing movement for electoral reform was handed a powerful lever to argue for proportional representation in all parts of the United Kingdom. It was given a further impetus by the need to legislate for elections to the European Assembly. In this case the retention of the traditional voting system meant that for the very large European constituencies, the effect of a fairly small swing of opinion to any one of the major parties meant a distorted electoral result, predictably with no Liberal representation and many more unfairnesses than in a general election with a large number of constituencies being involved. It was the manifest unfairness of retaining the 'first past the post' system which led a majority in the Labour Cabinet in 1977 to conclude that a system of proportional representation through a regional list was the preferable system for elections to the European Assembly. This view was formed before the decision was taken to enter into negotiations over the Liberal-Labour agreement and was one of the reasons why it was possible for the principal negotiators on behalf of the government, James Callaghan and Michael Foot, to promise that the proposal for a regional list would be put to a vote in the House of Commons. It was, however, against the interests of the Liberal Party that their negotiators did not insist that the continuation of the agreement was dependent on a successful outcome of that vote. Such a firm declaration would have ensured that the government kept to the principle of collective responsibility and that all who wished to remain Ministers would have then voted both for the principle of the

European Assembly inherent in a genuine acceptance of the 1975 referendum result and for the regional list system, since this reflected the Cabinet majority. It may or may not have influenced a sufficient number of backbench Labour MPs to support the legislation. It was an opportunity which may never recur to take a decisive step towards electoral reform across the whole of the United Kingdom.

Whatever the merits of electoral reform, and it is impossible to argue that the 'first past the post' system is the fairest system, reform will not come on its merits. It will come because it is forced on one or other of the major parties as the price they have to concede for remaining in government at a time when the balance of votes is held by a group of MPs who decide to combine and oppose the government and threaten another election. The debate about electoral reform lacks reality because the public sense that it is not an argument about merits but about power. The two major parties, Conservative and Labour, fear electoral reform. Since 1945 both the major parties have had an equal share of government and they would prefer a system they know, in the belief that this pattern of alternating power will continue.

Yet the system is producing an increasingly indefensible basis for forming a government with the power of absolute decision. In 1951 a Labour government could poll 40 per cent of the electorate and receive more votes in number than the Conservatives and still lose the election. They could poll a mere 28 per cent of the electorate in October 1974, however, and remain in government until May 1979, when the Conservatives won a big majority, but still only with the support of 33 per cent of the electorate. The Liberal Party has by any standards of fairness been appallingly treated. That in February 1974 they should have polled 6 million votes, 19 per cent of the electorate, and yet won only fourteen of the seats provides fuel for justified criticism of the system. But the system can claim in its defence that its power of adaptation is considerable, that it did ensure that from February 1974 to May 1979, when for most of that period the Labour government was in a minority, it had to listen more than it would ever normally have done to the views of the minority parties and that, although the Labour government formed no formal coalition, it reflected minority party views. Though attention was focused on the Liberal-Labour arrangement or pact, there were numerous deals and arrangements made between the Labour government and the Scottish Nationalist Party, the Welsh Nationalist Party, the Ulster Unionists and the Social Democratic and Labour Party. The Ulster Unionists demanded the acceptance of more Westminster MPs for Northern Ireland. The Scottish Nationalists, despite divisions within the Parliamentary Labour Party, demanded priority for devolution. There were the obvious manifestations but there were many other understandings and accommodations.

The basic argument remains that the justification for the present voting system is that it produces a coalition within parties and that both Conservative and Labour are normally forced by the very electoral system to remain broad-based political movements reflecting a wide spectrum of views, and that a coalition within a party allows, because of its better discipline, for more decisive government than a coalition formed across the parties. Yet the post-war history of Britain, particularly since Suez in 1956, demonstrates convincingly that the record of government in Britain is no better and in many cases a lot worse than the record of continental European governments where coalitions across the parties are more frequent, as are changes of government in Belgium, Holland and even Italy. The record of German governments from the 1950s onwards and of French governments since General de Gaulle, both with different systems, is clearly better than that in Britain. Anyhow the 1940-5 coalition was one of the best governments Britain has ever had. There was a form of coalition by tacit inter-party agreement between 1910 and 1915 and from 1977 to 1979. Britain has had single party government with total control for only forty-eight of the years up to 1980.

When the arguments and the mass of books and pamphlets on the subject have all been weighed, the question of electoral reform will be resolved by the pressure of power politics, not by merit or by constitutional theory about coalitions or the two-party system. If, for example, the Labour Party continues to narrow its electoral appeal and ceases to be a broad-based coalition it would split as would the Conservative Party. If that split were followed by the return of thirty MPs belonging to a new party, and if they were to vote in combination with the Liberal Party and other minor parties after an election, they could very well hold the balance. They could all insist that they would not vote for a Queen's Speech which did not contain a referendum to be held within three months on a specific 'yes' or 'no' vote to a specific electoral system which they would put forward. The two major parties would be forced to choose and either one or other might accept, or the Queen might have to agree to another election. If at that election the result again gave the minority parties the balancing power to insist on a referendum even if the two major parties refused to put such a commitment in the Queen's speech, the Queen would have to ask one of the minority parties to form the government and it is hard to see how the referendum proposition could be refused by parliament. If, as would be likely, judging by repeated opinion polls a referendum resulted in support for the specific system of proportional representation proposed again, it is hard to see how parliament could refuse to pass the legislation. The chances of such a sequence of events occurring are hard to assess. It nearly happened in February 1974 and became slightly more likely in 1977. It is possible that it may occur in 1984 and is certainly more likely than that electoral reform will come about as a result of logical argument and persuasion. It could arise from fear where a government, sensing electoral defeat because of a world economic recession and factors outside its control, while still holding a parliamentary majority, introduced electoral reform as the only way of protecting the country from the danger of an extremist government from either the Right or the Left. But even this would presuppose a readiness of the Prime Minister and other key figures to admit the possibility of electoral defeat, which is an unlikely admission since the more extreme the Opposition the more they would hope that they would win. The case for proportional representation for the Scottish, Welsh and regional Assemblies is that in order to win public acceptance their Assemblies must reflect national and regional views without becoming the vehicle for separatism or being controlled 100 per cent by one party – which could easily happen under the present electoral system.

Some people argue that the Treaty of Rome will itself force electoral reform in Britain in the context of the 1985 European Assembly elections. There is no clear justification for this belief, since the Community, having once accepted that the British parliament should choose its own system, would be likely to accept that this would happen again. Any British government ought to recognise that the distorted result from the 1980 election damaged the United Kingdom's reputation in Europe, and at home damaged for Labour voters the very concept of European Community. It is, however, very probable that the argument that introducing proportional representation for European elections would make it more likely that it would eventually be introduced for Westminster elections would again persuade most MPs to vote for the continuation of the 'first past the post' system.

It may seem depressing to discuss these issues in such *Realpolitik* terms, but as long as the two major political parties represent broad coalitions the political realities will continue to ensure that in their own self interest they oppose electoral reform. The October 1980 Labour Party Conference has, however, called in question more than any other single event since the 1931 economic crisis whether the Labour Party has the cohesion necessary to remain a broad coalition. The result of the internal arguments within the Labour Party may well determine whether electoral reform is forced on to the statute book in the 1980s or whether the present system continues unchanged. The best system of proportional representation to adopt would be the system that has operated successfully in the Federal Republic of Germany which allows predominantly for constituency MPs, but with a supplementary list system. No party receiving less than 5 per cent of the vote is eligible for representation and this stops a mass of small parties developing.

The constitutional changes discussed in this chapter are far-reaching. Yet they build on and synthesise existing patterns in the constitution and in the present structure of government. They take account of much of the debate on the constitution over the last fifteen years and they combine both decentralisation and devolution. They will need to be championed and argued for, since they will offend many vested interests in Whitehall and elsewhere, but they represent a new way forward while extending democracy and while retaining at every stage the unity of the United Kingdom.

15

Local Government

In 1851, sixteen years before the first major move towards universal suffrage, most of our present problems and tensions between local and central government were perceptively forecast: 'It is by independence of thought and conduct to be only acquired by the habit of being continually called on to express an opinion upon, and to take an active part in, the management of the affairs of their own district, that men can alone ever be really fit to elect representatives to Parliament or the local Council, or to form sound and respectworthy opinions on the conduct of such representatives . . . Free institutions do not, then, exist and national independence can never be ensured nor individual independence and fore-thought ever characterise a people unless true local self-government is fully and freely exercised in every district throughout the land.'[1]

The issue of popular identification with decision-making processes is as vital today as it was over a hundred years ago. However, the truth is that the average citizen's involvement is still largely restricted to periodic elections, and the habitually low turnout at local government elections is an indicator of a fairly general apathy. There is a widespread belief that local government is not 'local' but an arm of central government, that councillors lose touch with their locality when elected and that local government officials have a 'civil service' mentality. Many of the criticisms made in Chapter 13 about Whitehall can be applied as strongly to the Town Hall. It is ordinary people's sense of alienation from the process of decision-

making that breeds this harsh scepticism. But how to overcome it and how to involve people in the decisions that affect
their lives is an extremely difficult problem. As Professor
Donnison, who served for years as the Chairman of the
Supplementary Benefits Commission, has written: 'The electorate is likely to remain sceptical about public services and
their professional staff. Thus governments will have to take
more seriously the capacity of ordinary people to do things for
themselves ... We need not just more nursery schools, but
more mothers running their own playgroups with more
support and training from the state.'[2] It is this faith in the latent
ability of people to help themselves and to help each other,
given adequate support, that is so often lacking among experts
and professionals, planners and managers, and administrators
and politicians. Their scepticism is not without foundation,
but if the assumption that people are not able to help
themselves is allowed to go unchallenged, democracy itself is
threatened.

It is this scepticism which has motivated much of the
current criticism of local government, has allowed central
government to erode local government's autonomy and has
underpinned the movement towards centralisation. Of course,
the need to involve people in the decisions that affect their
lives is widely acknowledged and a great deal of lip service is
paid to it. The fact is that the opportunity to participate in
decision-making at a local level is still denied to most people in
Britain, and attempts to generate interest and action at local
neighbourhood or community level often meet with suspicion
and open hostility from those whose function it should be to
generate just this interest.

The quality of people's lives, whether in town or country, is
of concern to socialists, and while much attention has been
focused on the problems of city life, many rural areas face both
similar and particular problems. For example, the depopulation
of parts of North Devon, inadequate or non-existent public
transport, unpredictable seasonal employment and low wages
all contribute to the same sense of isolation and alienation that
people living in cities have.

It is all too apparent that many people feel they have no say in any changes in their neighbourhood; that their wishes and needs are not recognised by a remote and impersonal council bureaucracy; and that their elected representatives are not available to listen to grievances. That is not to denigrate the dedicated work of many councillors: Many of them are well aware of the justified criticism of their role and function.

The definition and identification of a community can never fit within an exact, precise and rigid formula. The pattern of social, cultural and economic life, the local centres for education, shopping, meeting and worship, transport facilities and means of communication – all these have their influence.[3] One sociologist has defined community boundaries – 'as far as you can push a pram' – and this serves at least to remind administrators, with their car and mileage allowances, that the people they serve have a different focus. The reasons why people feel alienated from their neighbourhood or community are complex but the results are all too apparent: vandalism, violence and crime increase, and the very fabric of life becomes threatened. The development and fostering of a 'sense of community' must be the task of both National and local governments.

As the 1977 White Paper of the Inner City pointed out, 'too little attention has been paid to the economic wellbeing and to the community life of the Inner City areas and the physical fabric in some parts is badly neglected or decayed.'[4] The same White Paper not only identified the need for resources to be channelled to areas in need but recognised that 'involving local people is both a necessary means to the regeneration of the inner areas and an end in its own right. Public authorities need to draw on the ideas of local residents, to discover their priorities and enable them to play a practical part in reviving their areas. Self-help is important and so is community effort.'[5] Unfortunately there has been constant hostility and suspicion from many officials and elected representatives at all levels of government both nationally and locally when people actually do try to involve themselves.

The White Paper went on: 'There is scope for the development of new methods such as area management or neighbourhood planning – in which both members and officers establish closer links with the people they serve and seek to provide the local authority's services in a way more closely attuned to the requirements of the area.'[6] It is one thing to recognise the need for participation but another to suggest how it should be affected; the idea was mooted for new procedures that would enable the community to articulate its needs. 'In some places elected Neighbourhood Councils . . . may have a role in representing the communities' views and in mobilising voluntary effort.'[7] This statement recognised that the tiers of local government set up in the 1972 Local Government Act had failed to identify and respond to the needs of people living in Inner City Areas and that alternative structures might be set up to cater for particular local communities. This idea was based on the finding of the Inner Areas Studies undertaken by the government which called for greater sensitivity to the needs of the local people by public authorities, for the involvement of local communities, for closer integration of services, for better use of existing resources, for positive discrimination in favour of run-down areas and for changes in organisations, in attitudes and in policies.

Three separate organisations at present speak for neighbourhoods in England: the National Association of Local Councils (NALC) – representing some 8,000 parish councils in rural areas – small towns, and some larger urban areas. These bodies all have statutory status. Besides these there are the National Federation of Community Associations (NFCA) representing 500 voluntary community associations in all types of communities, and the Association for Neighbourhood Councils (ANC) representing the smaller number of non-statutory, democratically elected, neighbourhood councils and others who wish to secure statutory status for directly elected neighbourhood councils in England. The ANC believe that the present separation of these organisations, all with closely related, though not identical, aims and interests, is damaging to the cause of neighbourhood democracy and voluntary activity. They believe that neighbourhoods need a single representative voice to speak to each other, to central and local government, and to the general public, and that this could be achieved by bringing the three organisations much closer together, sharing facilities, cutting out duplication, and unnecessary misunderstandings. They do not expect such a body to become, like the ANC, a pressure group for extending statutory status, comparable to that of a parish council, to neighbourhoods in English towns and cities. The case for one group to speak for neighbourhoods in England is very strong and if it allowed those members who wish to press for statutory status to do so without committing those who disagree, it is hard to see any objection. Statutory status means direct democratic election, a right to limited precept on local authority rates, and accountability to local people through the electoral process. I favour it, but like the ANC I see it as a democratic right, an opportunity to be taken only by those neighbourhoods who positively want it. I see no merit in imposing a universal pattern, or forcing a different structure on communities who are happy with their own voluntary organisation. There is not yet probably sufficient agreement for any government to legislate. If it is to come about it will need a groundswell of support from the local people.

The issue that transcends arguments about statutory status for neighbourhood councils is the need to ensure that local government itself survives as a truly democratic force. Challenges to the autonomy, freedom and independence of local government are nothing new, but the present Conservative government is mounting the most sustained attack on its fundamental nature that it has ever experienced.

In contrast to the situation in the 1980s, at the start of the century local government was at the height of its power and influence. There had been a rapid expansion between 1870 and 1900 when local government expenditure rose relatively much faster than that of central government. By 1902 it was providing housing, sanitary services, police, road repairs and education, and some authorities were running train and bus services, providing water, gas, electricity, libraries, public entertainments, and owned docks and other municipal enterprises. Public health extended to municipal hospitals and covered maternity, child welfare and the mentally handicapped. Local government was even given responsibility for the unemployed until the Unemployment Assistance Board was formed in 1934. After the Boer War, during the years from 1904-14 with the exception of 1912-13, local government actually spent more than central government; today central government spends nearly twice as much.

It is only looking back that one can see the true extent of the shift from local to central government to statutory duties, responsibilities and resources in terms of employment and finance. Analysis of the comparative spending figures reveals some interesting trends.[8] As one would expect, central government spending leapt during both World Wars and was accompanied by large deficits, only to be followed by considerable falls in expenditure. Local government expenditure increased much more steadily and it always met its expenditure from its current income. Grant income from central government was 12 per cent in 1913-14, 27·4 per cent by 1939-40, and 36·9 per cent in 1947-5, when it jumped because of a major policy switch, to 39·8 per cent of total income in 1975-6. The extent of this particular switch is further emphasised if capital expenditure is excluded, revealing that in 1966-7 rates made up 33·8 per cent of income, grants 37·1 per cent and other sources 29·1 per cent but by 1976-7 rates contributed only 23·8 per cent of total incomes, grants had risen to 49·6 per cent and other sources provided 26·6 per cent. It is clear that the dramatic shift whereby central government became virtually the paymaster of local government is a relatively recent trend, starting in 1967 and increasing significantly in 1975. Central government grants, which at the start of the century when local government had its greatest powers, were a negligible source of finance, have now become the dominant source, at the same time as the powers of local government have declined.

These facts and the extent of the growth of the centralised state in Britain need to be stressed for a post-war generation that has forgotten the days of the powerful and often enlightened municipal authorities, a generation which tends to forget the great cultural traditions of cities like Manchester, the strengths of provincial England, and which accepts the dominance of London and Whitehall – as if that were the only possible form of government for Britain. The time is overdue for a reassertion of a different balance where local government recovers some of its former powers and influence and where a more variegated pattern of government matches the rich cultural distinctions between Devon and Derbyshire, Leeds and Bristol. It may be that the public mood is starting to sense that the sickening hostility displayed daily for a decade in the national press towards local government owes more to the centralised nature of that press than to any objective assessment of the weaknesses and strengths of local government. In April 1980 a Gallup poll at a time when the Conservative government was campaigning against local government spending showed that three people wanted better local services even if it meant higher rates for every two who wanted lower rates even if it meant worse services. What was even more surprising was that when asked if councils had enough independence from central government only 17 per cent said 'too much', 32 per said 'about right' and a healthy 34 per cent 'too little'.[9]

Some people argue that a shift of functions from local government to national government is inevitable in an increasingly complex industrialised society which is predominantly urban. Larger-scale institutions, it is said, are required to deal with long-range planning and nation-wide industrial strategies. The arguments are exaggerated, though there is a limited regional function distinct from local government. The regional offices of national government administer and co-ordinate regional strategies. Parliament has been responsible for placing a statutory duty on government departments to carry out or supervise functions which were previously the responsibility of local government, and then by leaving the exact means of administration often to be worked out by the Department concerned, has strengthened Whitehall. Civil servants have decided that while they are in control of much of the finance, responsibility cannot be delegated to local government for detailed policy-making and administration. So central government, because of increasing financial involvement, has increased its own powers and sought to curtail those of local government. Ministerial control of departmental decisions in the English regions is slight, in comparison to

Wales and Scotland, as is parliamentary scrutiny. Regional Assemblies would have a scrutinising function that the House of Commons is unlikely to be able to fill, but this function does not reduce the role of local government. The form of Regional Assemblies suggested in Chapter 14 does not affect local government but increases the accountability of the appointed water and health authorities and scrutinises the civil service.

An overwhelming case can be made in favour of restoring the strength of local government: 'Local government in England can and does help to secure an active democracy; increase the knowledge, competence and independence of the people; provide personally and locally responsive services; make possible the apt distribution of powers and duties; preserve central and local accountability and support yet more local sharing in decision and administration. It does so through its local legitimacy and independence of the centre. Each local authority has a professional administration responsible to members who are elected and thus accountable. In short, local government is a critically important constitutional and democratic institution.'[10]

What is needed is a rethink of political attitudes towards centralisation and decentralisation. In 1971 the Conservative government's White Paper stated that: 'A rigorous local democracy means that authorities must be given real functions – with powers of decision and the ability to take action without being subjected to excessive regulation by central government through financial or other controls ... above all else, a genuine local democracy implies that decisions should be taken – and should be seen to be taken – as locally as possible.'[11] Some people may therefore have been encouraged to hope that the 1979 Conservative government would, as part of its general attack on bureaucracy, start to challenge central government's interference with local government; and indeed, in the early months of the present administration much publicity was given to the abolition and relaxation of a wide range of petty and largely unnecessary central government regulations and controls. However, the 1980 Local Government Planning and Land Act introduced a block grant system which has the avowed intent of preventing a local authority from spending more than central government thinks it should. This legislation represents the single most centralising measure ever passed by a British parliament, with consequences that are hard to exaggerate. Yet there was no public outcry. A few newspaper editorials made reference to it but there was no sense of shock. Parliament debated the Act under a guillotine and despite a considerable undercurrent of discontent from Conservative local councillors and a revolt by a few Conservative MPs, including a former Secretary of State for the Environment, there was no perception that what was being enacted was a constitutional outrage.

The sad fact is that legislation reflected the Whitehall consensus for which successive Labour governments were as responsible as the present Conservative administration. Though during the passage of the Bill through parliament the Labour Opposition made most of the correct criticisms, they were unable to mobilise public concern about the fundamental constitutional nature of the measure, not just because they were constantly reminded of the actions and decisions of the previous Labour government but because the public sensed the ambivalence within the Labour Party itself on the issue of the priority to be given to local government. This ambivalence is too obvious to hide behind a barrage of political criticism and it needs now to be thought through; it is basically the same ambivalence that haunted the debate among socialists over devolution, but it also goes much deeper and reflects the historic divide between the centralist and the decentralist socialist philosophy.

The ambivalence is well marked by central government's attitudes to the sale of council houses, which was discussed in Chapter 5 on Inequality. It also ran through the debate about how to introduce comprehensive education. Anthony Crosland was right in the 1960s to seek first to persuade and pressurise local authorities to introduce comprehensive education and not to enact legislation. Legislation was rightly only introduced later when a few recalcitrant authorities were resisting a social reform that had been voluntarily accepted by the great majority of Local Authorities. It was therefore far less challenging to the autonomy of local government in education which, as in other areas of their responsibilities, should only be eroded very rarely by central government.

The case for a Labour controlled council to be the master of its own house and the vehicle for socialism was argued by G.D.H. Cole in 1921. He saw local authorities as 'the instruments of decentralised public ownership in a democratic socialist state'[12] and he recognised the necessity of reorganising local government since, 'the objections which apply to the highly centralised national state need not apply in the same way to smaller bodies exercising jurisdiction over more manageable areas, even if these bodies reproduce to some extent, on a smaller scale, the structure of the State itself.'[13]

The Labour Party's ambivalence was well described by its then Local Government Officer in an internal Labour Party minute on 'Minimum Standards in Local Government Service'. It argues that there was a problem for democratic socialists when their aim of ensuring a decent level of community services for everyone conflicted with the commitment to strong democratic local government. The conflict arose most sharply when a Labour government was in power nationally and at the same time a majority of Councils were controlled by the Conservatives.

It was admitted that there was strong pressure within the Party for a Labour government to impose on Conservative Councils Labour Party policy for community services. The pressure could be for legislation to impose new obligations such as to complete comprehensive reorganisation in education or to remove a discretion such as the right to sell council houses or to take away from local government the responsibility for a particular service like further education. Pressure could also come to tie government grants to spending on a specific service or part of a service, either education generally or in-service teacher training in particular, or to set minimum standards of provision for the chronic sick and disabled.

The Labour Party was warned that the hypothesis had only to be reversed for the dangers of this centralist approach to be clear. A Conservative government acting under the same centralist doctrine imposed its rent policy on Labour Councils in 1972 and is now imposing a duty on local authorities to sell council houses.

It was argued that there was no difference in principle between imposing a particular rent policy on Clay Cross and a particular Education policy on Tameside and that the Party's attitude to the two cases was fundamentally inconsistent. The minute powerfully restated the case for a sensible measure of local government autonomy. It reflected all that is good in the local government tradition.

'Firstly there is the argument for democratic pluralism. It is a characteristic of totalitarian regimes that they tolerate no rivals to the powers of the state – not in individual rights nor in democratic institutions. The power of the state is total, and totally centralised. Democratic socialists on the other hand belive in a wide distribution of political and economic power – among democratic local government, trade unions, pressure groups, political parties, the press and public and private enterprise. The justification for this plurality of centres of power is that freedom depends on being able to invoke the protection of many alternative sources of authority. It also recognises that man is simultaneously a citizen, a member of a local community, a worker, a consumer and an individual with a need to express himself in many different ways. Political pluralism is the counterpart of the mixed economy.

'Local government derives its political powers from the local electorate and its legitimacy is recognised by law. What the Party must accept is that the legitimacy of Tory controlled authorities is equal to that of Labour controlled authorities and that Tory councils must have the right to make "wrong" decisions.

'Secondly there is the argument from efficiency and sensitivity. Local authorities know their areas and their needs better than Whitehall and can apply appropriate solutions to local problems much more effectively. Thus if the Tory county of Berkshire spends less per head on its disabled than the Labour City of Manchester it *may* be because the disabled in Berkshire are better supported by the family, friendly neighbours, and voluntary organisations than they are in Manchester.

'Thirdly there is the argument from accountability. Those making decisions of local significance ought to be available and susceptible to legitimate pressure from local electors and local interest groups.'

It was a sensible and correct analysis but it does not represent the dominant views inside the present Labour Party. The decision-making structure of the party at the level of the National Executive Committee and at Conference as well as within recent Labour governments, has not allowed the traditional decentralist socialist voice of experienced local councillors sufficient weight. This was demonstrated in the summer of 1980 when a significant group on the NEC persuaded the party's Organisation Committee to adopt, against the overwhelming advice of the Local Government Sub Committee, proposals to give the constituency party or district party the deciding voice in drafting the local manifesto for fighting local government elections and the right to choose the leader of the local government group and the principal spokesmen. This proposal was fortunately referred back but its significance in this context relates to the important issue of why the Labour Party and Labour governments repeatedly ignore or underplay the views of their local councillors. The continued absence of any formal representation of local councillors on the NEC is one reason and the issues are well discussed in a Fabian Tract published in 1977, *Labour and Local Politics*[14] which argues for giving 'new life to the old ideal of municipal socialism basing it squarely upon the issues of equality'.

The problem is not new. William Robson complained in 1931 that the Labour Party lacked 'any adequate recognition of the immense problems and difficulties facing the groups of local councillors in the localities, the need for integrating national and municipal Labour Policy into a coherent unity, or the opportunities for leadership in municipal affairs.' The emphasis has long been on parliamentary and trade union activity, and Parliamentary Party Leaders have been no exception: Clement Attlee contemplated in 1935 the 'super-session' of local government during the 'period of critical transition' to socialism.[15]

It is impossible to move towards a more decentralised society without challenging the trend towards central government control of local government. For local autonomy to be a reality local authorities must have a degree of freedom to determine the range and standard of their services and to choose to increase or decrease the level of expenditure which they devote to those services. This principle may appear so obvious as hardly to need stating but it is now threatened by the power that the government has under the 1980 Act to reduce support to local authorities which overspend in the financial years from 1980-1. The government can now, at the routine yearly inflation adjustment known as the Increase Order, reduce retrospectively the level of grant that the local authority anticipated it would receive.

At no stage in the argument has central government been able to show that in order to ensure the proper running of the economy the Treasury needs to be able to exert this degree of precise control on the quantum of local government expenditure. The national economy contains so many variables and the margin of error is so wide in expenditure forecasts that absolute precision of forward estimating is impossible. Local government expenditure is, in contrast to so many other expenditures, self-financing, so the problem is not one of deficit accumulation but relates solely to overall levels of expenditure. The evidence is that, far from being out of control, local government expenditure has been held by a combination of pressures and constraints very close to the levels asked for by successive governments.[16] The 1978 government expenditure forecasts had local government spending falling by 13·6 per cent in 1980-1 compared to 1974-5, whereas it had central government spending rising by 7·7 per cent over the same period. The consequences of having a few authorities overspending are very marginal to the management of the national economy.

Local government becomes a public issue once a year in early April when the rates bill arrives and for a few weeks there are angry denunciations of waste and bureaucracy as the rating system becomes the butt of many people's anger. Very rarely does any central government resist the temptation to distance itself from this public mood. It has often encouraged the criticism and sometimes responded in the heat of the moment by indicating that it would reform the rating system. Instead of a mutual respect between central and local government there has been growing antagonism. In 1966 the then Minister of Housing and Local Government, Richard Crossman, was determined to have a serious examination of local government and two Royal Commissions were established, for England under the chairmanship of Lord Redcliffe-Maud and for Scotland under Lord Wheatley.[17] Astonishingly neither of the Commissions was asked to examine local government finance. The Redcliffe-Maud proposals for unitary authorities came too late in the lifetime of the Labour government to be implemented, though they were accepted in principle. The new Conservative government in 1970 cavalierly abandoned the Commission's major recommendations and legislated for a two-tier structure of local government under the Local Government Acts of 1972 and 1973. Under the Water Act 1973 local authorities in England and Wales also lost their responsibility for water, sewerage and sewage disposal. The 1974 reorganisation itself triggered a major political controversy over local government, with allegations of 'Empire building' due to the substantial rates increases and the overlapping of responsibilities of the two tiers. There were many complaints of extravagance, particularly over the new system of councillor attendance allowances and lavish buildings contracted by the old authorities. The general rate revaluation of 1973 also meant that some people whose property had been reassessed had to face rate demands several hundred per cent higher than before. The average increase in rate demands sent by local authorities to domestic ratepayers in England and Wales was a little under 30 per cent but this average figure concealed increases from over 160 per cent to decreases of 9 per cent. Coming at a time of high and increasing inflation all these factors combined to unleash a general outcry in the spring of 1974 to which the newly elected Labour government had to respond. On 27 June the Secretary of State for the Environment announced the appointment of a Committee of Enquiry under Frank Layfield, QC, 'to review the whole system of local government finance in England, Scotland and Wales and to make recommendations.' The Committee was asked to work quickly and the report was published in May 1976.[18]

The Layfield Committee, however, came up with embarrassingly radical proposals. They argued that the level of government grant determines the amount of local autonomy and that over the last twenty years autonomy had been eroded as the grant had steadily risen to the then level of 60 per cent. They felt that autonomy had also been reduced by Whitehall setting national targets in the key services of education, police, fire, social services and roads, services which in 1975-6 accounted for over 80 per cent of total spending. The results, they argued, were confusion over who was responsible for rate increases, a lack of financial control because the increase of grants had encouraged local authorities to provide higher levels of services which the government would pay for, and an uncontrolled increase in spending and rates. The most important findings were that local autonomy would be increased if local authorities were given some financial independence and that government grants should be reduced to 50 per cent of spending, that rates should be at two thirds of their present level, and that a local income tax should be introduced at 11p in the pound.

A note of reservation by Professor Day argued that the majority report was wrong to reject a 'half way house' solution by which the government should set minimum standards in services and pay for them entirely, and that there should be a clear division of responsibilities between local and central government. He argued that unless this was done, the creation of financial institutions which give greater formal powers to authorities to raise revenue from sources such as a LIT would be unlikely to achieve any greater degree of effective local autonomy than the political will of the government would be prepared to tolerate'.[19] The majority report rejected this view because it felt that minimum standards could not be easily defined and costed. Professor Day denied this, saying that the difficulties were exaggerated and that such costing systems had already been worked out for the NHS which, though provided nationally, has significantly different costs in different parts of the country. The analogy with the NHS is somewhat unfair in that health authorities have no independent source of finance. The Layfield Report majority argued, however, that the introduction of national minima 'would impair the ability of local authorities to consider the best balance of provision within their areas as a whole and would introduce distortions in the allocation of resources'.[20] Also, 'If as seems possible, the cost of meeting minimum standards were to account for a large proportion of local government expenditure, a division of financial responsibility on this basis would tend to place the major share of responsibility with the government'.[21]

The Committee estimated that LIT would cost about £100 million per annum and the Inland Revenue would need to employ about 12,000 more staff. The tax would be levied by the metropolitan districts, non-metropolitan counties and by the Scottish regions, all of which would retain rating. Rating would be the sole tax for metropolitan counties and for non-metropolitan and Scottish districts, and all authorities would have grants. Rating, they argued – to many people's surprise – should be retained because it was felt that it is a visible and efficient tax, cheap to administer and difficult to avoid. However, since it does not take account of ability to pay and neglects the earning non-householder, it was recommended that it be supplemented by LIT and that a number of rating reforms be initiated. Rates, it was felt, should be based on the capital value of a property rather than on the rental value, that regular and frequent revaluations should be undertaken and that rates should be paid by instalments, as is the case in Scotland.

The Committee considered that a LIT was a 'serious candidate as a new source of local finance' as it alone suffered a substantial yield and contributed to the accountability of local government. A number of possible schemes were considered. Scheme A was based on local assessment and collection whereby the Inland Revenue would provide local authorities with the necessary information to assess the tax. This scheme had very high administrative costs. Scheme B was on the lines operating in a number of other countries whereby the LIT is based on an end-year assessment for both local and national taxes. This was ruled out due to the Inland Revenue's policy of minimising the number of taxpayers requiring an end-year assessment. Scheme C was based on self-assessment and was rejected as the costs were put at £200-250 million (1975 prices), representing 50,000 staff. The Committee came down in favour of a LIT within the present administrative framework. However, the estimated cost of £100 million annually and the 12,000 extra staff thought to be needed offered a marvellous target for local government's numerous Whitehall critics and was used unscrupulously by the centralists within the government to defeat the scheme. Referring to Scheme C some analysts have criticised Layfield on the grounds that, 'No satisfactory explanation was provided of how this remarkable high figure was derived. Not only does the £200-250 million estimate for self-assessed LIT wildly exceed the estimated costs of an officially administered version, but it is in the same league as the £249.8 million that it cost to administer all Inland Revenue duties in 1974-5'.[22]

The Inland Revenue have ruled out self-assessment since they argue that it would be costly to examine a proportion of returns to check for fraud and that there would be no incentive for taxpayers to render prompt returns. To which it may be replied that 'neither of these operations incurs such staggering costs abroad . . . there is no reason why taxpayers cannot be provided with an incentive to file prompt returns that have been completed accurately by a specified date. The Committee did not recommend self-assessment for income tax, local or otherwise.'[23] A number of countries levy a LIT, normally at a single rate. In Finland the rate varies between 13 and 18·5 per cent, Norway 18·5-22 per cent, Italy 8·9-14·7 per cent. Sweden is a good example of local and national taxes being almost totally integrated, with low administrative costs.

Much now depends on the detailed design of the forthcoming computerisation of the PAYE system. The danger is that its design will be decided with little public debate and with the centralist civil servants closing political options under the guide of technical decisions. Only in Scotland is PAYE at present fully computerised. A pilot scheme is being carried out at six offices in the Midlands and a report has been completed on the implications for a national network. The evidence of the Chairman of the Inland Revenue, Sir William

Pile, to the Public Accounts Committee is suspiciously vague on the degree of flexibility that will be built into the computer system. By 1985 computers, he thought, would be able to handle self-assessment but, 'We could not switch to an expenditure tax and use that same system. We could not, I think, introduce a LIT because there could be too many rate bands for employers to operate'.[24] In addition the kind of self-assessment that could be handled would have to be different from the American system and a very different system would be needed if a comprehensive LIT with multiple rates were adopted. Others argue that if we switched to self-assessment a LIT could be easily introduced. It is vital that this area is opened up to public debate, and examined in depth by a Parliamentary Select Committee before any irrevocable decisions are made.

The 1977 Labour government Green Paper was a most disappointing and negative response to the case for radical reform. It reflected every conceivable Whitehall prejudice and was deeply centralist in outlook. It rejected LIT for the following reasons: ' . . . the Government do not accept that local accountability depends on the proportion of revenue raised locally; or that any clear advantages would flow from the introduction of LIT. The freedom of local authorities to vary the LIT rate would have to be closely constrained so that it did not unduly complicate central government economic and financial management and there would need to be some equalisation of the proceeds of the tax between richer and poorer areas. Partly for these reasons, it seems highly questionable whether the great majority of electors could be made aware of the LIT element in their normal PAYE deductions so as to achieve the Committee's objective of securing an effective local discipline on local authority expenditure decisions. The Government are not convinced, therefore, that the case for the introduction of LIT has been made.'[25]

This response neglects the fact that there are 15 million domestic ratepayers and 24 million income tax payers, and therefore 9 million people who are already contributing to the finance of local government without many of them realising the full extent to which they are doing so. Layfield recommended that LIT be integrated into the national tax system and that notices of coding by the Inland Revenue should indicate to each taxpayer the local taxing authority. This would not be necessary under self-assessment, since the employer would calculate how much tax to withhold and then would add on a percentage to take account of LIT. Under a system of self-assessment a LIT would require far fewer additional staff than the 12,000 estimated by the Inland Revenue, since a local tax like the provincial tax in Canada would necessitate only the use of different withholding tables and the addition of one or two lines to the tax return. Against this must be set Sir William Pile's evidence to the PAC that a LIT with multiple rates would require a new computer system.[26] It is unclear whether the same objections would apply to a self-assessed LIT since he did not discuss this kind of tax, though he did say that self-assessed PAYE could be undertaken by the computer system if certain conditions were met.[27]

The Green Paper also rejected the localist approach recommended by Layfield because it 'would involve a surrender by central government of a large part of their present influence over local services'. It argued that since Layfield was set up the financial climate had changed so much that the need to control expenditure had become dominant, and, moreover, that LIT would involve large differences in the taxes paid in different parts of the country. Instead the Labour government proposed for consideration and discussion with local authorities a unitary grant by which ratepayers would pay roughly the same rate poundage for a similar level of services regardless of where they live. This would have the result that 'ratepayers would be in a position to ask, if the rate poundage were above the standard rate poundage, whether their local authority was less efficient or was providing services to a higher level than other authorities'.[28] Yet Layfield did recognise the real concern of national governments to control the level of spending as part of the overall management of the economy and recommended that LIT, if introduced, should be accompanied by a local spending regulator whereby the government could take from authorities a rising proportion of the revenue they were raising if the overall increase exceeded a certain level that had been set nationally. As a disincentive to excessive expenditure the amount of spending which could be financed by successive increases in local taxation would be progressively less. But Layfield was concerned that: 'the powers [of central government] should be expressly designed to meet the government's concern with economic management and should involve no wider intervention in local government affairs than is needed for that purpose.'[29] This was a sensible recommendation but one which has been ignored by successive governments since.

Layfield considered that the local tax regulator did not undermine the accountability of local government to the electorate and, further, was capable of being 'made sufficiently powerful and flexible to provide the government with the control it needs'.[30] A second control was also suggested, by which the national government could specify the proportion of capital expenditure to be borne out of revenue rather than from borrowing. It was noted that this control has been adopted in Denmark and that, 'It could be used selectively, with different rates of revenue contribution by region, type of authority or purpose. It could be applied or varied at comparatively short notice.'[31] The amount of borrowing could also be influenced by interest rates and by regulating the terms of access to the Public Works Loan Board. A better relationship between central and local government, in which each party attempts to keep the other informed of its requirements, would also help to secure better management of the economy: 'If local authorities are to be in a position to take account of the government's policy on national requirements they need to be given a better appreciation of that policy than they have had in the past; and the government in formulating those requirements needs better information as to their implications for local authorities.'[32]

The Green Paper did not discuss this point; in fact, generally it did not bother to rebut the arguments of Layfield but simply stated that the government wished to retain control over expenditure. It was not only the Treasury who rejected Layfield's case for LIT. The 'protectionist' school of Cambridge economists also alleged that the 'fatal confusion' in Layfield was that it presumes 'local autonomy to derive uniquely from its power to raise local taxes, thereby ignoring the autonomy from a grant that is not hypothecated'.[33] They argued that grants should be distributed on the basis of norms of standardised expenditure set for each authority and did not accept that this would undermine local responsibility since the local authority would be deciding the distribution of the grant unfettered by central government. It is a very limited view of responsibility which believes it right to separate decisions over the size of expenditure and its financing from its distribution, and not surprisingly identifies the 'protectionist' economists with a centralist philosophy. 'The Cambridge economists interpret responsibility narrowly and fail to take into account the political implications of the financial arrangements they advocate. Both central government and local authorities are elected; they have political bases and behave politically. They will seek political advantage for themselves from a grant system. When grant is high local authorities will try to place responsibility on the centre, claiming that local problems cannot be tackled because grant is inadequate. When it is so dependent on a large grant, that is also unstable, a local authority is transformed from a body that takes its own decisions in response to local pressures to become itself a pressure group on the centre urging more grant. It seeks to make out that it is a special case with distinctive features that the existing grant settlement has not taken account of. In turn the centre will respond with inspection to check up if the special case is justified and if the need to spend is present. So the departments are pulled into the detailed affairs of local authorities by a high level of grant.'[34]

The Labour government had set up the Layfield Committee as an act of political expediency to defuse a potentially serious political row: it soon discovered, however, as evidence from the various Departments began to be given to the Committee, that there was certainly no predisposition in Whitehall to favour any proposal for fundamental reform. It was the Department of the Environment in its evidence to Layfield that first introduced at a bureaucratic level the concept of the unitary grant which later became the foundation of the 1980 Act, and there has been much misunderstanding about its parentage and about who at various times supported it. The unitary grant was discussed by Layfield as the most appropriate form of grant, should government want to assume the major responsibility for local government expenditure and determine the spending patterns of individual authorities. However, since Layfield rejected this centralist model, the unitary grant was also examined in the context of the localist solution as a device for redistributing government grant while also giving local authorities responsibility for raising more of their own finance by means of LIT and rates. The Green Paper concealed the departmental origin of the unitary grant proposal, giving the impression that it came from elsewhere, and did not reveal the detailed discussion of its implications and consequences in Layfield. 'Disingenuousness could scarcely go further . . . The Green Paper stands as a classic case of a threat to democratic institutions created by carelessness, muddle and poverty of thought.'[35]

Admittedly the Green Paper was not, like a White Paper, firm government policy, but that is a poor excuse. The foundation was laid for the 1980 Act by a Whitehall consensus which certainly covered the Department of the Environment and Treasury officials who had initiated the unitary grant, at least for five years, from 1975 and through the periods of responsibility of three Secretaries of State for the Environment, Anthony Crosland, Peter Shore and Michael Heseltine. It underlines how important it is to ensure that collective ministerial approval is given to Departmental evidence to Commissions of Enquiry and how unwise it was for the few of us in the Cabinet who were in favour of Layfield's 'localist' option to let a Green Paper float a dangerous concept like the unitary grant under the pretext that the government was not committed.

The 1979 government actually made the political decision to legislate to introduce the block grant, which is the same as the unitary grant, though they have attached to it some particularly obnoxious sanctions against overspending. But the 1980 Act – hard though it may be for socialists to admit – was merely the most offensive aspect of a trend that had continued unchecked during the period of a Labour government. The intent was clear: to shift decision-making to the Department of Education and the Department of the Environment. The essential decision that must now be taken, if local government is not to lose its autonomy, is quickly to find and agree an alternative source of finance and to accept as an essential first step the Layfield recommendation that government grant should not be above 50 per cent of local authority spending.

In the early years at least of any switch to a new source of local finance the Layfield judgment that rates should be maintained is probably correct, though since the Conservative government has delayed the revaluation that was due the anomalies will increase and the potential take decrease. It is hard to see a Conservative government abandoning the derating of agricultural land and building which was introduced in 1929, but as Layfield indicated there are strong arguments for opening up this additional source of finance for local authorities. The 1979 Conservative government is pledged to abolish rates at some future date and this, along with the general public dislike of them, makes it unlikely that the rating system can ever recover wide national acceptance. The case for its retention is, however, stronger than is ever acknowledged by the general public and any new tax would soon make rates more acceptable in retrospect.

There are a number of alternatives less well-known and less documented than LIT. It might be feasible to incorporate rates, which are a property tax, with a new wealth tax. The property element of a wealth tax would go to provide local authority finance, but that portion levied on investments and objects of value could go to the Treasury. Local sales tax, though criticised by Layfield, is another possibility, particularly if it could be levied at a regional level and then distributed to local authorities on a per capita basis. Similarly, an additional specific regional petrol tax is an option which would have the advantage of taking some account of shifts of population such as summer tourism, which put additional costs on local authorities but is more attractive as a source of finance for national and regional assemblies. It is probably wiser to accept the introduction of an additional source of revenue initially as a supplement to rather than a substitute for rates. Then as the rates are frozen the revenue coming from the new tax could be built up, and only when the teething problems that surround the introduction of any new tax are over would the rating system be abandoned. Rate income is too large and too certain a source of revenue for it to be prudent to risk abolition without knowing the exact impact of a new tax.

Once a local authority has a buoyant source of finance the whole debate about local finance changes. Provided some mechanism such as the regulator proposed by Layfield is introduced to discourage local authorities from using their revenue raising powers without regard to their cumulative macro-economic effect, all that is needed is to find an acceptable mechanism for distributing the grant. Since the 'resources' and 'needs' elements have now been abandoned and the block grant put in its place, there have been strong arguments for moving towards a total simplification of the grant system and for introducing a simpler distribution based more on population.[36] One advantage claimed for the block grant is that the assessed needs expenditure per head and the standard rate poundage will be openly declared. But local authorities fear that this will lead to pressure for uniformity and loss of autonomy and argue that even if some deprived authorities were to lose some grant revenue, it is better to have a known grant which is not controlled by Whitehall. They fear that under the block grant system 'local government will become a pressure group rather than a government, arguing its case at national level together with other pressure groups.'[37]

Though the case for simplification is emotionally very attractive, particularly while fears of central government interference have yet to be tested by experience, it needs to be considered with caution. It is potentially dangerous to abandon any way of channelling central government money into areas of highest need, because social needs may be highest in areas that are depopulating and have a low income, and have little chance of raising much local revenue from rates or from any additional source. A redistributive formula, if it could be openly negotiated, is compatible with local autonomy provided it is accompanied by greater freedom for local authorities to raise their own finance. Failure to recognise this has been the basic mistake behind all the discussion of the unitary/block grant. The flaw in the previous system was the automatic increase in central government's grant when a particular local authority decided to increase its spending. This meant that the Rate Support Grant was not a fixed sum and if local spending increased as a result of local decisions during the year it did affect the government's expenditure forecasts and did require supplementary estimates. If local government has the freedom to raise its own finance, then how central government fixes its grant is predominantly its affair. If the central government grant is reduced in size then the local authorities' flexibility in raising revenue makes any readjustment more tolerable. They can offset central government decisions over redistribution and need in their grant by a local decision to raise extra revenue. Central government could act on its responsibility to try to ensure overall national standards and to stimulate spending in specific areas as a result of national policy, but local government would retain the right to challenge the priorities of central government from its own financial resources.

Central government must protect the education service from the growth in the private sector. Legislation to ban charging fees for private education touches on major issues of human rights (see Chapter 17). In 1978-9 local authorities spent £45-50 million supporting pupils at independent schools. Central government paid a further £37 million in boarding school allowances to public servants, mainly in the armed forces but also in the diplomatic service. It is legitimate and right to phase out this financial support for the private sector and to make tax changes as a disincentive to the growth in private education. But this will need to be accompanied by an increase in the quality and number of boarding places available in local authority schools for non-handicapped pupils, which in 1978 in England and Wales numbered only 8,900. Improving local authority schools remains the best way of curbing the growth in private education.

A redefinition of responsibility between central and local government and the greater financial independence of local government is the only way to revive local democracy and reverse the stultifying embrace of Whitehall.

16

Community Care

The Greek physician, Herophilus, observed some 2,000 years ago that illness 'renders science null, art inglorious, strength effortless, wealth useless and eloquence powerless'. Society at times seems to have understood the levelling impact of illness and has so far been prepared to judge health issues against a broader framework of values than most other activities. The National Health Service, which established the principle of medical need rather than ability to pay as the sole determinant of health care, has despite adverse professional and political comment been supported by the large majority of society, as opinion polls have repeatedly testified. People appear to sense that the NHS embraces within its legislative structure a philosophy which has a near-universal appeal and believes, as Aneurin Bevan wrote, that, 'Society becomes more wholesome, more serene and spiritually healthier if it knows that its citizens have at the back of their consciousness the knowledge that not only themselves but also their fellows have access when ill, to the best that medical skill can provide'.[1]

This concept of serenity is interestingly evocative and reminds us of the extent to which the 1946 National Health Service Act helped to ease the anxiety and distress which a combination of illness and the need to find the money to pay for health care could bring. The existence of the NHS is a constant challenge to the values of the market place; it persistently asserts that there are other values than those determined by money, and it helps to foster the spirit of altruism within society.

At a time when so much of the political debate centres on economic growth, incomes and profits, it is salutary to remember that peace in society does not come when everyone is paid the same amount of money but when 'everyone recognises that the material, objective external arrangements of society are based on principles which they feel correspond with their subjective ideas of justice'.[2] The NHS because it corresponds to most people's subjective idea of justice has had its basic framework maintained intact by successive governments and it appears that it may withstand even the doctrinaire distrust of all public services of the 1979 Conservative government.

Critics of the NHS point to the increase in administrators and the fact that 'there was one administrator or clerk to every 9·5 occupied beds in 1965 and one to every 5·6 occupied beds in 1973'.[3] But such a comparison does not take account of the immense increase in the number of patients using NHS facilities. Between 1949 and 1974 despite a fall of 14 per cent in the number of beds, the number of people coming through the hospitals increased by 87 per cent, and the average length of stay was halved. This was brought about by a great increase in the services offered. The number of bottles of blood issued increased four times, the number of pathology tests four and a half times, the number of ambulance journeys three and a half times; all this involved extra administrative burdens, but also demonstrated a return in terms of the more efficient use of resources. In long-stay hospitals there has been a differentially larger increase in the number of staff, not to increase efficiency but to improve standards of care, which were very low. There have also been dramatic changes in medical technology: the replacement of heart valves, the introduction of heart pacemakers, kidney transplant operations, the artificial replacement of hips – all involving extra staff and extra costs. The cost of new diagnostic techniques has risen beyond the rate of inflation. The real cost between the 1950s and mid 1970s of a pathology auto-analyser rose eight times, head X-ray and radiotherapy equipment thirteen times. Between 1949 and 1974 the expectation of life at birth rose from 66·3 to 69·1 years for men, and from 71 to 75·3 years for women; the infant mortality rate was halved, while the maternal mortality rate fell to one ninth of its former level.[4] These improvements were not due solely to the NHS: housing improvements and the generally improved standard of living played their part; but there can be little doubt that millions of people have experienced a quantifiable improvement in the quality of their lives since the introduction of the NHS.

The two major priorities for the health service now are to orientate it towards community care and prevention of illness. This is a long way from being achieved. Indeed the new Conservative government's attitude, as spelled out in *Patients First*, places far too great an emphasis on hospital and medical services and not nearly enough on community services, on the links between the NHS and the social services and on the related area of local government responsibilities. Unfortunately for those who – not unreasonably – baulk at further administrative changes, it is impossible to avoid the conclusion that the necessary orientation towards community care and prevention of illness cannot be achieved within the present overcentralised and bureaucratic structure. The report of the Department of Health and Social Security Working Group on Inequalities in Health published in 1980 once again highlights the wide differences in mortality rates and the incidence of chronic sickness between the occupational classes for both sexes and at all ages. At birth and in the first month of life, twice as many babies of Class V 'unskilled manual' parents die as those of Class I 'professional' parents. In the next eleven months four times as many girls and five times as many boys die. In later childhood the ratio of deaths between Class V and Class I falls, but then increases again in early adult life before falling again. Class differences are particularly marked for diseases of the respiratory system. What is really worrying is that the health of the unskilled and semi-skilled worker during the 1960s and 1970s has actually deteriorated relative to Class I, as has the class differential for children aged 10-14. There is evidence of a marked class difference in the use of the preventive health services, but it is interesting that primary health care, the most decentralised part of the NHS, has achieved more equity in terms of access.

379

The community needs to be encouraged to identify with and take more responsibility for its own community and health services. This can most easily be achieved if the health service is decentralised. Parallel with this development must be a recognition on the part of central government of its key role in developing preventive health measures. Legislation promoting such measures is urgent. So is a greater readiness to concentrate on the monitoring of health and care and the improvement of standards throughout the NHS rather than on the management of the service, which should be the prime responsibility of the new district health authorities.

It has become a fashion among politicians, journalists and field workers to castigate the administrator in the health service, as in other spheres of activity. We can easily make the administrator the butt for the frustrations that really stem from national economic decline and the inability to match higher expectations with the necessary resources. It was parliament and the Conservative government's legislative reforms of 1972 and 1973 for local government and the NHS which increased administrative staff and costs. The build-up to this legislation started in 1967, when Kenneth Robinson was Minister of Health, with proposals for bringing together the separately administrated elements of health care, the hospital service, the local government health and social services and the family practitioner services. But these proposals were criticised then by myself and others for their centralist civil service orientation.[5] They were followed by Richard Crossman's proposals, when he was Secretary of State for Health and Social Security, which reduced the strength of the regional tier and gave a more local structure; only to be followed by Sir Keith Joseph's unqualified acceptance of the report by the management consultants, McKinsey, recommending the restoration of regional authority and the retention of centralised control by the Department. In the event, parliament perpetuated the undemocratic structure of appointed authorities and spawned yet another centralised bureaucracy, in the name of reform, in which neither was administration streamlined nor the decision-making made quicker and more decisive.

A major reason for the failure of these administrative reforms has been that the reformers – whether civil servants, Ministers or MPs – have refused to confront the real dilemma: decentralisation or continued centralisation. In the NHS the issue of local control has been fudged at every decision point and the result has been an uneasy and often unworkable compromise between a civil service run Department of Health and Social Security and health administrators running, in effect, three other layers at the Regional, Area and District level with members of the medical profession as individual decision-makers holding most of the power.

The Royal Commission on the National Health Service, established by the Labour government in 1975, had the opportunity to challenge the centralised structure of the NHS but failed to grapple with this issue. Some argue that 'the job of a Royal Commission is consensus engineering'.[6] While that may be the correct approach for a Royal Commission in constructing its recommendations, it should not apply to its analysis of the issues under its scrutiny. Past Commissions of enquiry have sometimes produced very fundamental critiques. In 1892 the Chadwick Commission's 'Report on an Inquiry into the Sanitary Conditions of the Labouring Population of Great Britain' challenged the then current belief that disease was all the fault of the undisciplined and unclean labouring class and that all that was required was greater discipline and individual responsibility. It argued instead that disease was transmitted among the labouring classes by environmental pollution resulting from overcrowding, lack of drainage and inadequate water supply. This led to the Private Act of Parliament introduced by Liverpool in 1846 for the appointment of the first Medical Officer of Health, the Public Health Act of 1848 and, later, the great Public Health Act of 1875. This set the climate for preventive medicine, making staggering improvements in health care which far outweigh the significance of drug treatments; it is now in the 1980s that we should again look to preventive medicine for major improvements in health care.

The Royal Commission on the NHS in its report[7] dismissed the gloom and the doomsters and rejected the naive belief that responsibility for health issues could be taken away from parliament or that a revival of health insurance offered a credible method of financing the service. It is to the Commission's credit that it was, in its own words, content to eschew 'blinding revelation' and that it made a series of detailed but evolutionary recommendations for adaptation supporting the altruistic philosophy which inspired the creation of the NHS. Yet its analysis of the way in which the longer term structure of the NHS might develop was disappointingly unimaginative.

On 5 October 1945 in his first memorandum to the Cabinet, Aneurin Bevan wrote, 'We have got to achieve as nearly as possible a uniform standard of service for all'.[8] He rejected a local government system of care because he felt it would make the achievement of such uniformity impossible, arguing that 'there will tend to be a better service in the richer areas, a worse service in the poorer areas'. Even in 1945 this argument did not convince all his colleagues. The Home Secretary, Herbert Morrison, argued for continued local control of the public health system. In 1937 the aggregate finance of the 1,100 voluntary hopitals was in the red, with government grants preventing collapse. In 1946, of the 480,000 beds in the system, four out of five were in municipal hospitals.

The argument over centralised or local control has continued ever since, and now goes much wider than the single question of whether the NHS should be under local government control. The Royal Commission did not perceive that arguments on this issue go to the roots of the financing of the NHS, its control and the whole orientation of health care in its widest sense, community, environmental and preventive. It never considered separately elected health authorities or objectively reviewed the arguments for and against central control. It was wise to reject immediate fundamental changes, but it could have charted a course for the future within which the structural adaptations of the early 1980s to the Areas and the Districts could be set in context. As the Commission's own research points out, 'the irony is that despite [Aneurin] Bevan's argument for a national service in 1945 central government has been more successful in eliminating the grosser variations in the distribution of resources in some local authority services than in health.' Education was cited, by the Royal Commission as the best example, where central government allocation has, by using clear national criteria, been able to keep variations within very tight limits. The Commission quoted for example in its evidence that the coefficient of variations between pupil/teacher ratios for 104 local authorities was 7·6, whereas the population/general practitioner ratios from 98 Family Practitioner Committee areas showed a coefficient of variation of 10·5. Such evidence as there is shows that a national service is not a necessary, let alone a sufficient, condition for achieving a 'uniform standard of service'.[9] This is very important since many socialists justify centralisation on the grounds that it promotes equality.

It is worrying that, after over thirty years of the National Health Service, the provision of health care, however it is measured whether in terms of expenditure, bed allocations or manpower distribution, still shows dramatic variations between health districts, and among health areas and regional health authorities. The inequality of provision has its roots in the fact that instead of concentrating on essentials, priorities and policies, Ministers and parliament have connived at the myth that they control the whole service, becoming bogged down in detail while effective control has passed to the central bureaucracy. The failure for the first fifteen years of the NHS to do anything other than to hand out money on the historic allocation pattern to the English regions would never have been tolerated by the English regional health authorities if they had owed their position not to government patronage, but to the people of their region by election. In marked contrast, Scotland, with its own Secretary of State, has been able to extract a 24 per cent advantage over England in health resources, and Wales has been brought from well behind to a position where they have now a slight advantage over England. Nor would the relationship between hospital and community have been ignored for so long if the voice of the local areas had not been so weak in relation to the region and to the Department. The dominant share of hospital health resources given to London was not just historic but part of the Whitehall-

London bias that is another characteristic of centralised government. Central government listens to the teaching hospitals and to the Royal Colleges, and Westminster-based politicians to the London doctors they consult and know.

An example of the centralist tendencies within the NHS was its resistance to the implementation of the Resource Allocation Working Party (RAWP) recommendations which were aimed at correcting geographical inequalities. The London-based health service unions supported the London teaching hospitals and refused to face the logic of the facts of London's preferential resource allocation. Attempts to redress sectoral and class inequalities have met the same resistance from the powerful Royal Colleges where the interests of the surgeons and the general physicians predominate. There are admittedly imperfections, statistical crudities and physical problems associated with the allocation of resources and it is very difficult to define need criteria objectively[10] but the fact that problems of allocation have been given such low priority in the first thirty years of the NHS reflects its continued insulation from provincial and local pressure.

It is, of course, insufficient to allocate resources on the basis only of hospital need. In inner city areas and in particular in London, where there is over-provision of hospital services, there is under-provision of community services and a need for a more refined allocation system for personal social service needs. The introduction of joint financing in 1975, with NHS money being available for joint projects with social services, was an attempt to help the integrated development of community care.

The disadvantage of central allocation to the health regions is that they are appointed bodies more influenced by professional and hospital pressures than by democratic community priorities and they can very easily distort their allocation by the way in which they make allocations to their own Areas and Districts. In London, where there is over-provision of acute services in the centre but poor provision at the periphery and where in between the community health services are of uneven quality, it has never proved possible to redistribute hospital resources for the benefit of London's relatively poor community services. A sensible re-examination of London sub-regional allocations has been completed, but the proposals of London University to close and merge teaching facilities and post-graduate hospitals have met predictable resistance. The institutional resistance is so strong that rational argument rarely determines the correct distribution of resources. Democratic and media pressure could have a more important influence and until Nottingham, Leicester, Sheffield and Plymouth openly challenge the dominance of London in the decision-making process within the NHS, they will continue to be deprived. The NHS must reinforce local control and establish sufficiently sensitive criteria for central allocations, whether of money or of manpower, to be made direct to district health authorities and not through the regions.

The regions argue that there are dangers in encouraging local health authorities to think in terms of self sufficiency, that they will develop overlapping facilities and opt for prestigious projects. Local duplication has been a theoretical danger for the Education Service as well, whether for Polytechnics, Colleges of Technology or Teacher Training establishments; but in marked contrast to the Department of Health and Social Security, the Department of Education and Science has accepted local-national partnership, concentrating on the development of the school inspectorate and on research and development. In Scotland the Health Authorities Revenue Equalisation (SHARE) allocates across a population of 5·2 million people to fifteen Health Boards of very different size, with a spread of population from the Islands (68,000) and Borders (100,000) to Lothian (756,000) and Greater Glasgow with 1,059,000. It is clear from Scottish experience,[11] with complex patient crossflows, regional and sub-regional specialities and leading hospitals, that it is feasible, as well as desirable, to allocate direct to the new local health authorities below regional level.

The Royal Commission recommended the removal of an administrative tier and the government decided in 1980 to form new health authorities from existing single district areas, either by merging existing districts or by dividing areas. The

flexible approach, as recommended by the Commission, with
no single criterion predominating, was the right solution, and
it could have minimised the damage to effective collaboration
between the previously matching boundaries of the area
health authorities and local government social services departments. But the government's approach has been to allow the
regions to play down the importance of retaining conterminous boundaries with Social Services. In the South West
region, Cornwall has always been a single district authority
and there will be little change under the new arrangements. In
Devon, where four districts were created in 1974, a single
district health authority as proposed by Devon County
Council would have been very large. There has always been an
overwhelming case for looking afresh at the local government
boundaries in Devon and creating in Plymouth a metropolitan
district so that a new health authority could be conterminous
with social services. The South-West Regional Health Authority
wants Devon to have four district health authorities, which will
produce little, if any, saving in administration and will only
serve to enhance the region's control. In Somerset, which in
1974 was a two-district authority, a merger produced some
economies and this pattern will continue. In the multiple
district areas, in big cities like Birmingham, division into a
number of authorities will, however, create considerable
problems. In Liverpool, a multi-district area has already been
developed into a single district area. But conterminosity will
be impossible in big counties like Kent. Unfortunately some of
the new authorities will be too small to have proper services for
mental illness or mental handicap and, where the social
services are not conterminous, there will be problems over
joint funding and joint planning. With only four local
councillors out of sixteen on the new authorities, the influence
of local government will be deliberately reduced.

The Health Service has been limping back from the despair
which followed the 1974 reorganisation and it needed to be
cajoled gently into a more efficient and effective organisation.
The creation of so many new district health authorities is very
unlikely to produce the £30 million saving in administrative
costs and manpower claimed by the government in 1980. The

government would have made more economies if it had made fewer authorities.

A study by health administrators estimated that creating 180 district health authorities with an average of only 2,051 beds, in comparison to 90 with an average of 4,200 beds, will substantially increase management staff costs and add an extra overall cost of over £30 million. It is probable that the best trade-off between cost-efficiency and community identification would have set a figure of around 120 new authorities. By creating some 200 the government will make it easier for the regions to retain their managerial stranglehold, so that the apparent effect of decentralisation will be illusory.

London's health services need to be reorganised as an entity. The temptation must be resisted to impose a health authority pattern, which ignores borough boundaries. The individual's identification with the London boroughs which were introduced in 1964 is only just beginning to become a reality and if the new district health authorities bear no relation to the borough boundaries, the problem of identification will become even more difficult. There is a strong case for a radical change in the boundaries of the four metropolitan regional health authorities and for introducing an elected, single Greater London Health Authority, and readjusting the boundaries of the surrounding regions, creating a single Southern region. People in the areas around Greater London are not unreasonably demanding their own health facilities and are reluctant to travel into central London for hospital care as has been accepted in the past.

Apart from questions of organisation, the danger of the changes being introduced in the 1980s by the Conservative government is that they are tending to reject the philosophy of the wider definition of health implicit in the 1974 reorganisations. The hospital is again becoming the focus of health decisions and priorities, with doctors dominating the discussion. Sir Keith Joseph is apt to go around openly confessing the error of his ways in being responsible for the 1974 reorganisation, but he and the government of which he is again a member ought not to replace repentance with a reversal of the concept that was involved in that reorganisation, that of bringing together hospital and community. The new conventional wisdom is rediscovering the importance of the ward sister. Important though it is to improve the administration of the hospital, there is no case for reverting to a hospital-orientated health service, for forgetting the fundamental value of integrating fully the range of community services for patients and families and for failing to establish a far higher priority for preventive care.

Once the new authorities are established, the question will have to be answered to what extent they are to be given real freedom to manage. Should they in addition to a central financial allocation have the right to raise local finance? Health has – unlike Education – never had a local constituency for higher spending; the hybrid democracy continued in the new health authorities and in the regional authorities still has no power to raise money, other than through local lotteries. They are the creatures of government control, lacking the power of independent action that comes only from some measure of financial independence. No health authority is capable of setting the pace or of experimenting against the Departmental trend. There will continue to be an endless moan from health authorities about the inadequacy of their resources or a resigned acceptance of the government's financial decisions.

It is the undemocratic structure which has proved to be both inefficient and ineffective. There are many hard-working, informed people appointed to health authorities who, for many years, have given their time and energy without financial reward to the National Health Service. Their authority, however, stems from the central government who appointed them; they are often remote from and unknown to the locality they serve, and they have been more influenced by professional and hospital pressures than by democratic community priorities. The local authority nominees, while injecting some element of local accountability, accept a considerable curtailment of their normal democratic freedom and feel inhibited and restricted. It is a sad fact that the Health Service is represented by an amorphous and undemocratic authority, a Quango which should be abolished and replaced by democratically elected bodies. The Royal Commission seemed to hold out the vague possibility of change if some form of regional government was introduced. Meanwhile it wanted regional health authorities to continue but argued that they should be made directly accountable to parliament instead of, as at present, to the Department through the Permanent Secretary. The Commission explored the local government option, but not the localist approach. It met at a time when the Labour government had unwisely rejected in a Green Paper the Layfield Committee's recommendation for Local Income Tax (LIT).[12]

An illustration of the lack of accountability of the regional health authorities is the response of the National Health Service to the interim report of the Committee on Mentally Abnormal Offenders published in 1974. The Report, rightly, demanded urgent action to build secure psychiatric units in all the health regions in England and Wales. The prisons were becoming overcrowded, with psychiatric cases often being held in prisons simply because there was nowhere else for them to go. They were often refused entry to psychiatric hospitals by the consultants, who hold absolute authority over admissions. The basic inhumanity of holding mentally ill people in prison with no proper facilities for their case was highlighted, and public concern was considerable. As the Minister of Health responsible, I allocated £3 million for secure units, overriding the argument that the money should come out of the already-fixed allocation for the regional Health authorities. Seven years later the position in the prisons is worse. No regional secure units have been built, some of the regional authorities have not even produced any plans, most of the money went on other aspects of the NHS, and only a few hundred interim secure places have been found. This scandalous state of affairs has been tolerated by government, by parliament and by the civil service. In most other situations this would be regarded as a misappropriation of funds. But no one is held accountable. No one person can be identified as responsible and no one's job is at risk. If this had occurred in local government, parliament and Fleet Street would have responded by loud protests, but the flabby committee consensus which permeates the NHS in Whitehall and in the regions makes it impervious to criticism.

But an equal responsibility lay with the Home Office to ease the pressure on the psychiatric hospitals by reducing the overcrowding in prisons, introducing shorter sentences, and relying more on Community Service Orders. Instead nothing was done by successive Home Secretaries. Prison over-crowding has reached a scandalous state. The Dutch government have shown that sending fewer people to prison and for less time can make a dramatic impact on reducing the prison population. But the structure of government in Britain allows for no effective co-operation between the sentencing policy of the courts and the admission policy of the psychiatric con-sultant in the NHS. There is a case for some independent medical review procedure where the court or the prison authorities and the doctors are in conflict. This is a co-ordination of effort which the Regional Assemblies, suggested in Chapter 14, with responsibility for health and the power to question Home Office Ministers and officials could well promote.

At least the Royal Commission sensed that something was wrong with the accountability of the régional authorities; but the Government rejected its recommendations. The present unsatisfactory system, therefore, lives on. The civil service retains nominal responsibility, Ministers refuse to devolve democratic authority, parliament remains an ineffective rubber stamp, and the health service continues to be smothered by a blanket of corporatist inertia.

The Royal Commission was given evidence from Sweden pointing to the value of redirecting control from the centre to the local area[13] which, had it been imaginatively projected and built on, could have come like a breath of fresh air into the Report and, at a later stage, into the NHS. The Swedish County Health Authority, or *Landsting*, is elected every three years by proportional representation; the *Kommun* is their equivalent of our local authorities. A *Landsting* raises a local health tax as a percentage of taxable income or of income left after deduction of tax-free allowances. The percentage in 1975 varied from 9 to 11 in the 24 different *Landstingen* and averaged 10·21 per cent. To take an example, the Malmönus *Landsting* serves a population of 480,000. It has an Assembly of 109 elected members which meets several times a year, and whose most important meeting is in October, when the budget and local tax rate are decided. In 1975 it spent £257 million and the tax rate was for 10 per cent of taxable income. Between assembly meetings the administration is run by an Executive Committee consisting of fifteen members. Senior medical and administrative staff attend the meetings.

In Britain it would be neither necessary nor desirable to adopt the Swedish pattern wholesale and if elections to the health authorities were made by proportional representation and if health service representation on the authority was maintained, the fear that authorities would be endlessly dominated by one party would diminish. Involving over a hundred elected people in general policy, though not in management, is an interesting concept. In some ways this wider involvement is provided for already in the NHS by Community Health Councils (CHCs). The CHCs have been a success and it is helpful that, after initial doubts, the government has decided they should continue. Their members are representative of the locality and help to bridge the gap between executive authorities and the voluntary groups and the wider community they serve. The government would be very unwise to curtail CHCs' activities either by financial restriction or directive.

In Sweden, the government provides 21 per cent of the total income and makes equalisation grants to the poorer counties where the taxable income per head is lower, so that the available money per head is roughly the same. Central government retains authority over the allocation of doctors and other strategic decisions. In Britain, central government, having been for over thirty years the sole financier, would have to continue for some time as the major source of finance. The amount that might be raised for health locally would need to take account of the financial burden put on LIT for local government finance. It would be necessary for central government to determine that proportion of NHS expenditure which could be accepted as being locally determined by the health authority and this would have to be compatible with overall national economic management.

It will be argued by some that, rather than having separate health authorities, health should be put under local government. Apart from the ferocious resistance such a move would meet from the doctors, there is a case for separation on merit. Health authorities would attract candidates for election different from those standing for local government, and if the election dates were the same for both, turnout would not be a problem. The new health authorities account for a major amount both of local expenditure and of local employment, and, unlike local authorities, they have now established the principle of industrial democracy, having as full members representatives of some who work within the service. The authorities have benefited from the value of the professional and scientific involvement of these representatives. They should, however, be elected by the people they represent as the Labour government proposed when I was Minister of Health, and not be selected as they are now. The professions and the Health Service trade unions are solely responsible for not taking up that specific offer of industrial democracy, which demonstrates the all too familiar resistance to the implementation, where more than one union is involved.

Once the members of new health authorities were elected it would be right to look very carefully at the results in Northern Ireland of the 1973 decision to integrate health and personal social services. This is again an area where the Royal Commission's analysis was disappointing. It commented that 'the demographic change which will be the greatest single influence on the shape of the NHS for the rest of this century, is the growing number of old people and particularly those over 70. This will increase the need for long-term care. In addition, demand for services for the mentally ill and the mentally handicapped are likely to grow'[14] – but its conclusion was against a merger under the present system. Yet an integrated, localist approach would produce a structure far better able to cope with this demographic challenge than the present one, which has done little to translate into practice all the rhetoric about community care. If integration were made part of a major shift towards democratic control of the NHS, it would be far more acceptable to the social services which, under the present centralised system, rightly fear that they would be dominated by the medical profession.

From 1974 to 1979 the Labour government tried very hard to redirect resources into the 'Cinderella' areas of mental illness and mental handicap, geriatrics and disablement. Even the previous government had, with Sir Keith Joseph as Secretary of State, demonstrated its concern with the publication of the White paper on the Mentally Handicapped which had been started under the previous Labour government. In 1976 the National Development Group for the Mentally Handicapped was set up under Peter Mitler and the White Paper on Mental Illness was published. Within the health and social services spending areas, the joint financing of community projects was introduced, and other changes were made whereby the Hospital Advisory Service became a Health Advisory Service to work with the Social Work Service, and with a remit to draw the health and social services together. But despite all this activity, the Royal Commission, three or four years later, could find little evidence of any real shift in priorities towards the disadvantaged specialities. The resistance to change is strong, particularly from consultants in the acute illness sector protecting their specialities, and from trade unions unwilling to see any closures among the acute general hospitals, which they see primarily as employers of their members. The mass media, too, are geared to the dramatic surgical health story and show only sporadic interest in the chronic specialities.

The more the case for community care is put openly to local people, the more local people will have to face up to solving their problems locally and argue about priorities. The evidence is now clear that an unelected centralist authority is incapable of facing these issues. The process of electing people to the health authority means that the rate payer and tax payer will be involved in arguments about what they should contribute financially. Similarly, the greater the discussion locally about co-ordination between health and social services, between hospital, hostel and home, the more likely we are to see genuine community care and sensible planning.

The localist approach will still necessitate central government involvement in inspecting and upholding minimum standards. As a major financier, central government will still have the right to demand that its priorities are followed and will still have a responsibility for allocating resources on the basis of need. The Regional Assemblies advocated in Chapter 14 on the Constitution would take over the strategic responsibilities of the present appointed regional health authorities and plan regional and sub-regional facilities. This would mean a much reduced function for central government, which could then concentrate on its real tasks: the overall strategic planning of the NHS and financial and manpower distribution, which would include the protection of Cinderella areas like mental illness and handicap. To carry out these strategic functions the professional staff in the regions and in the Department should be integrated. The current separation between civil servants in the DHSS, who have little or no experience of managing the health service, and health administrators in the regions is wholly illogical. The suggested regional health authorities would work with the regional health administrators and the regional water administrators and this would be their only executive function, as opposed to their advisory and scrutiny role.

The extraordinary career structure in the NHS, which stops at the regions and offers no opportunities at the centre for health administrators, but grafts on civil servants to run the headquarters, damages the NHS. Under the 1973 Act a special health authority can be created and this could employ the small number of specialised medical and administrative staff which would be needed in the national health service in the DHSS, together with a small number of civil servants to deal, for example, with the Treasury. This would strengthen expertise on health service problems within the Department and provide better accountability to Ministers. This change should be made anyway, before the creation of regional assemblies, for it is necessary in its own right. The Regional Assemblies would be charged with securing co-operation between local health authorities, but most of the all-embracing powers of the existing regional health authorities would be transferred down to the local health authorities.

The argument for giving elected district health authorities the power to raise finance remains unchanged. So long as the new authorities are wholly centrally financed, the feeling that their money is in some way a bonus from afar will continue to reduce the discipline of prudent housekeeping and any concern to ensure that some commitments could be financed locally. The DHSS will continue, at times of national financial stringency, to reduce brutally their allocation without regard to local circumstances. The regions, insulated from local commitment and concerns, also take decisions from a distance and local schemes are cancelled at great cost and great inconvenience. This cycle of financial irresponsibility is endemic to the present system. The public will always dislike any form of taxation, but putting a larger proportion of the burden of financial responsibility for local health services on local health authorities and through local democratic management on to local people means that they are more likely to pursue steadier capital investment programmes and to plan more realistic forward revenue spending. The separate capital and revenue allocation system should also be abolished, increasing the scope for flexible planning. The introduction of LIT for health and local government services will not allow vastly greater overall expenditure levels. There will be the same resources to tax locally as is done centrally, but the relationship between taxation and local services will become much clearer. The partnership between local and central NHS would continue but, just as it is vital to shift the balance towards greater local financial responsibility for local government, so it is vital to accompany the administrative reforms of the past decade in the NHS with the radical innovation of giving the new health authorities access to an independent source of finance.

A decentralised health service will mean that government and parliament will be unable to continue woefully to neglect their responsibilities to promote the health of the nation. One example of this neglect is the confinement of the NHS to being just a sickness service. Another is the craven attitude of successive governments to those two powerful commercial interests, the tobacco industry and the alcoholic drink industry. The evidence of the increasing harm that the widespread promotion and use of these two products does to the health of the nation is now incontrovertible. The dangers were spelt out in the first-ever government publication aimed at influencing the general public's attitudes to health;[15] they were reiterated in the report of the House of Commons Expenditure Committee[16] and then accepted in the White Paper *Prevention and Health.*[17] But all that followed was the usual exhortation and a useful new duty on cigarettes with a tar yield of over 20 mg.

Yet smoking causes lung cancer, chronic bronchitis and coronary artery disease, which now have an incidence of epidemic proportions. There is also a very worrying increase in smoking among the wives of unskilled men, and the number of women aged 45 to 65 who die from lung cancer has increased sharply. All advertising of cigarettes should be phased out except at the point of purchase, sporting and cultural sponsorship should be banned for a period of years to allow time for adjustment and the possible finding of other sponsors, non-smoking areas should be widely extended and enforced, and the most harmful tobacco products totally phased out of production. The difficulty is that the government lacks the statutory reserve powers without which negotiations with the tobacco industry are bound to result in inadequate measures. In 1975, after a considerable internal fight within the bureaucracy and among Ministers, the Labour government made the decision in principle to legislate by a short one-clause Bill to put tobacco products within the scope of the Medicine Act. There was a strong case for making such a change by regulation through a statutory instrument, extending the scope of the Act, but since the tobacco industry might have challenged its vires, it was decided that the matter would be best dealt with by primary legislation. The decision having been taken, sadly, no place was found for it in the 1976 legislative programme and instead another inadequate voluntary agreement was negotiated with the industry. It is not enough just to blame resistance from the Department of Industry, the sponsoring Department for the tobacco industry, or from the Treasury, fearing a fall in revenue. The real problem is a lack of Ministerial resolve, fearing to follow the advice of Health Ministers and listening instead to the vested interests of the newspaper and advertising industries, couched in the humbug of supposedly protecting the freedom of the individual. The advantage of using the Medicine Act is that it would put tobacco products firmly into a medical background, allow the government to be guided by specialist medical advice, introduce a range of statutory processes covering advertising, sales and the ingredients of cigarettes and provide an elaborate appeals machinery for the tobacco industry which has been proved to be fair by the pharmaceutical industry. Once government has the Medicine Act behind it, the whole balance of power in its relations with the industry will be transformed.

The use of the Medicine Act for alcoholic drinks can also be fully justified. Both tobacco and alcohol can be addictive, both damage health, both need to be directly controlled if the health of the nation is to be improved. About half a million people in England and Wales have a serious problem with alcoholic drink and in Scotland the situation is proportionately much worse. Alcohol not only damages the health of the drinker, but has serious social consequences, leading to the break-up of marriages, battered wives, battered children and much misery and degradation. Thirty years ago a bottle of whisky cost 45 per cent of the average man's disposable weekly income; through most of the 1970s it cost less than 20 per cent and consumption has quadrupled. The case for curbing advertising, reducing the alcoholic content of spirits, limiting sales outlets for the higher alcoholic content products and supporting a major education campaign grows ever stronger.

Another area where government has been absurdly weak is over fluoridation. The Royal College of Physicians, after the most careful assessment of the evidence, has confirmed that the fluoridation of water supplies is completely safe and that it substantially reduces dental decay, yet less than 10 per cent of the population receive water with added fluoride and many water authorities are finding the pressure to cease fluoridation hard to resist as central government refuses to give a decisive lead. Yet fluoridation could cut dental decay by half and the resources released could revive the dental health service which is drifting fast into being a predominantly private system.

The inability of successive governments to act on the evidence is revealed again over seat-belt legislation. If all drivers and front-seat passengers wore seatbelts up to 14,000 serious and fatal injuries a year could be averted, and NHS could be saved immense effort and well over £50 million could be directed to other areas. It is as if no one has learnt a thing from the evidence of the breathalyser which, though its effect has worn off and the legislation needs to be toughened, has probably saved over 200,000 road casualties since 1967. Yet this legislation was very nearly not even introduced and probably only a Minister of Transport with a nerve like Barbara Castle's would have been prepared to take on the formidable campaign that was mounted against it on the emotive grounds that it interfered with people's liberty.

We also need statutory food labelling for health and education. A mother needs to know that a can of Coca Cola contains the equivalent of ten lumps of sugar. She also needs to know the fat content of food, what are the synthetic ingredients and its calorific value.

The attitude of governments to preventive health resources over the past few decades needs to be compared with the situation that would have arisen if central government in the last century had refused to lay down statutory public standards but had relied instead on persuasion and education and had said that it was up to individuals to boil their own water supply. If one compares, for example, the amount of ministerial time and effort, parliamentary legislative time and scarce financial resources spent by the Labour government of 1974-6 on phasing out pay beds from NHS hospitals with the fact that they did not then find time to tackle smoking or seat-belt legislation, one must wonder about the real social priorities of the Labour Party. It is even more revealing that legislative reluctance has often been rationalised by saying that what is involved is an interference with people's freedom; yet so were the measures taken to prevent typhoid and tuberculosis.

Allocating money for screening programmes requires no

legislation, simply a readiness to challenge current spending priorities and to re-allocate resources. To be cost-effective screening must concentrate on high-risk groups. Breast cancer screening once a year for women in their fifties could reduce annual deaths by 3,000 and cost around £30 million. The problem is to ensure that it would be taken up by the high risk groups. Monitoring all pregnancies in women over forty, and drawing fluid from the sac around the unborn baby, with abortions in those cases which show the chromosome abnormality associated with what is popularly known as mongolism, would have cut the number of children born with this abnormality in 1973 in England and Wales by 14 per cent – at a cost then of less than £8,000 per affected mother.

Yet legislation and screening are not enough. There is also a need for a positive programme of intervention to promote better health, and early childhood has been identified by the Working Group on Inequalities in Health as the period of life at which intervention could most hopefully weaken the continuing correlation between health and class. This means shifting resources towards ante-natal, post-natal and child-health services. An interesting example of what can be done has been analysed by Dr Marsh, a general practitioner in Stockton on Tees.[18] It means improving the quality and coverage of general practice and community nursing in those areas where the health statistics show above average mortality or morbidity rates. It means also, as the Royal Commission recommended, integrating the Family Practitioner Committees with other services, as is already done in Scotland and in Northern Ireland. It means concentrating on providing better day care for children under five and bringing together education, social services and voluntary agencies. In order to do this central government needs to have better statistics but also the means for monitoring progress and conducting special studies in selected areas, seeking out the best method of reaching agreed objectives, particularly if extra finance is to be provided from central government to locally autonomous health and local authorities.

The Department of Health and Social Security already has a potential independent assessment body in the Social Work

Service, but it has not developed anything comparable to the authority and independence that the Department of Education and Science's School Inspectorate enjoys in its relationship with local education authorities. Nor has the Health Advisory Service developed the necessary bite to insist that its recommendations should be seriously considered, though it has done useful work in trying to improve standards in the areas of mental illness, mental handicap and geriatrics. An essential accompaniment to a more decentralised structure for the NHS must be an enhanced role for central government as the advocate of improved standards of care, and along with that the fostering of an 'auditing' mentality at every level within the health and social services. Doctors must take more into account that they make economic decisions as they prescribe for patients, order diagnostic tests, admit patients to hospitals and determine their length of stay. As variations in treatment, results and costs which stem from individual doctors' decisions show a pattern impossible to justify, the scrutiny of clinical work by fellow doctors is starting to win acceptance. So is the fact that medical care has to be rationed by the public and by politicians, and this too is helping to shift attitudes within the medical profession. As long as doctors were able to invoke politicians' rhetoric about a comprehensive service as an excuse for not making choices, the debate about the NHS concentrated solely on the quantity of money and of services. Now it is focusing more on priorities, choice and standards of care. This debate needs to be pushed down to the district level and the community confronted with specific local choices.

The scale of provision for home helps, meals on wheels, disablement aids and specially adapted housing for the disabled determines whether disabled people can stay and cope at home or have to be kept within the NHS. Yet decisions on these matters are often made in terms of budgetary restraints wholly divorced from NHS needs or resources; and, similarly, NHS decisions which affect community services are often taken wholly apart from the financial situation and forward plans of the local authority. It is very easy for each to shuffle the responsibility off on to the other. There are, however, new and interesting developments. The hospice movement is a new approach to caring for the terminally ill and it is now developing a service for people who wish to die at home, giving them specialised care in the home rather than taking them away from the environment they know. With imagination and a structure for overcoming the institutional and administrative barriers, community care can transform the lives of the disabled and the elderly.

Without a really radical shift in the pattern of care, there is little chance that society will be able, either physically or financially, to care for its ageing population. It will require new techniques and new attitudes: the scale of adaptation needed has so far barely been perceived. That the government in 1980 could assert that integration between hospitals and community services 'has been substantially achieved' reflects an unreal complacency.

The main role of central government must be to protect the NHS. A small private health sector does not seriously damage the health service but if that sector grows the distortion it can introduce in terms of the rational allocation of skilled people and specialised facilities can harm the NHS. It is legitimate and right to phase private medicine out from within the NHS and for government to take financial and other measures actively to discourage the growth of the private health sector. In 1980 3,366,000 people estimated to be covered by private health insurance, and if the 1980 growth rate were to continue it would be 10 million by 1985. Legislating to ban private health is an issue of human rights discussed in Chapter 17. The result of the last Labour Government's attempt to phase out pay beds in NHS hospitals was a substantial increase in the waiting lists for NHS patients, caused by industrial action and a growth in private health insurance. There are lessons to be learned from this, one of which was the Labour Government's inability to grasp the fact that without a financial inducement for hospital consultants to opt for a full-time commitment to the NHS there was insufficient inducement for them to acquiesce in a policy which threatened many with reduced earnings. Improving the quality as well as the quantity of provision of the NHS is the best way of curbing the growth of the private sector.

401

17

Freedom with Security

Slowly it is becoming recognised that one of the dangers of corporatism is that the Welfare State can provide the cover and justification under which the government and bureaucracy bring forward for the best of motives, measures which challenge basic civil liberties. In its efforts to provide for the welfare of the citizen, society also extends the right of authority and the police to monitor and observe the life of the citizen, to computerise and hold information, sometimes to transfer information obtained for one purpose for use in another context. The Left, in the days when they were not the government or the provider, felt able to be both the champion of the Welfare State and the champion of libertarian principles, not afraid to attack government for any tendency to encroach on civil liberties. The welfare tradition and the libertarian tradition were not in conflict. But once socialists won power they began to accept the steady encroachment of authority and the reconciliation of freedom with security became not just a theory but a practical reality.

The simplest definitions of a state revolve around the notion of the monopoly of the use of force, and any state must therefore define the conditions and circumstances under which it permits the lawful exercise of that force. It normally entrusts the exercise of that monopoly to a professional police force and the armed services. In Britain, traditionally, there have been close links between the community and the police, whereas the state has had unfettered control over the armed services. Since society invests in every citizen 'powers to arrest

402

without warrant and to use reasonable force in the prevention of crime',[1] the police should be seen as specialists, as 'citizens in uniform', but identified with the community as fellow citizens. They should act on behalf of the community, acquire specialist skills and expertise, but always depend on, and know that they depend on, public support for their success. The authority of the police is acceptable if there is a disposition, in the average person, generally to support the institutions of the state and the authority of the law. If the relationship of trust breaks down, then one of the areas where tension between the individual and the state makes itself most immediately felt is that of police-community relations. At worst, the police then becomes a force for repression, deriving its authority not from a general acceptance of its methods and objectives but from the simple exercise of the monopoly of the use of force.

In Britain, parliament has wisely never accepted the argument for a national centrally-controlled police force and so far for a variety of reasons the actual numbers of police have remained lower than for most of our continental neighbours. Our police, though now often trained in the use of arms, do not normally carry guns; riots and demonstrations are usually handled without bloodshed and today's police have no offensive device for use against crowds which have not been in the possession of our police forces since 1829.

As Britain has become more and more centralised, so the authority of those in power becomes ever more distant, and the policies they pursue are likely to become more confrontational. We are already seeing in Britain a tendency for police methods to change and for centralist pressures to begin to take effect within the institution of the police itself. We need a rational debate about the role of authority in democracy and the issues affecting law and order, but a new and dangerous polarisation seems to be developing between, on the one hand, those on the extreme Right who argue that simply strengthening the forces of law and order will cure the complex problems of crime, alienation and public disorder which infect our society, and, on the extreme Left, those who argue that alienation and repression come essentially from an authoritarian and unaccountable police force. The one group seems to view the police and society as static entities: the other, equally unsubtly, sees a vast conspiracy in which the police force is lined up with all authority as 'baddies' against a small and 'saintly' band of good and progressive campaigners against injustice.

The Conservative Party, especially under Mrs Thatcher, has portrayed itself as the party of law and order. It has both exempted the police from expenditure cuts and assured them that their pay will keep pace with inflation, and has seemed in fact to be adopting the police as its special constituency – it is perhaps symptomatic that in the 1979 parliament, the Police Federation re-appointed the same Conservative MP that had previously been its parliamentary adviser, thereby breaking the tradition of having an Opposition MP as their spokesman. The Conservatives are, of course, perfectly entitled to try to win votes out of 'law and order', but the danger is that the Labour Party, which has in the past resisted pressure from within to become anti-authority, is responding to the Conservatives styling themselves as the 'Police Party' by becoming the 'Anti-Police Party'. Such a polarisation, if it develops, will be damaging and even potentially dangerous for the country, because it would appear that a key national institution had been appropriated by one political party.

Socialists should not forget that surveys have repeatedly shown that the British police are strongly supported by public opinion. In 1975 an independent survey by Dr William Belson of the London School of Economics found that 90 per cent of people supported the police and thought they did a good job; no less that 60 per cent were 'very satisfied' with the police's work. Another poll[2] has largely confirmed these findings. Only doctors were thought to have greater honesty and higher ethical standards than the police: the people interviewed put solicitors, businessmen, MPs, local councillors and trade unionists lower down the list. A northern survey[3] put the picture a little more in context, showing that while in general the population is pro-police, there is much greater scepticism about police conduct among the young generally and in particular among minority ethnic groups and in inner city areas such as Moss Side, Manchester. Nevertheless, this survey found that 77 per cent of those in the North-West as a whole thought the police were doing a good job.

Public opinion, however, though important, cannot be the final arbiter, for on civil liberty issues the general public can be remarkably insensitive, particularly where there is a racial background to a particular problem. The press in Britain has the best record of safeguarding human liberties, and active political groups championing minority rights – often, but not invariably, on the Left – have usually ensured the vigilance of parliament.

The Labour Party, which once had a proud record, has recently tended to shrink from challenging the established order: when in government it has both endorsed the secrecy which obscures debate and has been reluctant to risk the odium of public opinion by championing unpopular libertarian causes. The 1966-70 Parliamentary Labour Party was markedly more radical on these issues than that of 1974-9. This weakening of the libertarian tradition has been criticised by the socialist historian Professor E.P. Thompson saying 'the ambivalence within the "Left" towards civil liberties is the most alarming evidence of all that the libertarian nerve has become dulled, and carries with it a premonition of defeat.'[4]

Socialist politicians must not be afraid to be seen to champion a proper role for the police in modern society. To allow the present police to be depicted by its critics as an evil reactionary force on the side of conformism and the status quo is to abdicate responsibility. It also lends credence to a point of view that, generally speaking, is not supported by the facts. Any human society has to face up to the need to restrain the lawless and ensure that the law is observed. The history of the police in this country means that we start off with a long tradition of democratic, community policing on which to build. What we need now is to revive and identify that tradition in order to apply it to life today.

The public has been highly critical of the introduction of the panda-car and of the disappearance of the neighbourhood 'bobby', and in many areas the policeman is now back on the beat, proving not only a deterrent against crime but providing a friendly and accessible symbol of authority to the population as a whole. Not surprisingly, some neighbourhood police have themselves been critical of the approach to the community of outside mechanised squads lacking the close relationship which they themselves have built up on the beat. The Chief Constable of Devon and Cornwall, Mr Alderson, commented on the drift in the last fifteen years 'from what was primarily a foot-patrolling preventive force into a mobile reactionary force' and noted that there had been a 'gradual alienation of the police from the public which alters not only the nature of policing but the police officers themselves'. Recognising the growth of criticism which he felt to be unfair, he recommended that 'the police response ought to be to make it clear that they represented no particular class and to get close enough to the public for ordinary people to be able to put attacks into perspective and realise that such criticism did not tally with the police officers they knew.' This is wise advice. While some people criticise the police for playing any part in social activity designed to prevent crime, the evidence is that this social contact increases the social awareness of the police. This is particularly important at a time when the police have not been immune from the trends towards bureaucratisation and centralisation that are evident in other areas of our national life.

There is concern about the accountability of the police and the replacement of the old Watch Committees in the cities and boroughs and the Standing Joint Committees in the counties – which often exercised a considerable degree of political control over the local force – the new Police Authorities are larger and some people feel ineffective in making the police force democratically accountable. In the past twenty years since the Royal Commission on the Police the number of separate police forces in England and Wales has declined from around 150 to 43. Increasing use of the National Computer – it dealt with 33 million transactions in 1978 compared with 18·5 million in 1977 – also means more centralisation, as does the nationally co-ordinated training system, which gives the police a stronger sense of professionalism. In 1978, police strength stood at 109,975, while in the financial year 1977-8 total expenditure on police services in England and Wales stood at just over a billion pounds (£1,064,094,000), and expenditure has continued to rise.

The treatment that citizens – particularly members of minority groups – receive from the police and the relationship between the police and the citizen are key indicators of the democratic health of a society. Totalitarian states such as the Soviet Union and fascist states such as Chile can be characterised by the way they use their police force, and in particular secret or political police, to underwrite the whole political system. A state where the police work within clear legal guidelines, and where their authority comes not from the use of force or because of any privileges they may enjoy, but because they are supported by and derive their authority from the people, is a truly democratic state, whatever the professed ideology of its government. Policemen tend, like many professional groups such as servicemen, lawyers and doctors, to be conservative in their attitudes: their job requires them to enforce the law as it is, or as their senior officers see it, rather than to embrace or champion changes or reforms in society.

It is easy for a policeman, captain, judge or surgeon to feel that there is so much unlawful behaviour about that with more law and order, or with what is sometimes called a 'moral lead' from politicians, many of society's problems could be cured. Law and order is therefore a natural conservative issue, emphasising the failures of man rather than of the institutions of society. The extreme Right, and in particular the National Front, tends to claim that there is no evil in society that is not attributable to some group that needs to be either refused entry to Britain, deported or in some way taught a lesson. At the other end of the spectrum the anarchic Left argues that all society's institutions are rotten, and that law and order is a farce designed to maintain a social order characterised by exploitation and repression.

What society has to do is to choose between freedom and freedom from crime[5] and to establish the style and level of policing necessary to protect the public from crime while not making the individual vulnerable to arbitrary police behaviour. Socialists should not need to be reminded that, while the use of force is distasteful to some in almost any circumstances, there are many more, the majority, who wish to be protected from crime and thuggery. In general it is not Conservative voters who are most vulnerable to many forms of crime – hooliganism at football matches or vandalism on council estates, being mugged in darkened streets, coming home from the bus-stop or the station. Those who make up the Conservative Party's 'natural' suburban constituency and who are most vociferous over crime are more likely to take cars from home to work or entertainment and to live in areas with a lower crime rate. Yet regardless of position in society or the Party they support, all voters have the right to protection from these evils and the law must operate to protect everyone, whether they come from the immigrant community or are 'disgusted Tunbridge Wells'.

A welcome feature of the way Britain has handled police matters is the absence of a national police force. Although some small democratic countries, including Denmark, Finland, and Norway, have successful national police forces, such a development should be firmly resisted for Britain. The 1962 Royal Commission on the Police stated that the creation of a national force would not be 'constitutionally objectionable or politically dangerous' but it would, at a time when more and more of the levers of power have been passing to the centre, be a major and serious step in the move towards a centralised state. It would make for less identification and accountability to the community but, above all, it would give central government – through its politicians and civil servants – direct or indirect control of a vital institution. The diffusion of authority is one of the most important structural safeguards against the abuse of authority, which is much easier under a centralised structure.

The Royal Commission made a serious attempt to grapple with the central/local dilemma, and it pointed to the two often conflicting objectives of accountability and efficiency. The 1964 Police Act envisaged police forces under the direction and control of the chief constable being 'adequate and efficient' in terms of resources; while the police authority had powers to deal with general questions of policing policy though not with personnel or other matters which were under the chief constable's authority. Central government, in the form of the Home Office's financial and general control, working with the Inspectorate-General of Constabulary, acquired a much greater role in establishing priorities and standards than ever before. The Royal Commission concluded that the chief constable should 'be subject to more effective supervision than the present arrangements appear to recognise' and this view was accepted by the then Home Secretary. But the working of the Act has tended to exclude the police authorities from discussing policing policy and their right to acquire information has been restricted. Chief constables have tended to claim that 'operational' matters are their sole concern but this terminology is not used in the Police Act, which gives the police authority responsibility for providing 'an adequate and efficient police force in their area'. It is time that police authorities challenged the limitations that have been placed by practice, not statute, on their powers. It is time a police authority challenged – if necessary in the courts – the limited interpretation of its powers and if these are then found to be as limited as some say, the case for further legislation will be much more convincing. There is a case for a police authority which feels that a Special Patrol Group should not be established in their police force insisting that this is a decision for them, not for the chief constable.

The reduction in the number of police forces began with the 1964 Act and has been a part of the general attempt by central governments to rationalise administration by creating larger units. In England and Wales there are now 31 county forces, 10 combined forces covering two or more counties, and the two London forces, the City and the Metropolitan; while the eight Scottish forces and the Royal Ulster Constabulary bring the national total to 52. Each of these police forces, with the exception of the Metropolitan Police in London, is placed under a police authority made up of two-thirds local councillors and one-third local magistrates. As in many aspects of local government, police forces have become so large and extensive geographically that the Devon and Cornwall Police Authority, for example, finds it difficult to comprehend the scale of the operations. People who live in Penzance and serve on the

Police Authority may not have the same interest in the police of Barnstaple as they would in the police of St Ives. The matter of size together with the growing professionalism of the police has tended to make it difficult for police authorities to retain a grip on their functions in overseeing the efficient use of resources and they come to rely on the judgment of the chief constable and Her Majesty's Inspector of Constabulary. There should be no further police mergers and in some cases there is scope for splitting the larger forces up into smaller units.

The Metropolitan Police is placed under the authority of the Home Secretary who is, of course, accountable to the House of Commons. In practice the House of Commons does not give the attention to policing matters which a local police authority would be able to give in, say, a county police area. The Metropolitan Police provides national as well as local services and this ensures that Britain has some of the advantages of a national police force without its disadvantages. It provides protection for foreign embassies and it is the international link, through Interpol, of the British police with their foreign counterparts. Yet there is a case for a more effective system of police accountability in London, while leaving the Home Secretary with total responsibility for these national services. A Special Select Committee set up within Parliament – a Committee of Members drawn from the Metropolitan Police area, perhaps in some kind of associations with elected councillors from the London boroughs – might be able to exercise closer scrutiny than is possible at present.

Many local councillors, both Conservative and Labour, have expressed strong views about the working of the new system and this is not just nostalgia, for the present system poses some real problems of democratic accountability. In London it is possible to claim that the present arrangements make local involvement and accountability almost impossible, and in some other areas, even though elected local representatives and magistrates sit together on the police authority, there is often the feeling that much of what happens in local policing is in fact controlled from Whitehall or is at least the result of co-ordination between the forces. Many police authorities meet relatively infrequently, some as little as once every four months. Chief Constables who have a good and informal relationship with their authority members will say that they learn from them a great deal about the local area and how it is governed. Conversely, the involvement of local elected leaders in the problems of policing is good both for the leaders and for their Parties. But they must feel that they have real responsibility or good councillors will not serve on police authorities, preferring to spend their time in areas where their decision-making capacity is stretched and they feel responsible and involved.

Some people are critical of the 'new breed' of chief constables who have become well known national figures, speaking out not only on questions of police policy but also on general moral issues, sometimes using the mass media with considerable effect to put their points of view. It was Sir Robert Mark who in a BBC Dimbleby Lecture blazed the trail for outspokenness by senior police officers when he attacked some members of the legal profession who defend criminals in court and suggested major changes in the law relating to the rights of persons accused of criminal offences. The present Metropolitan Police Commissioner, Sir David McNee, has also entered public controversy by – probably rightly, as events have turned out – refusing to ban marches by extreme Right-wing groups.

This subject was discussed in his Annual Report for 1979 by the Chief Constable of Devon and Cornwall, Mr J.C. Alderson, who wrote: 'The Police should not be used to put down freedom of expression or protest but merely to facilitate it within the law. There are times, however, when in order to preserve order the police will have to educate the public through the media and other avenues of communication as to the desirability of curbing protest from time to time. It is essential that this should be understood in a plural and multi-racial society since that which might be inoffensive in a homogeneous society can be extremely offensive in a heterogeneous society.' Here Mr Alderson was referring to the activities of racist groups who organise marches, often through racially mixed neighbourhoods and in the presence of counter-demonstrators. In such cases the Chief Constable refers the

411

matter to the local authority by saying that he believes that if the march does take place public disorder is likely to get out of hand and a serious breach of the peace is likely to take place. He therefore asks the local authority to seek a ban from the Home Secretary, under the Public Order Act of 1936, that the planned march may not take place. In practice Chief Constables have rightly felt it their duty where feasible to protect the right to demonstrate even of the most obnoxious of demonstrators. As a result, a number of highly controversial demonstrations have taken place involving the National Front, with counter-demonstrators claiming that the police were 'supporting racism' and some even going so far as to argue that, since in their view the police had neglected to protect the victims of racism, they would themselves break up the demonstration. It is a difficult balance. The Chief Constable of the West Midlands Police Force sought to ban marches by the National Front and was supported by the local authority, which wished to prevent both public disorder and public expenditure.

It has been suggested that public demonstrations are no longer important in British politics – and a Home Office Consultative Paper published in 1980 suggested as much – the right to demonstrate is, however, vital to the maintenance of our democracy. Demonstrations allow people to vent their feelings and to carry a message directly to the intended target, be it a government, town council or a community generally. The Home Office paper went so far as to suggest that 'speakers' corners' in major cities might be an adequate substitute. The Metropolitan Police, in their evidence to the House of Commons Select Committee, stated that the number of demonstrations in the Metropolis had doubled in ten years, and stood at 482 in 1979. Others have pointed out the great cost of policing controversial marches, often involving large police operations on public holidays. In a recent paper produced for the Runnymede Trust, Andrew Nicol has shown that the right to demonstrate has always been costly: and he argues that violence in past demonstrations, such as the Gordon Riots, and Luddites, Peterloo, Cato Street and the Chartists, was in every case much more serious than anything we know today. Nicol also reminds us that in 1888 alone there were 1,400 demonstrations in the Metropolitan area. Administrative convenience or cost cannot be used as a pretext for curtailing the right to demonstrate.

At present Chief Constables have considerable discretion in matters of public order: under the Public Order Act 1936 processions can be banned for up to three months, it may cover all processions or only a class of processions, and may be made effective in all, or part of, the police district. The Commission for Racial Equality – among other organisations – has suggested that this is not a satisfactory situation, and put forward the proposal that processions should only be banned if they are likely to 'stir up hatred against any racial group'.

Should such demonstration be allowed? Which should take precedence, the right to demonstrate or the right to be free from racial abuse? The present position is extremely delicate, and it has had the effect, almost certainly desired by the extremes of both Right and Left, of making it appear that the police are particularly concerned to protect the National Front. The police are right in saying that the public will need to be educated about the limits to which certain freedoms can be taken when the freedom of others is put at risk. For instance, incitement to racial hatred remains a criminal offence, yet very few if any prosecutions for racial incitement have taken place as a result of National Front demonstrations, even when demonstrators have poured racial abuse on any black or Asian person unfortunate enough to be seen by them. The right to demonstrate is a precious freedom and demonstrations either re-routed or curtailed should be allowed if at all possible, but in a multi-racial society extreme care has to be taken to avoid unnecessary violence and racialism. The decision rightly should remain with local policemen, councillors and magistrates, who are in a far better position to judge than any Minister of the Interior would be.

Another type of publicity occurs when chief officers, like Mr Ken Oxford in Merseyside after the inquest on the Kelly affair, sometimes feel it necessary to speak out in order to defend their men and to keep up their morale. Possibly thinking of the Californian example, where Police Chief Ed Davis of Los Angeles became a Republican contender for the governorship

413

of the state, some people have suspected certain British police chiefs of having ambitions going beyond the confines of the conventional police career. There is no evidence for this suspicion. Mr Alderson, of Devon and Cornwall, has been criticised for his advocacy of community policing and is liberal in many of his views. The Chief Constable of Greater Manchester, Mr Anderton, appears to be more of a fundamentalist and has also been criticised for some of his statements. On the whole this diversity is no bad thing, and Chief Constables in this country have usually been very careful to keep well away from statements which could be construed as party political. They obviously feel, however, that there is a specific police viewpoint which is not getting across. What we are seeing is not so much the entry of policemen into politics as an increasing confidence of the police in themselves as an interest group with its own interests and concerns to put across to the general public. This is a welcome development: and to the extent that the media sensibly do not allow police chiefs a totally uncritical hearing, it forms an extension of police accountability to the public. It is better to have a Chief Constable who is well known and on whom responsibility can be pinned than an amorphous and anonymous leadership which stays out of the limelight.

The Police Federation – the only trade union, by law, to which policemen may belong – is a slightly different case. While some of its spokesmen have tended to speak in strident tones in recent years, their behaviour is no more than characteristic of trade union leaders about to enter negotiations. It is up to policemen to decide if their public representation is to be by tough, abrasive spokesmen provoking controversy rather than by counciliatory, quiet negotiators. An idiotic pronouncement by a police trade unionist on some aspect of society and its attitudes to crime may raise the morale of a certain type of police officer but certainly does not enhance the standing of the police in the community at large. But strenuous efforts need to be made to ensure that the Police Federation does not see its allies and friends in parliament as being confined only to the Right wing of the Conservative Party.

The French political scientist Maurice Duverger has pointed

out that 'if democrats blindly assume that the police are their enemies, then they will in fact become their enemies'. It is therefore absolutely essential that the constitutional position of the police in this country should be carefully considered by socialists and that serious efforts should be made to improve the existing machinery for police accountability to the public. It is to be hoped that the police will not resist establishing more clearly than at present that police authorities do have a serious democratic role in the overall formulation of policy for their force and should not act as merely the cyphers of the Chief Constable, their only sanction being the negative one of financial control.

At the level of the man in the street or in a police station, more specific questions arise. It is essential if the British public's trust in the police is to be maintained and strengthened that there should be a credible system for dealing with complaints against the police by members of the public. Under the Police Act of 1976 a new procedure was set up with the establishment of an independent body, the Police Complaints Board, to consider those complaints which, after investigation by the police, are proceeded with. The appointment of outsiders to the Board and its independence from the police was a major innovation which caused unease in police circles. Police anxieties over this reform have been shown to be grossly exaggerated. The Board dealt in 1978 with 11,881 complaints but recommended that formal charges should be brought in respect of only fifteen. Investigations carried out by the police are undoubtedly very thorough; indeed many serving officers are privately critical of the considerable resources which forces devote to the detailed investigations of complaints.

HM Chief Inspector of Constabulary in his 1978 Report, points out that in that year 22,999 members of the public took the trouble to write letters of appreciation to the police for the way they did their job. But the public finds the 'success' rate of complaints remarkably low. There remain controversial cases, like that of Liddle Towers who died in 1976 from injuries allegedly received from policemen, and Blair Peach who died in the Southall demonstrations in 1979. In both these cases coroners' inquests – an inappropriate form of investigation anyway – failed to clear the police of some of the suspicion generated by strong campaigns blaming them for the deaths. In future it will be mandatory for the coroner to hold an inquest in every such case and such inquests will be held before a jury selected on the same basis as juries are selected for ordinary courts.

The controversy surrounding the 'Operation Countryman' enquiry into alleged corruption in the Metropolitan Police has also aroused suspicions that 'cover-ups' and the closing of ranks occur in the police force when certain complaints are made. Obviously it can only be to the good of the police in general if the incompetent or malevolent in their ranks are weeded out quickly and efficiently. But policemen do tend to close ranks when criticised and the results on occasion are far from satisfactory for public confidence. The police themselves need to be brought to understand that, particularly at a time when they are attracting strong support from the Right, they must be more careful to be seen to be unafraid of investigation. In addition more effort must be made to increase the confidence of the ethnic minority groups in the way the Board operates – it still has no black or brown members.

One reason for having, in the police, a strong and impartial mechanism for enforcing the law and a judiciary independent both of the House of Commons and of the Executive is that they have thereby a clear authority to protect minorities. Unpopular laws can be enforced when necessary without politicians being involved or fearing that they need to change the law in order to win votes. The protection of racial minorities is, almost by definition, not a task likely to be supported with relish by most of the population. We are very unlikely ever to allow a populist tyranny to develop, but as parliament, in response to the wish for greater accountability and the pressure for a move to delegated rather than representative democracy, makes more use of referenda, there are strong grounds for giving minorities fundamental rights and the protection of the law.

Despite strenuous efforts by the police and the Home Office, recruitment into the police service from minority ethnic groups remains at an extremely low level and there is now in many inner-city areas a high degree of misunderstanding and enmity between the police and young blacks, an enmity which has on both sides, strong racial overtones. As long ago as 1967 the late Sir Joseph Simpson, then Commissioner of the Metropolitan Police, spoke of the 'deteriorating background to the pattern of police and immigrant relations' in London. The police have responded by giving a good deal of attention to community relations; officers have visited the West Indies and the Asian countries to study the background of recent immigrants to Britain, courses have been held to help senior officers learn about race relations and the Metropolitan Police has a Community Relations Department at Headquarters and a network of community liaison officers in the divisions.

In community relations, as in policing in general, the conflict between the right to freedom and the right to be free from crime creates difficult dilemmas for the community. The police officer needs to carry out his duty, but he also needs to have understanding and support from the community. In many inner-city areas the police do not live locally, indeed, a high proportion of London police are not Londoners, and tend to bring in the values and attitudes of the communities where they live. Where those values are those of the outer suburbs – with its stress on individualism and achievement – they clash with the values of solidarity and clannishness which are characteristics of, for example, young black unemployed people of Caribbean origin. In the outer suburbs people will support the police and expect energetic action against burglaries and crime: in the inner city the police may be regarded as unwanted and rejected agents of the 'powers that be', a government which appears uninterested in the plight of the inner-city populations. A Liverpool police officer once observed that the inner-city areas are society's 'dustbins' where unwanted groups are dumped. The trouble, said the officer, was that the police were given the job of 'sitting on the lid' of the social dustbin.

The Ombudsman in his 1979 Annual Report wrote about the dilemma of balancing basic rights, just laws, good movement and popular feeling in relation to a particular case

417

affecting gypsies: ' . . . Three main conflicting obligations in this case were: the established policy of not chivvying a special group of people, gypsies, away from unauthorised encampments when there is nowhere else for them to go; the duty there must be on any administration to protect the interests of the law-abiding majority of the community; and the requirement to obtain for the whole body of taxpayers full value for surplus government land when it is disposed of.' In this case the Ombudsman took the side of what he called the 'law-abiding majority of the community' but frequently justice may not lie on the side of what is perceived to be the majority, but rather with extremely unpopular minorities. How should individual rights be guaranteed in a society in which the individual often appears to be sacrificed to the interests of the big battalions? We tend to think our record in upholding human rights is unique, but the doctrine of the unfettered legislative freedom of the House of Commons means that there is no check on a House of Commons which might wish to pass repressive or illiberal legislation or to attack the position of vulnerable minorities. A few other democratic countries have so developed their systems that it is far from certain that the UK can claim to have now the best record in human rights.

One simple, not perfect but nevertheless helpful, decision would be to utilise the international code of human rights in the European Human Rights Convention and the United Nations Covenant on Civil and Political Rights, in ways which extend the rights of British citizens. We ratified the International Covenant on Civil and Political Rights in May 1976 with reservations and derogations, but we have yet to ratify the Fourth Protocol of the European Convention. We in Britain are as aware as any member of the Council of Europe of the real effectiveness of its human rights machinery because we have been taken to the Court and to the Commission both by states and by individuals. Where complaints against the British government have been upheld as in the Northern Ireland case involving interrogation methods action has been taken. Applications lodged with the Commission or the Court in Strasbourg have for instance led to improvements in the system of appeals for immigrants entering the country and to new regulations about the right of prisoners to have access to the courts, and could well provide a check on telephone tapping. The experience may not be particularly comfortable but gradually in Britain we have accepted that the human rights machinery provided for under the European Convention has become an integral part of that empirical process by which over the centuries individual liberties in Britain have been expanded and reinforced. This process is the foundation of our democratic way of life. There will always be room for improvement in safeguarding the rights of the individual, in Britain as elsewhere in Europe; that the authority and meticulous standards of the Court and Commission are now engaged alongside our own national institutions in helping us to make these improvements is something wholly to be welcomed, not treated with insular suspicion.

We need to contribute to discussion and debate about what can or should be done to make the European Convention even more effective. The Committee of Ministers needs to be opened up to public scrutiny to avoid suspicion that it is biased in favour of member states. Individuals should in addition be given direct access to the European Court of Human Rights and the enforcement machinery could be strengthened. The system has been subject to constant development over the years. The First and Fourth protocols to the Convention added substantive new rights. A number of technical improvements have been made. Work is in hand on the more effective application of basic standards to particular problems relating for instance to press freedom and to the threat to privacy by data-processing banks. An inter-governmental committee of experts on which the UK is represented has explored the possibility of adopting certain rights embodied in the International Convenant on Civil and Political Rights which are not explicitly covered by the European Convention. We should be more positive in welcoming this development.

At present the Convention is not fully implemented and not all the member states accept all its provisions and those of its protocols. Four countries do not accept the compulsory jurisdiction of the Court; five do not recognise the right of individual petition: eight, including Britain, have not ratified the Fourth Protocol, although we have signed it. This protocol guarantees certain rights relating to the liberty of the person and to freedom of movement. There are some arguments, though they are mostly exaggerated and wrong, for the UK not at present ratifying this Protocol: but arguments in favour of ratification are much stronger. It would introduce a permanent guarantee for certain important rights fundamental to a democratic society over and above the transitory concerns of Ministers in the executive. A British government might well have to introduce two or three reservations and might have to consider making an additional derogation to take account of the 1976 Prevention of Terrorism Act. There are clear precedents for making such reservations and they would not need to be permanent. Ratification would advance the tally of rights protected within the UK from 17 to 21 and would complete our acceptance of the European system of enforceable rights.

Should the Convention be actually incorporated into UK law? Although some oppose such a development on the grounds that the Convention could be used by the opponents of trade unions to attack them and some lawyers have argued that to define rights in a positive way would be contrary to the traditions of British law, which has traditionally set out what is not permissible while leaving it understood that everything else is permissible, the effect would undoubtedly be to enhance individual rights by giving individuals access to the courts if they thought their rights had been infringed. In cases involving press freedom, prisoners' rights, or the tapping of telephones, it would be possible under the Convention for specific grievances to be given a proper hearing where this is at present not so.

Some people object to accepting international human rights provisions because they see that it could fetter the freedom of a Labour government to ban by law the private education of children or the practising of private medicine. The UN International Covenant on Economic Social and Cultural Rights, which was ratified by the Labour government in 1976, in Article 13(3) obliges the state parties 'to have respect for the liberty of parents and, when applicable, legal guardians, to choose for their children schools other than those established by the public authorities'. The European Convention on Human Rights in Article 2 of the first protocol obliges states to respect the rights of parents to ensure education and teaching in conformity with their own religious and philosophical convictions. In a judgment on the interpretation of this article it was seen as guaranteeing the freedom to establish private schools and as 'safeguarding the possibility of pluralism in education, which possibility is essential for the preservation of the "democratic society" as conceived by the Convention'. This adds a further complexity to the issue. Socialist governments, which have generally been the keenest to try to establish international codes of conduct for the protection of minorities and civil liberties, could find their own freedom to act as they might feel best limited by international criteria. Yet the same international criteria pose a very considerable restriction on the freedom of any Right-wing government wishing to introduce racialist legislation or to restrict minority rights. It is desirable, as argued in Chapters 15 and 16, for government to withhold all financial support and encouragement from private educational or health provisions, and to separate private from central government sponsored activity. As Minister of Health I was deeply involved in the phasing out of pay beds in NHS hospitals and faced serious industrial action from hospital consultants. I have never charged nor ever will charge a patient; and my own children go to state schools. But I do not accept that it is legitimate or compatible with the values of a democratic society, in the 1980s, as the Labour Conference decided, to ban the charging of fees for private education or private health without first having a sustained period of socialist government giving positive support to the public educational and health services and discriminating actively against private educational and health services. These services might then wither away to be of little significance, and the extremely disturbing choice avoided of whether the price of abandoning society's libertarian values was worth the social advantages. The onus of proof lies on those who wish to destroy a human right. The European

Convention on Human Rights is a powerful external check on all governments who ratify it and not easily flouted.

Another controversy is whether or not the adoption of a Convention on human rights should be entrenched, as is the Bill of Rights in the United States. In this country this would mean that the Convention should prevail over existing legislation if a court should decide that an Act is in violation of it, while all legislation passed subsequent to the passing of the Convention should be interpreted in line with it. This would challenge the present total freedom or sovereignty of parliament, yet it would be an important safeguard for human rights in this country. There needs to be careful debate about this issue. The important first step is to ratify the Convention and to ensure that all individuals have remedies available if their rights have been violated.

The enhancement of individual and minority rights could not only counter present trends towards bureaucratisation and centralisation but could also increase the prestige, and therefore the legitimacy and authority, of the whole process of law and order in this country. This is not something to be feared by the Left; socialists have far more to gain from the entrenchment of the rule of law than the Right, provided socialists are prepared to ensure that the full weight of the law is put at the disposal of every citizen. At present, many millions of people whose income is above the Legal Aid limit have no access to the law because they cannot afford to meet its spiralling costs. This must be remedied. Neighbourhood law centres, with young lawyers working for a salary and bringing low cost legal advice could ensure that the law was the friend of the under-privileged and disenfranchised. Nothing has been more depressing than the inability of Labour governments seriously to challenge the restrictive practices and remoteness of the legal profession. There are arguments for having a Minister of Justice answering for all aspects of law and order. But whatever the merits of this, and it is bound to raise anxiety about putting so much power into one person and one Department's hands, there is a strong case for the Lord Chancellor and the Department being answerable to the House of Commons and not being tucked away in the House of Lords.

Terrorism is now an international security issue posing the threat of anarchy and disorder. Not only is the political motivation often international but it is often aided by international finance, backed by governments and given access to sophisticated weapons. It is sad but inevitable that, in countering the threat, governments will have to re-examine many past attitudes and introduce measures which do encroach on civil liberties. It is even more than normally necessary, therefore, to have some international as well as national checks on such legislation. The British legislation for dealing with terrorism in Northern Ireland is annually reviewed by parliament but to have to justify these powers in international forums is an important safeguard. Just as our legislation to counter terrorism must be scrutinised with great care so must our techniques for countering it. This means that the price for accepting more restrictive legislation must be a greater readiness to examine and devise new methods for democratic accountability to cover the relationship between the police and the armed services and the intelligence and security services which have become even more important in tracing and thwarting potential acts of terrorism.

We need to be very careful to maintain the distinction between police functions and the role of the armed services. When the police practically never carried arms that distinction was easy, but the activities of urban guerrillas and international terrorists have put more people and more buildings at risk. The siege of the Iranian Embassy in May 1980 aroused public admiration and respect, and tough action against terrorism will be supported, but it would not have been right for a special police unit to have stormed the embassy, following, as is now known, a policy to shoot first. This was rightly judged to be an operation for the army and the specialised SAS. It was also right that the decision to deploy the armed forces should have been made by politicians, the Home Secretary and the Prime Minister.

In Northern Ireland defining the separate roles of the military and the police has been one of the major priorities of the politicians wishing to build up the effectiveness of the Royal Ulster Constabulary and to pull soldiers off the streets.

Tight political control of the military becomes ever more necessary when the armed forces have been drawn in to aid the civil power, as in Northern Ireland for over ten years. It is vital that there is no blurring of roles between the SAS and police units such as the Special Patrol Group (SPG). The decision to tighten control over the SPG and above all to rotate police through their groups at frequent intervals is very necessary. There has also been too much glamour publicity about the SAS and the role of the armed forces in support of the civil power. Any prudent democratic government makes contingency plans for their use in this way but it creates a very bad impression to sensationalise them.

The two areas of national security which have hitherto remained outside any form of parliamentary scrutiny are the Security Service, MI5, and the Intelligence Service, MI6. Only in 1980 was it formally admitted that MI6 existed, the previous practice having been to answer no question about any aspect whatever of its work. Both are covered by secret expenditure votes subject only to an authorisation to parliament signed by the Permanent Under-Secretaries of the Home Office and the Foreign and Commonwealth Office and Commonwealth Secretary and their respective political heads, the Home Secretary and the Foreign and Commonwealth Secretary. There is no formal ministerial Cabinet Committee, though there is an Intelligence Co-ordinator in the Cabinet Office working under the Secretary to the Cabinet and both services come under the overall supervision of the Prime Minister; the head of each service is also answerable directly to the Prime Minister. The system that has evolved is reasonably effective; because the two Ministers know that there is no one else responsible for these matters, which are never delegated to junior Ministers in the Department. With no other democratic scrutiny, they are more likely to watch this area with special care, since their responsibility is so personal that they are very vulnerable if anything should go wrong. A development which has at times been suggested but which would be most inadvisable is for the two services to be controlled by the Secretary to the Cabinet and formally answerable only to the Prime Minister. It is a very important constitutional and democratic safeguard that Ministers other than the Prime Minister are directly answerable for each service and have the main responsibility. Centring control of both on the Prime Minister would be a dangerous accumulation of power.

Nevertheless, a sense of unease has built up over the years about the present arrangements. It surfaced most recently over the revelations concerning Anthony Blunt. It rightly amazed many people that the then Prime Minister, Sir Alec Douglas Home, did not know about Blunt's confession or about the decision to grant an amnesty. There may or may not have been a political motive in keeping it quiet. It is a fact that a prosecution in the atmosphere of early 1964, following after so many other security scandals, particularly the Philby case in 1963, would have been a political embarrassment with potentially important electoral consequences. It is also hard to see why the Prime Minister was not involved in the decision to allow Blunt to continue to be associated with the Royal Family through his appointment, initially made in 1952, as Surveyor of the Queen's Pictures and his later appointment in 1972 as an Adviser on the Queen's Pictures and Drawings. The then Home Secretary should have informed the Prime Minister.

It is claimed that the procedure is now sufficiently tight to prevent such an omission in future. But a more fundamental question is whether the circle of knowledge should be confined only to government. Between 1951-64 the Conservatives held continuous power; during such a long period practices could easily have developed in the security field that might have been very undesirable. Yet apart from the civil service only a handful of politicians, all of them from one party, would have known of those practices. The United States has a powerful Congressional check on the security service. In Britain there is no parliamentary accountability. There is a democratic case for widening the circle to include a few senior politicians from at least the main Opposition party acting as a Committee of Parliament. The Committee would accept restrictions dictated by legitimate security considerations. Special arrangements would have to be made for it to meet and question witnesses, and for handling any paper work and for reporting its conclusions. The individuals would need to be Privy Councillors but not necessarily former Ministers, though it would be desirable for them to have experience of how government works. The House of Commons should, however, know that the money it authorised was being spent in a manner fully compatible with the standards of a democratic state. The objections are predictable but not sustainable. Ministers would still retain ultimate control over what is revealed; there would be many actual operations which by their nature require that the minimum number of people know of them, but the principles which guide operations could be discussed and the senior people most concerned questioned. The mere existence of the Committee would ensure that the Home Secretary, Foreign Secretary and Prime Minister accept the detailed workload of their supervisory responsibility; and that they never became mere cyphers, signing authorisations for telephone tapping or for operations without reading carefully and therefore being able to justify their decisions later to their parliamentary colleagues.

Legislation in this area is fraught with genuine difficulties. Creating ad hoc enquiries or giving special powers to a judge or distinguished individual is no answer to the democratic case for accountability. That accountability must be to the House of Commons. The security services will fear that a Committee of MPs would lead to the same reduction in effectiveness that the FBI and the CIA suffered – so it is loosely claimed – as a result of Congressional scrutiny. The evidence for this claim is in any case highly debatable; it is an allegation not so much against the specific Congressional Committee as against the whole mood of openness in the US, particularly after Watergate – the leakiness of the official bureaucracy and the demands of the whole of Congress that details about individual security cases be revealed.

It will be argued that any movement towards greater openness always leads to further disclosure, that secrecy and security are inseparable and that disclosure to anyone is a slippery slope. But there is a counter argument: if the security services resist the present trend of opinion, what is now only a limited demand for scrutiny will grow, and the action that will eventually be forced on governments could lead to an

426

avalanche of disclosures. Already by damming back information in other areas of government the system is compensating by increased leaking. To admit the existence of MI6 may be logical, but there was much to be said for the previous wholly illogical, even farcical, position, where everyone knew MI6 existed but its existence was never formally acknowledged. Now there is growing pressure to reveal more information about its activities. If we embark on what will certainly be a course of selective disclosure there will be difficulties in defining exactly where we stop. There are advantages in recognising instead the logic of settling for detailed parliamentary scrutiny and accountability. We should entrust such detailed information to a few people charged by parliament with responsibility for all aspects, and we should accompany this by a refusal to allow disclosure of details piecemeal under specific pressure publicly through parliamentary questions and debate.

In maintaining the balance to ensure freedom and security the task of the democrat, whether or not a socialist, is to share and legitimise authority but not to abolish it. But in legitimising authority socialists must be zealous in the defence of liberty and be prepared also to challenge authority and to rub against the grain of public opinion in order to protect minority rights.

PART FIVE
International Socialism

18

The Internationalist Tradition

William Clarke, one of the original Fabian essayists and a radical journalist, wrote in 1896 before the launching of the *Progressive Review*: 'the real crux of politics is not going to be Socialism and anti-Socialism, but Jingoism and anti-Jingoism.'[1] It was a perceptive prediction, and the passions centred around nationalism, patriotism or jingoism have indeed haunted the debate amongst socialists – whether it is on their attitude to war or their attitude to the present-day conflict of opinion over defence policy and Britain's membership of the European Community.

It is worth surveying the past in order to gain some insights into present-day divisions over internationalism amongst socialists. In September 1900 when the 'khaki election' was called, the newly-formed Labour Representation Committee and its fifteen candidates had to decide their attitude to the Boer War in an atmosphere of overwhelming patriotic senti-ment. The ILP opposed the war; the Fabian Executive refused to condemn the war; and a referendum of Society members voted against taking a position, many supporting the war. The trade union leaders were cautious, knowing many of their supporters were susceptible to jingoistic appeals. Ramsay MacDonald, who had opposed the war, thinking it unnecessary and unjust, circumvented the problem by announcing he intended to fight the election upon Leicester rather than Johannesburg; 'upon the problems which faced the wage earners rather than the problems of the capitalists who did their mining for gold and diamonds in South Africa by black labour.'[2]

431

Ramsay MacDonald, who was for the next thirty-four years to have a crucial influence on British foreign policy, took an active interest in most aspects of foreign affairs; he travelled extensively and regularly attended Socialist International meetings from the time of his election as secretary of the Labour Representation Committee in 1900. He had a wide range of contacts, particularly in the German Social Democratic Party. This made him very critical of the government's German policy as it developed; he felt it to be provocative and based on an incapacity to see good in any German. When MacDonald became Chairman of the Parliamentary Labour Party in 1911 he had already developed a deep scepticism about the government's war-mongering policies. He was particularly suspicious of Winston Churchill, who became First Lord of the Admiralty in 1912. In 1913 MacDonald wrote that Mr Churchill was a very dangerous person to put at the head of either of our fighting services. 'He treats them as hobbies.' On 3 August 1914, the day before war was declared, MacDonald in the House of Commons gave the considered view of the Labour Party. 'So far as we are concerned,' he said, 'whatever may happen, whatever may be said about us, whatever attacks may be made upon us, we will take the action that we will take of saying that this country ought to have remained neutral.'[3]

But it was not long before MacDonald's peace emphasis began to conflict with the pulse of patriotism flowing in the country and the Labour Party. On 5 August the Parliamentary Labour Party supported the government's request for war credits and MacDonald immediately resigned as Chairman, feeling he had been disowned. The Labour Party was divided between the ILP, who were predominantly pacifists, and the trade unionists, who predominantly supported the war. In May 1915 Arthur Henderson joined the Cabinet and inexorably the Parliamentary Labour Party, influenced by trade unions, was drawn into supporting conscription, by default. Ramsay MacDonald, who continued to argue against the war, was vilified in the country and criticised by the Party, yet he never supported the pacifist arguments, seeing that this was no guarantee of peace. In 1917 he published *National Defence*, an interesting study reflecting the anxieties, ambiguities and ambivalence of much socialist thinking on foreign affairs – much of which is relevant to the present day.

MacDonald's biographer writes that 'his analysis of power politics lacked a strategy by which a different system of international relations might gradually be put in their place. His solutions, were in fact, not solutions at all. They were elaborate attempts to deny that there was a problem to be solved. The people, it turned out, were pacific after all. They had merely been misled by secret diplomacy and the bugles of war.'[4] Yet it was these very policy ambiguities which proved – as appears to be the case for every leader of the Labour Party apart from Hugh Gaitskell – to be MacDonald's strength, for during the years of his opposition to the war he widened his appeal in the ILP and to sections of the party who passionately felt the war was wrong, while still retaining the respect of many pro-war trade unionists. Arthur Henderson resigned from the Cabinet when the Labour Party Conference in August 1917 voted in favour of the resolution – which he supported – to send delegates at the invitation of the Petrograd Soviet to a Conference of the International at Stockholm. The Labour Party was now no longer so formally linked to Lloyd George's government, even though some Ministers still served. More importantly, Henderson and MacDonald now agreed on the need for a negotiated peace, not military victory, with no annexations or indemnities. Yet in the 1918 election the Labour Party won only 59 seats; the anti-war section lost all their seats and both MacDonald and Henderson were out of the House of Commons.

In February 1919 the Conference of the Second International opened in Berne in an attempt to influence the Paris peace conference and rebuild the International. MacDonald moved an amendment which was carried, arguing that a League of Nations should not be a League of Governments, a League of Cabinets, but must be a League of Parliaments, a League of Peoples. But it was not to be. The League of Nations was to be a League of victorious nations, and the eventual peace treaty was attacked by MacDonald as 'an act of madness unparalleled in history'. He predicted that the German worker would feel an economic slave to other nations and that this would jeopardise peace. Even so, in July, when the peace terms were put before parliament, only one Labour MP voted against the government.

The Second International was split between the pro-war British Labour Party and the majority German Social Democrats on one side, and the anti-war parties, the ILP and the German Independents on the other. Two important resolutions were discussed: the Branting resolution, which was carried, asserting that socialism would develop only on the basis of parliamentary democracy and free speech, and the Adler-Longuet resolution, which was lost, warning against ostracising the Soviet regime and insisting that membership should be open to all socialist parties conscious of their class interests.

While MacDonald was uneasy about the Second International and criticised it, he was under no illusions about the Third International. He fought against the ILP being taken in by Leninism and joining the Third International, and used his anti-war credentials to hold the position. More than anyone he was responsible, at a crucial moment in its history, for holding the British Labour movement to democratic socialism.

In April 1922 the executive of the Second International, the Vienna Union and the Third International met in Berlin, the first time for eight years that all the differing factions had met together. The meeting ended with the Second International agreeing to take part in a general conference, and the Third International promising to cease infiltrating trade unions and Social Democratic parties as part of a tactic of splitting and destroying them. At a further meeting in May, it was clear that any unity had been shattered; the Russians had made an agreement with the Germans and then denounced the Second International. In May 1923 the Second International and Vienna Union met in Hamburg and the Labour and Socialist International was established. Meanwhile, in the 1922 election Labour won 142 seats and became the official Opposition, and MacDonald, who was returned as an MP, became the Leader of the Parliamentary Party.

In 1923 the dominant issue was foreign affairs. The Reparations Committee had declared Germany in default of deliveries of timber and of coal; French and Belgian troops moved in to reoccupy the Ruhr and the German Mark collapsed. In March a conference of socialist parliamentarians from France, Belgium, Italy and Britain was held in France with Léon Blum in the chair, but the initiative was Britain's and MacDonald played a leading role.

In November the British election was called on the issue of free trade, with Baldwin convinced that some form of protection was needed to fight unemployment. MacDonald and the Labour Party were riding high, confident in the House of Commons, eloquent in the country. Labour won 191 seats. The NEC, the General Council and the Parliamentary Labour Party all voted that, should the need arise, a Labour government should govern without compromising itself in any coalition, even though it was in a minority.

On 22 January 1924, the Labour government took office and MacDonald decided to be his own Foreign Secretary, realising that the German reparations crisis, which he knew well, was going to be a crucial issue. Attention was focused on improving relations with France, which had become the *bête noire* of some in the Labour Party; the new British government was not prepared to offer France an automatic military guarantee against German actions, but it wanted French troops out of the Ruhr and had to try to persuade France that her apprehensions about Germany were exaggerated. The French were seen by the public as bent on revenge. Germany was judged no longer a threat and the mood in the Labour Party was tending to be isolationist, with MacDonald asserting the need for a responsible role for Britain.

Eventually, on 16 August, the inter-Allied Conference in London hammered out the first negotiated agreements since the war. It was a domestic and international success for the new government, and was followed in October by the Assembly of the League of Nations accepting the Anglo-French resolution calling for a disarmament conference to be held in June 1925. Through the Geneva Protocol France felt Britain was committed to a system of collective security and Britain felt France was committed to disarmament. The government fell, having lost seats in the October election, which itself was influenced by the storm over the Zinoviev letter, and so the problems and the strength of its commitment to the Protocol could never be tested. On 4 November 1925 MacDonald ceased to be Prime Minister. It had been a short period in office, and for the first time a government's record had been marked more by success abroad than at home.

The years up to the 1929 election were dominated by domestic issues, but during the election campaign the Labour Party played on the people's fears of a drift towards war. On 28 May, in a crucial broadcast, MacDonald was able with authority to ask what had happened to British foreign policy since 1924: 'Failure to come to an understanding with America; failure to be of assistance to the Committee of the League of Nations preparing for a disarmament conference, a military agreement with France which would have been a serious setback to disarmament . . . and remember what the next war is to be like. The old lines which divide combatants from non-combatants, the weak and the diseased from the strong and the robust, men from women and children, will all be obliterated and civilisation itself assailed, and from sea and sky will be brought a heap of ruins.'[5] On 30 May the Labour Party won an overall majority with 287 seats; a gain of over 130.

Ramsay MacDonald became Prime Minister and, after a row and against his inclination, appointed Arthur Henderson as Foreign Secretary. It proved an unhappy relationship. The first international issue of importance was the Reparations Conference in The Hague in September which was dominated by the Chancellor Philip Snowden, negotiating toughly to uphold British interests, though the successful outcome was helped by Henderson's diplomacy. The other main foreign policy issue facing the new government was to correct the deterioration in Anglo-American relations which had arisen from failure to agree at the 1927 Geneva Conference on restraining naval ship-building programmes. The Prime Minister made a very successful visit in public relations terms to the United States in October to see President Hoover. Although the visit produced no specific new agreement, it greatly improved the character of Anglo-American relations.

In January 1930 the Five Power Conference with the United

States, France, Italy and Japan opened. It dragged on until April, eventually stopping new battleship construction until 1936 and restricting submarine building, and contained a Three Power Agreement between Britain, Japan and the United States covering the detail of the future ship building programme. Agreement with the French proved impossible because of Britain's traditional reluctance to guarantee French security and assume defence obligations over and above those entered into by other member states in the framework of the Leage of Nations.

In 1929 the Irwin Declaration affirmed Britain's intention to give India dominion status. In March 1930 Gandhi started his campaign of civil disobedience and the Simon Report on India was published a few months later, the report of a Commission to which Clement Attlee had been appointed when the Party was in Opposition. Nationalist feeling would never have been satisfied by the Simon Report findings, and so a round table conference on India was called, in which the Prime Minister and not the Foreign Secretary was closely involved. The divergent communal interests and aspirations were not resolved and the ILP and other Labour MPs strongly supported the Indian National Congress in their demand for complete independence. In the debate on the conference in the House of Commons in January 1931 the government announced its intentions to transfer responsibility for Indian affairs to provincial governments with provincial legislatures, and to have a central executive responsible to a federal legislature. Winston Churchill attacked the proposals, demonstrating as always that his judgment over India was clouded by imperial grandeur. Baldwin, however, savaged Churchill and held to the attempt to develop a bipartisan policy towards India.

In July 1931 the Seven Power Conference in London met in the midst of the international financial crisis, and agreed the measure of a standstill on non-governmental international credits to Germany.

The Labour government of 1929-31 can fairly claim to have made reasonable progress in holding the international situation. As judged by history, its most important achievement was to start the process of decolonisation that led in 1935 to the Government of India Act and to the decision of Clement Attlee as Prime Minister to grant India independence after the Second World War. It was also to provide a central theme of Labour Party foreign policy from then on to decolonise in Asia and in Africa, grant early independence and to try to establish a new framework of equality between new and old nations in the Commonwealth. Arthur Henderson, though overshadowed by the Prime Minister in some areas, showed a firm commitment to the principles underlying the League of Covenant, and in the value of collective responsibility. He earned the respect of many as one of the few sensible Foreign Secretaries in the inter-war years. When the Labour government collapsed in 1931 it had a reasonably successful record in foreign affairs.

The First World War was an experience which not only the Labour Party, but the whole British people, wished never to repeat, and it had a crucial impact on the Party's attitude to foreign affairs until 1940. As a comprehensive study of Labour's foreign policy put it, 'the terrible experience of those four years had demonstrated, beyond any doubt, the total unprofitability of war; an intellectual grasp of this fact was alone sufficient to set the nations in irreversible motion towards a new and better era.'[6] In effect, the Party, in its fervent wish to see a more equitable international system, and in its strong opposition to war, voiced widely held sentiments, but failed to identify or to emphasis the practical difficulties of bringing about the state of affairs it advocated.

From 1931 onwards the Party never had to face its idealism being put to the test of reality. The divisions in the Labour Party were, therefore, essentially about the nature of war and peace: dispute with those who opposed war totally was inevitable, but there were also throughout the 1930s bitter arguments over the roles of such bodies as the League of Nations and the Socialist League. Many socialists argued that a new international order, based on the League, would banish war forever; war was seen as part and parcel of capitalism; and world citizens would grow up owing allegiance, not to nation states, but to the League and its ideals of war-free world. It was common to denounce power politics and an international system based, as many in the Party depicted it, on a capitalist society and on the law of the jungle and the survival of the fittest. The Party's proposals to end the system were based on advocacy of pooled sovereignty to halt aggression, and universal total disarmament – concepts which it was often insufficiently recognised would not advance very far without the support and concurrence of the whole world community, many members of which were, and were likely to remain, like the US, capitalist countries.

In 1934, after years of striving idealistically for disarmament, MacDonald wrote in a memorandum which has continuing relevance, that Britain had gone further in disarmament than any other country in the world. Though some people argue that if Britain under the National Government had accepted the disarmament plan put forward by President Hoover at the 1932-33 Disarmament Conference all would have been different. The United States had professed disarmament but their actions were felt by many, not just by MacDonald, to be contrary to their declaration. MacDonald wrote that Japan was putting itself in a position to fight a war in the Far East and that Russia was undoubtedly the most heavily armed nation in Europe. Admitting that Britain had diminished its fleet very substantially, both in men and material, and that its air force was only the fifth in Europe MacDonald lamented that no one thought of following Britain's lead, that disarmament by example had completely broken down and that Britain alone was not in a position to lift effectively a little finger to protect itself in the event of trouble. He continued sadly, 'For the moment we are continuing the policy which has been mine from the beginning. But I am only too well aware that at any moment it may be changed, not because this or any other Government wants it, but because it is forced upon us by the refusal of other nations to keep down their arms . . . The outlook is most depressing. Mankind seems to be bent upon its own ruin.'[7]

Another issue which tested the Labour Party leadership in Opposition in the inter-war years was the question of sanctions against Italy. It is possible to believe that Mussolini's aggression in Abyssinia could have been prevented if Anthony Eden as

Foreign Secretary had proposed oil sanctions against Mussolini. Eden's action in removing sanctions was opposed by public opinion, and Philip Noel-Baker won a by-election in Derby on 9 July 1936 in which the Abyssinian question featured prominently.

The conflict between idealism and realism dogged the Party all through the 1930s and over the appeasement years. If the League of Nations had been used with courage maybe the war could have been averted but it would have required many different statesmen to change their attitudes. The foreign policy debate that took place inside the Labour Party caused the resignation of the pacifist Lansbury as leader of the Party and his replacement by Clement Attlee. Yet while 'collective security' remained the policy of most of the Party's supporters, it was also held that since any potential aggressor would be deterred by collective security, rearmament was unnecessary. Hugh Dalton and a small group of Labour MPs refused to go along with this policy and defied the Party line, but as usual the issues were confused. Some Labour MPs voted against the Defence Estimates as a way of voting in favour of the League of Nations. Yet Attlee, as party leader, 'criticised every demand for arms made by the National Government until after the outbreak of war in 1939'.[8] The period following the general election of 1935 was marked by deep and bitter divisions within the Labour Party about the approach to be adopted to Germany's growing military strength. In retrospect it may now seem curious that the 'realists' were then in control of the extra-parliamentary Party, with Hugh Dalton, a supporter of British rearmament, as Chairman of the National Executive Committee, and Ernest Bevin, simultaneously Chairman of the TUC, also advocating a tough policy; while the Parliamentary Party was dominated by pacifists and anti-militarists. The NEC and the TUC, working through the National Council of Labour, put a resolution to conference that year which supported the government's rearmament programme, which was carried.

Dalton felt very strongly that the feelings of individual party members on the subject of disarmament were not being adequately represented by the Parliamentary Party, and he therefore became a strong advocate of constituency delegates being elected to the NEC. Although the unions generally opposed this proposal, Bevin was persuaded by Dalton to agree to it, and it was approved by the 1937 conference and came into effect at once. In the late 1950s – and again in the early 1980s – the position was reversed. It was constituency delegates and the constituency section of the NEC who were the unilateralists. Although some left-wingers were elected to the seven constituency seats which then became available, the net effect, as Dalton had calculated, was to strengthen his attempts to disassociate the party from the so-called 'Popular Front' – an alliance of Left-wingers and the Communist Party who feared that rearmament would bring British participation *with* Hitler in his war against Soviet Russia. A tough policy of implementing Party policy then followed. Constituency parties which had advocated the 'Popular Front' policy were disbanded, and new, loyal, Parliamentary Labour Parties were set up in their place. The NEC expelled Stafford Cripps, Charles Trevelyan, Aneurin Bevan and George Strauss from Party membership. As A.J.P. Taylor observes, 'In this odd way, the Labour Party entered the war against Hitler, locked in conflict with its most vocal opponents.'[9]

When the crisis finally came on 10 May 1940 and the Germans attacked France and the Low Countries, the Labour Party decided – that same day – that the military situation called for Winston Churchill as Prime Minister. A party which had become increasingly confused and incoherent in its attitudes to war – on the one hand opposing the National government's rearmament programme, on the other calling for armed support for the Spanish Republic – suddenly found itself joining in a wartime coalition pledged to oppose the fascist dictators by force. Attlee became Churchill's deputy, and important Cabinet posts were filled by Labour leaders. Ernest Bevin became Minister of Labour and National Service, Hugh Dalton Minister of Economic Warfare, Herbert Morrison Home Secretary and Stafford Cripps Ambassador to the Soviet Union.

The significance of these changes was in influencing the policies and outlook of the Labour leaders: ' . . . comparatively unversed in the responsibilities of office, free to moralise against the stupidity of those in power . . . where once they had been but leaders of a party almost permanently in opposition, they now became the governors of a whole nation, who were daily led deeper into the multitude of bewildering administrative tasks of total war . . . whatever their previous impulses in matters of foreign policy, they had no choice in their new roles but to keep ideas of British security, power, and national interests uppermost in their minds.'[10] Although the divisions in the Labour Party between 'idealists' and 'realists' in matters of foreign policy have their roots in the learning experience of Labour leaders in government, there was always a divide within the Party between, generally speaking, the political wing and the trade union wing on these issues. This difference in approach has been ascribed to the trade unions' more developed 'sense of power'. Trade union leaders, for example, used to the techniques of collective bargaining, more readily understood the role of the threat of the use of force, and the actual use of force, in international negotiations and of the need for some leverage in any negotiations. Their approach tended to be more pragmatic and less theoretical than that of the political wing: they were the natural 'realists'. It was Ernest Bevin who told George Lansbury to 'stop hawking your conscience around from body to body asking to be told what you ought to do with it'. Nevertheless the idealistic, moral and pacifist voices in the Party traditionally play an important role in balancing harder militaristic arguments.

Though the Labour Party has been the voice of anti-imperialism, strangely its attitudes have sometimes been based, unconsciously, on wholly unrealistic assumptions about Britain's true position in the world. Socialist politicians as much as Conservative politicians from the 1930s to the present day have talked in terms that assume that the view of a British government will automatically prevail in the world. The renunciation of war or of a particular form of arms by a socialist Britain is assumed to be a gesture which of itself will produce a major change in world attitudes and affect the decisions of other nations. In 1930 the imperialists saw Britain as leading the world in its military might and economic strength, but its socialist leaders had a similar rather grandiose vision of Britain as a 'moral' leader. So, paradoxically, many of the actual attitudes of imperial Britain were shared by those who intellectually disapproved of such things: socialists sought to impose, not markets for British goods or the Union Jack, but their view of what constituted a moral, peaceful, socialist world.

The internationalist rhetoric of British socialism has throughout its history been vulnerable to the criticism that it contained more than a tinge of moral superiority. Sidney Webb was scathing in his criticisms of the leaders of the Independent Labour Party – they were hopeless little England-ers, high-minded men of inaction who proved to be, with regard to the British Empire, mere administrative nihilists.[11] Today there are many so-called 'Left-wing' socialists who talk about wanting a wider socialist Europe while being hostile to the socialism of most European political parties. A further complication for the internationalist rhetoric of British socialism is that some trade union members and Labour Party suppor-ters have been and still are as imperialist and as chauvinist as some Conservative supporters. Yet Labour voters have never been alienated *en masse* from the symbols of King, Queen and Country and have always been proud to respond to patriotic appeals to save the nation from Nazism and Fascism and this is a praiseworthy sentiment that has given the party hitherto its national standing. Most Labour Party leaders have understood and reflected the solid common sense of the majority of their supporters and have been prepared to risk polarising feeling between themselves and the party activists. Most trade union leaders of the past also stood firm against their activists. At the start of the 1980s all that appears to have changed.

It is, however, more than a simple division between 'idealists' and 'realists' which explains some of the divisions which have appeared amongst socialists over foreign policy. The hankerings after neutralism are deep-seated and tend to reappear in any period when the Conservatives are in govern-ment and heighten cold war rhetoric. As Britain's power base shrinks fewer and fewer people can credibly maintain that Britain alone can change the face of the globe. The risk is that internationalism in both major political parties will give way, not to realism, but instead to a narrow nationalism. The emotional nostalgia for a world position which was beyond our financial means characterised the post-war period. The Labour government after the Second World War still maintained that Britain could somehow 'go it alone' and spent more on defence in 1945-50 than any other country outside the communist bloc; they also rapidly rearmed in 1950-1 for the Korean War. Suez polarised attitudes as did the issue of our membership of the European Community. The 1964 Labour government maintained the East of Suez military posture, against inter-party opposition even after the end of confrontation with Indonesia, and only very reluctantly reassessed its world role under great financial pressure and pulled out from bases in Singapore and the Persian Gulf. The controversy over the Labour government's attitude to the United States' role in Vietnam also created bitter division within the Party.

The major international question, which, however, dominated post-war Party debates was what attitudes should be towards the Soviet Union. It had long been an axiom of Labour Party belief that the Soviet Union was not expansionist or imperialist like other great powers: many Labour Party members were full of admiration for the Soviet Revolution and the sacrifices the Soviet people had made in the war, and many looked forward to a period of close co-operation with the Soviet Union after the war. 'Left can talk to Left' had seemed a powerful and convincing slogan to many voters in 1945.

The Labour Party has not been unique among European socialists in wishing to pursue distinctive policies towards the Soviet Union. The SPD, which under Schumacher had taken to the streets in 1955 to oppose German membership of NATO, changed its position in the late 1950s following the Soviet invasion of Hungary. Just as the Soviet coup in Czechoslovakia in 1948 had the effect of drawing a clear dividing-line between communists and socialists, so the Soviet invasion of Hungary in 1956 and of Czechoslovakia in 1968 reinforced that line. Throughout the 1960s, for Willy Brandt, the European Community was always important as part of a structure, a 'European Peace Order' which would ensure peace with the Soviet Union and a secure Germany; and Willy Brandt's *Ostpolitik* became the dominant theme of Germany's foreign policy. The Italian Socialist Party under the leadership of Pietro Nenni, which had been one of the few European socialist parties to advocate a neutralist foreign policy, changed its policy and supported NATO in the late 1960s. In France the French socialists supported General de Gaulle's withdrawal from NATO's military organisation, and also supported the nuclear 'force de frappe', as now does the French Communist Party.

The onslaught of Stalinisation in Eastern Europe and the build-up of the Cold War meant that democratic socialist parties had to look very closely at the facts of international life. The Labour government's wholehearted support for NATO seemed a long way from the time, only a few years earlier, when the Soviet Union's professed beliefs in peace and self-determination had been taken at their face value by many, if not most, of the members of the Labour Party. The reality of, first, Hitler's war, and second, of a Stalinist and expansionist Soviet Union, had converted many people to 'realism'. But the 'idealist' current was always there, and emerged when the Party went into Opposition.

It surfaced in a neutralist form initially over the rearmament of Germany in 1954, which provoked one of the most bitter debates. The issue was whether to accept Soviet terms for the neutralisation of Germany, with the almost certain withdrawal then of the United States from a military presence in Germany and the risk of the Soviet Union controlling Germany. Looking back it is amazing that the 'Bevanites' should have made such strong headway on this issue, Attlee only won in the Parliamentary Labour Party in February 1954 by a majority of two.

The Labour Party's opposition to Suez in 1956 was in parliamentary terms a unifying factor, though it caused bitterness amongst some Labour voters. It was interesting how fidelity to the UN Charter came through so strongly as the core of the Labour Party's case. French socialists were in contrast more divided about Suez and the merits of their government's action, together with the British government of Anthony Eden, in mounting the invasion of Egyptian territory. Many French socialists who were anti-imperialist supported the seizure of the Suez canal because they believed it was the only way to prevent the destruction of Israel, whose Labour Party was an active member of Socialist International. The Parliamentary Labour Party attitude to Suez was unpopular with some Labour voters who felt the Conservative government was right to have a go at Nasser; this section of opinion, which was normally inclined to be pro-American, was very critical of the US for, as they saw it, letting Britain down over Suez. The Left, traditionally anti-American, seized their opportunity and began to portray NATO, not as a defensive alliance against the Warsaw Pact, but as a symbol of British dependence on the United States. There were demands for Britain to lead a new alliance of third-force neutralist states. The Left tended to assume a British leadership of new blocs able to wield a force in the world, as moral examples. Once again one saw the socialist version of imperial nostalgia emerging 'in proportion as British power in the world declined'.[12]

In general, the Labour Party for its thirteen years in Opposition aspired to a more moral world order, whether neutralist or socialist, and it tended to take for granted that Britain, under a Labour government, would possess a moral superiority which would automatically thrust her into leadership. Subconsciously, notions of imperial superiority lingered on; and nationalism remained a deplorable feature of Labour Party thought on international issues. The European Defence Community was for others, not for Britain. The Messina Conference in 1956 which led to the Treaty of Rome was ignored or dismissed despite the enthusiasm of French socialists. Paradoxically, the very rhetoric of internationalism helped to disguise this innate nationalism. Alliances and groupings were resisted because better, wider groupings were said to be more appropriate. Few Labour Party members argued seriously against the fundamental objectives of NATO, but they tended in quite large numbers to be resentful of American hegemony, and therefore favoured larger groupings which would be less exclusive and which would leave scope for the exercise of Britain's moral leadership. The case of the unilateral disarmers was, in the late 1950s, in fact, a culmination of the 'idealist' tradition. The genuine pacifists were joined by the CND protest which was a curious blend of unreality and unconscious superiority: for Britain to renounce nuclear weapons would be a 'moral' example to the world, an act of moral leadership which, it was assumed, would be emulated by the super-powers. The belief that Britain by a combination of unselfish or disinterested acts would affect the course of world events, was crucial to foreign policy thinking in the Party. Hungary, in 1956, was soon forgotten though Czechoslovakia in 1968 was another rude shock to those who had convinced themselves that the Soviet Union's influence was benign. The British trade union movement was eventually rallied in 1961 to vote down unilateralism. But in marked contrast to most other democratic European trade unions, it continued to have close contact with the official trade union movements in Eastern Europe, and when it was confronted by the Polish strikes in 1980 for free trade unionism the TUC establishment reacted very slowly and unimaginatively.

The 1980 Conference decision to dissociate from the nuclear deterrence strategy of NATO has therefore a long history. It also reflects a debate which is occurring in other socialist parties. In Norway, Denmark, Holland and Belgium there are pressures within their socialist parties against nuclear weapons and NATO and the outcome of the debate among British socialists will have some influence on them. The German SPD which also reflects this debate has a powerful political constraint, in that if there was any fundamental change the Liberal FPD would leave the coalition with the SPD and form a coalition with the Christian Democrats, as they have done before.

No issue illustrates more markedly the Labour Party's foreign policy divisions than its attitude to the European Community. The 1945-50 Labour government resisted moves towards European integration, despite the previous internationalism of its leaders, and despite the fact that many of them, during and after the war, had developed personal friendships with continental socialist leaders. The leadership that had been at Potsdam, that had lived through the heyday of the British Empire, was not able to adjust to the post-war realities of Britain's position, although even then there was a group of Labour MPs and Party supporters keenly interested in European integration. In 1962 Hugh Gaitskell spoke for the majority when he spoke out against entering the Common Market, reminding the Conference of Britain's 'thousand years of history' and recalling the Commonwealth connection in an emotional reference to the sacrifices of Vimy Ridge in the First World War. Yet while in the early 1960s it was still just possible to see the Commonwealth as Hugh Gaitskell tended to do as a substitute for the European Community, and the European Free Trade Area, EFTA, as an alternative grouping, these soon became less credible alternatives.

The Labour government in 1967 and again in 1970 felt driven by economic and political realities to attempt to negotiate British membership of the European Economic Community. In the 1970 General Election both the Labour and Conservative Parties maintained that with the 'right terms' British entry was desirable. In 1970 the new Conservative government under Edward Heath began to negotiate terms for British membership. The two former Labour Ministers most closely concerned with the preparation for the 1970 negotiations, George Thomson and Michael Stewart, felt in 1971 that the terms the Conservatives had negotiated were very similar to those which a Labour government would have negotiated and accepted. The Parliamentary Labour Party, supported by the NEC and Conference, under the leadership of Harold Wilson, adopted a contrary view, and there was a clear majority for a policy of opposition to the 'Tory terms'. Despite this, 69 Labour MPs, believing entry to be in the national interest and despite varying degrees of reservation about the terms, voted for entry, against a Three Line Whip.

When Labour returned to power in 1974, serious divisions over membership of the European Community had been circumvented by the Manifesto commitment to renegotiate and to accept the verdict of a national referendum on whether Britain should stay within the Community. In June 1975 seventeen million people voted to stay, against eight million people who voted to withdraw, and it was believed that a majority of Labour voters had voted 'Yes'. But divisions over the European Community were never simply between the Left and the Right. While some of the Left explained their opposition to the Community in ideological terms – the Community being seen as a capitalist device to exploit the workers – many on Left and Right agreed that for them the key political issue was not the acceptance of the mixed economy but the question of British sovereignty. The issue of sovereignty united many Labour Party members, but also Labour with Conservatives, particularly those like Enoch Powell from the Right wing of that Party. For the Labour Party Douglas Jay and Peter Shore, both on many issues on what is commonly defined as the Right of the party, became the spokesmen for the 'anti-European' section. Peter Shore made an impassioned speech on the subject at the 1972 Party conference. 'I did not come into Socialist politics in this country . . . ', he said, 'to connive in the dismantling of the power of the British people as represented in their Parliament and in their Government.' In the 1980 Conference it was Peter Shore who refused to consider another referendum, arguing that this was an issue which only required a Manifesto commitment to amend the 1972 European Communities Act. There was no common political strand linking people, across a broad spectrum of Party opinion, who were opposed to EEC membership, but a view of British sovereignty, identity and national feeling was an instinctive cause of much of the opposition.

The old division between the 'idealists' and the 'realists' within British socialism was now joined by an even more powerful division between the 'nationalists' – the 'go-it-alone' school – and the 'internationalists' – the 'working-with-others' school. The common thread linking the 'idealists' and the 'nationalists' however, was the assumption that Britain was different: the economy and political systems of other EEC countries presented a threat to British sovereignty. They were dismissive of the fact that similar considerations did not seem to present a threat to other countries or other socialists. For them to accept a European role for Britain meant accepting that Britain was just another country, one among many in the modern world. Though they knew Britain was no longer one of the richest or the most powerful, they seemed to want to believe that what was past was only temporary: the greatness of Britain could return if only parliament remained sovereign, unfettered, supreme. As Professor King described it, 'the anti-Europeans, in one way or another, resisted the modern world; the pro-Europeans, by contrast, accepted it. They accepted the mixed economy; they accepted, however reluctantly, the division of Europe; they accepted the fact of Britain's economic and political decline. They believed that, outside Europe, this decline would be accelerated; they believed that, inside it, it might be reversed . . . The pro-Europeans not only accepted the modern world: by and large they liked it and wanted to embrace it. They did not mind Britain giving up some of its "sovereignty"; on the contrary, they were exhilarated by the idea of the leaders of different nations meeting together to try to solve their common problems.'[13]

What was most depressing for the future direction of the Labour Party was that on an analysis of attitudes, it emerged that the older Labour MPs were more likely to be pro-European than younger MPs, in marked contrast to public opinion in the country, where the young were in favour of the EEC. The older members, perhaps because they had lived through the experience of the war and the subsequent division of Europe, were more attracted to the overall political arguments; they had also built up contacts with fellow socialists on the Continent. Younger Labour MPs voted against EEC membership in greater numbers because of the prevalent ideology of the Left in Britain. This was hostile to NATO, held that a wider Europe was desirable, and used social democrat as a term if not of abuse, certainly of identification with 'pink socialism' –all right for continental Europe but not for Britain. As Professor King wrote – though they would have denied that he was right – theirs was ' . . . the politics of imperial nostalgia, of xenophobia mixed occasionally with anti-Catholicism.'[14] This will seem a harsh judgment, but the attitude which an experienced political scientist, Professor Anthony King, detected in anti-EEC MPs was more explicable when one considers that Labour MPs represent a party where the activists see themselves increasingly as in permanent opposition to the system and structure of a capitalist country, a country which has seen over a relatively short period a massive contraction of its international power and influence, and a marked fall in its relative economic strength. The old idealist internationalism has been tinged with a disdain for the harsh realities of the modern world and a belief that Britain can manage on her own. The new nationalism of many so-called 'Left wing' socialists is in many respects a continuation, in vastly changed circumstances, of this older tradition.

While other socialist parties in Europe have faced up to the difficulties, chosen a course and stuck to it, the Labour Party has twisted and turned, racked by divisions over whether membership of the Community is compatible with Socialism. Yet Labour Party members in Britain, particularly those who have opposed British membership of the Community, sometimes fail to take into account the serious debates which their fellow socialists in other member states have had, and continue to have, over their countries' membership of the Community. In France, for example, although it was a socialist Prime Minister, Guy Mollet, who signed the Rome Treaty for France in 1957, the French parliament only approved French membership by 322 votes to 267 – and many French socialists have been critical of the Community. When Mollet took France into the Community it was of course a new and untried body and some socialists could see in it the embryo of a fairer, socialist order in Europe. Mollet himself saw Europe as a united Europe acting as a 'strong, not neutral, but independent power between, on the one hand, "impulsive America, slow to take in the facts" and "a threatening Soviet Union".'[15] But by the 1970s the Left of the French Socialist Party were seeing the EEC as too close to the United States. François Mitterrand, the socialist leader, took very strongly the line that Europe was a prerequisite to socialism, rather than a barrier. Attempts by the Left wing to investigate a new grouping, possibly based on the newly democratised states of Southern Europe, plus Italy and France, foundered when the extent of the economic integration and interdependence

451

already attained by France in the EEC was realised.

In Germany similar divisions occurred in the SPD. During Schumacher's leadership, the party opposed moves towards European integration, and German re-unification was the main foreign policy issue in German politics. During the 1950s the SPD became strongly pro-EEC, but whereas French socialists, like most of their British counterparts, have been more or less united in resisting moves towards federalism, the German party has clearly stated that its long-term aim is European unity. In 1975 a specially appointed 'European Commission' of the party not only recommended the adoption of a European Federation as an ultimate objective, but also recognised the need for the redistribution of resources within the Community to benefit the poorer areas. The Young Socialists saw in the European ideal a means of tackling the problem of multinational corporations and co-ordinating socialist policies and the new generation of German socialist leaders have developed close relationships with their French socialist counterparts. In practice German governments, particularly that of Helmut Schmidt, have been highly critical of the way the Commission and the Community works, and have preferred to do business through close consultation with fellow member-governments, particularly with France, rather than give more power to the EEC Commission. No German government has been as federalist in practice as its position might imply. The Dutch and Belgian socialists are all committed to Community membership and tend to be federalist in rhetoric if not always in action where there is a conflict with a specific national interest.

The dissatisfaction with the European Community in Denmark and in the socialist parties in the Community is, unlike much of the so-called 'anti-common market' sentiment in the British Labour Party, not based on a rejection of the ideals of the Community. There is an awareness on the Continent, though not in Britain, that the Community is itself an ongoing negotiation rather than a static entity. Other members negotiate both to uphold their national interests and the interests of the Community. What marks Britain out is the dichotomy between the Labour Party's attitude to negotiate flexibly within any system nationally to improve it, and its demand to renegotiate or to withdraw from the European Community or from its alliances. The Labour Party – one of whose elements is the trade union movement whose *raison d'être* is negotiation and bargaining – ought to have an important contribution to make to an evolving European community and to international arms control and disarmament. Instead, at the 1980 Conference the Labour party committed itself, three years before it could even be in a position to implement such a decision, to withdraw from the European Community, to unilateral disarmament and the rejection of any defence strategy based on nuclear deterrence.

Most serious issues confronting the world can only be solved by multilateral action. Britain is a member of the European Community, of the Commonwealth, and of the North Atlantic Treaty Organisation, three organisations which should continue to define our foreign policy. Our membership of the United Nations and its specialist agencies, and our common interest in world security and a stable world economic order bring us into constant negotiation with other nations. It is a cliché that we live in an 'interdependent' world; it is a fact that almost no decision affecting foreign policy is now taken without at least consultation with our partners and allies. It is not the true path of socialism to talk and think in terms of unilateral action, based on a unique perception, in this country, of what we think is good for the rest of the world. Fellow socialists abroad, especially in Europe, have had to confront the same choices and dilemmas which too many socialists in Britain have refused to face. While only we can choose our future policies, we can learn much from the experiences of socialists in other countries; and given the nature of the modern world it is only in concert with others that we shall be able to deal with world problems.

19

Negotiate and Survive

It would be a fool who lightly decried the movement of protest over nuclear weapons, who disparaged its motives, or who denigrated or dismissed its purpose. Peace is so fragile, the way forward to ensure that it is maintained so fraught, and the complex problems and issues so fiercely debated that any movement which engages the public conscience and public passions cannot be wholly wrong. Those who seek peace may differ on methods and means, but we have a common end and must try to agree on facts, and narrow our differences wherever possible so that our common purpose is not overshadowed.

The government's pamphlet *Protect and Survive* which, among other things, has been derided for its assertion that white-washing windows and wrapping one's head inside a jacket make a realistic contribution to defence against a nuclear attack, asserted that a full scale nuclear attack on Britain could leave over 20 million survivors, of whom some 15 million could remain alive and well, and that people should know what to do should war threaten. The Soviet government has a very similar approach to civil defence but the danger of emphasising protection is that it gives the impression that nuclear war is being contemplated. The Home Secretary, Mr William Whitelaw, in a letter to Northern Ireland Secretary, Mr Humphrey Atkins, on 24 May 1980, defended the government's policy saying, 'Regrettably the UK has always been an obvious target in any military aggression against the West, because of its political, geographic, and industrial importance rather than because of its nuclear weaponry. Protective measures should not be regarded as ineffective solely because they are simple in concept. The white-washing of windows can provide very effective protection against fire resulting from the heat-flash from nuclear explosions. It must be recognised, however, that home defence arrangements, important as they are, must be geared to what the country can afford.'

It should surprise no one that the government, having triggered a debate which accepts that Britain is a target for nuclear attack, and that argues for millions of pounds more to be spent on civil defence, should face a protest against the whole concept that Britain should do or say anything which makes it a target for such an attack, and a rejection of any defence strategy which even admits such a possibility. A powerful reaction was the pamphlet, *Protest and Survive*,[1] written by the historian, Professor E.P. Thompson, parodying cleverly the title of Her Majesty's Stationery Office's publication, though published for the Campaign for Nuclear Disarmament and the Bertrand Russell Peace Foundation.

What was surprising was that the Labour Party could within eighteen months of losing an election switch the basis of its whole defence policy since 1961 and become committed again at the 1980 Conference, though this time by an unopposed vote, to a resolution urging unilateral disarmament and a Manifesto commitment 'opposing any British participation in any defence policy based on the use or threatened use of nuclear weapons'. The 1979 Election Manifesto reaffirmed its support for NATO, never mentioned abandoning Polaris patrols or nuclear deterrence but renounced a new generation of British nuclear weapons or a successor to the Polaris nuclear force. The systematic erosion of policy and of principle began in discussions before the Special Conference at Wembley in May 1980 when it was decided that since the policy document mentioned and quoted from the 1979 Manifesto, it was acceptable not to vote against endorsing the whole document, despite the damaging unilateral wording which said 'the Labour Party opposes the manufacture and deployment of Cruise missiles and the neutron bomb and refuses to permit their deployment in Britain by the United States or any other country'. The sequence of events is more revealing about the true state of the Labour Party at the start of the 1980s than anything else. Party management predominated on an issue central to the country's defence policy as the Party drifted towards unilateralism. No doubt before the next election the position will be pulled back by the trade union block vote being mobilised to support a form of words less challenging to the central deterrent posture of NATO and of the credibility of our membership of the Alliance. No doubt any future Labour government would attempt to continue the Polaris patrols pending multilateral negotiations and to bury some of the other specific commitments made in Opposition on defence, as in 1964 the Labour government buried its commitment to remove US nuclear bases and continued with Polaris. But if this is done in this way those who are now genuinely protesting and who believe that they have won the argument will be driven not just to despair with the Labour Party but to disillusionment with democratic politics. The Labour Party is also now committed by Conference decision to the European Nuclear Disarmament (END) movement which promotes in its Manifesto a common object: 'to act as if a united, neutral and pacific Europe already exists. We must learn to be loyal, not to "East" or "West", but to each other, and we must disregard the prohibitions and limitations imposed by any national state. It will be the responsibility of the people of each nation to agitate for the expulsion of nuclear weapons and bases from European soil and territorial waters, and to decide upon its own means and strategy, concerning its own territory.'

Protest aimed at peace is not worthless; on the contrary, no one should dismiss the legitimacy and effectiveness of protest within the political process. Protest does have influence in countries that democratically elect their leaders but much less in countries that do not. Protest needs to be made, needs to be encouraged, but it will not of itself be sufficient. Governments will have to be convinced, decisions will have to be taken as a result of bargains struck between nations, compromises forged between Heads of government. The depressing development would be of a mutual contempt; the protesters of the politicians and the politicians of the protesters. In such a climate there will be no debate, merely a dialogue of the deaf, in which fear replaces reason, prejudice reinforces reaction and the world slithers into a Third World War which no one wants, everyone fears and from which we would be lucky to emerge as well as General Sir John Hackett and others have predicted.[2]

The argument against the underlying philosophy of *Protect and Survive* is put simply that, if despite the deterrent effect of the armed forces of ourselves and our allies, war breaks out, and escalates to nuclear war, who should be protected?

The Home Secretary reveals the paucity of his approach when he reminds us that 'home defence arrangements, important as they are, must be geared to what the country can afford', and then goes on to advocate spending to ensure that the ruling establishment survive – the Royal Family, central government and local government politicians, the admirals, air-marshals and senior administrators all survive. But millions of others lose their lives. Money is to be spent on sub-regional headquarters; the governors will go underground, the governed will stay on top.

One does not have to be a cynic to wonder about such an arrangement, and whether it would not concentrate the mind of the governors better on the implausibility of limited nuclear war if they were in line to die with their fellow citizens. The late United States Chief Justice, Earl Warren, demonstrated the ethical basis for such a strategy when he asked, on being given a special pass admitting him to a secret relocation site of government, what arrangements had been made for Mrs Warren; on being told there were only 2,000 places and no room for wives he said, 'If she's not important enough to save, neither am I', and he returned the pass. It is difficult to justify on administrative grounds but impossible to justify on political grounds such an openly selective system of home defence. The Soviet Union, Switzerland, and Sweden have opted for nationwide cover for all citizens, implausible though such cover is. It has been estimated in Britain that a shelter programme putting 10 per cent of the population in deep shelters, 15 per cent in basement shelters and the rest in survival shelters would cost £8,000 million. The government having decided that home defence must be geared to what the country can afford, and yet having decided it can at the same time afford £5,000 million for the Trident missile system, it is not surprising to find a considerable measure of scepticism about the genuineness of the government's intention to protect against nuclear attack. It has also stimulated an opposition to the whole defence philosophy. What started as a harmless political gesture in response to pre-election commitments to the civil defence lobby within the Conservative Party has, as is often the case, developed a momentum of its own. While the Red Cross, the St John's Ambulance Brigade, the WRVS and the Royal Observer Corps may feel their voluntary effort is at long last being recognised, millions of other citizens who have previously been able to relegate the horror of Hiroshima and Nagasaki to the darkest recesses of their minds, now feel a new or revived fear and apprehension.

Yet while fear of nuclear war is again creating in some people a growing mood of protest, in others it is prompting support for the government's increased military spending programmes. There is as yet no sign that it is providing the stimulus to negotiate, to replace the polarised emotions of protection and protest with a concerned demand that all governments negotiate genuine, not cosmetic, arms control agreements which really will lessen the risk of nuclear war. Fear having been aroused by the government, there is little to be gained by trying to play down the horror. A new debate over nuclear strategy was coming anyway. Afghanistan and its effect on détente has coincided with European anxieties, however unfounded, about US leadership; and the difficulties over SALT II revealed a hard-line stance amongst some in the US who seemed ready to contemplate a limited nuclear war.

The decision to allow the US to start making plans to deploy its cruise missiles in 1983 if there has been no previous arms control agreement, and to retain the UK deterrent, was bound to stimulate an argument over whether Britain was likely to become more of a Soviet target than we were already. We have, in fact, always been a target and there is a tendency to forget that the US have operated from UK bases with nuclear weapons since the early 1950s, using B29 bombers, then B47s,

458

F45s and today F111s as well as submarines from Holy Loch.

END's view that it is credible for East and West in Europe to act now as if a 'united, neutral and pacific Europe already exists', is absurd when Europe is neither united, neutral nor pacific. It is very hard to believe that the peoples of Eastern Europe are going to have a determining influence on the policy of the Warsaw Pact when one considers the continuing struggle over free trade unions in Poland, to name but one human rights' issue. Loosening up the political rigidities of Eastern Europe is a much to be desired objective. The emergence of Helsinki monitoring groups, despite the consequences for individuals, is a triumph for the free spirit. But to argue from this that such people will be able over the next few years to bring about significant nuclear disarmament in Eastern Europe by directly influencing their governments is not only to indulge in a pipe-dream but to misread the military philosophy of the Soviet Union. The Soviet leaders will negotiate with other governments, as the SALT dialogue has shown, but they are as concerned about balance as the United States and very fearful of any dramatic or bold steps. While I share most of the protesters' concerns about the risks and dangers of nuclear war and of using terms such as 'limited' or 'theatre' nuclear war, I believe along with, I suspect, millions of other people, that to embark on a course of unilateral disarmament, neutralism or disengagement from NATO and to act as if the Warsaw Pact's military strength did not pose a threat to our independence is profoundly dangerous. In essence it would risk repeating in the 1980s all the mistakes of the 1930s.

The key issue is not protection versus protest; the question is whether protest can be the springboard for political action; the trigger for negotiation and agreement. As the late Admiral of the Fleet, Earl Mountbatten of Burma, said on the occasion of the award of the Louise Weiss Foundation Prize to the Stockholm International Peace Research Institute at Strasbourg on 11 May 1979: 'To begin with we are most likely to preserve the peace if there is a military balance of strength between East and West. The real need is for both sides to replace the attempts to maintain a balance through ever-increasing and even more costly nuclear armaments by a balance based on mutual restraint. Better still, by a reduction of nuclear armaments I believe it should be possible to achieve greater security at a lower level of military confrontation. As a military man who has given half a century of active service I say in all sincerity that the nuclear arms race has no military purpose. Wars cannot be fought with nuclear illusions which they have generated. There are powerful voices around the world who still gives credence to the old Roman precept – if you desire peace, prepare for war. This is absolute nuclear nonsense and I repeat – it is a disastrous misconception to believe that by increasing the total uncertainty one increases one's own certainty.'

It is important to start bringing to disarmament and the whole argument about the feasibility and the desirability of a nuclear-free Europe in particular, let alone to unilateral disarmament, a greater intellectual astringency on terminology and definition, and more honesty in quoting from eminent people's speeches, than has been obvious so far on the part of all the participants. Lord Zuckerman and the late Lord Mountbatten are often quoted in a way which suggests they have said that Britain should unilaterally abandon all nuclear weapons. This is not, and has never been, the case. Both played a prominent part in negotiating and following through to deployment the original Polaris Agreement. Lord Zuckerman advised me on nuclear matters from 1977 to 1979 when I was Foreign Secretary. I share many of his anxieties about nuclear strategy. He warns of the three dangers; the first being that if we go on talking about the use of nuclear weapons as though this was a real option in world politics, then they will be used. The second danger being 'a technological trend which aims at obliterating the critical difference between nuclear weapons on the one hand and so-called conventional weapons on the other'. Lord Zuckerman then argues the central case against the protectionists contemplating limited nuclear war. 'We persuade ourselves that nuclear weapons can be made small and precise, and not as harmful as an equally precise conventional weapon with more destructive power. In my view this trend undoubtedly lowers the nuclear threshold, at least partly because it encourages people to believe that nuclear weapons (for example, so-called neutron bombs used ostensibly to hold up a massive tank incursion) can be real weapons of choice. This leads into the third danger I see – the growing belief that nuclear weapons could be used in what is now fashionably called a "theatre war". I do not believe any scenario exists which suggests that nuclear weapons could be used in field warfare between two nuclear states without escalation resulting.'[3]

These three dangers are real and form some common ground with the arguments in *Protest and Survive*, and need to be faced up to. Anxiety about them lay at the root of Lord Mountbatten's call for the banning of Tactical Nuclear Weapons, but we do his memory, action and words, a disservice by implying in any way that this is a unilateralist stance when in fact he urged us all to 'set about achieving practical measures of nuclear arms control and disarmament'. CND now tends to invoke the decisions of the Canadian government after the UN Special Session on Disarmament over non-nuclear weapons in Europe, to support their case for unilateral disarmament. Those who seek to invoke Canadian policy would do well to ponder the words of Pierre Trudeau in the foreword to the book, *The Dangers of Nuclear War*, explaining the double strategy of the Canadian government:

'It has participated actively in efforts to slow down and eventually reverse the nuclear arms race, through such means as research into seismic verification techniques, contributions to negotiations on partial arms control measures, and appeals for a ban on the flight testing of new strategic delivery vehicles and on the production of fissionable material for weapons purposes; and it has sought to restrict the use by other countries of Canadian nuclear technology and materials to peaceful purposes, through the application of full-scope safeguards. We have not called into question the principle of nuclear deterrence itself, nor in consequence have we endorsed appeals to the nuclear powers never to use nuclear weapons; for we have accepted that in the world as it is the system of nuclear deterrence is essential to our security. We have also believed that Canada must contribute her fair share to

461

Western defence arrangements as long as threats to Western security exist. Canadians decided thirty years ago that neither unilateral defence policies nor unilateral disarmament policies were appropriate in a nuclear world. Most thoughtful citizens agree, by and large, that national security is both a matter of military deterrence and of arms control. The balance to be struck between them will vary from time to time, but the concept of balance is important. Ever higher levels of deterrence may impose intolerable strains on control procedures; but if arms control measures give rise to lack of confidence in deterrence the political consequences can be equally dangerous.'[4]

What END underestimate is the extent to which large unilateral steps towards disarmament will actually impede progress in overall disarmament. Large steps not only remove the incentive from some countries to negotiate matching responses but can also destabilise relations and destroy the atmosphere of confidence between nations which has to accompany any significant arms reduction. It should not be forgotten that in 1977 President Carter offered the Soviets a disarmament package which proposed deep cuts even to 50 per cent. This was probably too large a step for the Soviet bureaucracy to endorse. 'Yet had the President "hung tough" on his proposals it is hard to see that the Soviet Government could have gone on blindly opposing them. Here, after all, was the first comprehensive disarmament package from a Super Power to approach the package that the Non-Aligned had developed in the CCD during the Sixties and Seventies in Geneva; one, moreover, which would properly fulfil Article VI of the Non-Proliferation Treaty on which the CCD had insisted.'[5]

The Soviet Union view of détente is summarised by Professor V. Kortunov in the Soviet journal *International Affairs*, May 1979: 'In the world arena, the Communist Party of the Soviet Union consistently pursues the Leninist policy of peaceful co-existence of states with different social systems and streng-thening of overall peace and security . . . For the Soviet Union and other socialist states, the policy of détente constitutes a struggle to create favourable conditions for Communist construction and for the development of the world revolutionary process; for the capitalist countries it is an effort to protect the bourgeois set-up in the new historical situation, to hold back social progress and use expanding inter-state relations to further their own class interests.' Whatever the different interpretations of détente, the situation in the 1980s is in some sense less dangerous than it was at the time of the Cuban missile crisis, when the whole world sensed that civilisation was perilously close to the nightmare of self-destruction. It was a time in Khrushchev's evocative words, 'When the smell of burning hung in the air.' Yet the smell of burning is not just confined to the dramatic headline-catching situation. It hangs threateningly but inscrutably over every military strategy and operation. Since 1962 the Soviet Union has redressed any major military imbalance between itself and the United States particularly over nuclear weapons and it relies, as does the West, on nuclear deterrence. Those who criticise nuclear deterrence are not prepared to recall the predictions of the protesters and the unilateralists from Hiroshima onwards that nuclear war was imminent, inevitable and that it was inconceivable that a balance of terror could deter. Yet to argue that deterrence has worked is not an acceptance that it will go on working; this is why there is no substitute for negotiation and why the pessimistic acceptance of nuclear war in *Protect and Survive* is unacceptable.

The arguments and the philosophy of both *Protect and Survive* and *Protest and Survive* can be briefly summarised. The protectionists accept the theory of nuclear deterrence, but believe we can live out a nuclear exchange. They build their defence strategy on the possibility of a limited nuclear war. They buttress this with an established position which accepts a distinction between tactical and strategic nuclear weapons. They accept the validity of a tactical nuclear weapon strategy, want the neutron bomb, accept the concept of the Eurostrategic balance, and advocate land-based cruise missiles in Europe. While they accept the need for arms control negotiation they insist that at all stages it is perfectly balanced and symmetrical, and are reluctant to consider any step like involvement in negotiations, depicting this as destabilising and dangerous.

The protesters, on the other hand, reject the theory of nuclear deterrence and despair of disarmament by negotiation. They desire a pan-European movement of people who demand of their politicians the de-nuclearisation of Europe and the ending of the two military alliances. They favour Britain becoming a neutral state. They want Britain unilaterally to give up all nuclear weapons, in the belief that this moral gesture will be matched by other European countries, East and West; and their definition of unilateral disarmament involves not just Britain giving up its own nuclear weapons, both tactical and strategic, but also the removal from the UK of all US nuclear forces, air, maritime or land based, which at present contribute to the NATO nuclear deterrent strategy.

The public debate about nuclear weapons has been dominated by these two polarised positions, as if there is no alternative viewpoint. There is a negotiator's alternative, which takes as its central premise the need progressively to reduce the volume, the cost and the sophistication of arms, both conventional and nuclear, and is prepared to take calculated risks in order to achieve greater progress than hitherto in the various forums for multilateral arms control. The alternative position is based on deterrence and the belief that unilateral disarmament undercuts a determination to achieve multilateral disarmament by negotiation.

Both protection and protest are in their different ways a counsel of despair if they are taken as the basic premise of a strategy. To counter despair, those who believe in the theory of nuclear deterrence while rejecting unilateral disarmament, must devise a credible strategy of multilateral negotiations in order to survive. It is insufficiently recognised that there are a number of politicians, scientists and military men in Britain and in many other countries who are not so starry-eyed as to believe in unilateral disarmament but who have for some years challenged the established consensus from inside and outside government. Some idea of the contrast in thinking can be seen by comparing the views of three former recent British Chiefs of the Defence Staff.

Field Marshal Lord Carver, who has publicly argued against a Trident system, said in an article in the *New Statesman* of 15

August 1980, 'We should take our share, as we do, of manning theatre nuclear weapon delivery systems, including those which use American warheads, so that the allies are seen to share the responsibility, the odium and the determination to use them if need be . . . ' He warns one against believing that even if the Soviets could be persuaded to disband their tactical or theatre nuclear armoury and retain only a strategic force directed at the USA and China, one should think of conventional warfare as being a comparatively harmless affair. 'The Yom Kippur War of 1973 reminded us of the purely military effects of modern warfare. In a contest that lasted less than three weeks, with limited forces in a limited area, both sides lost about half of their tanks and a quarter of their aircraft. To provide sufficient material to last out a prolonged major conventional war demands immensely expensive industrial effort, and its use would bring about a devastation in the area of operations.'

Yet in sharp contrast to what Lord Carver says about NATO's tactical nuclear weapons strategy, Admiral Lord Hill-Norton, a former Chairman of the Military Committee of NATO who wants Britain to buy Trident, thinks it is idle to suppose for a second that we can fight a battlefield nuclear weapon. He said, in *The Times* of 18 August 1980: 'I believe with Hermann Kahn, that once you cross the nuclear threshold you have taken an irreversible step which is almost bound to lead to a strategic nuclear exchange, which in turn is almost bound to lead to the end of civilisation . . . I will go to my grave being certain that if you let off a neutron bomb anywhere in Europe you have gone 90 per cent of the way to triggering a strategic nuclear exchange.' The real as opposed to the propagandist argument against the neutron bomb is that it does make it more likely that a battlefield nuclear exchange will be started.

Air Marshal Sir Neil Cameron in a lecture to the Royal Society of Arts on 30 April 1980 also criticised the concept of limited nuclear war when he said, 'that so-called battlefield or nuclear weapons are not means of winning military victories. That is a conclusion to which NATO has inevitably come, through the work of its Nuclear Planning Group over a dozen years or more ago . . . The warfighting school of nuclear theorists has lost the argument in the West. The role of nuclear weapons is to deter war – all war – not just nuclear war, between East and West.' A scepticism of tactical nuclear weapons is perhaps more prevalent amongst naval officers than army or air force officers, but apart from Lord Mountbatten and Lord Zuckerman there are a number of political leaders who have never believed that it was credible to expect a politician to authorise a battlefield nuclear exchange.

It is often alleged that the Soviets have a nuclear warwinning strategy and the views of the late Marshal Vasily Sokolovsky, who was their Chief of Staff in the 1950s, are quoted from his book *Military Strategy*. Also the fact that many Warsaw Pact exercises and planning are based on the first use of nuclear weapons is often cited. But the Soviet Union thinks the same about NATO exercises and plans. There are undoubtedly Soviet militarists and politicians who think limited nuclear war is a credible strategy and that the Soviets can win, and the same opinion exists in the United States. We should not ignore the fact that while there are, as I have indicated, people who challenge this view in the West, so there are important voices who also challenge that view in the Soviet Union. In a rare interview in the *New York Times* of 28 August 1980 Lt. General Mikhail Milshtein said, 'We believe that nuclear war will bring no advantage to anyone and may even lead to the end of civilisation. And the end of civilisation can hardly be called victory. Our doctrine regards nuclear weapons as something that must never be used. They are not an instrument for waging war in any rational sense. They are not weapons with which one can achieve foreign policy goals. But, of course, if we are forced to use them, in reply to their first use by an aggressor, we shall use them, with all their consequence, for the punishment of the aggressor.'

The reasons for Britain's and Europe's nuclear strategy goes back to the early 1950s, when the conventional defence forces of NATO were widely felt to be outnumbered 5-1 by the Warsaw Pact. Some even put it as high as 10-1. Even though NATO's conventional forces have been considerably improved since then, NATO still does not feel confident enough in its conventional forces to guarantee that it could repulse a

Warsaw Pact conventional attack. For this reason NATO has refused to agree to a declaration subscribed to by China and proposed by the Soviet Union that they would never under any circumstances use nuclear weapons first if they were under attack. NATO has therefore made it clear to the Warsaw Pact that if it were overrun by conventional forces the Warsaw Pact could not assume that NATO would not retaliate with nuclear weapons. Gradually over the years the so-called doctrine of the flexible response has meant that NATO has acquired, as have too the Warsaw Pact, a whole range of battlefield nuclear weapons and weapon systems capable of striking behind the battlefield area. Various attempts at producing coherent nuclear guidelines have been made by NATO to guide the military field commanders and ensure political control and the same has been done by the Warsaw Pact. The result has been one of differing options but with considerable doubt about whether many of the options would ever be contemplated. The best expert opinion concludes from the available evidence that the only consequences of moving from a conventional military exchange in Europe to a nuclear exchange might be a temporary lull but that this would be followed by an accentuation of previous trends, though at a much greater level of destruction. An American strategic thinker, W. McGeorge Bundy, with experience both inside and outside government has written, 'the confusion over strategy in NATO has been almost continuous, but in this respect constructive. NATO's incoherent mixture of deployments, conventional and nuclear, tactical and strategic, while it has served no serious war-fighting scenario, has none the less served the common peace. There is here a tantalising paradox which applies also, in a different way, to the general strategic balance: war-fighting at the level of thermo-nuclear exchange has become unreal as an object of policy, but a real capacity for it, and the possibility that it could happen are real elements, vital elements even, in the calculus that keeps the peace.'[6]

It is hard to envisage war in Europe. Certainly, while NATO remains as strong as it is at present a major Warsaw Pact attack, with or without warning, against NATO is extremely unlikely.

It is most likely to arise out of a miscalculation. For example, if there were strike action in East Germany, following a rising trend of militancy in Poland, it might lead to the deployment of Soviet troops. This might then be resisted by the East German strikers. Part of the East German army might join the strikers and the East Germans might appeal for West German help. The West German government might mobilise its forces but refuse to help, and would try to cool the situation. But armed West Germans might anyway cross the border to help. This would be resented by the Soviets. Despite warnings, the crossings continue. The Soviets might then retaliate into West Germany, and the conflict could escalate, despite both Germanies and both military pacts having no wish to engage in direct military conflict. The danger of an 'incoherent' NATO strategy is that not everyone is tough-minded in his analysis and that an option which might strike many politicians as fanciful could become, almost by default, the accepted wisdom for the military.

It is time openly to abandon the option of a limited battlefield exchange of nuclear weapons and to accept the logic of the studies and research which have all pointed to the fact that most of NATO's nuclear systems, particularly the short range battlefield systems and systems where the range ensures they can never reach into the Soviets' own territory, can neither bring about military defeat nor pose to the Soviet Union an unacceptable risk. The arguments for NATO initiating a short range battlefield nuclear exchange are unreal. In the event of an all-out conventional attack the only sensible political nuclear response would be to authorise a demonstrative nuclear explosion in an unpopulated non-military area of the Soviet Union as a warning that the nuclear threshold was about to be crossed. A battlefield response would have less value as a warning and be almost certain to invoke a similar battlefield response by the Soviet Union. In the case of an accidental attack it would be folly to authorise a battlefield response; here the only option would be to respond conventionally, yielding what ground one had to in the hope that the attack would be countermanded and to use the already negotiated machinery for political dialogue and exchange in order to abort the action. Such agreements were first signed between the US and the Soviet Union in 1977. In the most likely of any form of attack, one which stems from a miscalculation of a local incident, the main thrust of any response should be political, to defuse the political tension which had provoked the incident, and here a battlefield nuclear response would be folly.

The politicians must ensure at all times that there is no power for NATO's military commanders or Soviet military commanders to take a battlefield decision to release nuclear weapons – even if a sensitive military installation was overrun. Whereas the NATO guidelines are clear about the need for political authorisation, the tradition of a field commander putting his blind eye to the telescope did not die with Admiral Lord Nelson. It is dangerous to allow the military commanders to believe that battlefield nuclear weapons might ever be politically authorised, and to allow them to plan and exercise on the possibility.

There would be great security advantages in negotiating away all of NATO's and the Warsaw Pact's short range battlefield weapons and putting this as a higher priority than some of the strategic arms limitation issues, important though they are. This would mean NATO abandoning Lance missiles, short range nuclear capable aircraft, nuclear artillery, atomic mines, Nike Hercules missiles. NATO has some 7,000 nuclear weapons, 5,000 of them situated in West Germany; at least 65-75 per cent of these could go without any loss in capability and incidentally release a considerable number of US armed personnel currently guarding the security of these systems. Though the French would probably not participate, the broad aim of such a negotiation would be to cover all nuclear systems with a range not covered in SALT II within an arms control agreement related to, if not part of, the SALT process. It would cover formally the US and British long range bomber aircraft and US and British strategic ballistic nuclear submarines, and informally, in the sense that they would be taken into account, the French force. The aim would be to stabilise at equivalent, preferably reduced, levels with the Soviet Union's SS-20, SS-4 and SS-5 missiles if they continued in service, Backfire and

Blunder/Badger aircraft if they remained in service, Golf Class submarines and SSM3 cruise missile carrying submarines. Within this sort of arrangement it might be possible to exclude all nuclear weapon systems from a part of continental Europe. This would be a negotiated disengagement, but in order to convince the West Germans that this would not increase the risk of a conventional attack taking a slice of their territory, they probably need to have a feeling that the absence of battlefield weapons would be covered by land or air based cruise missiles and would not be content to rely on long range aircraft or intercontinental ballistic missiles. It is the West Germans, above all, who need to feel confident in any change of strategy. They have as an act of policy shown no wish to acquire their own nuclear weapons but they are a crucial power in central Europe and have made a decisive contribution to détente. We must take account of the fact that they appear to believe that the capability of the Soviet Union to attack Western Europe with weapons like the SS-20, quite separate from their central strategic forces targeted on the United States, represents a new and destructive political threat to Europe. This is presumably whý Chancellor Schmidt raised the issue of a Eurostrategic balance in 1977. This is what has underlain their wish to upgrade the Pershing missile and for the US to deploy land based cruise missiles in Europe, and why they were, in particular, very concerned about any future limitation on cruise missiles in the SALT process. If some cruise missiles were based in West Germany near the French, Belgian, Dutch border, this might given the necessary reassurance while any SS-20s were still deployed by the Soviets. Cruise missiles would not need to be deployed in the battlefield area, though they could be targeted into the battlefield area.

Whether an area of nuclear disengagement, on both sides of the border between the two Germanies, could be negotiated as a nuclear-free zone is therefore predominantly an issue of West German confidence. It is not a new idea; it was an FDP representative in the West Germany Parliament, Dr Pfleider, who, in 1952, first put forward the idea of 'disengagement in Central Europe'. The idea re-surfaced a little later during the discussions of the so-called Bonin Plan, but only assumed international importance at the Berlin Conference of 1954, when Sir Anthony Eden came out with the idea of a Central European zone of arms limitation and control. Eden later submitted a variant of his proposals – an idea of a 'demilitarised zone between East and West' – at the Geneva Summit Conference of 1955, and at this meeting Marshal Bulganin, then premier of the Soviet Union, declared 'that the Soviet Government was of the opinion that their eventual objective should be to have no foreign troops remaining on the territories of the European states'.

Two years later, in 1957, Hugh Gaitskell made a set of very far reaching proposals. Stressing the explosive nature of the Eastern Europe situation, his proposals related to Germany, both East and West, Poland, Czechoslovakia and Hungary and, it was hoped, might also cover Romania and Bulgaria. It was entitled 'A Neutral Belt in Europe' and three conditions were laid down: firstly, the Oder-Neisse frontier should be accepted, secondly, NATO should be preserved, and thirdly, US forces should remain in Europe. In the autumn of the same year, 1957, the so-called Rapacki Plan, providing for a nuclear-weapons-free zone comprising Poland, Czechoslovakia, East Germany and West Germany, was presented to the UN General Assembly. Details of the plan were handed to the governments involved through a memorandum dated 14 February 1958. It provided that:

1 The states located in the zone would undertake the obligation not to manufacture, maintain or possess nuclear weapons and not to permit the installation on their territories of such weapons;

2 the nuclear weapons powers should undertake not to maintain nuclear weapons in the armaments of their forces stationed on the territories of these states;

3 not to install any installations or equipment in those territories for servicing nuclear weapons, including missile launching sites;

4 not to transfer such weapons or equipment.

An amended version appeared on 4 November 1958. Its main thrust was: 'A freeze on nuclear armaments in the

471

proposed zone: and a reduction of conventional forces simultaneously with the complete denuclearization of the zone carried out under appropriate control.'

Again an amended version was put to the Committee of 18 Nations in Geneva, on 28 March 1962. The proposal envisaged that the proposed zone would be open to any European state wishing to accede. Its purpose was 'to eliminate nuclear weapons and to reduce armed forced and conventional armaments within a limited area in which these measures could help to reduce tension and substantially to limit the danger of conflict.' Although the final version appeared to bear some resemblance to the British ideas, the Rapacki plan was rejected primarily because the United States and the then West German government were not keen, although later Helmut Schmidt said that it could with advantage have been explored more carefully.

The NATO governments never seriously worked out what the implications for military planning in the area would have been after carrying out such a plan. In those days the fear was that it would make West Germany vulnerable to attack, but now that the strategic ballistic missiles have become so accurate, this has become less of a problem. Now, even though there are still some command and control problems, a Polaris or Trident missile can be fired from hundreds of miles away from under the sea and be targeted in a tactical battlefield sense to land within yards of the chosen area. The US land based missiles fired from Nevada are even easier to target, so in theory the arguments against removing nuclear weapons from Europe are less strong as the difference between tactical and strategic weapons becomes blurred. Also, since Hugh Gaitskell's suggestion the policy of *Ostpolitik* has transformed relations between East and West Germany. The frontier question is now settled, they have established major economic and trading links and the Berlin situation appears reasonably stable. The Soviet Union have also seen that the West is not prepared to act militarily to exploit internal dissent within the Warsaw Pact and never contemplated action in 1956 over Hungary, in 1968 over Czechoslovakia or in 1980 over Poland. This accommodation was institutionalised in the

Helsinki Final Act signed in 1965 and though détente has not stopped, nor could it, or should it, stop the ideological war, it has produced a measure of confidence in terms of crisis management and an accepted discipline in terms of solidifying the current map of Europe.

Against such a background the possibility of negotiating the abandonment of short range battlefield nuclear weapons and an area of disengagement is greater in the early 1980s than it was in the late 1950s but it will still require a massive shift in attitudes to arms control on both sides that may be impossible for President Reagan and his administration to contemplate.

If a limited nuclear-free zone could be negotiated, it might be possible at a next stage to extend it by giving up all airborne nuclear weapons systems and/or all land-based missiles other than those based in the US and in the USSR. To achieve sufficient confidence to allow such far-reaching agreements the United States, Britain, France and the Soviet Union would need to agree to negotiate arrangements to enhance the survivability of existing nuclear submarines carrying either ballistic or cruise missiles. It would need to cover a ban on active trailing of such submarines and the establishment of large areas within the Arctic Ocean – so as to be away from naval operational areas – where there would be a ban on all anti-submarine warfare techniques, and particularly on the placing of under-water hydrophones, which promises to be an era of expansion if it is unchecked by negotiations. Negotiations would enhance the value of existing French and British deterrent systems and those of the US and Soviet submarine missile fleets. It should make it possible to downgrade the current strategic debate over the so-called Eurostrategic balance and for all to accept the asymmetry inherent in the geography of Europe, whereby a limitation of land based missiles to Soviet and US territory will always favour the Soviets since they can target their SS-20s on Europe whereas there is no equivalent, if one excludes French land based missiles, even if US cruise missiles are deployed. For some time US strategic missiles have had a multiple targeting strategy on Soviet military installations, as well as on Soviet cities, quite independent of European based systems and though there has been a lot of comment on the new Presidential targeting directive 59, it is not wholly new. The anxiety this new targeting strategy arouses stems from its apparent linkage in some people's minds to the acceptability of limited nuclear war or a first strike potential. By highlighting the switch made some time ago to include military targets the new directive has lent credence to the view that a missile exchange could be limited to military targets.

If such a series of phased agreements could be contemplated, guaranteeing the invulnerability of the US and Soviet submarine missile systems, then the US might feel able to delay and eventually cancel the vast expenditure necessary for the deployment of the MX missile, though it is hard to see the Soviet Union ever giving up its land based missile systems. The advantage of both sides relying primarily on an invulnerable submarine deterrent force is that they are clearly second strike systems and this could bring a greater degree of mutual confidence in the intentions of all sides to avoid a first strike strategy, which is missing at present between the US and the Soviet political leadership.

It is very necessary, given this undercurrent of scepticism in both NATO and the Warsaw Pact about limited nuclear war and different perception about what is the currently accepted strategy, that a discussion is started within NATO and the Warsaw Pact which seeks to challenge the militarists and tries to negotiate a newer, more acceptable means of deterrence. When Chancellor Schmidt met President Brezhnev in Moscow in July 1980 the Soviets declared their readiness to start negotiations on medium range nuclear weapons without either waiting for the ratification of the SALT II accord or requiring that NATO's modernisation plans be rescinded. If progress is to be made before the completion of the SS-20s' deployment and before the modernised Pershing and cruise missiles are scheduled for deployment it is urgent to have discussions.

There is a strong case, which I advocated as Foreign Secretary, for Britain, France if she wished to, and West Germany and perhaps one other Warsaw Pact country to be involved as negotiating partners, not just to be consulted on these discussions. It was this case, for Britain to use the fact of its possession of nuclear weapons to join in such a new and wider forum for negotiations, which I argued before the 1980 Special Party Conference. It would be impossible to sustain such an argument if a Labour government in Britain had decided to abandon nuclear weapons, for neither the US nor the Soviet Union, already sceptical about widening the participation in SALT, would then see any case for the UK to be present. All the signs are that the US will not seek to involve Britain, and the present British government appears to have no wish to be involved. It is deeply sceptical about disarmament negotiations and seems actively to want US cruise missiles in the UK rather than reluctantly accepting the need to deploy them if negotiations over the Soviet SS-20 missiles do not succeed. West Germany also may not want to be involved. But how long can Europe effectively opt out and allow critical negotiations for its security to be handled by a US President with no direct European involvement? The 1980s are different from the 1960s when the SALT process started, the leadership role of the US has been eroded and may never again carry the same automatic authority in Europe. We are moving from an era of consultation into an era of partnership. The task of President Reagan is to give leadership to the Alliance without destroying the relatively new concept of partnership. But the European countries will have to contribute as partners, particularly Germany, France, and the United Kingdom.

In discussion with President Brezhnev and Mr Gromyko I found them ready to consider carefully and sympathetically the case for British involvement and possibly that of other countries in any discussion on arms control that focused on Western European security. The Labour government gradually became convinced that there were advantages in involving Britain in future SALT discussion provided that West Germany wanted our involvement, and we would have preferred it if they too would participate in any discussions affecting nuclear weapons located in either the Soviet Union or Western Europe and targeted on each other's territory. We were not prepared to involve Britain as the only Western European country, unless this was positively welcomed by our European allies, nor would we have wished to be involved if either or both the United States or the Soviet Union were obviously unenthusiastic.

I am very wary of accepting the concept of a Euro-strategic balance as distinct from the overall East-West global strategic balance. It was Chancellor Schmidt who first raised the question of the so-called Euro-strategic balance in 1977 and it is West Germany which has argued strongly that the SS-20 should be discussed in SALT III. Once raised, the issue has to be grappled with in SALT, yet new intercontinental nuclear missiles have an incredible accuracy. This new-found accuracy challenges all strategic thinking since it questions the vulnerability of second-strike nuclear forces and emphasizes once again the superiority of the submarine platform for a second-strike strategy. It also makes it possible to target these weapon systems as part of a theatre strike strategy. The distinction between strategic weapons and theatre weapons has therefore become increasingly blurred and makes for considerable confusion in discussions over the so-called theatre balance or Euro-strategic balance.

SALT II has a Joint Statement of Principles to apply to SALT III. This undertakes to deal with the Protocol to SALT II which commits the United States not to deploy ground and sea-launched cruise missiles of a range over 600 km until 31 December 1981. SALT III is therefore committed to discussing the very weapons systems on which Western European countries, following the NATO decision over deployment, have a crucial interest. The United States has satisfied her Western European allies that nothing in SALT II prevents the deployment of cruise missiles in Europe within the time of their availability. Nor does SALT II prevent the US from passing on strategic nuclear technology and weapons delivery systems, such as Trident and cruise missiles, to Britain or to France.

Yet it is clear to everyone that the tensions over these and other issues engendered by SALT II did not strengthen confidence within the Alliance. The European fuss over the cruise missiles was exaggerated and if there was any criticism it was more applicable to commitments entered into by President

Ford and Henry Kissinger than to the actions of President Carter and Cyrus Vance. Similarly the misunderstanding over the neutron bomb stemmed from delay in Europe's forming a position, particularly West Germany and Britain. We, in retrospect, could, and should, have given a much earlier lead and it is nonsense to blame President Carter alone. As a consequence of the European delay in deciding their position, when President Carter came to make the actual decision to deploy he found NATO was itself seriously divided. In the run up to the Special UN Session on Disarmament President Carter was right to avoid a decision which would have split NATO and given the Soviet Union a wonderful propaganda weapon. But this experience should give us all pause for thought, particularly since NATO finds its inner cohesion stretched again over the cruise missile deployment decision.

To what extent are these tensions the endemic accompaniment of a purely Soviet-American negotiation which concerns itself with crucial European-American matters, and will they recur again? To what extent are they due to lack of proper consultation within the Alliance and can they be cured by better consultation procedures and more discussion within NATO before decisions are taken? I am convinced the tension is endemic to a bilateral dialogue and will not be removed by better consultative procedure within NATO. The US and Soviet bureaucrats are bound to be apprehensive about any change being undertaken in their bilateral discussions. The politicians, aware of the difficulties of reconciling differences, may be less resistant to questioning whether SALT I has not now reached the limits of usefulness of that particular framework. The all-powerful international position of the US is being eroded and, to some extent, this erosion affects the Soviet Union's position as well. The United States is forced to operate more within a collective Western framework and the Soviet Union has to take some account of non-aligned views and of potential divisions within the Warsaw Pact.

All the signs are that for the 1980s the US leadership role in the West is no longer automatically accepted by France and West Germany. We cannot any longer simply acquiesce in the establishment of SALT III on a bilateral basis. Fortunately for

477

the peace and security of Europe, West Germany has been economically strong. This has given it the national self-confidence to be adamant that it does not wish to become a nuclear weapon state. West Germany and France now have a very close political relationship but all of this cannot be taken completely for granted. Economic decline in Germany and a souring of Franco-German relations could bring back many anxieties about Germany's role in Europe.

Both West Germany and France have important economic relations with the Soviet Union. Apart from France, West Germany, far more than any other Western ally, has been apprehensive about US policy towards détente, from human rights to cruise missiles. It is the West Germans who stand both to lose and gain more than any other country over the outcome of SALT. Standing on the sidelines as at present, West Germany does not have to take a firm position on SALT negotiations; it is tending to sit back and then, if it feels dissatisfied with the outcome, that only serves to weaken its confidence in the US defence 'guarantee. West German involvement in the negotiations would not mean in any way acquiring nuclear weapons. West Germany already has a sophisticated nuclear power industry. Involvement will not mean that it will acquire more new information. Yet by being party to a decision on SALT III it would reinforce SALT's credibility. The lesser alternative is to add only Britain at the negotiations on SALT III, which would allow another communication channel to our fellow European allies.

The US Administration would not have faced a fraction of the Congressional problems with SALT II if Britain and West Germany had been full partners in the actual negotiations. Public statements of NATO support for SALT II are not the same thing as European participation, especially if accompanied by well publicised private doubts at various stages of the negotiations. A multilateral negotiation would also be less likely to polarise views inside the United States. There is no reason why a key non-nuclear weapon state like West Germany should not be involved in the negotiations, even if on some sensitive issues, for example on warhead technology, it excluded itself from the exchange of information. The Soviet

Union could obviously oppose West German involvement or counter by insisting on the involvement of East Germany or another Warsaw Pact country, but instead she might see advantages from involving West Germany, as a way of making any agreement with the US stick and deal with substantive Soviet concerns. At present, fears of arousing suspicion about West German nuclear intentions, the reaction of her continental partners, perhaps in particular France, and sheer inertia, are all factors in the West German apparent reluctance to be involved.

If the Federal Republic refuses involvement, and if Britain's other European allies wish, Britain should welcome becoming a full negotiating partner in SALT III. It would be an extension of British involvement in the Comprehensive Test Ban (CTB) talks. The present British government has not hitherto wished to be involved, as much as anything else for fear that this would mean that Polaris or its replacement, the submarine-launched Trident, or cruise missiles would be on the table at such negotiations. The weakness of this argument is that Polaris, or the Trident missiles the present government have decided to purchase, will be on the table anyway, even if Britain is not present. Britain's mere presence or absence would not mean that the Soviet Union would allow the United States to exclude the British contribution from her overall numbers. Britain's presence would allow public opinion to take a far more balanced decision on the future of Britain's nuclear deterrent and set that decision in the context of European security and arms control negotiations. Britain would be free to go ahead purchasing new missiles if she so decided at any time she wished, for SALT has not prevented the US or Soviet governments from making weapon decisions during the negotiations.

Britain will carry little credibility in asking other non-nuclear weapon states to take arms control more seriously if she is not even prepared to participate in negotiations herself because of the fear of including her own nuclear weapons. Britain cannot easily justify, only on grounds of national deterrence and national military requirements, her continuation as a weapon state. Her possession or discontinuation of nuclear weapons has a very high political content. Ensuring West Germany stays non-nuclear and that France is not the only European nuclear weapon state are political, not military, objectives, as is ensuring that our public commitment to disarmament is to use our nuclear knowledge constructively in all arms control forums. Not being a super-power, Britain can with skill help to bridge gaps in understanding between the two super-powers and between the non-nuclear weapon states. Britain's dilemma is the cost of remaining a nuclear power. Afghanistan has revealed a worrying difference in perception about détente between Europe and America. While West Germany is the key country for closing the difference, Britain also can exert an influence, provided she does not just mirror US perceptions but remains sensitive to European concerns.

A wider membership of SALT III will take time to achieve. It may not be accepted initially and substantive negotiations over SALT III will take time. If it starts at least as a purely Soviet-American negotiation then consideration will need to be given to other forums for discussing Euro-strategic issues.

The Mutual Balanced Force Reduction talks have had, since 1975, a nuclear component through the West's Option III offer, but few would argue that this forum could or should be expanded in this way. It is better for the Mutual Balanced Force Reduction (MBFR) talks which have become hopelessly bureaucratised through many years of inertia and political neglect, to concentrate on making progress with the new Western proposals. This limited Phase I proposal follows closely a proposal which I, when Foreign Secretary, put to West Germany in early 1979. MBFR needs a political impetus and a commitment to meet at Foreign Minister level which NATO agreed in principle in Washington in 1978. Again West Germany has a key role which so far it has not fully exercised. Strategic arms negotiations are very complicated, deal with highly classified material and as I argued in *Survival*, the journal of the International Institute for Strategic Studies, in May 1980, there is a need to keep to a small group of nations. Indeed one of the strongest arguments against widening the membership of SALT will be the problems of multilateral negotiations. Yet there are powerful arguments against creating a new separate negotiation to cover Western European concerns. To do so will reinforce the concept of a Euro-strategic balance and could of itself contribute to the danger of separating US strategic policy from that of Europe. If it were decided to keep unchanged the existing forums of SALT, MBFR and CTB and Helsinki it would be worth considering whether any linkage could be established.

Progress on confidence-building measures could have been made in Belgrade had that conference not focused so heavily on human rights. The Madrid meeting had the advantage of the wider 35-nation Helsinki membership, but with it goes the disadvantage of numbers and certainly this is no forum for strategic arms control decisions. Discussion over the future structure of arms control, whether or not one widens SALT III, must face the desirability of French participation in some form.

At long last France is taking a serious interest. President Giscard attended the UN Special Session. France has taken her place at the enlarged Geneva disarmament talks and she proposed a European Disarmament Conference in 1978. This proposal for the 35 Helsinki countries plus Albania to discuss arms control, excluding nuclear weapons, across the breadth of Europe from the Atlantic to the Urals is starting to arouse more support. It was conceived before the French elections in a wish to take an initiative over disarmament which would have a specific French imprimatur. It has since become a more central part of French foreign policy. It is rooted in the French dislike of block to block negotiations, and her belief that the MBFR remit of the Central Front is too narrow. Many countries, including Britain, have always been reluctant totally to reject the proposal because they wished to encourage France into international discussions on arms control. West Germany, as part of its bilateral relationship, has been more positive than any other NATO country in encouraging the French proposal. A radical and positive role for a European Conference would be if it could be scheduled for some years ahead, say 1982-3, and be the forum which would bring together and co-ordinate decisions taken in the framework of

SALT, CTB, MBFR and Helsinki. Yet to carry any conviction or to have any hope of success such a Conference would need to be able to bridge the gaps between France and West Germany on the one hand, and increasingly Britain and the US on the other, before there could be progress with the Soviet Union.

To avoid creating a new structure it might be worth taking Berlin as the focus. Quadripartite machinery between the Soviet Union, America, Britain and France as the four occupying powers already exists. Also existing is the Bonn Group for co-ordinating views between France, Britain, West Germany and the United States. Not only do these meet at official level but also regularly at Foreign Minister level and, from time to time coinciding with Economic Summits, at Heads of Government level. At Guadeloupe the four Heads of Government were acknowledged to have discussed security issues. It is worth considering whether a grouping of five – the Soviet Union, the United States, West Germany, France and Britain – would be an acceptable steering group to act as a link between the existing arms control forums which affect European security. In this way highly secret nuclear weapon systems might be discussed and some coherence and political leadership be given to the present disparate and disappointing arms control negotiations. It raises sensitive issues and must not undermine the existing very successful Berlin machinery, which is of course designed for a different purpose. But one of the difficulties in international affairs is to introduce any new forum without so adding to numbers of countries involved that the forum cannot negotiate successfully or exchange highly classified information.

The whole area of arms control and disarmament needs, after Afghanistan, a fresh impetus. The United States, Soviet Union and Western Europe are all now embarking on yet another twist to the already spiralling arms race. Afghanistan should not be the excuse for turning back either on SALT or on the sustained pursuit of realistic détente. It should rather be the stimulus to try once more to re-establish a genuine bargain in which both sides gain important objectives and in which both sides trade off gains by accepting restraints.

It would be possible, if such a degree of arms control could be negotiated, for the UK to reconsider the relevance of its own independent deterrent, though the existing Polaris covers Britain's needs for at least the next twelve to fifteen years. My position, which has never varied since I first became involved in nuclear deterrence, as Under Secretary for the Royal Navy in 1968, has been a strong commitment to negotiating nuclear arms control agreements. I opposed the purchase of Poseidon to replace Polaris in 1970, when I was on the Defence and Overseas Affairs Sub-Committee of the Expenditure Committee. I thought it was militarily unnecessary and something Britain could not afford to spend so much defence money on. Both in and out of government I opposed the Trident system as a Polaris replacement on similar grounds. It is impossible to purchase Trident without major reductions in what we might otherwise spend on the conventional defence forces. There is an argument that we can extend Polaris well past 1995 by cannibalising A3 missiles and with a prudent programme of replacing equipment at the time of refits. Certainly Polaris hull life will now last much longer than was once feared. By 1990 there may have been a transformation of weapon technology, with important advances being made in laser technology. No one can predict the future, nor is it easy to predict the progress of arms control and disarmament over the next decades. If in 1990 there was still felt to be a need, for European political reasons – which have always been more important than military reasons – for Britain to retain its own deterrent, then we should consider purchasing cruise missiles to be fired from the existing torpedo tubes of our hunter-killer submarines. This would provide the UK with an ability to threaten a second strike, capable of inflicting unacceptable damage on a few Soviet cities in the unlikely event of a breakdown in NATO or, even more unlikely, of a uniquely threatening situation developing for the UK in a general East/West war. It would not be as sophisticated or as effective a system as Trident. Nor would it be sufficient for the US, whose strategic needs are very different, but it would be a lot cheaper and financially supportable for the UK. To argue the economic limitation is no more than a realistic judgment of what is the size of the UK defence budget we can afford, since it is already distorting other expenditure priorities. No decision, on this basis, would be needed over whether to replace Polaris for ten years, during which time the UK would contribute fully to NATO's deterrent as at present, and would also contribute constructively as a nuclear weapon state to discussions over détente and arms control in every possible forum. It would allow Britain to argue now for a five-year ban on nuclear tests in the Comprehensive Nuclear Test Ban discussions.

The criticism made about secrecy attached to nuclear decision-making in Britain by many of those who also oppose the policy is well founded. Professor E.P. Thompson writes in *Protest and Survive*: 'The name of the game, on both sides, is mendacity. Indeed "deterrence" might itself be defined as the biggest and most expensive lie in history, and it was, in effect, defined in this way by our Defence Secretary, Mr Pym, in the debate on 24 January 1979. "Deterrence is primarily about what the other side thinks, not what we may think".'[7] This is not mendacious, and even though secrecy has been taken to absurd lengths within Britain it is as of nothing compared with the Soviet Union. Too much secrecy is not for me a new criticism; concern about defence decision-making stimulated me to write a book[8] arguing for more openness, for the creation of a climate in which defence decision-making operates sensibly, sensitively and objectively in the interests of every citizen, and saying that it would not be achieved by avoiding the difficult moral and humanitarian issues that any defence policy inevitably raises, and that it could only be achieved by a far deeper public involvement in the discussions of military affairs.

Protest and Survive criticised the decision not to announce formally the existence and details of the Chevaline programme, hardening the Polaris A3 missile warheads, until the programme was completed. 'A programme costing £1000 millions which had been carried out in the deepest secrecy, and without the knowledge of the full Cabinet, and in defiance of official Labour Party policy, on the authority of Mr. Callaghan and two or three of his particular friends.' As Foreign Secretary in 1977 I did not think the savings justified a political row. But it is important to correct the impression that there had been no debate even though there had been too little debate. As long ago as 1972 I wrote [9] that it may be that the pessimism over SALT leading to a really effective limitation on ABM deployment will prove to have been misplaced. In which case, some argue, the need for a 'hardening' programme to increase the penetration of the A3 missile will not be vital. But the British government seems to have taken the pessimistic view, for it appears that in late 1970 it decided to embark on a 'hardening' programme.

There were a number of articles about the problems that the Soviet antiballistic missile (ABM) systems would pose for Polaris, and about cost increases to the Polaris improvement programme, in the British press all through the 1970s, and specific references were made to a modernised Polaris warhead programme. The main newsworthy facts announced by Mr Pym were not so much the formal confirmation of the existence of the programme but the codename Chevaline and its cost, which had been escalated considerably.

Criticism of the absence of parliamentary debate and general parliamentary accountability is fair; compared with the US the poverty of public debate on defence matters in the UK generally, and particularly on nuclear issues, is a disgrace. But at least over the last decade there has been a marked improvement, particularly in the specialist press. The decision in 1970 to establish the new Expenditure Committee with a Defence and External Affairs sub-Committee with a remit covering defence policy followed by the creation of a specific Defence Select Committee in 1979 is very important. MPs are beginning at last to subject defence decision-making to detailed scrutiny. The Expenditure Committee carefully analysed the case for purchasing the Poseidon missile in the early 1970s and came down against the purchase and for continuing with Polaris, so the 'all-party consensus' as some disparagingly refer to, does not always follow the militarists' preference. But at the time that the decision to continue with Polaris was made it was also decided to improve the system's capability against ABM defences by 'hardening' and the addition of sophisticated penetration aids. The decision was made early in the 1970s by a Conservative government. The decision in 1974 for the Labour Cabinet was not whether to start the programme but whether or not to cancel it. The government had to consider whether the Soviet Union would ever deploy more ABMs of a more advanced kind than the fairly primitive Galosh system around Moscow, but by then this was unlikely and our programme should have been cancelled.

Modernising it did not mean Multiple Independently Targeted Re-entry Vehicles, a programme incompatible with the two Manifestos issued by the Labour Party in 1974. The promise not to purchase a second generation missile system was a commitment in fact scrupulously upheld by Mr Callaghan as Prime Minister, and before the election no decision over the whole complex of issues involved in deciding what, if anything, to do after Polaris was ever contemplated by the last Labour government. It was deliberately decided, in deference to the previous Manifesto, to ensure only that any new government had all the necessary information to take informed decisions.

One of the questions which I thought needed to be answered was whether the degree of urgency that the military felt for a decision in 1980 was really essential or whether the life of Polaris could not be further extended to give time to see whether a SALT III negotiation could be established which would cover European nuclear weapons, and in which Britain and West Germany might be directly involved as participants in the negotiations. It is wrong to allege that after revealing the detail of Chevaline Mr Pym 'held other, "second strike" secret material back as a further deterrent' in the debate in the House of Commons in order to induce Labour politicians to give silent assent. No decisions were made so there can be no embarrassment, and when they would have had to be made there would have been, as the Labour Party promised in their 1979 election Manifesto, a 'full and informed debate about these issues in the country before any decision is taken'. This is stressed because by innuendo and smear the myth will take hold that the last Labour government was party to the decision to invest in the Trident system, thus buttressing the prejudices of those who want to believe that there is no democratic control of the military, and no difference between the political parties.

Professor Thompson writes, 'Now I am not an expert in these matters, and I do not usually follow the specialist press'. This humility, however, does not stop him from alleging, 'why the air is fouled-up is that the military and security elites in both blocs, and their political servitors, cannot pursue their expensive and dangerous policies without continually terrifying the populations of their own countries with sensational accounts of the war preparations of the other bloc.' It is important to his political philosophy to talk of 'political servitors' and 'mendacious rhetoric', for it can then buttress his jaundiced view of Britain, 'digging even deeper bunkers for the personnel of the State, distributing leaflets, holding lectures in halls and churches, laying down two weeks of supplies of emergency rations, promoting in the private sector the manufacture of Whitelaw shelters, and radiation-proof "Imperm" blinds and patent Anti-Fall-Out pastilles, and "Breetheesy" masks, and getting the Women's Institutes to work out recipes for broiling radio-active frogs. And it is also necessary to supplement all this by beating up an internal civil-war or class-war psychosis, by unmasking traitors, by threatening journalists under the Official Secrets Acts, by tampering with juries and tapping telephones, and generally by closing up peoples' minds and mouths.' An academic discussion! Spare us such disclaimers, Professor Thompson – yours is a brilliantly written political tract in which the object of attack is the Established Consensual Opinion of the Realm. Yet how strange that such an anti-establishment figure should so consistently invoke a section of the establishment, though a splendidly robust and atypical part, to buttress his arguments, in the shape of Lord Mountbatten and Lord Zuckerman.

There are important disarmament negotiations continuing which are not just centred on Europe. A nuclear test ban would for the first time demonstrate to the non-nuclear-weapons states that the countries with nuclear weapons were starting to take their commitment to stop vertical proliferation or sophistication of nuclear weapons seriously, and they would therefore carry more weight when they argue with other countries for the full implementation of the Non-Proliferation Treaty, NPT, and for other countries to help in the curbing of horizontal proliferation or the spreading of weapons to non-weapon states.

It is ten years since the NPT came into force, and there are now 115 signatories. India exploded its own nuclear device in 1974 and has refused to sign the NPT; it is watching Pakistan's nuclear development programme with care and meanwhile keeping open its options on nuclear weapons. Pakistan shows every sign of continuing to develop a nuclear weapon capability, completely ignoring US representations, and those of France and the UK, to desist. This was happening even before the invasion of Afghanistan, which will only serve to increase the Pakistan leaders' resolve. Israel undoubtedly has the capability to deploy nuclear weapons, which it can fulfil at any moment. South Africa is on the brink of developing a military capability. Were Brazil and Argentina to develop a nuclear capability it would mean ignoring the Treaty of Tlatelolco which seeks to make Latin America a nuclear-free zone. South Korea can probably be restrained for a little longer by the US. Iraq's intentions are unclear. The possible link between Israel and South Africa is a very disturbing nuclear issue though the possession of nuclear weapons will have little relevance for the sort of guerrilla warfare and urban violence which faces South Africa. It is unlikely now that any of these countries will be influenced to halt or slow down any currently planned developments by a CTB agreement, but it could make it easier for them to stop new developments or to delay existing developments.

Britain has played an important part in the London-based Nuclear Suppliers Club in trying to reduce the risk of proliferation, again showing there is scope for a positive constructive use of Britain's position as a nuclear weapon owning state. In this area Britain could take a lead by completely opening up establishments like Windscale for international inspection and trying to get all states with nuclear weapons to accept that the size of their plutonium stockpile cannot continue to be held secret if there is to be a genuinely open international check on the plutonium cycle for all states, whether they have nuclear weapons or not. Britain, which played a constructive role in the London summit of the Seven in 1977, should also try to ensure that the decision to establish the International Nuclear Fuel Cycle Evaluation Group is now followed by full implementation of all the recommendations in the agreed report which was published early in 1980.

The protesters seem to wish to depict Britain as being uninterested in and unimaginative over arms control and disarmament; in fact the record is not a bad one, though it could well be improved. In the UN Special Session in 1978 the British role was widely judged to have been a leading one and the British delegation helped to construct the formulation of the final document. I asked Lord Philip Noel-Baker, a Nobel Peace Prize winner, to be part of that British delegation, which served to emphasise to Third World countries that we were not approaching the Session in a negative or militaristic mood. James Callaghan, as Prime Minister, made a major speech to the Session as did many other Heads of government. The challenge now is to ensure that substantive progress is made at the 1982 Second Special Session to ensure progress in the second decade of disarmament. We need to ask why some measures of disarmament have succeeded and others failed. How the future trend towards greater arms expenditure can be checked at the early stage of research and development. These are some of the objectives of an Independent Commission on Disarmament and Security Issues which has been set up under the Chairmanship of Olof Palme and of which I am a member. It hopes to stimulate progress on disarmament as hopefully the Brandt Commission will stimulate progress on development, and influence the UN Special Session in 1982.

The first Disarmament decade during the 1970s produced some very limited progress. It started with the entry in force of the Non-Proliferation Treaty, and the Treaty on the Prohibition of the Emplacement of Nuclear Weapons and other Weapons of Mass Destruction on the Sea-bed and the Ocean Floor in 1971. The only actual measure of disarmament was the Biological Weapons Convention of 1972. The Strategic Arms Limitation Agreement of 1972, the 1977 Convention Banning

489

the Military Use of Environmental Modifications Techniques and the signature, though not the ratification, of the second Strategic Arms Limitation Treaty in 1979 were all worthwhile but progress was very disappointing. The arms race continued and easily outstripped the measures to control it, with too many agreements being cosmetic. Apart from the Antarctic there were no new regional arrangements such as the Treaty of Tlatelolco in Latin America and the Non-Proliferation Treaty review Conference of 1980 has been unable to produce a new momentum and build on the findings of the International Nuclear Fuel Cycle Evaluation Report. There is a chance, though a dwindling one, of agreement on the Comprehensive Test Ban negotiations. The French proposal for the establishment of an international satellite monitoring agency, having its own observation satellites, would allow the world community as a whole to participate in the effective verification of arms control agreements. Discussions in the revamped Committee on Disarmament now involve France and China and may be able to achieve more. The Committee has highlighted four major disarmament issues to be covered by working groups: security guarantees for non-nuclear weapon states against nuclear attack, a comprehensive programme of disarmament, the prohibition of radiological weapons and a complete ban on chemical weapons. The use of chemical weapons in wartime is prohibited by the Geneva Protocol of 1925 but it is full of drafting weaknesses and gives scope for varying interpretations which has allowed poison gases to continue to be made for retaliatory purposes and has given rise to dispute over riot control gases such as CS gas. Both the Soviet Union and the US have developed gases that can completely paralyse the human nervous system in a fraction of a second. The fact that the world is poised on the brink of an escalation in manufacture and deployment of these most horrifying weapons should be every bit as much a cause for concern as the build up of nuclear weapons. The growth of anti-satellite weapons and new forms of anti-missile weapons shows the danger we face of the arms race escalating into space.

Other issues for the 1980s are to seek to reverse the lack of progress on limiting sales of conventional arms. Third World countries with scarce resources who purchase arms, as is their sovereign right, are being sold sophisticated weapons by both East and West, with both of them paying too much attention to profit and ignoring the warning of the Brandt Commission when it drew attention to the fact that: 'While the prevention of nuclear war remains the first ambition of disarmament, "conventional" (non-nuclear) weapons account for 80 per cent of all arms spending. In fact all the wars since the Second World War have been fought with conventional weapons, and in the Third World, where they have killed more than ten million people. In some of these wars, such as in Korea and Indochina, the major powers were actively engaged; in others they have been in the background. Some of the most lethal wars have been fought with "small" arms. The Lebanese civil war, for instance, has caused more deaths than all four Arab-Israel wars. The war in Cambodia is an even more tragic example. The North's sales of conventional weapons to the South are increasing. These represent 70 per cent of all arms exports.'[10]

It is inconceivable that the developing countries will ever accept that the rich developed countries should withhold from them their sovereign right to purchase weapons for their own country. That is a recipe for neo-colonialism and has already been resented over the developed world's restrictions on nuclear power technology for developing countries. The developing world concentrates all its political pressure on the nuclear weapons held by the few nuclear weapon states, a vital issue, but not the only issue, or in terms of world development the most important issue. What is needed is an imaginative radical change in the UN over world security issues away from national dominance and towards a new world security order.

Until the sending of Russian troops into Afghanistan, and, a year before, the flying in of large Cuban forces into Ethiopia, there was a growing confidence about the chances of peace in the world. The threat of a war between the major powers appeared to be wildly improbable. It seemed that a mutual fear of nuclear destruction might have ushered in a new era. But we have now seen in the suspension of SALT II and the debate preceding it how a delicate negotiation, arrived at through painstaking effort, can be placed in jeopardy by internal political arguments which a United States President cannot always be certain of controlling, as well as by external events to which a President feels he has to respond.

It is not only political factors which can disturb this balance. Advances in science and technology, whether in the nuclear weapon field or in that of chemical and biological warfare, or the erosion of the Nuclear Non-Proliferation Treaty, could quickly alter significantly many of the political equations. In the case of non-proliferation the Treaty has given us limited respite, but many countries have not signed it and not all who have signed will remain signatories if circumstances do not soon change and if no progress is made towards other disarmament measures. Conflicts keep breaking out with conventional weapons and the last decade has brought danger and destruction in the Middle East, South East Asia and in parts of Africa. These are all reasons why we should not become complacent in the face of the failure to date of the United Nations to handle the problems of world security as we had once hoped, and of the UN Special Session on Disarmament to make significant progress. A new approach to security problems is urgently needed. One such radical new approach was contained in *The Reform of Power*, which though published in 1968 may yet prove to be prophetic of developments in the direction of a safer and more stable world order.

At the time of its publication the book received respectful if guarded reviews, with the expected criticisms of those detailed arguments which disturbed the reviewers' own prejudices. Leonard Beaton's pungent remarks about the defects of the UN and the unreality of the General and Complete Disarmament plans bandied about by the major powers ruffled many feathers. It has also been easy to argue about the difficulties surrounding some of his ideas, such as the proposal to assign national forces to a World Security Authority in much the same way as is done for NATO. But the specialised agencies of the UN such as the World Health Organisation have been a success, in part becase they are staffed by specialist experts, not by diplomats. There are obviously many difficulties over such a proposal in the present uneven world political climate. But none of these detailed criticisms diminishes the force of the basic concept. This is that while it is hopelessly unrealistic to suppose that the Sovereign State is going to disappear in the foreseeable future and that it must therefore be assumed that national security will remain a primary concern of all states, there is none the less a mutual international security interest which is not at present adequately expressed in the form of a functional international institution. As Beaton put it: 'there is a national security interest and a world security interest; both are proper objectives of national policy.'[11]

He therefore proposed the setting-up of a World Security Authority charged by the participating powers with the responsibility of developing and giving substance to their mutual security interests. Some of the obvious candidates for its concern are the strategic arms balance; the non-proliferation of nuclear weapons; the working out of convincing defence guarantees to non-nuclear powers under threat from a nuclear power; and the development of peace-keeping forces to avoid the involvement of major powers in local conflicts.

The precise machinery which would be needed to carry out these functions will require long, detailed debate and negotiation. It would need to be linked to the United Nations Security Council but in a way that would allow it to develop as an authoritative independent body, attracting a dedicated international staff composed of experts in the military, scientific and political field. It is essential that they should be capable of gaining the respect and confidence both of governments with differing ideologies and of world opinion.

In my view it would need to handle much of its work on a regional basis. I doubt whether Latin America or Africa can make a very valuable contribution to the discussion of European security problems – or for that matter that Europe can make much of a contribution to Africa's security problems and I have always opposed the idea of a European intervention force as a relic of colonial attitudes. The Authority should be designed to handle the supervisory elements in all arms control and disarmament agreements. It may well be that to begin with it would be allowed by member states only to handle a number of comparatively minor matters, but as it gained practical experience, as nations came to appreciate its value, and as they became acclimatised to this new way of looking at security problems, it could play an increasingly central role in international affairs.

There may be some scepticism as to whether it would be possible to gain world-wide support for the creation of such a body. Would the Soviet Union, for instance, find it unacceptable? I am not convinced that they could oppose it if it was endorsed by the UN Special Session in 1982. It demands no surrender of sovereignty unless such surrender is willingly accepted by the particular nation itself, as would be the case if international inspection were agreed to verify a disarmament measure. In the present Comprehensive Test Ban negotiations the Soviet Union, the United States and Britain have virtually agreed on the siting of monitoring equipment on their own territory. The Soviet Union, faced by African support for a United Nations Transitional Assistance Group to go to Namibia for UN supervised elections, has not used its veto, nor did they do so over a similar proposal at one stage for Zimbabwe.

Then again the evidence of the SALT talks, the willingness of the USSR to participate in MBFR and the European Security talks, and the co-operation with the USA in working for a ceasefire in the Middle East, all lead to the conviction that most countries, and not least Communist countries, now see the advantage of approaching the subject of world security in a manner which is no longer expressed in simple adversary terms. As an early 1970s' report of the Committee of Nine to the North Atlantic Assembly put it in examining the problems of détente: 'European-American security policy during the next decade means in essence to pursue simultaneously two seemingly contradictory objectives: maintaining an adequate military balance and promoting a détente with an adversary who thereby also becomes a partner.' The partnership concept carries within it tensions inherent in its contradictory objectives, and détente does not mean friendship.

In a world which now possesses a destructive capacity which can turn our planet into a lifeless desert, we have by a mixture of good luck and good judgment so far achieved a rough balance of power which, despite recent events, still makes a major war unlikely. The whole human history and experience tells us, however, that such a period of balance is likely to be short-lived. There are dangerous signs now that could be the signal for an irreversible deterioration. We ought to seize this moment of pessimism and fear to create a world system which would attempt to ensure that the inevitable fluctuations in the power equation will be handled rationally and peacefully. The path Leonard Beaton proposed, with modifications, represents the best and possibly the only hope for achieving a warless world. As he says: 'The way forward is to create a central professional military organisation to discover where the common security interest is and to administer it. Such an organisation may eventually help to widen the area of concerted action but it should not depend for its creation on a pre-existing alliance relationship. A certain concert of the powers is needed, for example, to operate the International Civil Aviation Organisation. Without such a concert, world aviation would be impossible. But this mutually valuable technical objective does not depend on dedication to perfect amity; nor has it required governments to concede ultimate control over their own air space. There was a common interest to be served; it required specialized technical skills; and the necessary organisation was created in common to solve the common problems.

'Once such an organisation had come into existence in the security field and governments knew its working and understood its character, its responsibilities would expand to the extent that governments identified common security interests. In any one period that might be very much or very little, depending on the skill with which the institutions were managed and on the political climate in the world. No doubt there would be periods when the system would do well to survive and continue to discharge its most pressing obligations. But as in federal states, there would be a natural tendency for power to accumulate at the point at which problems could most easily be solved. All the evidence is that on the great security issues this would be at the centre.

'A chess board is either black with white squares or white with black squares. In going from one to another, the board need not be changed at all. The powers similarly are now organised on a sovereign basis with international arrangements. They could go over to an international system with sovereign arrangements with no essential alteration in their present capacity to defend themselves and their allies. But they could create the technical and military context and perhaps the political conditions in which their common servants could achieve the common object of severely limiting or even abolishing war which may otherwise elude them.'[12]

The inertia in many areas of disarmament stems from the negotiators becoming firmly bureaucratic and institutionalised.[13] Progress depends on consensus – the military have an inbuilt caution expressed in the doctrine that 'everything must be balanced and simultaneous' – so movement is very slow. Step-by-step changes with a political impetus offer a much greater chance of progress, and the risks of this have to be offset against the risks of continuing as we do at present. The problem is that each country or group of countries is hesitant to make the first move. We are in danger of being inhibited by the wish to march in step towards disarmament and no one is prepared to be the first to break ranks. To achieve movement towards disarmament governments must be prepared at times to take the initiative as part of a coherent strategy to achieve momentum in all multilateral negotiating forums. It is the emphasis on large unilateral steps, divorced from the context of any multilateral negotiation, which is unrealistic.

Protest and Survive was right to argue that 'deterrence is not a stationary state'; it must be buttressed by constant negotiations for peace, but they must be real negotiations based on bargains, nor just on concessions. Deterrence, however, need not be a 'degenerative state'; certainly no more of a degenerative state than the spectre of unilateral disarmament would be – undertaken for the best of motives but achieving no response. Eventually this would lead to a vulnerable state where freedom is threatened and the choice is subjugation or war.

The task in the 1980s is to prevent an appalling conclusion similar to the failure of the 1930s. The need for peace should be a driving ambition for every politician. Its morality needs no elaboration. Yet sincere people differ over how peace can best be guaranteed. Pacifism is a belief, often carried with great conviction, but history warns against believing too easily in the good intentions of other nations, particularly those who have different political ideologies from our own. Sadly, to ensure peace we have to be prepared to defend ourselves and our country. The task for socialists is to spend on defence only what is necessary and to strive constantly to reduce the levels of armament worldwide and to creat a mood of greater confidence and trust between nations. In a nuclear age to protest is understandable, to protect is inevitable, but only if we negotiate will we survive.

20

The Community of Twelve

Predictably, the early years of British membership of the European Community have been full of difficulties. These have been essentially part of the adjustment process which faces every member state on accession but they have been magnified by our size and complicated by our history. Some people argue that the lost opportunity was in not participating from the outset in the creation of the Community. In retrospect, however, it can be seen that no British politician could have persuaded the British public to accept the necessary commitment at the Messina Conference in 1956; and historians will probably conclude that it was necessary for the building of the European Community that it started only with the original six continental countries.

The first essential priority was to build up Franco-German understanding, an outstanding achievement which could not have been so completely successful without the framework of Community membership. General de Gaulle's veto on British entry in 1962 was not as unfortunate for the Community or for Britain as some have portrayed it. It was in fact a perceptive calculation, a mixture of national self-interest and European vision that led de Gaulle to the conclusion that France had to establish herself more firmly, economically and politically, and the federalist tendency within the Community be more clearly destroyed, before France and in part the Community itself would be able to withstand the difficulties of absorbing British membership. In 1970 President Pompidou correctly saw that as Prime Minister Edward Heath had the political

498

resolution that would be needed for Britain's entry and judged that the time had come – which some believe General de Gaulle had always envisaged would come – when Britain's entry had become inevitable. Understandably France and the other member states, fearing British industrial competition, attempted to safeguard their own interests and the terms negotiated by Britain were recognised even at the time to have been tough.

The hard-headed view in 1972 – supported by subsequent events – was that Britain could improve the terms and that, since the Community is in a state of permanent negotiation, there would be every chance for the deal to be improved. No one could predict whether or not Britain's industry would find and develop new export opportunities but it was clear this was going to be a major problem for Britain in or out of the Community. Our access to traditional Commonwealth markets was becoming increasingly limited and if we could not sell into the Community it was not unreasonable to ask where we would be able to sell our goods. Since 1972, the year before Britain's entry to the EEC, our trade with the other eight member states has increased to represent nearly half of our total exports. In 1972 34 per cent of our total visible imports came from the EEC, while by 1979 the proportion had risen to 45 per cent, and in 1980 the proportion was still rising. In 1972 30 per cent of our exports went to the other member states and by 1979 it had reached 42 per cent. In the first six months of 1980 43 per cent of our visible exports went to EEC countries and we bought from them 41 per cent of our total imports, this dramatic improvement owing much to our cutback in consumer spending. On any analysis the European Community was by October 1980 the most important market for Britain.

The 1980s will see major changes in the European Community and many of these changes can be made to help Britain's position in the Community. It can certainly be argued that a combination of British reluctance to pursue her own interests single-mindedly, plus a widespread feeling among the original Six that the three newcomers simply had to accept the Community as it had always been, made it difficult for some essential changes – such as reform of the Common

Agricultural Policy – to be pushed through. But it is now clear that, without radical reform, the CAP, already responsible for a large percentage of Community resources, will push the Community into bankruptcy as the member states refuse to increase their VAT contributions. Hitherto attempts by the incoming Three, Britain, Denmark and Ireland, to seek changes in any aspect of the Community have been resisted by the Six on the grounds that new members had to play by the rules, they could either leave or have a special 'second-class' or 'two-tier' membership. There always was a reluctance among some of the original Six to accept that a Community of Nine was more than the original Six plus Three – and the whole Community had to evolve together. The Community of Ten – with the addition of Greece – will also have to face that its character will change. The Community of Twelve will present an even greater challenge, which is starting to emerge as Spain and Portugal's negotiations begin to throw up practical problems that need resolution. The Spanish membership in particular will force a reappraisal of the Common Agricultural Policy. Spain needs to import some agricultural products, particularly milk and dairy products, which are in surplus in the northern part of the Community, so Spanish membership is in the interests of a number of members. It will thereby have a beneficial effect on such an obvious scandal as the 'butter mountain'. But at the same time, Spain's own agricultural sector produces, often working in small units, wine, grapes, tomatoes and peaches which are already produced by the 'Mediterranean' members of the Community, Italy, France and Greece. Without radical reform the Common Agricultural Policy cannot hope to support Spanish agriculture financially. The existing basis will have to change. The French, who will become net contributors to the EEC Budget, may well suddenly switch and become the advocates of national support for agriculture, having benefited hitherto from Community support. In the new German coalition the stranglehold on agricultural policy of Herr Ertl, the FDP's Agricultural Minister, which was so dominant in the 1970s will be modified by the acceptance of the need for changes by both parties in the 1980 election. The justifications of the Common Agricultural Policy has been that it helps to support poor farmers and to save sectors of the agricultural economy that would otherwise collapse into ruin and unemployment. No socialist should unthinkingly decry this contribution, which has had a vital social purpose in some of the continental countries and has also been a factor for political stability. But many of these social objectives could be better achieved, not through the blunt and wasteful instrument of the Common Agricultural Policy, but through a combination of national support under conditions to prevent distortion and of imaginative use of the regional fund to help with restructuring the agricultural industry, just as the regional fund, if it were expanded, could satisfy British needs in areas of industrial dereliction. No one can deny that for some time there will be a continued need to provide social assistance to poor farmers on the continent. The renegotiation of the British budgetary arrangements will come up in 1982; the Common Agricultural Policy will have to be in part at least restructured by then, and at the very latest by the time of Spanish accession, which may possibly be delayed until 1984. Britain must ensure that she is not excluded from the Franco-German axis and that a triad develops which could shape the identity of the Community of Twelve. Despite the gloom and the pessimism and lack of confidence about Britain's role in Europe, the opportunities for fundamental change from within are likely to be immense in the 1980s. The derisory election result which the Labour Party deservedly earned in the 1980 European Assembly elections is a warning against believing that the electorate is attracted by the obstructive unilateralist approach to Community negotiations. The electorate well understands what any trade unionist knows: that a government which goes to Brussels merely to obstruct and block is unlikely to bring home much from such negotiations. The NEC draft Manifesto for the 1979 Assembly election was ill judged in tone and in content; so much so that even anti-market candidates virtually disowned or ignored the wording. A straight withdrawal ticket in the next election will obviously win support with a sizeable part of the electorate but it will also mean that many longstanding socialists when faced by the choice – withdrawal and vote Labour, or abstain or vote for another party – will not vote Labour. Anyhow by October 1983, the earliest likely time for the election, the Community's problems may be such that reform will have been already forced upon it. The 1981 budget has been savagely criticised by the European Parliament for increasing agricultural aid while cutting back on social and regional expenditure – a measure which, even though it was estimated to increase British food prices by 4 per cent, was supported, in addition to France and Germany, by the British government. The European Parliament has been united in its opposition to the whole budget procedure, and the crisis has led to a political crisis between the parliament and the Commission. The real crisis will come, however, when the Council of Ministers is faced with demands for extra funds because the 1 per cent VAT ceiling no longer meets the Community's requirements. Out of crisis will come change – substantive and long overdue change – and all the member states will negotiate toughly to protect their essential interests. But British interests are in this situation majority interests. We are no longer urging reform in a minority of one. All member states know the Community is grossly over-extended in the field of agricultural support and that it must face the need to reassert Europe's manufacturing interests and put a far higher priority than hitherto on industrial investment to provide employment. The United States non-oil investment in Britain was only 22 per cent in 1972 of their Community investment, yet it was 33 per cent by 1976 and 50 per cent by 1980.

It is almost incomprehensible why against such a back-ground in October 1980 the Labour Party Conference passed, by a two-thirds majority, Resolution 15 which urged the Labour Party 'to include the withdrawal of the United Kingdom from the European Community as a priority in the next General Election Manifesto'. Not only did the NEC, predict-ably, rule out a referendum of the British people before withdrawal but so did Peter Shore, speaking on his own authority without any consultation with the Parliamentary Committee. So within five years the Party which had, in 1975, given the British people the chance to determine their own destiny, had decided that a Labour government would come into office committed to withdraw. It is important to trace the background to this development in order to see the extent to which recent pretensions to being a Party committed to widening democracy are sincere, or whether the European Community is being used as a front for the manipulation of the power struggle within the Party. This means quoting what politicians have actually said, and some need to be quoted in detail.

At the 1962 Labour Party Conference Hugh Gaitskell put all his new-found authority, as the leader who had at the last Conference in 1961 reversed the 1960 Conference commitment on unilateralism, against the case for British entry into the European Community. Whatever the merits or otherwise of the detailed arguments, Gaitskell's opposition at least ensured that the issue could not become a Left/Right issue within the Labour Party.

His biographer objectively sums up Hugh Gaitskell's position: 'He shared neither the Commonwealth illusion of a few anti-Marketeers, nor their opponents' worry that the great opportunity, once missed, might never return. He always thought that a negative in 1962 might have to be reconsidered if circumstances changed, and never believed those changes would make reconsideration impossible. Some Marketeers feared that Britain would never again want to join because the Community would have moved so fast towards unification that Britain could never catch up; but Gaitskell saw that de Gaulle would prevent that development (enabling many other unenthusiastic Europeans to escape the blame for obstructing it). Other Marketeers feared that Britain would decline economically outside the Community, who therefore would not welcome her in; but Gaitskell never attributed European economic growth to the Market, and always believed that domestic developments would depend on domestic decisions – notably the quality of British political leadership, and the response to it of the British people.'[1]

The Common Market ceased to be a dominant issue in British politics after de Gaulle's veto and hardly became an issue in either the 1964 or 1966 General Elections. The next watershed in the Labour Party's attitude to the EEC came in

May 1967 when in the House of Commons 260 Labour MPs voted for Britain to apply to join the Community and thirty-five Labour MPs voted against. In 1970 Labour's Manifesto *Now Britain's Strong, Let's Make It Great To Live In*, said, 'we have applied for membership of the European Economic Community and negotiations are due to start in a few weeks' time. These will be pressed with determination with the purpose of joining an enlarged Community provided that British and essential Commonwealth interests can be safeguarded.' On 28 October 1971, 365 MPs, among them 69 Labour MPs, voted to join the European Communities on the basis of the government's White Paper, while 244 voted against, among them 39 Conservatives and Ulster Unionist MPs. In the four-day debate many MPs spoke, and I put my views before the House of Commons in the following words: 'I do not believe that it will be a painless period when we enter the Community. I believe that a good deal of the propaganda in favour of the Common Market, particularly on the economic issues, has been slanted and unrealistic. I do not wish any of my constituents to think that in advocating entry to the Community I am offering them automatic prosperity. But I do believe that a radical party, a party that wishes to see change, should not be afraid of accepting challenges, and I believe, as the best judgment I can make, that the economic advantages of Britain's entering are likely to emerge progressively over the years.

'I freely admit that the terms are not ideal. I believe my right hon. Friends would have achieved better terms, but the issue is whether we should reject the concept of European unity. When I talk about European unity, I am talking in part about our concept of nationalism and internationalism. I find that one of the most dangerous facets of modern life and, indeed, of our history over the last 50 years is the scar of nationalism. I believe in internationalism as an article of faith. Of course that means that one gives up sovereignty, and a lot of the debate in this House has been focused upon sovereignty, and rightly so, because this is a central matter to many of the people who fundamentally do not wish us to go into Europe. They do not wish to give up any measure of sovereignty, and the debate today on regional policy has shown the reluctance of hon.

Members to give up power from this House; they do not wish to give up any power that we exercise as a nation and put ourselves into the decision structure of other nations because it involves compromise. It involves not always getting one's own way. It is, however, foolish to try to sell the concept of the EEC and not admit that this means giving up some sovereignty. Of course it does, and I believe it rightly does. I believe this is one of the central appeals of it.'[2]

Three weeks earlier I had faced a reselection conference after boundary changes for the new Devonport Constituency in Plymouth and I had felt it right to warn the GMC before they voted to adopt me as their candidate that I intended to vote for British entry and to do so despite a three line Whip to vote against. I do not regret to this day that decision to vote for British membership of the Community. I believe that vote was a true manifestation of parliamentary democracy where MPs exercised their judgment of what was in the best interests of the country – some suffered the penalty for exercising that constitutional right, some were not re-adopted, others faced major problems in their constituency. There is no way that that can be prevented if an MP goes against the democratic decision-making of his own party, but the fact that on both sides of the House of Commons Conservatives as well as Labour MPs chose freely what they felt was the right course demonstrated the strength and health of parliamentary democracy.

On 10 April 1972 I resigned as junior Opposition spokesman on Defence when Roy Jenkins, Harold Lever and George Thomson resigned after the Shadow Cabinet first rejected, then accepted, a referendum, though I had privately argued against resigning and in favour of fighting to win a referendum. In both the General Elections in 1974 the Labour Party in the Manifesto promised a referendum on the terms that would emerge from the attempt at renegotiation. On Thursday, 5 June 1975, 17,378,581 people – 67·2 per cent – voted 'Yes' to stay in the Community and 8,470,073 people – 32·8 per cent – voted 'No'. All the regions of the United Kingdom voted 'Yes' except the Western Isles and the Shetland Islands. The *Guardian* described the result as, fullhearted, wholehearted and cheerful hearted. Tony Benn said, 'I have just been in receipt of a very big message from the British people. I read it loud and clear.' It is a strange rewriting of history that by 1980 on the eve of the Labour Party Conference at Blackpool, Peter Shore could refer to that same referendum as 'persuading a sullen and bemused nation to vote against their instinct and their interest'. There was no sullenness or bemusement. Some, undoubtedly, now regret their decision but the result at the time was a true reflection of public opinion.

The European referendum came about because of Tony Benn's advocacy that the Labour Party should choose this as the preferable way of dealing with the issue. In fairness it is clear that this was not a sudden decision taken opportunistically in 1971. In 1968 when he was Minister of Technology he argued in favour of the British application to join the EEC and predicted in Bonn in February that year that 'the political opposition to our membership will be ineffective because the nationalistic arguments upon which it is based are becoming increasingly irrelevant'.[3] In May 1978 at Llandudno Tony Benn began to argue about the desirability of referenda though not specifically relating it to the EEC, but as a way of sharing responsibility with the electorate. In November 1970, in a letter to his constituents, Tony Benn argued the case in detail for a referendum on British entry to the European Community, well before the issue became a Left/Right issue inside the Party: 'But would an election fought on the Common Market help very much? If both parties were in favour there would be no choice offered to the public. And if one party was opposed to it this would not be a good way of reaching such an important decision. In some constituencies there would be candidates from both main Parties who were personally in favour; and in others candidates who were personally opposed which would deny to many electors the right to make their voice heard. Moreover it would be quite wrong to expect a life-long supporter of one party who deeply believed in its philosophy and policy to vote for the other party just because he or she agreed with them on the Common Market issue. No General Election could allow people to record a separate vote on the Common Market question. This has not only to do with whether the terms are good or bad. There are both Labour and Conservative voters who on political grounds wouldn't want Britain to join the Common Market even if you could prove conclusively that they would be far better off financially if we did join. And there are also people who would still think it politically desirable even though it did mean higher prices and a lot of painful changes in the short run. It is for these reasons that we have got to consider the use of a unique mechanism to help us reach a unique decision. The case for a referendum on the question of Britain's entry is, in my opinion, immensely powerful if not overwhelming. If people are not to participate in this decision, no one will ever take participation seriously again.'[4] All these arguments apply with equal relevance in the 1980s, but in addition there is the fact that the referendum once having been conceded on this specific issue it is peculiarly hard to justify its abandonment.

What is interesting about Tony Benn's advocacy of the referendum in his 1970 letter is that he accompanied it by a statement of his own position which shows that not only was he in favour in principle then of entry, though later he was against the terms negotiated, which is a question of judgment – but he had also changed his position by 1979 over parliamentary sovereignty as well, which is a question of principle. 'In the post-war years I was very hostile to the idea of a Common Market. I did not like the strong anti-Russian cold war bias that lay behind it, since the reconciliation between the Communist world and the West seemed, and still seems, to me to be at least as important as the reconciliation between France and Germany. I was afraid that the EEC would be inward-looking with no interest in the developing world and would forever be dominated by Conservative forces. None of these fears now seem to be so justified. Willy Brandt's Eastern policy and rapprochement with the USSR is of great significance. One other factor which changed my view was the enormous growth of international companies which are now, in many cases, bigger than nations and growing more rapidly. If man, as man, does not organise himself into bigger political units the international companies will run the world and we shall be like

Parish Councillors in our Parliaments with little say in what happens. Big power requires big politics if little people are to be protected. The world is so small that Britain alone cannot separate itself from world influence nor prevent its destiny being affected by what happens abroad. Nor should we suppose that merely joining the EEC will solve all our problems for us. It will not. Of course we can stay out and stand alone, but we will still find that European, American and Russian decisions will set the framework within which we would have to exercise our formal parliamentary sovereignty.'[5]

In 1970 Tony Benn could still talk sensibly about the reality of our formal parliamentary sovereignty. The most depressing aspect of the argument about British membership of the Community was by 1979 the way the Left had absorbed much of the xenophobic language and narrow nationalism of the more traditionally minded anti-marketeers. In 1963 Tony Benn was one of the most trenchant critics of this type of attitude when he wrote that : 'the idea of Britain joining the Common Market is emotionally very attractive. To throw open our windows to new influences, to help shape the destiny of a new community, even to merge our sovereignty in a wider unit – these offer an exciting prospect. By contrast the xeno-phobic, parochial delusions of grandeur fostered by the Beaverbrook press appear petty, old-fashioned, and reaction-ary. But the issue must not be decided by either of these emotions. A political decision of this magnitude calls for a cold, hard examination by each of us of what is involved.'[6]

Against such sentiments, which at least set criticism of the Community in genuine internationalist context, it is very hard to understand why the issue of parliamentary sovereignty should have become such a dominant issue with Tony Benn and others on the Left. In 1979 he had so aligned himself with the arguments used so often by Enoch Powell, Michael Foot and Peter Shore that he actualy sponsored the European Communities (Amendment) Bill, which sought to amend the 1972 European Communities Act. The Manifesto commitment in the May 1979 General Election, however, only said, 'The Labour Government will legislate to ensure that British Ministers are accountable to the House of Commons before making any commitment in the Council of Ministers. Enlargement of the Community will provide the opportunity for seeking changes in the Treaty of Rome, which would enable the House of Commons to strengthen its powers to amend or repeal EEC legislation. This would involve consequential amendments to the 1972 European Communities Act.' As Foreign Secretary, I had opposed that commitment in the Clause 5 meeting between the Cabinet and the NEC. I was in a minority of one when I raised fears that its tentative reference to Treaty amendment would eventually be firmed up to become a unilateral commitment, not, as stated, something which could arise out of negotiated multilateral changes in the Treaty of Rome as a result of enlargement. It was therefore no surprise to find this statement progressively tightened up as soon as we lost the election. The document adopted by the 1980 Wembley Special Conference had a firm commitment to 'amend the 1972 European Communities Act so as to restore to the House of Commons the full control of all law-making and tax-gathering powers now ceded to the European Communities'. This wording was then included in the NEC draft Manifesto. Tactically the strategy of Peter Shore and Michael Foot has been clear for some time; it is only to ask for a Manifesto commitment to amend the Act and then to be free to arrange to withdraw without a referendum. This strategy was upset by the pressure from John Silkin and others in 1980 for withdrawal to be included in the Manifesto. This made the issue much sharper, and of course forced the question of a referendum back on to the agenda. The traditionalists like Enoch Powell whose objection to the European Community is rooted in their attitude to parliamentary sovereignty have never liked referenda. The Blackpool Conference decision commits the Party to total withdrawal in the Manifesto. At present Peter Shore and Michael Foot are keeping to amendment of the European Communities Act and presenting this as a lesser option than withdrawal. They have been joined by Denis Healey who would probably hope to be able to finesse the issue away by negotiation and not use the power that amendment of the Act gives in such a disruptive way that it would lead to withdrawal. There are, however, immense dangers in going along with a commitment to amend the Act unilaterally and for anyone who is seriously interested in staying within the Community there is only one credible strategy: that of multilateral improvement, whereby change comes first from negotiation and co-operation, and the legislative power to take unilateral action is taken only as and when necessary as part of the overall negotiating strategy. This was the approach agreed by the Labour Cabinet in an all-day meeting in the summer of 1977 and outlined in some detail to the Labour Party in the published letter to Ron Hayward by the then Prime Minister, James Callaghan, in September before the Annual Conference.

The case for multilateral improvement is that already using this method Britain has changed some of the arrangements in the Community which were against our interests. After four years of attrition by 1981 we can claim to have forced the majority of the member states to recognise that the Agricultural Policy must be changed. Nor should we underestimate the changes taking place within the political system of many of the member states: the Left is becoming more radical and restive with the Community as recession bites in all member states. The German SPD is now taking reform very seriously and promised reforms in Community structures during their 1980 elections. British socialists are not the only ones in Europe arguing for a redistributive budget affecting all member states. On questions of trade and industry, and particularly as far as selective import controls and managed trade are concerned, the policy of many member states is changing and particularly that of their socialist parties. The document agreed by the Labour Party and the TUC in the summer of 1980, *Trade and Industry: A Policy for Expansion*, with its emphasis on controlling import penetration, is compatible with membership of the Community – provided that any government shows a willingness to negotiate with others, and does not simply put its wishes down on the table as an ultimatum, and recognises that in any multilateral deal concessions will have to be made on some issues to gain essential demands.

As unemployment rises in the other member states there is already a more receptive climate for challenging the status quo on trading policy. This is happening particularly in the Benelux countries, usually the most reluctant to make any movement away from the traditional Commission interpretation of the Treaty. Socialists in the Dutch Labour Party, the PvdA, are becoming much more critical of the Community; the same is occurring in Belgium where the socialist-orientated trade union, FGTB, is showing a readiness to consider new initiatives. The German trade union confederation, the DGB, has long pressed for a more active use of the social fund and as the economic downturn affects the German economy they too are now pushing much harder than in the past for industrial and social reforms. In France the CGT and the CFDT are already campaigning for changes in the Community's industrial policies as are some in the Socialist Party. In Italy, with a large state sector in industry, even right-wing coalition governments often support arguments for greater freedom for state inter-vention and less interference from the Commission. Within the Socialist Party, PSI, and, to some extent in the Italian Communist Party, there are voices arguing for more funda-mental change, such as the largest union in Italy, the CGIL.

It is nonsense to believe that only in Britain is there to be found a desire to change the Community. On the sensitive issue of political union there is unanimity between the French and the British in resisting federalism, with the Gaullists and the Communists being rather firmer on this issue than the French Socialist Party. This operates as an effective blocking mechanism. In Denmark the Social Democrats are quite explicit about national sovereignty and want their parliament, the *Folketing*, to be able to control all important Community decisions. In Britain parliament can easily do this if it shows the will and it does not need an amendment to the 1972 European Communities Act. A very well-developed parlia-mentary committee system such as the Danes have, where Ministers discuss their negotiating position in private well in advance of adopting a position in the Council of Ministers, is a sensible compromise in balancing the need for parliamentary control and yet freedom to negotiate without one's tactical position being known to other member states. There is, too, a small but vocal Left socialist party in Denmark which is opposed to the Community. The main Greek opposition party, PASOK, is socialist and hostile to the Community and will be a force for change even if they do not form the government at the next election. A socialist government in Britain which had established good relations with other socialist parties in Europe, but which nevertheless was prepared to negotiate toughly, would be able to form shifting alliances with socialist groupings and other governments on different issues and would rarely be speaking and voting alone on any of the major reforms advocated by British socialists whether for or against the EEC.

The unilateral approach on the other hand rejects co-operation and negotiation. Its advocates have varying motives. The main thrust has come from those who are hostile not simply to the terms but to the whole concept of Community. This is the Enoch Powell, Michael Foot approach. Peter Shore expressed it in a meeting on the eve of the October 1980 Conference, 'The heart of the matter, the bone in the throat, is precisely the power that the Westminster parliament has ceded to the European institutions, the powers that are the birthright of the British people; powers that permit the Commission, the Council of Ministers, the European Court to impose their legislation, to levy their taxes, to adjudicate on all disputes between us and them that arise within the wide ranging ambit of the Treaties we signed.' A similar approach to the Community comes in Enoch Powell's words. He wrote in the *Spectator* in October 1980 depicting membership of the Community as being, 'to swear allegiance to a Europeanism that is incompatible with the existence of the United Kingdom as a free, parliamentary nation.' There are many arguments against the European Community but for socialists to identify with Right-wing nationalists and to advocate national sovereignty as the core reason for opposition is a perversion of every internationalist sentiment that socialism has ever stood for. The depressing feature of the current position of the Labour Party is that so many people are content to go along with the sovereignty argument by endorsing as a tactical position the amending of the 1972 European Communities Act. As a lever to be used on a specific issue in negotiations, no one can deny the possible need to amend the Act. It could have been necessary, for example, in 1979 or in 1980, in order to withhold VAT payments when the Budget contribution negotiations were stalled. To amend the Act for its own sake is, however, to take the power to withdraw from the Community, without actually stating clearly to the electorate that withdrawal will happen, just that it might happen. It is potentially a backdoor method of leaving and ought to be recognised as such. It is absolutely consistent with the fundamentalists' objection to the Community and also their tactical position that the advocates of this strategy reject a referendum. They want to take the legislative power to withdraw in a Manifesto, but for parliament alone to decide whether to withdraw. It is a strategy which had constitutional propriety on its side prior to the 1975 referendum. But the right to a referendum having been granted, it would be a constitutional outrage to do anything other than either to fight an election on a clear Manifesto commitment to withdraw, or to offer the right to a referendum before taking any decision to withdraw. A referendum was endorsed by the TUC Conference in 1980 and this may be accepted by the Labour Party, but even this is a depressing recipe for a mix of hesitant hostility to continue towards the European Community for a number of years, when we could be contributing constructively with our fellow socialists.

It was unfortunate but not all that surprising that after the transitional period had expired in 1977 the financial contribution that Britain made to the European Community became the most visible sign of economic imbalance, with Britain as the largest contributor in 1979. This was widely judged by all shades of political opinion in Britain to be unjust and intolerable. Those in Britain who always argued that entry was against our interests fairly claimed that their predictions on this issue had been fulfilled. Those who argued that the terms, though not ideal, still justified entry, believed that the Community would honour the pledge it gave Britain that 'if unacceptable situations should arise, the very survival of the Community would demand that the institution find equitable solutions'. The financial adjustment negotiated in 1980 goes some way towards honouring that pledge, but there is much more that needs to be achieved. The negotiations over Britain's financial contribution started under the Labour government in 1978 in the European Council of Heads of Government held at Bremen, continued at the next Council in Brussels and again at the meeting in early 1979 in Paris. They were continued by the new government at the European Council meeting at Strasbourg, then at Dublin and an interim arrangement virtually settled at the spring meeting in Brussels in 1980. Mrs Thatcher negotiated toughly and well – apart from lifting the farm price freeze which was central to the carefully constructed negotiating position inherited from the Labour government in the summer of 1979. That mistake, for which the Foreign Office was largely responsible, led to the débâcle in Dublin. Britain had no leverage and the issue had to be postponed until the farm price review came round again in 1980.

During those three years spanning Labour and Conservative governments a distinctive and new strand of opinion emerged in Britain, a determination to fight for essential British interests without worrying too much if this caused ill-feeling among our European partners. It was the view which I presented to the Labour Cabinet in its all-day review of EEC policy in the summer of 1977, and though the Labour government was criticised for fighting abrasively for reform of the Community from within, it was a popular policy in the Labour Party and in the country. This tough view was, after an initial and unreal honeymoon period, also adopted by Mrs Thatcher in the autumn of 1979. It was a view that the Foreign Office resented and resisted. It was a policy that was firm; that Britain should remain a full member of the Community, should take no interest in two-tier membership or association but should be tough and resolute in asserting Britain's rights as a full member, in the correct belief that Britain had been hesitant and weak in upholding its legitimate interests during the early years of membership: it was perhaps inevitable that this stance should have started to emerge only after the referendum in 1975, and to have built up steadily after the transitional period ended in 1977.

A Britain determined but not destructive can contribute positively to the Community, but there has to be give and take and North Sea oil is a potential negotiating lever. Member states such as Germany and France want to be able to rely on purchasing North Sea oil; with imagination Britain could use a tough depletion policy to ensure that during the middle 1980s any surplus oil production over and above that which gives us self sufficiency is either kept in the ground or is stored as strategic reserve available for the Community as a whole. This would be an imaginative policy combining both self-interest and Community solidarity. The Community as a whole is weakened if any member state feels a deep sense of injustice. It was vital to fight for a fair financial contribution and risk inflaming a bitter and dissatisfied public, only too ready to blame all its ills on the Community because some of its ills were related to Community membership. It would be foolish to deny that a critical stance carries with it considerable dangers. It could still lead to a progressive isolation of Britain within the Community; it has probably contributed to the development of anti-EEC feeling in the country and in parliament, but this should not be exaggerated. Most of the key figures who oppose the Community in the Labour Party have never accepted the result of the referendum. They will never want negotiations to succeed. Those who genuinely want Britain's membership of the Community to succeed must stick to a firm negotiating strategy.

In terms of Budget contributions the Community must be based on fairness rather than equality if it is to remain viable. The value of membership cannot and should not be weighed only in arithmetical terms. But a realistic minimum for the medium term viability of any member state's membership is that there should not be a deep sense of injustice within any state over its financial contributions. Given that economic convergence between the economies of the member states is so elusive, and likely to remain so, there is a limit to the tolerance of divergence from the mean for each member state. Such a principle was alluded to in Britain's initial negotiation and formalised in the financial mechanism agreed in Dublin in 1975. Because of the effect of North Sea oil on our balance of payments this mechanism proved to be inadequate since it could not be triggered while we were in surplus. Past experience of the Community indicates that after the 1980 agreement, perhaps some time around 1983, Britain will again negotiate a mechanism which prevents us, as the seventh smallest GNP of the Community of Ten, becoming again a major contributor to the Community Budget. Another limit to the tolerance of divergence from the mean relates to the import-export ratios for any member state in their overall trading relations but including intra-Community trade with other member states. The question is only just emerging as an issue – in Britain it is the source of much of the anti-Community economic opposition. As the recession bites, however, socialists and economists in the Community are seeing that it will be as much an issue of major concern for them as it is for us in Britain.

As a result, again, of the differing economic strengths between the member states it is quite possible for the balance between imports and exports to become so wide that some voluntary arrangement for restraining imports, even from other member states, will become necessary. There is nothing in the Treaty of Rome to prevent a reasonable measure of protectionism being applied within the Community, nothing in the Treaty which precludes the sensible application of selective import controls as a result of give-and-take and negotiations. Reason dictates that there must be a level of import penetration which is simply intolerable for any member state, and an adjustment mechanism for restraining a marked imbalance is again a realistic minimum for the viability of any member state's membership. It is no answer to such an issue to invoke the sanctity of market forces. It is absurd how little recognition is given by the anti-market socialists in Britain to the fact that the Community is already strongly protectionist in many sectors. While Britain rightly complains about the Common Agricultural Policy, urging radical reform, yet we use the Monetary Compensation mechanism to tax imports of food which increases our food costs while protecting our own agricultural industry. Other member states find this very illogical. The Community was initially called the Common

Market but there has never been an absolute free market in agricultural products and while that remains, as it will, it is impossible to argue in logic that there must be an absolute free market at all times in all industrial products. The 1980s will demonstrate that the UK is better able to take selective protectionist action within the framework of the Community than by acting alone, that there is less risk of retaliation and that the Community is able to be the main vehicle for a policy of selective import controls. This is therefore an area where British socialists should be combining with European socialists to challenge some of the free market theologians in the Commission for not everyone in the Commission is against selective action, or managing trade. Yet it must be done in the full recognition of one of the Brandt Report's most easily forgotten recommendation that 'the North should reverse the present trend towards protecting its industries against competition from the Third World and promote instead a process of positive, anticipatory restructuring. Industrial adjustment policies affect other countries closely and should be subject to international consultation and surveillance.'

In 1980 the French government banned sheep imports and defied the Community's highest legal court to make it clear that a certain import level was intolerable for them. The French were prepared to assert their national interest, to defy the Community rules even in the agricultural sector which gives them substantial benefit. It was perhaps unwise for us to make an issue of principle out of the lamb restrictions; for Britain may need to take similar restrictions against other member states' imports covering some sensitive products for our own economy, probably in the industrial sector. In any Community it is preferable for all forms of import restrictions to be negotiated and not imposed unilaterally. Britain has a strong interest in developing the concept of what the French government call 'orderly marketing arrangements'. In the 1980s the European Community must grapple realistically with the issue of trade imbalance.

It is obviously easier to handle import restraint if it concerns extra-Community trading patterns such as are emerging over Japan; but it may be necessary to cover intra-Community trading patterns as well. Otherwise we shall increasingly rely on a whole series of covert restrictions which seek to circumvent market forces and this will undermine the spirit of the free market within the member states of the Community. Many Community member states have already made bilateral agreements with Japan to limit Japanese import penetration, with special arrangements covering steel, shipbuilding, computer technology, textiles and cars. An informal restriction over Japanese cars has operated in Britain since 1975 and has been modestly successful: Japanese imports in 1975 represented 9 per cent of the UK market, while in 1979, despite a rise in overall car imports from 33 per cent to 56 per cent, the Japanese share was just under 11 per cent, imports from other EEC countries having risen from 20 per cent to 38 per cent and those from other countries from approximately 4 per cent to 7 per cent. The EEC is nevertheless facing a mounting trade deficit with Japan. In the first half of 1980 it was 4.8 billion dollars, and it was likely to be a total deficit of 8 billion dollars for the whole year. Japanese car exports to the EEC in the first half of 1980 grew by 23 per cent in volume and 10 per cent in value in comparison with the first half of 1979 and it was the other member states who suffered the most penetration. France's increase was 58 per cent and Germany's 31 per cent. The EEC sold very few cars in Japan during the first half of 1980 and overall imports from the EEC fell by 2 per cent in value. There will be growing pressure in the early 1980s for the EEC to take action to limit Japanese imports and that pressure will not come from the United Kingdom alone.

In the 1980s the British government may have to choose either to give up supporting British Leyland financially or to negotiate temporary import ceilings to limit car import growth, not only from Japan and other countries but also from our fellow member states, such as Germany, France and Italy, who present for the United Kingdom a more difficult problem than Japan. There is not much difference in principle between the French action on sheep imports and possible British action over car imports. The question of import penetration in sensitive sectors may face other Community countries as the economic recession deepens. All the economies of the Nine moved deeper into recession in 1980 and unemployment is rising in all the countries. Greece, which joined the Community as a full member in 1981, has no economic growth. Spain, a highly protected industrial market, will face special difficulties in the middle 1980s when it becomes members of the Community. One can expect initially a total rejection of import restraint from the Commission, and, judged by past attitudes, resistance from the Federal Republic of Germany will be strong because import restraint is clearly not in their interests, at least for the time being. But as the recession begins to make an impact the case for action to protect gathers momentum. We have seen the Commission exercise powers under the Treaty of Paris to impose quotas on both extra- and intra-Community levels of steel production. There is no doubt that if the British government had made more imaginative use of the finance available in the provision of the European Coal and Steel Community Fund it could have eased the rundown in British Steel.

Another major industry which has required protection is the textile and clothing industry. In 1980 these industries were still the United Kingdom's second largest manufacturing sector, with about 700,000 people employed; its exports made up 5 per cent of our total overseas sales. The two industries have had to make a massive adaptation since the war to new technologies, fibres and fashions. Since 1950 they have lost some 700,000 jobs, 280,000 of them in the 1970s. In the European Community the two industries provide an estimated 10 per cent of wage-earning industrial jobs. It was not easy to negotiate support within the Community for the Multi Fibre Arrangement in 1974, or to renew it in 1977, and there will be difficulties over its renewal in 1981. Yet the Multi Fibre Arrangement demonstrates the potential for orderly marketing between the industrialised countries and the developing countries. Some 68 per cent of the UK imports of textiles and clothing from low cost sources are now governed by forty-seven bilateral agreements negotiated by the Commission under the Agreement to run until 1982. Unfortunately in 1977 we managed to inject into the quotas only a very small element to take account of the social and economic needs of the very

519

poorest countries. We should in future be much tougher in negotiating larger quotas for the poor countries who most need them and be less sensitive to the claims of the more prosperous super-competitive developing countries like Korea, Hong Kong and Brazil, and be prepared to argue against the commercial interests of those member states who want to accept textiles from these countries in order to obtain access to their markets for Community produced products. As it is, there is too much evasion. Global ceilings have been breached, though this has not hurt the United Kingdom as much as it might have done because other countries have under-used their quotas and there is scope for greater vigour and toughness in implementing the agreement in both Brussels and Whitehall.

Widespread protectionism would hurt rich and poor countries alike, but some greater measure of orderly marketing arrangements is inevitable; the MFA points a direction in which the Community should be prepared to go with greater commitment than in the past. It also demonstrates the virtue of negotiating across ten countries with a flexibility of quotas between countries and giving scope for special treatment for member states and the least developed countries. All such marketing negotiations will have to take a pragmatic attitude and balance often conflicting trading interests between member states and between the Community and other countries. With skill, however, marketing arrangements can be devised which will be of mutual benefit to rich and poor countries. There is little logic or reason in the Community clinging to a Messianic belief in market forces in the industrial sector while it totally rejects the very same arguments for its own agricultural sector. It is unconvincing to argue the case against import restrictions solely because of their effect on developing countries when, over sugar in particular, Community protectionism has a harsh effect on primary sugar producing countries. What is needed are negotiations involving give-and-take as part of the world economic order.

Monetary stability is in everyone's interest. If the Community could agree arrangements to make sensible adjustments of temporary import balances then it would make it much easier for Britain to consider taking part in the exchange rate regime of the European Monetary System. We would need to undertake an initial devaluation and be assured about future exchange rate flexibility. Italy, for example, has been accommodated by a mechanism which allows the lira to float downwards. Certainly nothing could be worse than Britain's inability, because of high-interest rates and being a petrocurrency, to hold our exchange rate down to a realistic level in accordance with our true industrial competitiveness. Had Britain joined the exchange rate system in 1978 we would almost certainly not have experienced the 31 per cent revaluation of the pound against our major trading partners which was, by the middle of 1980, having grave repercussions on our exports and deepening our own domestic slump. A Community united behind a fair adjustment mechanism between its member states covering financial contributions, import-export ratios and an exchange rate policy would be in a far better position to negotiate orderly marketing arrangements with OPEC and Third World countries over our access to oil and their access to industrial markets, over commodity arrangements and methods of financing indebtedness.

Another major issue for the Community is the future development of the co-ordination of foreign policy within the framework of Political Co-operation. The member states sadly showed their disagreements in public over the Soviet Union's invasion of Afghanistan. Since Political Co-operation first began in 1973 there has, however, been a remarkable degree of unity and with this exception no difference of view emerging, at least in public. Admittedly, there have been differences of emphasis and style but there has all along been a striking degree of substantive agreement in most areas of foreign policy. On the Arab-Israel dispute, Iran, Vietnam and Cambodia, China, Cyprus, South Africa, Namibia, Zimbabwe, Angola, Zaire, Uganda, Ethiopia and Somalia, it was possible to detect nuances of difference but nothing disruptive. In many of these areas the actual process of Political Co-operation had helped to iron out differences of perception in part by the sharing of information and expertise, in part because of a readiness to compromise by others when confronted by a particularly strongly held view by one or more member state.

The area that has caused the greatest difficulty has been the whole complex of related issues hinging on relations with the Soviet Union. Difficulties first came to the surface in 1977 over the issue of human rights in the Soviet Union and policy towards the Soviet Union. It surfaced again over Soviet adventurism, whether by surrogates in Africa or arms sales and training in the Middle East and South East Asia. It was, however, Afghanistan which triggered off public differences in attitude among the member states. The inability of key member states to move quickly to co-ordinate a common approach to this major issue demonstrated how vulnerable the Community can be if it is disunited at a potentially dangerous time. A major difference over détente between Western Europe and the United States in the 1980s could sap and then erode the fundamental defence link that has preserved European security since 1941. This rift of opinion has no single, simple explanation but it does represent a drift of policy in the Federal Republic of Germany, France and Britain.

It is a drift which can easily be reversed – there are no villains or Machiavellian figures pursuing a pre-ordained policy. There have always been different foreign policy priorities in the three states which hold the potential for division: in shorthand terms, Germany has wanted Franco-German entente, the US defence guarantee and *Ostpolitik*; France has wanted national defence, Franco-German entente and an independent foreign policy with European co-ordination; Britain has wanted a strong NATO, a quadripartite understanding between Germany, France, Britain and the US and, because of the Commonwealth, attaches importance to the United Nations. It is not impossible to reach clear understandings within these different positions. It has been done in the past and it has been the linchpin of political co-operation, and the basis for close co-operation with the United States. In the past, before political co-operation existed, Europe decided to regard Soviet aggression over Hungary and Czechoslovakia as defensive action to protect Soviet interests.

In 1962, on the other hand, Europe had no doubt that the deployment of Soviet missiles in Cuba was an offensive act to promote Soviet interests and gave the United States total support for their action. Over Soviet aggression in Afghanistan there were differences of perception within Europe. In France and Germany many argued, rightly, that the Soviets acted defensively to protect their interests, fearing the humiliation of being forcibly ejected, along with Amin, by the Muslim rebels. This analysis saw that the Soviets had become progressively more involved with Afghanistan since 1953 and that they were fearful, first, of the political effects of the successful Iranian revolution and, second, of the prospect of a successful Afghan revolution on their own large Muslim population. That was why they felt they had to act ruthlessly to impose a leader of their choice. The other view, that of the political Right in Europe, and of the United States and of the British government, saw the Soviets acting offensively to promote Soviet interests. The collapsing Amin regime was – in that view – the excuse for the Soviets to occupy Afghanistan militarily. Afghanistan was deliberately chosen as a Soviet base to threaten the oil-rich countries around the Gulf and to support an eventual Marxist overthrow of the Iranian Muslims, when and if the revolution were to lose public appeal in the wake of severe economic disruption and anarchy, perhaps triggered by the consequences of Iraqi-Iranian conflict.

Gradually, in the months following the invasion, the United States and European perceptions began to coalesce. British socialists, out of government and unable to influence events, should recognise that Chancellor Schmidt's influence throughout this period was crucially important in upholding foreign policy objectives most socialists in Europe felt to be important. Germany refused to abandon détente, though the Germans did not send their Olympic athletes to Moscow; afterwards Chancellor Schmidt visited Moscow and was instrumental in persuading President Brezhnev to open talks on European theatre nuclear weapons in October 1980 and not wait, as the Soviets had previously insisted, until SALT II was ratified. The French and German influence helped to restrain the United States from using military force following the Iranians' seizure of the US diplomats and at a time of world tension tended to soften the more extreme attitudes of Mrs Thatcher and the British government. The history of 1980 shows very clearly how Britain, even under a Right-wing government, is influenced by its membership of the European Community, and how the European Community can exercise an influence on US policy which none of the member states could exercise alone. The European Community countries' support from 1977 to 1979 for the principled stance that the Labour government adopted, within a UN framework, over a genuine settlement and fair and free elections for an independent Zimbabwe was of considerable importance in resisting Right-wing pressures in the United Kingdom, which built up before the 1979 election. It was also a factor in helping to persuade the new Conservative government to give up its plan to recognise Bishop Muzorewa and instead to call the Lancaster House Conference. There were, of course, many other factors – US and Commonwealth attitudes perhaps the most crucial – but France and Germany could well have taken a different attitude, and the constant consultation within the framework of Political Co-operation was important. So also was the joint working of France, Germany and Britain with Canada and the US in the Five Western Security Council powers' initiative over Namibia. Britain also had an influence on French and Belgian policy over Zaire and in cooling the enthusiasm for a Western intervention force after Kolwezi. Italy had a helpful influence with France, Germany and Britain in developing policy with the US over the Somalian invasion of the Ogaden and in avoiding the West falling in with Right-wing pressure to support Siad Barre when he was in conflict with the OAU and then in holding Ethiopia back from invading Somalia.

It is also a harsh fact – which British socialists often refuse to face – that even in 1979 before our aid programme was sharply reduced, Holland was spending 1 per cent of its GNP on aid, Luxembourg 0·9 per cent, Belgium 0·85 per cent, France 0·7 per cent and Britain only 0·6 per cent, with Germany at 0·54 per cent overtaking us by 1980 in the Community league table of real commitment to the Third World as distinct from rhetoric. French links with their territories have tilted Lomé too much in the direction of French-speaking countries but the balance is being shifted back and, for all the criticism, none of the Commonwealth ACP countries would leave Lomé if Britain withdrew from the Community. The poor Third World countries who wish to remain non-aligned welcome the opportunity of having a special link with the European Community and Europe has been well in advance of the US in forming relationships with Mozambique and Angola. It has been possible to hold an overall Community position on the Middle East, and to make this position more realistic in relation to the legitimate rights of the Palestinians than has been feasible for the US or politically acceptable for Britain if we had been acting alone.

Yet no one in Europe should be under any illusion about the dangers of letting US public opinion build up a feeling of resentment that their friends and allies in Europe are not prepared to shoulder their share of the burden in responding to Soviet action worldwide. Since 1977 Britain has often acted as the hinge between the French and German perception and US perception. That hinge role is more a matter of personalities and attitudes than of countries. It was used very effectively by James Callaghan as Prime Minister with President Carter from 1977 to 1979. So far, at least, Mrs Thatcher has been unable to act as the hinge since she has apparently had few qualifications to make about the US government's perception, as it began to harden with the approach of the Presidential election in 1980. The growth of Right-wing opinion in the Senate in 1981 will strain relations. The hinge role for the 1980s will fall on the Federal Republic of Germany and particularly on Chancellor Schmidt who has gone out of his way to establish a close working relationship with President Reagan and will, one hopes, use his skills to make the crucial decision-making group of France, Germany, Britain and the US more coherent. Britain must make it clear while we are all for good Franco-German relations Europe cannot limit itself to the Franco-German axis.

Britain's membership makes it necessary for the Community to accommodate to the traditionally different foreign policy priorities of France, Britain and Germany. Britain is not, as some Gaullists depict, an American Trojan horse inside the Community. But we will want under any British government, whether Labour or Conservative, to ensure that the European Community evolves in a way that reinforces and does not weaken the North Atlantic Alliance. There is no more crucial relationship than the hinge between the US and Western Europe. If it operates effectively the sharing of perceptions leading to agreed action is the most vital influence for peace in the world. It can ensure that the search for realistic détente between East and West is not abandoned on the tide of Right-wing emotion in any of our countries. It can bring a shared understanding rooted in the different histories of the countries of the world. The task is to ensure that Europe and the US pursue a steady and persistent policy of realistic détente towards the Soviet Union and the Eastern European countries while at the same time making a prudent deployment of adequate defence forces. Only the most blindly prejudiced can believe that Britain in the 1980s could exert a more powerful influence on world affairs outside the European Community. The British electorate can decide to become an offshore island, a neutralist nation if it wishes, but let no socialist pretend that in doing so we shall increase our influence in the world and let no socialist deny the socialism of those of us who remain convinced that Britain's destiny is best served by remaining a member of the European Community and a firm supporter of the North Atlantic Alliance.

Notes

1 The Values of Socialism

1 Fabian Tract. No. 4, 1886. Quoted in C. Ward, 'Self-help Socialism', *New Society*, 20 April 1978.
2 F.A. Hayek, *The Constitution of Liberty*, Routledge & Kegan Paul, 1960.
3 R. Titmuss, *The Gift Relationship*, George Allen and Unwin, 1970.
4 J. Vaizey, *Whatever Happened to Equality?*, BBC Books, 1975.
5 M. Thatcher, *Let Our Children Grow Tall*, Centre for Policy Studies, 1977, p.4.
6 S. Lukes, *Essays in Social Theory*, Macmillan, 1977, p.111.
7 I. Bradley, *William Morris and his World*, Thames and Hudson, 1978, p.37.
8 K. Popper, *The Open Society and its Enemies*, Routledge & Kegan Paul, 1966, vol. 1, ch. 10.
9 Isaiah Berlin, 'The Hedgehog and the Fox', in *Russian Thinkers*, edited by H. Hardy and A. Kelly, Hogarth Press, 1978, p.22.
10 A.W. Wright, *G.D.H. Cole and Socialist Democracy*, Clarendon Press, 1979, p.136.
11 G.D.H. Cole, 'What Next? Anarchists or Bureaucrats?', *Fabian Journal*, April 1954.
12 Berlin, op. cit., Introduction, p. xv.
13 Michel Rocard, in *Le Monde*, 21 June 1977.
14 Cole, op. cit.
15 *North-South: A Programme for Survival*, Pan Books, 1980.

2 The Decentralist Tradition

1 W. Morris, in *Commonweal*, 25 January 1890.
2 M. Cole, *The Story of Fabian Socialism*, Heinemann, 1961, p.185.
3 G.D.H. Cole, 'Guild Socialism Twenty Years Ago and Now', *New English Weekly*, September 1934.

4　S. Webb, 'A Stratified Democracy', *New Commonwealth*, 28 November 1919.

5　Morris, op. cit.

6　C.A.R. Crosland, *The Future of Socialism,* Jonathan Cape, 1956, p.84.

7　C.A.R. Crosland, *Socialism Now,* Jonathan Cape, 1974, pp.65-6.

8　'The Miners' Next Step', quoted in H. Pelling, *A History of British Trade Unionism*, Penguin, 1971, p.141.

9　B. Webb, *My Apprenticeship*, Longman, 1926, p.377.

10　S. and B. Webb, *A History of Trade Unionism*, Longman, 1894, p.760.

11　*For Socialism and Peace*, Labour Party, 1934.

12　Quoted in R. Miliband, *Parliamentary Socialism*, Merlin Press, 1973, p.289.

13　R.H. Tawney, *The Radical Tradition*, Allen and Unwin, 1964.

14　*Local Government in England*, Cmnd 4040, HMSO, 1969.

15　*Local Government Finance*, Cmnd 6453, HMSO, 1976.

16　*Industrial Democracy*, Cmnd 6706, HMSO, 1977.

17　A. Crosland, *The Future of Socialism*, pp.521-2.

18　A. Crosland, in *New Fabian Essays*, ed. R.H.S. Crossman, Turnstile Press, 1952, p.42.

19　A. Crosland, *Socialism Now*, p.34.

20　A. Crosland, *The Conservative Enemy,* Jonathan Cape, 1962, p.127.

3 The Growth of Corporatism

1　R. Miliband, *The State in Capitalist Society*, Weidenfeld and Nicolson, 1969.

2　A.J.P. Taylor, *English History 1914-45*, Oxford University Press, 1965, p.1.

3　K. Middlemass, *Politics in Industrial Society*, André Deutsch, 1979, p.20.

4　Taylor, op. cit., p.507.

5　Middlemass, op. cit., p.22.

6　A.H. Halsey, A.F. Heath and J.M. Ridge, *Origins and Destinations*, Oxford University Press, 1980.

7　Miliband, op. cit.

8　C. Welch, 'Crosland Reconsidered', *Encounter*, January 1979, p.91.

9　G. Dalton, *Economic Systems and Society*, Penguin, 1974, p.149.

10　*Report of the Royal Commission on Trade Unions and Employers' Associations*, Cmnd 3623, HMSO, 1968.

11 J. Elliott, *Conflict or Co-operation? The Growth of Industrial Democracy*, Kogan Page, 1978, p.139.
12 R. Undy, 'The Devolution of Bargaining Levels and Responsibilities in The Transport and General Workers' Union, 1965-75', *Industrial Relations*, Autumn 1978, pp.44-56.
13 S. Walkland (ed.), *The House of Commons in the Twentieth Century*, Clarendon Press, 1979, p.277.
14 S. Holland, *The Socialist Challenge*, Quartet Books, 1975.
15 M. Kogan, *The Politics of Education*, Penguin, 1971, pp.44-5.
16 M. Meacher, 'It takes 2,700 to quango', *New Society*, 20 September 1979.

4   The Social Democratic Tradition

1   J. Braunthal, *History of the International, World Socialism 1943-68*, Gollancz, 1980.
2   Ibid.
3   Ibid.
4   The Frankfurt Declaration, quoted in Braunthal, op. cit.
5   W.E. Paterson in Paterson and Campbell, *Social Democracy in Post-War Europe*, Macmillan, 1974.
6   Ibid.
7   Ibid.
8   P.M. Williams, *Hugh Gaitskell, A Political Biography,* Jonathan Cape, 1979, p.570.
9   Ibid., p.631.
10 L. Kolakowski, quoted by Denis Healey in the Sarah Barker Memorial Lecture, 8 September 1979.
11 M. Kolinsky and W.E. Paterson, *Social and Political Movements of Western Europe*, Croom Helm, 1976.

5   Inequality

1   G.P. Marshall, *Social Goals and Economic Perspectives*, Penguin, 1980, p.159.
2   P. Townsend, *Poverty in the United Kingdom*, Allen Lane, 1979.
3   Marshall, op. cit., p.96.
4   N. Bosanquet and P. Townsend (eds), *Labour and Equality*, Heinemann, 1980, p.130.
5   Marshall, op. cit., p.78, and *Economic Trends*, no. 316, HMSO, 1980.
6   *New Society*, 27 July 1978, p.174.
7   Hansard, 30 November 1978, col. 298 and 1 May 1980, col.

660. Quoted in H. Parker, *Goodbye Beveridge?*, Outer Circle Policy Unit, 1980, p.28.

8   Hansard, 25 July 1979, col. 312 and 1 May 1980, col. 660. Quoted in Parker, op. cit., p.31.
9   *Social Trends*, 1979, table 6.26.
10 *Royal Commission on the Distribution of Income and Wealth, Report No. 6*, Cmnd 7175, HMSO, 1978, p.74.
11 Ibid., p.94.
12 Bosanquet and Townsend, op. cit., p.173.
13 R. Layard et al. *The Causes of Poverty*, Royal Commission on the Distribution of Income and Wealth, Background Paper No. 5, HMSO, 1978, table 3.16.
14 Marshall, op. cit., p.149.
15 Bosanquet and Townsend, op. cit., p.95.
16 *New Society*, 21 February 1980, p.398.
17 *Beyond Beveridge*, The Outer Circle Policy Unit, 1978, p.306.
18 Ibid.
19 Institute for Fiscal Studies, *The Structure and Reform of Direct Taxation*, Allen and Unwin, 1978, p.306.
20 *Beyond Beveridge*, p.50.
21 Ibid., pp.62-5.
22 Committee of Public Accounts, Minutes of 19 November 1979, para. 1045.
23 Ibid.
24 Ibid.
25 Ibid.
26 Committee of Public Accounts, Minutes of 26 March 1979.
27 *Economic Trends*, no. 316, HMSO, February 1980, p.86.
28 Bosanquet and Townsend, op. cit., ch.14.
29 *Housing Policy: A Consultative Document*, Cmnd 6851, HMSO, 1977.
30 D. Webster, 'Why Labour Failed on Housing', *New Society*, 17 January 1980.
31 B. Kilroy, 'Housing Finance – Why So Privileged?', *Lloyds Bank Review*, July 1980, p.43.
32 Ibid.
33 M. King and A. Atkinson, 'Housing Policy, Taxation and Reform', *Midland Bank Review*, Spring 1980, p.8.
34 Ibid., p.13.
35 *Local Government Finance*, Cmnd 6453, HMSO, 1976, p.170.
36 King and Atkinson, op. cit., p.13.
37 Ibid.

38   Ibid., p.14.
39   *Supplementary Benefits Commission Annual Report 1979*, Cmnd 8033, HMSO, 1980, p.24.
40   *Can Tenants Run Housing?* Fabian Society, Fabian Research Series 344, April 1980.
41   B. Kilroy, 'Labour's Housing Dilemma', *New Statesman*, 28 September 1979.
42   Townsend, op. cit., table 5.14, p.202.
43   R. Carroll, *The Two Wage Worker*, Fabian Society, Fabian Tract 470, Oct. 1980, p.10.
44   A. Halsey, A. Heath, and J. Ridge, *Origins and Destinations*, Oxford University Press, 1980.

6   Economic Policy

1   R. Harrod, *Reforming the World's Money*, Macmillan, 1965, p.77.
2   M. Stewart, *The Jeckyll and Hyde Years*, J.M. Dent, 1977, p.247.
3   'The Global 2000 Report to the President: on entering the twenty-first century', 1979.
4   W. Beckerman, *In Defence of Economic Growth*, Jonathan Cape, 1974, p.248.
5   F. Hirsh, *Social Limits to Growth*, Routledge & Kegan Paul, 1977, p.9.
6   *Commission of the European Communities Annual Economic Report*, 1979-80, November 1979, table 7.
7   D. Blake and P. Ormerod (eds), *The Economics of Prosperity*, Grant McIntyre, 1980, p.18.
8   Ibid., p.19, and *Cambridge Economic Policy Review*, April 1979, p.38.
9   *Cambridge Economic Policy Review*, March 1976, p.37.
10   Hansard, 23 May 1980, col. 393-4.
11   Bank of England, *Quarterly Bulletin*, June 1980, p.191.
12   P. Forsyth and J. Kay, 'The Economic Implications of North Sea Oil', *Fiscal Studies*, July 1980.
13   *Report of the Committee to Review the Functioning of Financial Institutions*, Cmnd 7937, HMSO, 1980, p.278.
14   *Cambridge Economic Policy Review*, March 1978, p.1.
15   R. Major, 'Britain's Trade and Exchange Rate Policy', *National Institute Economic Review*, November 1979, p.80.
16   *Cambridge Economic Policy Review*, April 1979, p.32.
17   C. Allsopp and V. Joshi, 'Alternative Strategies for the United Kingdom', *National Institute Economic Review*, Feb. 1980, p.98.

18 S. Brittan, *Steering the Economy*, Secker & Warburg, 1980, p.229.
19 Major, op. cit., p.78.
20 Hansard, 4 February 1980, col.39-40.
21 *The Government's Expenditure Plans 1980-81 to 1983-84*, Cmnd 7841, HMSO, 1980, p.10.
22 A. Walker, P. Ormerod and L. Witty, *Abandoning Social Priorities*, Child Poverty Action Group, Poverty Pamphlet 44, December 1979, p.15.
23 Stewart, op. cit., p.226.
24 Blake and Ormerod, op. cit., pp.48-9.
25 Ibid., p.49.
26 Ibid., p.45; *Financial Statistics*, September 1980, table 2.6, and *National Income and Expenditure*, 1980, table 1.1.
27 Stewart, op. cit., p.230.
28 D. Savage, 'Some Issues in Monetary Policy', *National Institute Economic Review*, February 1980, p.80.
29 Ibid., p.85.
30 *Report of the Committee to Review the Functioning of Financial Institutions*, op. cit., p.261.

7   Incomes Policy

1   A.R. Braun, *The Role of Incomes Policy in Industrial Countries Since World War II*, International Monetary Fund Staff Papers, March 1975, p.2.
2   F.T. Blackaby, 'The Reform of the Wage Bargaining System', *National Institute Economic Review*, August 1978, p.51.
3   'Incomes Policy', *National Institute Economic Review*, February 1976, p.75.
4   *Incomes Data Services International Report*, August 1979, p.1.
5   Braun, op. cit., p.23.
6   *Report of the Royal Commission on Trade Unions and Employers' Associations*, Cmnd 3623, HMSO, 1968, p.28.
7   A. Jones, *The New Inflation*, Deutsch, 1973.
8   A. Dean, 'Incomes Policies and Differentials', *National Institute Economic Review*, August 1978, p.46.
9   R. Elliott and L. Fallick, *Pay Differentials in Perspective: a study of manual and non-manual workers' pay over the period 1951-75*, University of Aberdeen Occasional Paper no. 77-07. Quoted in Dean, op. cit. p.47.
10 Dean, op. cit., p.48.
11 W. Brown, 'Incomes policy and pay differentials: the impact of incomes policy upon workplace wage determination in the

engineering industry, 1972-75', *Oxford Bulletin of Economics and Statistics*, February 1976.
12 S Henry and P. Ormerod, 'Incomes policy and wage inflation: empirical evidence for the United Kingdom 1961-77', *National Institute Economic Review*, August 1978, p.39.
13 Department of Employment, *Prices and earnings, 1951-69: an econometric assessment*, HMSO, 1971.
14 R. Tarling and F. Wilkinson, 'The Social Contract: Post-War Incomes Policies and their Inflationary Impact', *Cambridge Journal of Economics*, 1977.
15 Blackaby, op. cit., p.51.

8 Industrial Policy

1 Sir Alan Cottrell, *The Undermining of British Industry*, University of Southampton, Fawley Foundation Lecture, 1979, pp.7-8.
2 *Education, Training and Industrial Performance*, Central Policy Review Staff, HMSO, 1980, p.7.
3 *Outlook on Training: Review of the Employment and Training Act, 1973*, Manpower Services Commission, HMSO, 1980.
4 *Engineering our Future: Report of the Committee of Inquiry into the Engineering Profession*, Cmnd 7794, HMSO, 1980, p.74.
5 Hansard, 6 August 1980, cols 129-30.
6 S. Mukherjee, *The Costs of Unemployment*, Political and Economic Planning Broadsheet, no.561, 1976, quoted in D. Blake and P. Ormerod (eds), *The Economics of Prosperity*, Grant McIntyre, 1980.

9 Energy Policy

1 *North-South: A Programme for Survival*, Pan Books, 1980, pp.238-9.
2 J. Brodman and R. Hamilton, *A Comparison of Energy Projections to 1985*, International Energy Agency, 1979.
3 Lord Flowers, speech to Eye Constituency Labour Party, 12 May 1980.
4 Ibid.
5 Ibid.
6 *Report of the International Nuclear Fuel Cycle Evaluation Study*, 9 vols, International Atomic Energy Agency, Vienna, 1980.
7 Ibid., vol. 9.

10 State Intervention

1 *Report of the Monopolies Commission on the supply of Chlordiazepoxide*

and Diazepam, April 1973, House of Commons Paper no. 197.
2 *The Pharmaceutical Industry*, The Labour Party, 1976.

11 Co-operatives

1 P. Derrick, 'Industrial Democracy and Co-operative Owner-ship', *Industrial Participation*, Autumn 1977, p.13.
2 *The Banker*, August 1979, p.23.
3 *Farming Business*, Summer 1979, p.11. See also John Morley, *British Agricultural Co-operatives*, Hutchinson Benham, 1975.
4 *The Economist*, 24 June 1978, p.126, and 31 May 1980, p.98.
5 J. Hughes, in *Bulletin for the Society for Co-operative Studies*, Bulletin 38, April 1980, p.48.
6 P. Derrick, op. cit., p.16.
7 R. Oakshott, *The Case for Workers' Co-operatives*, Routledge & Kegan Paul, 1978, p.123.
8 Ibid, Chapter 10.
9 Ibid., p.73.
10 P. Derrick, *Co-op Review*, October 1979, and T. Eccles, 'Kirkby Manufacturing and Engineering' in K. Coates (ed.), *The New Worker Co-operatives*, Spokesman Books, 1976.
11 Alister Mackie in Coates, op. cit.
12 Quoted in C. Hird and P. Wintour, 'Workers need not apply', *New Statesman*, 5 January 1979, p.7.
13 Ken Fleet, 'Triumph Meriden', in Coates, op. cit.
14 *Guardian*, 13 December 1978.
15 Oakshott, op. cit., p.xvi.
16 *The Financing of Small Firms*, Cmnd 7503, HMSO, 1979, p.22.
17 B. Potter, *The Co-operative Movement in Great Britain*, 1891, quoted in D. Jones, 'British Producer Co-operatives' in Coates, op. cit.
18 S. and B. Webb, *A Constitution for the Socialist Commonwealth of Great Britain*, 1921, quoted by Jones in Coates, op. cit.
19 Jones, in Coates, op. cit., p.34.
20 Oakshott, op. cit., p.32.
21 Ernest Mandel, *Journal of the International Marxist Group*, volume 2, number 3, quoted by Coates, op. cit., p.19.
22 Coates, op. cit., p.23.
23 Rob Paton, *Some Problems of Co-operative Organisation*, Co-operatives Research Monograph no.3, The Open University, 1978.
24 Peter Abell, 'The Economic Viability of Industrial Co-operatives', *Public Enterprise*, April 1979.

25 TUC, 'Industrial Democracy: Report by the TUC General Council to the 1974 Trades Union Congress'.
26 Oakshott, op. cit., p.249.
27 Paton, op. cit., p.5.
28 *The Financing of Small Firms*, op. cit., p.23.
29 A. Clayre, *The Political Economy of Co-operation and Participation: A Third Sector*, Oxford University Press, 1980.

12 Industrial Democracy

1 Commission of the European Communities, *Employee Participation and Company Structure*, Bulletin of the European Communities, Supplement 8/75.
2 Quoted in J. Elliott, *Conflict or Co-operation? The Growth of Industrial Democracy*, Kogan Page, 1978, p.114.
3 *Report on the Committee of Inquiry on Industrial Democracy*, Cmnd 6706, HMSO, 1977.
4 *Industrial Democracy*, Cmnd 7231, HMSO, 1978.
5 T. Forester, 'Whatever Happened to Industrial Democracy?', *New Society*, 17 July 1980.
6 *In Place of Strife*, Cmnd 3888, HMSO, 1969.
7 *Industrial Democracy*, op. cit., p.9.

13 Parliamentary Government

1 J. Mackintosh, *Specialist Committees in the House of Commons: have they failed?*, The Waverley Papers, Edinburgh University, 1969.
2 G.K. Fry, *The Growth of Government*, Cass, 1979, pp.2-3.
3 R.H.S. Crossman, *Diaries of a Cabinet Minister*, 3 vols, Jonathan Cape, 1975-7.
4 E. Burke, *Speech to the Electors of Bristol*, 3 November 1774.
5 *Report of the Committee on Financial Aid to Political Parties*, Cmnd 6601, HMSO, 1976, p.56.
6 S.A. de Smith, *Constitutional and Administrative Law*, Penguin, 1971.
7 Crossman, op. cit., vol. 1, *Minister of Housing, 1964-66*, p.21.
8 N.C. Crowther-Hunt and P. Kellner, *The Civil Servants: an Inquiry into Britain's Ruling Class*, Macdonald and Jane's, 1980.
9 *Report of the Committee on Representational Services Overseas*, Cmnd 2276, HMSO, 1964.
10 G. Moorhouse, *The Diplomats: The Foreign Office Today*, Jonathan Cape, 1977, p.121.
11 D. Owen, *The Politics of Defence*, Jonathan Cape, 1972.

12   T. Barnes, *Open Up!*, Fabian Tract 467, Fabian Society, 1980.
13   S. Dresner, *Open Government: Lessons from America*, Outer Circle
      Policy Unit, 1980, p.132.
14   *Report of the Committee on Data Protection*, Cmnd 7341, HMSO,
      1978.
15   H. Fairlie, 'The Lives of Politicians', *Encounter*, vol. XXIX, no.2,
      August 1967.

14   Constitutional Reform

1   *House of Lords Reform*, Cmnd 3799, HMSO, 1968.
2   R. Crossman, *The Diaries of a Cabinet Minister*, vol. 3 *Secretary of
     State for Social Services 1963-70*, Jonathan Cape, 1977, p.355.
3   *Royal Commission on the Constitution 1969-73*, Vol. 1, *Report*, Cmnd
     5460, HMSO, 1973, pp.5-6.
4   Ibid., p.322.
5   Ibid., *Memorandum of Dissent by Lord Crowther-Hunt and Professor
     A. Peacock*, Cmnd 5460-1, HMSO, 1973, p.viii.
6   V. Bogandor, *Devolution*, Oxford University Press, 1979.

15   Local Government

1   T. Smith quoted in W. Thornhill (ed.), *The Growth and Reform of
     English Local Government*, Weidenfeld and Nicolson, 1971.
2   F. Gladstone, *Voluntary Action in a Changing World*, National
     Council of Social Service, 1979, p.3.
3   Cited in Circular 121/77, Department of the Environment.
4   *Policy for the Inner Cities*, Cmnd 6845, HMSO, 1977, p.1.
5   Ibid., p.8.
6   Ibid., p.9.
7   Ibid.
8   T. Burgess and T. Travers, *Ten Billion Pounds*, Grant McIntyre,
     1980, pp.23-36.
9   D. Lipsey, 'Councils of Despair', *New Society*, 31 July 1980.
10   Burgess and Travers, op. cit., pp.14-15.
11   *Local Government in England*, Cmnd 4584, HMSO, 1971.
12   G.D.H. Cole, *The Future of Local Government*, Cassell, 1921.
13   Ibid.
14   J. Gyford and R. Baker, *Labour and Local Politics*, Fabian Tract
     446, Fabian Society, 1977.
15   C. Attlee, *Problems of a Socialist Government*, Longman, 1935.
16   Burgess and Travers, op. cit., p.28.

17 *Report of the Royal Commission on Local Government in England*, Cmnd 4040, HMSO, 1969; *Report of the Royal Commission on Local Government in Scotland*, Cmnd 4150, HMSO, 1969

18 *Local Government Finance*, Cmnd 6453, HMSO, 1976.

19 Ibid., p.306.

20 Ibid., p.287.

21 Ibid., pp.287-8.

22 N. Barr, S. James and A. Prest, *Self-Assessment for Income Tax*, Heinemann, 1977, p.51.

23 Ibid.

24 Committee of Public Accounts, Minutes of 19 November 1979, para. 1039.

25 *Local Government Finance*, Cmnd 6813, HMSO, 1977, p.18.

26 Committee of Public Accounts, op. cit., para 1055.

27 Ibid., para.1045.

28 *Local Government Finance*, Cmnd 6813, p.11.

29 *Local Government Finance*, Cmnd 6453, p.248.

30 Ibid., p.250.

31 Ibid.

32 Ibid., p.247.

33 F. Cripps and W. Godley, *Local Government Finance and its Reform*, Cambridge University Department of Applied Economics, 1976, p.11.

34 G.W. Jones, 'Central-Local Government Relations: Grants, Local Responsibility and Minimum Standards', in D. Butler and A. Halsey (eds), *Policy and Politics – Essays in Honour of Norman Chester*, Macmillan, 1978, p.71.

35 Burgess and Travers, op. cit., p.94.

36 Ibid., p.180.

37 R. McAllister, *Local Government: Death or Devolution?*, Outer Circle Policy Unit, 1980.

16 Community Care

1 A. Beavan, *In Place of Fear*, Heinemann, 1952.

2 R. Titmuss, *Commitment to Welfare*, Allen and Unwin, 1968.

3 R. Bacon and W. Eltis, *Britain's Economic Problem: Too Few Producers*, Macmillan, 1978, p.35.

4 D. Owen, *In Sickness and in Health*, Quartet Books, 1976, p.28.

5 D. Owen, B. Spain and N. Weaver, *A Unified Health Service*, Pergamon Press, 1968.

6 R. Klein, 'Living with its disabilities', *British Medical Journal*, 6 October 1979, p.848.

7   *Report of the Royal Commission on the National Health Service*, Cmnd 7615, HMSO, 1979.
8   Memorandum by the Minister of Health to the Cabinet, 5 October 1945, Public Records Office CAB/129/3.
9   Resources Allocation Working Party, *Allocating Health Resources*, Research Paper, No.3, Royal Commission on the NHS.
10 *RAWP Deals*, Radical Statistics Health Group, 1979.
11 A. Mitchell, *Resource Allocation Scotland*, Chartered Institute of Public Finance and Accountancy, Conference Papers, 1978.
12 *Local Government Finance*, Cmnd 6813, HMSO, 1977.
13 M. Wynn and A. Wynn, 'Administration and Financing of a Health Service: A Note on Swedish elected County Health Authorities and the Swedish County Health Tax', Evidence submitted to the Royal Commission on the NHS.
14 *Report of the Royal Commission on the NHS*, op. cit., p.379.
15 *Prevention and Health: Everybody's Business*, A Consultative Document. HMSO, 1976.
16 *Preventive Medicine*, Report of the Expenditure Committee, House of Commons Paper 169-i, HMSO, 1977.
17 *Prevention and Health*, Cmnd 7407, HMSO, 1977.
18 G.N. Marsh, 'Obstetric audit in general practice', *British Medical Journal*, 1977, vol. 2, pp.1004-6.

17   Freedom with Security

1   S.A. de Smith, *Constitutional and Administrative Law*, Penguin, 1971.
2   *Sunday Times*, 16 March 1980.
3   *Listener*, 24 April 1980.
4   E.P. Thompson, *Writing by Candlelight*, Merlin Press, 1980, p.20.
5   B. Whitaker, *The Police*, Eyre and Spottiswoode, 1964, p.67.

18   The Internationalist Tradition

1   Quoted in D. Marquand, *Ramsay MacDonald*, Jonathan Cape, 1977, p.56.
2   Ibid., p.73.
3   Hansard, vol. 65 (1914), col. 1831.
4   Marquand, op. cit., p.206.
5   D. Carlton, *MacDonald versus Henderson: The Foreign Policy of the Second Labour Government*, Macmillan, 1970.
6   M.R. Gordon, *Conflict and Consensus in Labour's Foreign Policy*, Stanford University Press, 1969, p.40.
7   Marquand, op. cit., p.757.

8   Gordon, op. cit.
9   A.J.P. Taylor, *English History, 1918-45*, OUP, 1965.
10 Gordon, op. cit., pp.91-2.
11 Ibid., p.19.
12 Ibid.
13 A. King, *Britain says yes: The 1975 Referendum on the Common Market*, American Enterprise Institute, 1977.
14 Ibid.
15 Roger Quilliot, *La S.F.I.O. et l'exercice du pouvoir 1944-58*, Paris, 1972.

19   Negotiate and Survive

1   E.P. Thompson, *Protest and Survive*, Spokesman Pamphlet no.71, 1980.
2   J. Hackett et al., *The Third World War, August 1980, A Future History*, Sidgwick and Jackson, 1978.
3   Lord Zuckerman in F. Griffiths and J.C. Polanyi, *The Dangers of Nuclear War*, University of Toronto Press, 1979, p.164.
4   P. Trudeau, Foreword to Griffiths and Polanyi, op. cit., pp.ix-x.
5   E. and W. Young, 'Marxism-Leninism and Arms Control', *Arms Control*, May 1980, p.23.
6   W. McGeorge Bundy, 'The Avoidance of Nuclear War since 1945', in Griffiths and Polanyi, op. cit., p.32.
7   Thompson, op. cit., p.8.
8   D. Owen, *The Politics of Defence*, Jonathan Cape, 1972, p.235.
9   Ibid., p.207.
10 *North-South: A Programme for Survival*, Pan Books, 1980, pp.119-20.
11 Leonard Beaton, *The Reform of Power*, Gollancz, 1968.
12 Ibid.
13 D. Owen, *Human Rights*, Jonathan Cape, 1978, p.133.

20   The Community of Twelve

1   P.M. Williams, *Hugh Gaitskell: a political biography*, Jonathan Cape, 1974, p.748.
2   Hansard.
3   *Speeches by Tony Benn*, Spokesman Books, 1974, p.94.
4   Ibid., pp.97-8.
5   Ibid., p.99.
6   Ibid., p.93.

Index

advisory bodies, and corporatism, 52-3
Advisory Conciliation and Arbitration Service (ACAS), 265, 271
Afghanistan, Soviet intervention in, 317, 458, 480, 482, 488, 491, 521, 522, 523
Africa, 492, 493, 522
aged, care of, 83, 392, 393, 401
agriculture: co-operatives, 238-9; EEC policies, 500-1, 502, 510, 516
Aitken, Jonathan, 308
alcohol, and health, 396, 397, 398
Alderson, J.C., 406, 411, 414
Alexander, Sir William, 52
Algeria, 204
Anderton, C.J., 414
Anglo American Venture Management, 230
Angola, 521, 525
Arafat, Yasser, 61
Argentina, 488
Armstrong, Sir William, 291
Association for Neighbourhood Councils (ANC), 355-6
Atkins, Humphrey, 454
Atomic Energy Authority (AEA), 197, 203
Attlee, Clement, 363, 437, 438, 440, 441, 445
AUEW, 47
Austria: corporatism, 52; industrial democracy, 282; nuclear power, 201; socialism, 61-2; trade union relations, 69; wage bargaining, 148, 159, 161

Bagehot, Walter, 315
balance of payments and North Sea oil, 126-7
Baldwin, Stanley, 435, 437
ballots: industrial democracy, 261, 268, 270; interest group democracy, 50; secret, 285-6
Bangladesh, 18, 300
Bank of England, 144, 212
banks: co-operatives, 237, 243; investment, 143-4; loans to worker co-operatives, 254-6
Barclays Bank, 104
Barre, Siad, 524
BBC, 317
Beaton, Leonard, *The Reform of Power*, 492-6

Belfast, 338, 343-4
Belgium: EEC membership, 452, 511; energy policies, 195; foreign aid, 524; foreign policy, 524; industrial democracy, 274; opposition to nuclear weapons, 447; socialism, 67-8; state intervention in industry, 173; state subsidies, 183
Belize, 300
Belson, Dr William, 404-5
Benn, Tony, 170-1, 175, 224, 325-6, 506-8
Berlin, 482
Berlin, Sir Isaiah, 10-11, 12
Bertrand Russell Peace Foundation, 455
Bevan, Aneurin, 377, 382, 441
Beveridge Report, 75, 82, 84, 86, 89, 91
Bevin, Ernest, 40, 41-2; Marshall Plan, 57; prices and policy, 151; and rearmament, 440, 441, 442; support for NATO, 59
Biafran war, 308
Bingham Report, 304, 306
Biological Weapons Convention (1972), 489
Birmingham, 106-7
'black economy', 95
Blum, Léon, 435
Blunt, Anthony, 309, 425
Board of Trade, 289
Boer War, 431
Boots (Chemists), 104
Boyle, Andrew, 309
Boyle, Lord, 52, 294
Brandt, Willy, 63, 445, 507
Brandt Report, 18, 19, 21, 191, 489, 491, 517
Braunthal, Julius, 56, 57
Brazil, 488, 520
Brezhnev, Leonid, 474, 475, 523
Bristol, 1980 riots, 106
British Aerospace, 174, 176
British Airways, 174, 176
British Army: in Northern Ireland, 337-8; prevention of terrorism, 423-4; relations with politicians, 288-9, 290
British Communist Party, 58, 441
British Empire, 112-13
British Gas, 173, 176, 177, 204-5, 217, 335, 336
British Leyland, 220, 235, 236, 518

Namibia, 300, 494, 521, 524
National Association of Local Councils (NALC), 355
National Board for Prices and Incomes, 164
National Coal Board, 173; energy policy, 195; North Sea oil interests, 212; private industry accounting practices applied to, 44, 176; wage bargaining, 27, 161
National Conference of Employers' Organisations (NCEO), 40
National Development Group for the Mentally Handicapped, 393
National Economic Development Council, 152
National Economic Development Organisation, 183
National Enterprise Board (NEB), 159, 173, 229-30, 234, 273
National Executive Committee (NEC): EEC policy, 448, 501, 502, 509; House of Lords reform, 324-5; local government policy, 363; 1930s rearmament, 440-1; unilateral disarmament proposals, 441; worker co-operatives, 248-9
National Federation of Community Associations (NFCA), 355
National Front, 407, 412, 413
National Health Service (NHS), 29, 289, 366; administration, 380-1, 386-7, 394-5; corporatism, 49; decentralisation v. centralisation, 51-2, 379-87, 393-5, 400; finances, 136, 388, 391-2, 395; pay beds, 421; and the pharmaceutical industry, 230-4; preventive medicine, 395-9; reform, 32; size of, 53; undemocratic nature of, 388-93; value of, 377-9
National Incomes Commission, 152, 164
National Institute of Economic and Social Research, 155
national insurance, 92
National Oil Account, 212, 214
National Plan, 183, 184
National Union of Mineworkers (NUM), 27
National Union of Railwaymen (NUR), 28
nationalisation: centralism v. decentralism, 23-37; Clause IV controversy, 64-6; government policies, 115-16; incomes policies, 161-4; and industrial democracy, 274-5; industrial policy, 173-80; size of undertakings, 53
nationalism, 15; see also internationalism
neighbourhood councils, 355-6
Nenni, Pietro, 445

Netherlands: co-operatives, 251; EEC membership, 452, 511; foreign aid, 524; freedom of information, 311; industrial democracy, 274; natural gas, 205; North sea gas revenues, 128; opposition to nuclear weapons, 447; prisons, 390; public expenditure, 136; socialism, 63-4; trade union relations, 69
neutron bomb, 455, 461, 463, 465, 477
New Age, 27
new towns, 99, 107
Nicol, Andrew, 412-13
Noel-Baker, Philip, 440, 489
North Atlantic Treaty Organization (NATO), 61, 306, 453; British membership of, 526; Labour Party attitude to, 455, 456; nuclear weapons policies, 465-84; proposed disengagement from, 459, 464; socialist attitudes to, 59, 444, 445, 446-7, 450
North Sea oil: and Britain's EEC membership, 515; and economic policy, 125-8, 129; energy policy, 206-19; revenues, 144
Northern Ireland: constitutional reform, 336-46; control of terrorism, 423-4; economic decline, 121; government of, 332-3; health care, 392, 399; human rights, 418; referenda, 284; violence in, 327
Norway: freedom of information, 310-11; incomes policies, 148-9; industrial democracy, 274; local income tax, 368; oil resources, 133; opposition to nuclear weapons, 447; police force, 408; public expenditure, 136
Nuclear Non-Proliferation Treaty (NPT), 488, 489-90, 492
nuclear power, 16-17, 196-203
Nuclear Suppliers Club, 488
nuclear weapons, 200, 201, 454-97; civil defence, 454-5, 457-8; socialist opposition to, 447; test ban, 487-8
NUPE, 164

Oakshott, R., 250, 253
Official Secrets Act, 308-9
oil: and Britain's EEC membership, 515; and economic policy, 125-8, 129; energy policies, 189-94, 196-219; revenues from North Sea, 144
Oil Taxation Act (1975), 113
Ombudsman, 311-13, 314, 417-18
one-parent families, 84